DISCOVERING A. S. J. ALLEN

A Story of Skinfolk, Kinfolk, and Village Folk

by Alonzo Felder

Discovering A. S. J. Allen
A Story of Skinfolk, Kinfolk, and Village Folk
Copyright © 2022 by Alonzo Felder

ISBN: 978-1-949810-11-0

The Florida Historical Society Press
435 Brevard Avenue
Cocoa, FL 32922
http://myfloridahistory.org/fhspress

Cover design by Jon White
My Roots Foundation logo by Mia Felder Rowe

DEDICATED TO

Zayne, Wyatt, and Reese

Table of Contents

DISCOVERING A. S. J. ALLEN iii

A Story of Skinfolk, Kinfolk, and Village Folk iii

Preface 1

Introduction..3

Why Write *A Story of Skinfolk, Kinfolk,
and Village Folk?* 3

An African American Story; Not *the* African American Story 4

About the Post-it Notes, Bible, and Songs.....................................7

Who Am I? Why This Interest in Family History? Finding My
Way Home...11

In the Beginning 14

Discovering A. S. J. Allen 17

A Story of Skinfolk, Kinfolk, and Village Folk 17

About 3 o'clock Thursday Afternoon,
April 21, 1904 22

Understanding the Killing and the Surrounding Environment ...23

A Good Man 26

Definitions of Folks 29

SkinFolk 29

KinFolk...29

VillageFolk 29

Some Other Important Folk..32

    WorkingFolk 32

    DeadFolk 32

    YourFolk... 32

    Tell It All.. 33

    He understood the times 34

Alabama After the Civil War 40

    Differing ways of seeing the 1860s......................... 40

    Florida's Roots in Racism.................................... 42

Black Codes.. 45

African American Education....................................... 49

    Violent Deaths in Alachua County, Florida.............. 50

Kinfolk 53

    The Women 54

    The Lembrics.. 72

    The A. S. J. Allen Family 77

    The Reverend Albert Sydney James (A. S. J.) Allen, MG 79

    He Was Rebuilding Lives.................................... 83

    The Return to Dust 94

Remembering the orphans of A. S. J. and Dinah Allen
(ages at the time of his death).................................... 97

A Legacy to Be Proud Of.. 102

    The "Outsider" Story.. 104

The Importance of Offering Children an
Intergenerational Identity 106

The Importance of the Narrative.. 106

Skinfolk..109

The Problem of Identity 111

Black People...111

A. S. J. Raised his "Voice" to Help SkinFolks During
the Nadir of American Race Relations 115

A Preacher's Job, the Gospel, Education,
and Announcements 119

A. S. J. Allen's life shows God's love for folks and challenges
me to be like him...127

An Era of Racism, Bad Science, and Negative
Social Messages...129

Bad Science: Eugenics 129

Black Lives Matter, or Fighting a History of Being Dispensable
and Negative Press Coverage...131

Black Men as Demons 133

The Big, Bad, Black, Magical, Superman...................................135

The History of Whites Charged With Killing Negroes is Rare ...139

Help for the Poor and Uneducated 140

A New and Uninformed King Resulted in Israelite Slavery in
Egypt...145

The Law 147

Myth: Racial Purity 151

Connected Communities: Methodist, Jews, the Poor,
    and the Orphaned 153

Care for the Children Orphaned by the Tragedy 160

Florida African American Education and Lynching.................. 162

Linking Your Knowledge of Your Forefathers
    to Your Wellness 168

Black man's code, or the talk—how to behave—lessons
    every Black child learns from their parents........................... 172

Driving While Black.. 174

Shopping While Black.. 174

Village Folk 177

Who Were the "Us" in the Life of A. S. J. Allen? 186

Understanding Cousins.. 189

Fictive Kin, the Fraternities, Lawyers, and the Media 192

Fictive Kinship 192

The Lawyers... 202

Something New-Black Communities Fighting Back 205

Fraternal organizations 205

The Media... 209

Three Consequences of Telling a True Story 212

First, transgenerational trauma and transfer 212

Transgenerational Trauma Transfer 213

Historical trauma... 214

Descendants of slaves 215

Second, a violent death 216

Third-Bias 220

Finding Help and Hope Now That the Story Has Been Told 222

Your Folks 229

A Guide to Finding Your Folks 229

About Surnames 230

Surname Origins Linked to Occupation 235

Useful Tools 237

Newspaper Obituaries and Funeral Programs 237

Using Google 237

Using Census Records 241

Brief Word About Race and the Census 242

Research Mindset, Approach, and Methodology 242

Develop a Genealogy Research Plan 243

Snooping Away from the "Kids' Table" 246

Intergenerational Storytelling 247

Let's Talk to the Coworkers and Other Associates 249

Church Records 249

Records of Intentions to Marry 250

Records Documenting that a Marriage Took Place 253

Let's Look Around the Neighborhood. 257

Let's Check in with Others Who May Be Working on the Same or Similar Cases. 259

Due diligence: "Leave no stone unturned" 263

The Dash and the Mindset List of Fun Facts for
A. S. J. Allen's Lifetime 266

Your Legacy, Your Footprint, Your Stuff—Er, I Mean
Your Prized Possessions..278

Why Save Your Personal History for Future Generations? 278

Preparedness.. 279

Knowing and remembering you 280

How To Save Your Personal History for Future Generations.......281

1865-1904—Inventions and World Events He Missed 285

Epilogue 301

The Final Chapter, of the Book – Not the Story...........................303

The Backwards Church and More Graves................................. 312

My lullaby...313

The Rest of the Story with the Train 315

Another Story on Why A. S. J. Was Killed 316

Acknowledgments 321

My Kinfolk: 321

My Village Folk: 323

Appendix A – Working Folk...327

The Job Options Available to Our Ancestors.............................339

Jobs and Terms Associated with the Underground Railroad.......415

What it took to perform those jobs...416

Getting a job or doing a job involved more than
   just doing the job..419

Occupational hazards 421

How race and gender played a part in who did what work..........422

A Short History of Colorism 426

Online references related to occupations....................428

Appendix B – Dead Folk 431

"How would you describe the deceased?"....................431

The Ripple effect of loss..432

Waking the Dead...432

Recognizing and Grieving Secondary Losses 435

Sick Folk: Aging, Disease, and Death 440

Aging, medications, illness, and the like: Stories
   connecting to the keepers of your stories. 440

Ancient Disease Names Sometimes Used as "Cause of Death." ..445

Unusual or Odd Deaths 453

Grief, memorials, museums 454

What's good about them? 455

Memorials 456

Visits to burial grounds—cemeteries and graveyards.................457

The Unmarked Grave..461

Biography – Alonzo Felder...467

Preface

At times when I speak about family history, I've had folks ask me why I do this. "After all, the past is gone, you should put it behind." My answer reaches back to a metaphor that I read in a book by James K. A. Smith, *On the Road with Saint Augustine*. Smith tells that he got it from the photographer Sally Mann's memoir, *Hold Still*. And Mann says she quotes one of her father's diary entries. Still with me? It goes like this: "Do you know how a boatman faces one direction while rowing in another?"

To move forward, you have to face the past and do the hard work of rowing. This book represents me rowing.

Enter the *Sankofa* bird . . .

Sankofa (pronounced SAHN-koh-fah) is a word in the Twi language of Ghana that translates to "Go back and get it" (*san*-to return; *ko*-to go; *fa*-to fetch, to seek and take) and also refers to the Asante Adinkra symbol represented by a bird with its head turned backward while its feet face forward carrying its precious egg in its mouth. *Sankofa* is often associated with the proverb, "*Se wo were fi na wosankofa a yenkyi*," which translates as, "It is not wrong to go back for that which you have forgotten."

We make the world a better place by bringing a sense of history to the present world. Folks often say, forget the past and move forward. While that may be true, I believe that like the *Sankofa* bird, we must look back to what is precious while continuing to walk forward.

I like to look at history from the inside out, or from the micro level first, then the macro level. So, when I see and hear lessons concerning our national history, I always think, "Where were my ancestors while this event was going on? What were they doing when this was happening?" This helps me understand the context better.

Introduction

Why Write *A Story of Skinfolk, Kinfolk, and Village Folk?*

There is a universal message of family here in the telling of the story of A. S. J. Allen. His kin may be someone else's village folk, who may be skinfolk for another and on it goes. This is a story of connectedness.

For too long the story here in America has been one of class, where some folks are riding this ship in first class and others are in coach, as if somehow our seating really mattered.

In the aftermath of protests with athletes kneeling during the playing of the national anthem at sports events, Black Lives Matter protests over police killings of unarmed Black folks, women's marches throughout major cities, students marching to protest for stricter gun laws in the face of school shootings and such, our country has had to come to grips with a few things. We've had to increase our vocabulary. We now speak daily using terms like diversity, equity, and inclusion. The folks on the ship are starting to mingle. We are starting to look differently at our boarding passes and even recognize the differences in the passes we've inherited. Since A. S. J. was a man of color, this book cannot and will not avoid the topic of race.

John Bradshaw says, "We are all hurtling through space on a rock and we're all going to die. You would think we would be holding hands and singing."

We might want to learn to get along. Later on we will look at a poem called *The Dash*. This poem illustrates the importance of the "dash" that is written between the date of birth and the date of death on a tombstone. Throughout the poem, Linda Ellis calls us to think about how we live between those two dates.

> "If we treat each other with respect and more often wear a smile . . . remembering that this special dash might only last a little while."

An African American Story; Not *the* African American Story

I have found myself on more than one occasion, having to remind folks that the TV series *Roots* was the story of *one* family. Not *all* African Americans have Kunta Kinte as their ancestor. While certainly common, Alex Haley's story is by no means the *only* narrative for African American families. Many times, in discussing African American history, a mistake is made in ascribing a common narrative to all African Americans. The story is often related that all African Americans are descendants of folks who arrived here on slave ships, and we all have this history of abuse, enslavement, trauma, and suffering. Like many of my race, I have yet to discover the African roots of my folks who first journeyed here in America. My story begins with a free man of color from Alabama. And I will tell his story—not of enslavement, and trauma—but a story of achievement, success, and promise that was interrupted by a violent death.

There is no single narrative for all Black people in America. This fact became painfully obvious to me the day I came home from work and found my teenage son parading around the living room in baggy jeans and an oversized FUBU shirt, with a baseball cap on, turned so that the brim was covering his ear. Having never seen him in such "urban" attire, I questioned him as to what was going on. His explanation was, "Dad, I figured it was about time I started representin' my slave roots."

Okay, time out . . .

The only clue to my family's African origins comes to us from my cousin, Joyce Mills. She writes in her book, *Two Trees Standing*, that our common ancestors, Shed and Phyllis Lembric, used their original African names rather than "American" names post-slavery. The only problem here is we have no record of their enslavement. In fact, I have a video statement from my great-uncle Wilbert that he knew both his grandparents (Shed and Phyllis) and neither of them were enslaved. I found a death certificate for Phyllis, and on it her mother and father are listed as Millie and Lewis Harris.

Phyllis Lembric has a death date 01 Mar 1926 and was born somewhere in South Carolina. Records also indicate that her parents were born in South Carolina (not Africa).

> *Source*: "Florida, Deaths, 1877-1939," index, *FamilySearch*
> https://familysearch.org/pal:/MM9.1.1/FPZC-JCW: accessed
> 06 Jan 2013. Shed Limberic in the entry for Phillis Limberic,
> 01 Mar 1926.

Phyllis lived a long life and, near the end, seems to have cared for her aged mother. A death certificate for Phyllis shows her mom, Millie Harris, in the Florida State Census, 1867-1945. Her name is spelled in this record as Phillis Limberic.

As I write this, I am impacted by another piece of my family narrative. I was recently at a symposium where I was introduced to an author who has written about his family's diaspora in the state of Florida. His family escaped St. Augustine, Florida, in the early 1960s due to KKK activities against his family. Mine moved out of Gainesville into St. Petersburg due to racial violence. Within minutes of talking, we discovered that we share a common set of cousins. His relationship stems from the cousin's mother's side of the family and mine from the father's side. Both of us have family roots where racial violence caused the relocation of our immediate families from one Florida city to another.

There is no single narrative for all of us. There may be common points of convergence in all our stories, but I believe there is great danger in believing any group of people has a single narrative. The myth of "a single story" leads to stereotypes and shallow understanding of peoples and the times and places in which they live. If you take the time to explore an individual's perspective you will discover or develop an awareness about the unconscious nature of managing social and cultural stereotypes, including implicit associations. While I have no real objection to urban wear, my son and I had a long talk about the actual people from whom he is descendant. If you choose to "represent" a culture or make a statement via clothing, I think it's a good idea to understand your part in that culture, statement, or position. Occasionally I will catch a glimpse of some sagging pants, but at least now his wardrobe is a show of solidarity and not an attempt at family pride. This was a personal wakeup call for me. We must know, and our children must know, our true roots and take pride in our personal histories.

About the Post-it Notes, Bible, and Songs

As you read through this book, you will notice boxes serving as Post-it Notes placed throughout the pages. This feature tells you a little bit about the way that my brain works. As I read a book, I'm not keen to write in the margins or underline. However, I do tend to go wild with Post-it Notes to myself or the reader coming behind me. I use the notes to draw attention to items I see as important details in a book. As I write this book, a question that haunts me at every page is "Why?" You see, it is easy for me to get caught up in the story—it is, after all, my story. But why should you care? That's where the boxes serving as Post-it Notes come in. Each note contains a single question from the Do You Know (DYK) scale. The DYK scale is a measure developed by Dr. Marshall Duke and Dr. Robyn Fivush of Emory University. The scale is comprised of twenty questions seeking knowledge about family history.

Children who score high on the DYK scale are associated with higher levels of self-esteem, an internal locus of control, better family functioning, lower levels of anxiety, fewer behavioral problems, and better chances for good outcomes if faced with educational or emotional/behavioral difficulties.

The questions test knowledge of things that children could not possibly have learned first-hand, but from others through stories, writings, or other indirect resources. Mostly, this storytelling happens at family dinners and family occasions, and mostly it's the mothers and grandmothers who do the transmitting. Answer yes or no to the question and then stop to meditate on the materials you just read. There may be an additional thought right after the note. Answer the Post-it Note as it relates to your knowledge of your own family history. The more "yes" answers you give, the more likely you are to have the positive benefits of this "knowing" in your day-to-day life.

As you journey through these pages, there are times I want you to stop and ask, "Why is this important?" So, pause and reflect when you encounter a note in a box.

> *Do you know how your parents met?*
> *Y N*

Why should you care?
Because everybody's story matters.
Myth: Our stories are unimportant.

Something else to look for as you read, in addition to the note boxes, are Bible verses and quotations from the Hebrew Talmud and Midrash. I'm writing about a man who was deeply religious. You may not be a religious or even a spiritual person. Still, I invite you to not skip over these inserts. Read and take these verses as a way to understand my family's mindset, values, and views. I believe it is important, as we seek to interpret history, that we see events and read newspapers and other documents, not with our twenty-first-century sensibilities, but as the people who wrote and recorded these events experienced them. I invite you to take some time to walk in my great-grandfather's shoes. From my great-grandfather's generation on down to the current generation, there exists a passion for the God of the Hebrew Bible, for justice for the poor, the weak, the marginalized, and the despised folks of this world. This passion is understood best in light of Scripture.

As we journey here together through these pages, you will also get to know me. I've taught Bible and Sunday School classes, led small group Bible discussions, and taught and preached in settings throughout the United States and Africa. I am a member of a Jewish fraternity, served as an elder in my local Christian congregation, and worked as a missionary in the Third World. This is who I am. So, you see, it's impossible for me to write about my family without using some Bible. I am reminded of a family reunion held in Gainesville, Florida, some years back. There were about one hundred of us in attendance. The master of ceremonies wanted to include a moment to give special honor to some, and asked anyone in the room who was a preacher, elder, deacon, or some sort of church worker to please stand and be recognized. After sitting down, my son leaned over and whispered to me, "Dad, it would have been easier if he'd just asked the four or five of us who are *not* church workers to stand." Such is my family!

The other thing you will see as you journey with me here are "soundtrack suggestions." These are songs I associate with various themes we will discuss.

From old "Negro spirituals" that my great-grands would have sung, to folk, rock and roll, and country—I love music. I'm that guy who, when I hear a song on the radio, most of the time can tell you where I was, what I was doing, and who I was with the first time I heard it. Songs add flavor and meaning to life, and song references will show up throughout this book under "Soundtrack Suggestions." I believe songs are tools to help you navigate, make sense of, and process the tasks of living. Songs move our hearts. How many times have you heard a particular song, and you are instantly transported back in time to a certain place or time in your life?

When life is full of joy and wonder, or when it is hard or demands that I buckle down and get to work, songs help me get there. I believe that is why our ancestors sang as they labored. There is healing and therapy in the "whistle while you work" idiom.

I listen to music on the drive home from work, and it is not uncommon for me to arrive at my home and sit in the running car having an extended driveway moment because some song has come on the radio, and I just can't tear myself away from it.

I invite you to join me in such moments are we journey through this book. I will suggest a song and I do hope you will find a way to play it while you explore the particular chapter I've associated it with. Remember, songs are poems. So, as you go on this journey with me, sing. Call up whatever app you use to get your music, and at the suggested point, listen to the music and sing the words of the songs suggested.

Using the words of John Keating from the movie *Dead Poets Society*:

> We don't read and write poetry because it's cute. We read and write poetry because we are members of the human race. And the human race is filled with passion. And medicine, law, business, engineering, these are noble pursuits and necessary to sustain life. But poetry, beauty, romance, love, these are what we stay alive for. To quote from Whitman, "O me! O life! ... of the questions of these recurring; of the endless trains of the faithless ... of cities filled with the foolish; what good amid these, O me, O life?" Answer. That you are here—that life exists, and identity; that the powerful play goes on and you may contribute a verse. That the powerful play goes on and you may contribute a verse. What will your verse be?

I present this tribute to my great-grandfather, the Reverend Albert Sydney James Allen, as my verse.

Who Am I? Why This Interest in Family History? Finding My Way Home

"Those who have no record of what their forebears have accomplished lose the inspiration which comes from the teaching of biography and history" (Carter G. Woodson).

Marcus Garvey said, "A people without the knowledge of their past history, origin and culture is like a tree without roots." Our knowledge of our family and group identity gives us nourishment and helps us grow. This is true whether it is a religious identity, or an ethnic or racial group. Who we are as individuals in the world is anchored in our histories, and knowing these histories provides us strength and resilience. Being part of a cultural group, and participating in the passing on of stories and rituals that define a group history and a group identity is highly beneficial for adolescents." (Robyn Fivush, Ph.D.)

Soundtrack suggestion:
"Everyday People"
Sly and the Family Stone
Songwriter: Sylvester Stewart

The butcher, the banker, the drummer and then
Makes no difference what group I'm in
I am everyday people, yeah yeah

My family story has elements of racial injustices, the struggle for civil rights, and the desire for unity with all people, but this is not an Afrocentric narrative written just for Black folks. No matter your racial or ethnic background, my story includes you, too, for the fight for Civil Rights has always included people of non-Black groups, fighting with and on behalf of African Americans. In one sense, I hope you see in the following pages how, when one group fights, all groups fight. What affects one, affects us all, because we are all connected. As you will see, it takes all kinds of folks to complete this collection of kin folks, skin folks, and village folks.

I grew up as one slightly out of time with my peers. My mother was an only child; born to an orphaned Negro girl. At nineteen years old and unwed, my grandma entered the twentieth century. Momma turned forty the year I was born. Grandma was fifty-five. We all lived together in the house Grandma and Grandpa bought and assembled together in 1923.

Most of the kids in the neighborhood were a few years older. Because of my mom's age and the kids around me, I experienced life with loves of music, movies, books, and culture more befitting someone ten to fifteen years my senior.

So, while preteen boys my age were listening to the sounds of Bob Dylan, Aretha, the Beach Boys, the Beatles, Hendrix, Zeppelin, the Supremes, and the Temptations, I was just as at home with music icons like Ella Fitzgerald, Louis Armstrong, Billie Holiday, Nat King Cole, Elvis Presley, Chuck Berry, Fats Domino, Little Richard, and Jerry Lee Lewis.

I loved growing up on the south side of St. Petersburg, Florida. I heard stories of the wars (World War II, Korea, and Vietnam) and the drills during the Cuban missile crisis. I heard about the Great Depression in the 1930s, and how Mom used to dance the Charleston while sailors tossed coins at her feet down at the shore. I heard stories about sharecropping and peonage. About Jim Crow, segregation, civil rights sit-ins, marches, and protests. I heard and even experienced many of these things as a child.

When I went off to school, I loved history and "civics" (that's what we called social studies back in the day). It all made sense because I could place some of my folks in it. It wasn't until years later that I learned, when you couldn't see your people in the stories that are being told, it's hard to maintain a real investment in the stories. This is why history studies seem so boring for many of my classmates.

The author at ages one, five, and eighteen

My connections to history may have been somewhat easy. My social connections to the folks around me—not so much. As a school kid, I was always bothered by the fact that I did not look like my classmates. I so wanted to fit in that I tried to change my appearance in various ways over the years. My buckteeth, big ears, and red hair seemed to always make me stand out in a crowd. As an elementary school kid, I would often sleep with a headband or nylon stocking cap on in an effort to flatten my ears.

Anyone who's ever lived in Florida knows that the Florida sun (along with ocean water, which I loved) will bleach out your hair in about an hour. So, for me to have brassy red or light brown sun-bleached hair was pretty normal. The other Black kids at school would pick on me because of my big ears and red hair. I started coloring my hair black very early on in life.

It wasn't until I was in college, after the death of my grandmother, when I decided to take Grandma's family photo album and repair that tattered old scrapbook to give my mom a nicer book to keep her family memories in, that I began to notice something that had eluded me my entire life.

Most of the relatives in the book were fair-haired, big-eared people. I looked just like my family! Why had I lived so much of my life trying to look like folks I am not related to?

One of my life's passions has been about helping folks connect. I especially want folks to see how the stories told in school and the narratives in our popular culture played out with the characters of their own family, or at least with folks who looked like them. There is much benefit when we look at the great epic battles, conflicts, and victories of our nation and can see where our ancestors were. What role did they play in these stories?

> *Do you know which person in your family you look most like?*
>
> *AF*

"I don't speak because I have the power to speak; I speak because I don't have the power to remain silent" (Rabbi A. Y. Kook).

In the Beginning

I began this journey of family discovery because I felt alone. I had grown up as an only child with my mom and grandmother. When I began thinking about looking into my ancestry, my grandmother was dead, my mom was dead, and my dad, though not present during the bulk of my formative years, was also now dead. I was an orphan. Never again would I hear a voice call out to me and address me as "son." So much of my identity was defined by my position as grandson and son. All my life, I had just wanted to be a good son. Now, sonship was not possible. I was not ready to make friends with my new identity of not being "the son." I wanted to cling to sonship even though this was now an identity and role that I could no longer fulfill.

Social identity theory posits that people derive some of their sense of identity and self-worth from their group memberships (including gender, race, religion, politics, or even sports teams), and are highly motivated to maintain and protect a positive image of their social groups. (https://hbr.org/2020/02/research-bringing-up-past-injustices-make-majority-groups-defensive)

So it is easy to understand that I was dealing with a major broken relationship and identity crisis. This loss of identity and role was going to take a mammoth effort to deal with.

The only people on the planet who shared my surname and my

Mom and me   Dad

DNA lived in my house—my son and my daughter. They, along with their mother, my wife, are the family. Just the four of us—that was it! The next closest kin I could think of was a second cousin once removed. The shock of that realization was powerful. I felt that I now had to learn more about my family. My message to all reading this book is "Start now." If you do not know much about your ancestry, you should start asking questions and searching immediately. The living relatives you have are not getting any younger. Seize the day!

Soundtrack suggestion:
"Grandma's Hands"
By Bill Withers
Songwriter: Bill Withers
Grandma's Hands lyrics © Universal Music Publishing Group

Grandma's hands
Picked me up each time I fell
Grandma's hands
Boy, they really came in handy

Since I did not have any close family to talk to, I did what anyone in the twenty-first century would do: I turned to Google for answers! I downloaded some free software and built a family tree. I then created a website to house all my findings. In 2007 I made a significant discovery! A Google search of "A. S. J. Allen" turned up a book, *Emancipation Betrayed: The Hidden History of Black Organizing and White Violence in Florida from Reconstruction to the Bloody Election of 1920* by Dr. Paul Ortiz.

In the book, Dr. Ortiz told a story about my great-grandfather. Reading the book and then meeting Paul was a game-changer. Paul encouraged me to dig deeper and to find out all I could about A. S. J. Allen. The result was I did a rewrite of the story about A. S. J., and that rewrite was inserted into the current books and scheduled for incorporation into future versions/printings of the book.

My friend George Digsby told me, "No one ever sat around thinking, 'I am going to have a bunch of knuckleheads as descendants.'" He encourages and motivates me daily to realize that we are the answered prayers and dreams of our ancestors. I am the one A. S. J. was striving for.

Discovering A. S. J. Allen

A Story of Skinfolk, Kinfolk, and Village Folk

The Florida sun was especially hot, and beads of sweat formed big droplets that rolled down both their faces, as it beat down on their brown skins. She had twisted her long black hair up into a bun, and the two continued working the fields. A father and his daughter, they had worked hard all day, but that was nothing new. Ella was used to hard work. A motherless child, growing up as one of nine children on a north Florida farm. Her studies aside for a while, she was exactly where she wanted to be—side by side scratching in the hot dirt with her daddy; preparing to plant more beans, cucumbers, okra, peas, and sweet potatoes.

As they worked and talked, they noticed something odd in a corner of the field. With a hoe in one hand, and Ella firmly gripping his other hand, the pair walked over to investigate. They arrived to find the next-door neighbor constructing a new fence. Mr. Shaw was a White man in his forties. He owned the farm adjacent to the Allens'. A rather large stone marked the boundary line where the Shaw and Allen farms met. However, the newly constructed fence was clearly a ways over onto the Allen side. There was a boundary stone in the field; maybe he didn't see it? No, the stone had been moved. That is not right. Ella did not pay much attention to the men's conversation. Looking at the indentation in the ground, anyone could see where the stone had originally sat for a long time.

Albert Sidney James (aka, A. S. J.) Allen now lay dead in the field. The loud bang of the shotgun blast both startled and temporarily rendered Ella deaf. Her ears were ringing, and it seemed as if time was standing still. As she looked in horror at her blood-covered daddy, the seventeen-year-old stood there frozen in the moment. His precious, innocent blood was now seeping into the warm, dry Florida ground that he once claimed as his own. Following Allen's death, Oscar F. Niblack wrote:

> Now, not forgetting our friend and brother in the person of Rev. A. S. J. Allen, who was appointed to the Jacksonville charge, and went to his work with great earnestness and there labored faithfully until April 21, 1904, when he fell a victim to the power of death, leaving nine children without mother or father to care for them, we trust that our loss is heaven's gain, and we can but say:
>
> > Rest from thy labor, rest, soul of the just set free,
> > Blest be thy memory and blest thy bright example be.
> > Now, toil and conflict o'er, go take with saints thy place,
> > But go, as each has gone before, a sinner saved by grace.
>
> *Source: Journal and Yearbook of the Florida Annual Conference, Methodist Episcopal Church, Thirty-third Session*, p. 15. Held in Zion Church, Ocala, Florida, February 2, 1905. Published by the authority of the Conference and approved as the Official Record. Edited by the Secretary, Jos. M. Deas, D. D.

A. S. J. Allen

A few days earlier, on Easter Sunday, the Rev. A. S. J. Allen stood in the pulpit at Pleasant Plain Methodist Church and talked about the horrible killing of an innocent man. He told how those in power had unjustly killed this man over some dispute. Ella knew well the story of how the blood flowed from His side. She thought of the Bible story of Cain and Abel. Abel, the symbolic ancestor of every murder victim—the first innocent victim of the power of evil. Killed by his brother, for no good reason. He had done nothing wrong. To Ella, the scene that now played out before her felt like one of the Bible stories her daddy had often preached about.

> "And Cain said to Abel his brother, 'Let us go out to the field,' and when they were in the field Cain rose against Abel his brother and killed him. And the Lord said to Cain, 'Where is Abel your brother?' And he said, 'I do not know: am I my brother's keeper?' And He said, 'What have you done? Listen! your brother's blood cries out to me from the soil.'"
> (Gen. 4: 8-10)

Like other familiar Bible stories, like those of Abel, Uriah, Steven, and Jesus, this scene now unfolding before Ella just seemed senseless and unfair. The familiar Bible characters did not deserve their deaths, and her daddy had done nothing to warrant this. He had just wanted the neighbor to respect the boundary stone and move the encroaching fence. However, in the stillness of this deafening silence, A. S. J.'s dark red blood seeped in and then cried out from the ground. More than a few would hear its call and would show up.

Ella had no words to describe her feelings as she stood stiff with fright, awestruck at the sight of her daddy's blood. It was overwhelming, and her heart was a twisted, tangled ball of emotion—she felt fear, she was confused, stunned, shocked, and bewildered. She tried to make sense of the scene before her. She had been holding on to his hand and, in a moment, there was a loud boom, a flash of light, the smell of gunpowder, and now the sprinkled stains of blood. The ringing in her ears gave way to silence. Now there was no sound at all. Her daddy, who was never at a loss for words, was silent. Daddy was not moving. As other adults arrived, they rushed to shield her from the sight. It would be impossible for Ella to ever unsee this moment. Her little brother, Wilbert, and baby sister, Fannie, had now come from the house into the yard. "They should not see Daddy on the ground like this! Not all the blood. Oh, do not let the babies see the blood!" Ella thought to herself.

To the adults now congregating in the field, this scene made no sense. You just do not walk out of the house on a Thursday morning to work your land and end up dead by three in the afternoon. A. S. J. had escaped racial oppression and moved out of Alabama's harsh racist environment. He had crossed state lines to settle in a gentler land. Or so he thought. He had gone to school and learned to read and write. He would become a teacher. He was good at math and accounting. He was articulate. He would be ordained as a Minister of the Gospel in the Methodist Church. Well-mannered. Well-dressed. Until his wife's death a few years back, A. S. J. was a devoted husband. He'd fathered eight children with Dinah and adopted another. A hard worker who provided well for his large family. All nine children were well-groomed and being educated at the best Negro schools available at the time. He had done all the "right" things. So why was the Rev. Albert Sidney James Allen lying dead in a field? Why this violent death? Why was it that another Black life did not matter?

About 3 o'clock Thursday Afternoon, April 21, 1904

The story of how and why A. S. J. Allen was murdered is a painful one for me; you see A. S. J. Allen was my great-grandfather. As with many painful memories in Black culture, the story is rarely told. But oddly, when it is told, it is familiar. As a child, I would ask Grandmother about "the man in the picture" and she would simply tell me that he was her daddy, and he was dead. That was about all I could get out of her. I would ask Mom and the story she told was that he was killed in a case of racial violence. Such was the environment during Jim Crow law. Whites did not need a reason for killing a Black person; that's just the way it was.

NEGRO PREACHER KILLED NEAR ALACHUA

GAINESVILLE. April 23 - J. L. Shaw, a prominent farmer, who resides near Alachua, shot and instantly killed Rev. A. S. J. Allen, a negro preacher, about 3 o'clock Thursday afternoon in a difficulty which occurred over a fence which Shaw was building. Allen owns adjoining property and from the best information that can be learned, the dispute arose over a boundary line. The preacher and a few of his friends congregated to make trouble and Allen cursed Mr. Shaw and threatened his life, stating "that he would get even with him before the sun set." Mr. Shaw then shot Allen, killing him instantly.

Coroner Bell impaneled a jury of inquest which rendered a verdict of justifiable homicide, and Mr. Shaw was released.

Allen was pastor of Pleasant Plains M. E. Church, Jonesville, but made his headquarters in Gainesville. He was an educated negro and for several years was employed as a school teacher in this county. He was regarded as a troublesome negro and had few friends even among his own race. Notwithstanding this he seemed to gain prominence by his affable tongue. Four years ago he was applicant for the postmastership of Alachua, and it is said that he had the independent indorsement of many prominent Republicans, but for some reason he did not receive the appointment.

The Florida Times Union
Jacksonville, FL
Saturday, April 23, 1904
p. 3

In an interview with A. S. J.'s granddaughter (Ella's daughter), Essie Mae Singleton, advanced in years at the time we spoke, hinted at "something more." Essie Mae believed that there was more to the story than what the newspapers reported. Ella had told the story to her daughter, Essie. Essie was the one who told me that her mother was holding A. S. J.'s hand when Mr. Shaw fired off that fatal shot.

The news of A. S. J.'s murder rang out from Alachua County. History provides the account from multiple newspapers, including the *Florida Times-Union*.

Understanding the Killing and the Surrounding Environment

After reading these accounts, it is painful to see the racial bias of the times dripping from the newspapers. In the early 1900s, the nation was steeped in wild-west-like lawlessness, Black codes, and White supremacy. Eugenics was the accepted "science" and common knowledge of the day, and amidst the national climate of demonization and hatred toward Blacks, it is no wonder that four months go by before an arrest is made after A. S. J. was killed. The local newspaper reported Shaw's attitude was that "there would be nothing serious resulting from the arrest."

Across the United States, grand juries are used by federal, state, and county prosecutors to decide whether "probable cause" exists to support filing criminal charges against someone suspected of a crime.

When a statement of "No Bill" (written by the foreman of a grand jury) is written across the top of a bill of indictment, this means that the grand jury decided that the criminal charges alleged against a suspect have not been sufficiently supported by the evidence presented before it to warrant that person's criminal prosecution.

The Gainesville *Daily Sun* newspaper from October 10, 1904, carried this article announcing that J. L. Shaw, having been arrested for the murder of A. S. J. Allen, was exonerated following a Coroner's Jury investigation:

> J. L. Shaw of Alachua, one of the most widely known citizens of that area, was arrested in this city. Upon a charge of murder of Rev. A. S. J. Allen, a negro minister, which occurred at the place of Mr. Shaw, near Alachua, in February of the previous year, and the details of which are yet familiar to many readers of the *Sun*.
>
> Mr. Shaw was arrested by Sheriff Fennell while conversing with a friend on the street. He submitted coolly to his arrest

and accompanied the sheriff willingly, probably feeling that there would nothing serious result from the arrest.

At the time of the killing, a coroner's jury was impaneled and held an inquest, the jury entirely exonerating Shaw of the charge.

Walter M. Davis of Jacksonville and W. E. Baker of this city will be employed to assist the State in the prosecution of Shaw.

Mr. Shaw experienced no trouble in making bond, which was fixed at $2,500. Jesse I. Griffin of Jonesville and J. L. Mathews of Alachua are sureties. Evans Haile will represent the defendant in this matter.

On October 13, 1904, the Gainesville *Daily Sun* published an article stating that a grand jury did not indict Shaw:

The grand jury in the case of the State vs. J. L. Shaw of Alachua, charged with murder, without hesitation Monday afternoon returned a no bill—meaning that the defendant was not indicted. No difficulty was experienced in the return of this verdict.

It will be remembered that in February of the present year Mr. Shaw shot and killed Rev. A. S. J. Allen, a negro preacher who owned a farm adjoining his own near Alachua. The trouble between the two men emanated over a dispute between certain property lines, and it is said that when Shaw constructed a fence along a certain line, Allen became very angry, claiming that he was being encroached upon. It is stated that Allen made several threats to kill Shaw with a hoe, after which he started to the house for his gun. In the meantime Shaw went to his own home, procured a shot gun, and when he met Allen, and the negro again advanced upon him, Shaw shot him, he claimed, in self defense.

Mr. Shaw immediately surrendered to the officers. A coroners jury was impaneled, and after due and proper investigation exonerated Shaw in the matter, declaring that the act was one of justifiable homicide.

It was thought this matter was ended until a few days ago, when it is said a number of prominent colored Odd Fellows and Masons, together with the aid of some churches, agitated the matter of prosecution. They took the matter up with Attorney Walter M. Davis of Jacksonville, who associated with him Attorney Baker of this city. The attorneys succeeded in having the matter brought before the grand jury at this session of the court, but that body could not find sufficient evidence to reverse the verdict of the coroners jury, since they reported no bill.

Mr. Shaw's friends have felt confident that there would be no further trouble in the matter.

After the shooting, the local law enforcement officer arrived on the scene. That officer was Alachua County Sheriff L. W. Fennell. A coroner's jury was impaneled by Alachua County Coroner, E. E. Bell, six months after the shooting. Below, see the transcript of that record.

Alachua County Judgment Record 11
Fall term
Page 46
Monday Oct. 10, 1904

| *State of Florida* | *Murder* | *Andrew J. Feaster* |
| *vs* | *} No Bill* | *foreman Grand Jury* |

Joe Shaw

Page 25 lists the Grand Jury members as:

BT Thomas
John Serouse
LR Long
Fernando Sanchez
JB Coleson
TB Horn
RE Johnson

W Jackson
LD Tillman
GS Chamberlin
HL Perryman
CC Rountree
Isaac T Guinn
AR Kelly
CS Bennett
HS Rutledge
AJ Feaster
JM Turner

A Good Man

A good man is now dead, a community mourns and pushes against the status quo. A. S. J. Allen "fell to the power of death" but he was not one who in life would "play the victim." A. S. J. would not blame someone else for his troubles. His character had always been to take responsibility for the troubles he encountered. He would never ignore his part in the situation no matter how small. And now, in his death, the family and community would seek to understand the "why" of this horrible death.

He was killed over "something about a fence" said one newspaper that next day. Even in the reporting, one could sense that there was something wrong with this killing. A man with a hoe is no match for a man with a gun. And why were the accounts of the killing so varied in the details of who was present, what was said, and the depiction of all folks involved? There was little continuity in the various reports. The only consistent fact seemed to be that a "colored" man had questioned the actions of a "White" man. There have been, and continue to be, good and noble men among us. A. S. J. was such a man. Racism did not win. Evil won the battle that day, but evil did not win the war.

Now, over one hundred years later, as A. S. J. and Ella look down from Heaven, they see folks must drive along a stretch of road now named for the killer. You pass a gated community that bears his name. Then you turn into the Mt. Nebo Methodist Church grounds and cemetery. In that cemetery lies the legacy fruit of A. S. J. Allen. His children, grandchildren, in-laws, nieces, nephews, cousins, and more. They are all there; alongside the burial sites of folks from the community that he loved and worked so hard to build. From their graves, their voices attest to the legacy of a good man. No one knows exactly where A. S. J.'s burial site is. There is no stone marker for visitors to lay flowers. It is uncommon for lynching victims to be given a "proper" burial and marker. Local officials typically assign the body to a pauper's grave with little or no fanfare, lest too much attention be brought to the event. There is no decorative headstone to say, "Here lies a great man," but what remains is far more enduring.

"When they hurled their insults at him, he did not retaliate; when he suffered, he made no threats. Instead, he entrusted himself to him who judges justly" (1 Pet. 2:23).

A. S. J. Allen showed us how to live. He showed us how to build a community. He showed us how to have a righteous response to injustice. He has given one view of what a Black man at the turn of the last century looked like. And for some, he stands as a deviation from the usual story that is told. His life has inspired me to be a better man. This book is not a bitter diatribe about how the family was wronged by a hateful man or an adversarial system. Yes, we will look injustice square in the eyes. But this book is about family and legacy; about what a good man leaves behind.

My endeavors in genealogy and family history have been far less about mourning the dead, than an effort to celebrate the fact that such honorable folk as my great-grandfather LIVED!

Now, over a century later, there is nothing to be done about this tragedy. It is history; and as one of my favorite comedians, Lily Tomlin, has been reported to say, "I've given up all hope of a better past." It is what it is. It has passed!

What I have not given up hope for, and why I write, is so that we will acknowledge the tears, beginning with Ella's, that we as his "folks" have cried here on earth. The Psalmist says that God collects our tears, and he puts them away tenderly in a bottle. God knows that stuff happens. When it does, we can respond or react to it. One of the first responses is to shed tears. Tears cry out and say, "I feel. Join me in feeling. Do not let this event go unnoticed."

> You keep track of all my sorrows.
> You have collected all my tears in your bottle.
> You have recorded each one in your book.
> (Ps. 56:8, [New Living Translation])

The significance of A. S. J. and the impact of his life demanded that I write, not just about his life, but also about his life in the context of the community in which he lived. When all is said and done, I want to be a good man. I want to care about my God, my church, my family, and my community. Like my great-grandfather, I, too, want to care for the people in my community. Learning about A. S. J. has inspired me to be more.

Who showed up; who surrounded A. S. J. Allen? In the following pages, we will meet the folks A. S. J. cared for, the very folks who showed up when he was killed.

First, we will look at his skinfolk. A. S. J. spoke up for his skinfolk. His skinfolk were the African Americans freed from enslavement right around the time he was born; and those like him born free in the late 1860s. We will examine his kinfolk; the family he married into and the family he created, of which I am a descendant. We'll also take a glance at his village folks; the local community that A. S. J. invested himself in and who joined with others in his story.

Definitions of Folks

SkinFolk

Someone who is of your race or skin color but not biological family or friends.

My basic understanding is that the term is used in reference to POC (people of color) and carries with it the idea that sharing skin color doesn't necessarily unite people. In other words, "No, I am not related to that other Black guy Karen met in the next town over." A kind of pushback on the "You all look alike, so you must all be related" thinking that was common during the Jim Crow era. The writer, Zora Neale Hurston, seems to get most of the credit for popularizing the term. "All *my* skinfolk *ain't* kinfolk."

KinFolk

In anthropological or formal use, a person's blood relations, regarded collectively.

Synonyms: relatives, relations, kin, kindred, family members, family, kith and kin, kinsmen/kinswomen, one's own flesh and blood, blood relatives, connections.

A group of folks related by blood and/or marriage. The reference is to a set of relatives.

VillageFolk

No, this is not a reference to the popular band of the 1970s disco era; that was the Village People! For A. S. J., these are the African American community members of Central Florida, the Freemasons, and Odd Fellows. It will also include the lawyers and the Methodist Episcopal Church who all came together to support him and his.

This community also includes the fictive kin, play-cousins, and "other mothers" who function as family members in many communities.

"It takes a village to raise a child" is a phrase attributed to an Igbo and Yoruba proverb that means that an entire community of folks must interact with children for those children to experience and grow in a safe environment. The villagers look out for the children.

"The greatness of a community is most accurately measured by the compassionate actions of its members" (Coretta Scott King).

According to the announcement made in the June 16, 1904, issue of *Southwestern Christian Advocate*, approximately eight hundred folks showed up for A. S. J.'s memorial service.

To be clear, a main reason I became interested in A. S. J.'s story was that, after his killing, the community pushed back. I was taught in school that the beginning of the civil rights movement and Black folks "pushing back" against White supremacy happened in the 1960s. I was eager to know more about this event in 1904. I thought you would have to look years into the future, after 1904, before finding evidence of empowered Black folks fighting back against the casual taking of Black lives.

In that future time, post-1904, at the burial of a noted Black activist, Malcolm X, Ozzie Davis spoke the following words:

> Consigning these mortal remains to earth, the mother of all, secure in the knowledge that what we place in the ground is

and temporally. Four new churches are being built and many souls are being brought to Christ. But amidst all this, death came. Our beloved Elder, A. S. J. Allen, was shot to death by one Joseph Shaw (a white man) of the same community, over a trivial matter. April 21st, 1904. His funeral was attended in the new Mt. Nebo M. E. Church, which was just completed in time for said service. The pastor, Rev. T. E. DeBose, and members, deserve great credit for having built in so short a time such a creditable building. Its size is 35x55. The dedication sermon was preached in the morning by Rev. J. M. Deas of Gainsville. Memorial service was conducted by the Presiding Elder, assisted by Elders A. DeBose, John Wilson and others. Eight hundred people, more or less, were present. $40.00 were raised for church purposes. Pray for us, that we may continue the good work begun.

Death Announcement

no more now a man—but a seed—which, after the winter of our discontentment, will come forth again to meet us. (Ozzie Davis, Our Shining Black Prince, eulogy for Malcolm X)

Some Other Important Folk

Although not mentioned in the title, there are three other "folk" that are discussed in this work: WorkingFolk, DeadFolk, and YourFolk. These sections are meant to help you as you search for answers concerning your own family tree.

WorkingFolk

In times past, a person's work was so defining that many common English names are derived from the trades an ancestor was involved in. We will examine some of these. In Appendix A, we'll explore how to use our ancestors' occupations to find out more about them, their families, their race, their status in society, and possibly more about their character.

Included in this appendix is also a table of old job names, their current new name, and a description of the old job.

DeadFolk

Although at one time genealogy was stereotyped as the hobby of maiden aunts, grandmothers, and scrapbookers, family history has quietly become a national compulsion. There are TV shows now, like *Who Do You Think You Are?* and *Finding Your Roots*, who employ small armies of researchers to churn out complete family trees and uncover the interesting family narratives and storylines for folks. The focus here is on seeking the stories of the dead, but many times this involves talking to the living who may have a very real memory of your now deceased ancestor. So, the topics of grief and memorials are explored also.

YourFolk

As captivating and exciting as it is for you to read about my ancestors, I believe that more is to be gained for you personally when you can apply the things written here to your own family narrative.

In the final section of the book, I want to give you, the reader and researcher, insight into some of the tools and tips that I used to make my discoveries.

Tell It All

Does my story of my grandfather come with a bias? Yes. Will I attempt to be honest and truthful about his story? Yes.

At my father's funeral, testimony after glowing testimony was given by many grieving attendees. That is, until one woman rose and said, "I had to check my funeral program and make sure I was at the right funeral. I hear all these wonderful things you all are saying about him. But I went to school with him; knowed him all my life. I needed to make sure we all was talking about the same man."

So, in that spirit of "keeping it real," I offer my hope that this work does not come across like so many eulogies that "preach a man into heaven." My granddad, my dad, your dad, and every person you have ever known did both good and evil in their lives.

Having said this, every southerner knows there are some things we all hold dear and, well, sacred. These sacred cows are usually some combination of Jesus, Monday night football, Momma, and Grandpa—and not necessarily in that order. I look up to and admire this man and my whole desire to write this work has been to honor him. There are good things written about A. S. J. Allen. I have found next to nothing bad or ugly written about him. I am not under any delusions about my great-grandfather.

"The evil that men do lives after them; the good is oft interred with their bones" (William Shakespeare).

Aside from the death records, newspaper reports of his death, marriage records, census records, and church records, I have to date found one obscure "bad" reference to my great-grandfather. It was found in a Texas newspaper. The article accuses him of running a scam using a chain "Letter written by Jesus."

On Saturday, June 1, 1889, a New York paper, *The Truth Seeker: A journal of free thought and reform* published the article that referenced the *Gainesville Sentinel* newspaper of Gainesville, Florida. The article describes how A. S. J. Allen was profiting from a fraud involving the publishing of a letter supposedly written by Jesus Christ.

I have yet to uncover a copy of the alleged article where A. S. J. advertises and solicits money for this phony letter. In fact, one scholar has suggested that this reference may be an attempt to defame him and that the chain letter ad may have never existed. I do not find anything that leads me to suspect that A. S. J. ever showed traits of dishonesty or manipulation. Nor do I see the response to his death as a case of folks playing the "Black card" or of him or the community somehow "playing the victim." Most of the time, folks are at least partly responsible for the troubles they encounter. If someone is playing the victim, he is ignoring his part in the situation, no matter how small. The confrontation resulting in A. S. J.'s death appears to be one of an armed aggressor killing an unarmed and politically powerless man.

He understood the times

"And of the children of Issachar, which were men that had understanding of the times, to know what Israel ought to do" (1 Chron. 12:32).

A. S. J. Allen's life was devoted to the benefit of his contemporaries, the folks of his time—his generation. Over the years spent with them, A. S. J. acquired a familiarity with the wants and needs of the folks around him. The records show that he labored to supply their needs and alleviate their troubles.

> Though good men may, and must, do many things that will only yield fruit in after days, they will seek to have "understanding of the times," and to know what they ought to do to promote and conserve the welfare of those around them. Where there is want, they will strive to supply it; where there is ignorance, they will strive to dispel it; where there is weakness, they

will strive to uphold it; and where there is guilt, they will be pitiful and tender, if by any means the wrong-doer may be reclaimed. Think how soon the opportunity of helping will have slipped away from us. Our own "generation," how it is diminishing every day! In a very little while, we ourselves, as members of it will have disappeared.

Source: The Scriptural Ideal of a Good Man's Life and Death by C. M. Merry. https://biblehub.com/sermons/auth/merry/ the_scriptural_ideal_of_a_good_man%27s_life_and_death. htm. The Biblical Illustrator, Electronic Database. Copyright © 2002, 2003, 2006, 2011 by Biblesoft, Inc. All rights reserved. Used by permission. BibleSoft.com

THE Tyler, Texas, *Leader*, published by and in the interest of the colored race, thus exposes an old but pious fraud. It is hoped that the negroes may be wise enough to heed the words: "A religious gentleman by the name of A. S. J. Allen, of Gainesville, Fla., recently had a remarkable letter printed in the office of the *Sentinel* of that city. The letter purports to be from Jesus Christ, found eighteen miles from Iconium, sixty-five years after Christ is said to hav left the world. Copies of the letter are to be sold. Mr. Allen has struck a rich vein, and, owing to the general ignorance and credulity of the masses, he will perhaps coin many a dollar out of his pious fraud. The hoax is similar to the one practiced by cunning priests several years after the crucifixion of Christ. They sold, in all parts of the world, pieces of the cross on which he was crucified.

To understand why he was killed necessitates that we understand the times in which A. S. J. lived. We have to ask, "If he was living such a good life; fulfilling what we now call the American Dream, why was he killed?" Why wasn't he protected from this fate? Why was his killer not punished? Why are people of color not "protected" today from similar fates? If history teaches us anything, it teaches us that life is not fair. And if life was not fair then—well, we can suppose that it remains unfair.

"I have seen something else under the sun:
The race is not to the swift
or the battle to the strong,
nor does food come to the wise
or wealth to the brilliant
or favor to the learned;
but time and chance happen to them all."
(Eccles. 9:11 [NIV])

The death of A. S. J. Allen influenced race relations in Florida and my sense of identity. It has made a profound impact in shaping my life. Discovering A. S. J. Allen has brought me much inspiration. I am proud of my family heritage. Proud of the noble folks I've come to know through talks with older family members, photographs, marriage certificates, newspaper articles, and other paper trails they have left behind.

> *Do you know the names of the schools that your mom went to?*
>
> *Y N*

Why should I care?
Because we need a personal connection.
Myth: Someone else can write your story.

> BELLBOY: You know, Mister Clemens, I'm going to do you another favor today. You're always looking for good stories, right? Well, I've got a real humdinger for you. The story of my life. Now, I know you may think I'm young, but I've covered a lot of ground, and if I do say so myself, it'd make for some pretty fascinating reading. So, what do you think?
> SAM CLEMENS: About what?
> BELLBOY: About writing my life story. You and me. Literary partners, of course.
> SAM CLEMENS: Young man, I have a maxim that I have always lived by. No one is more qualified to write your story than you are.
> BELLBOY: Me? Be a writer? You think I could do that?
> SAM CLEMENS: As long as you write what you know. You got any passions, boy? Any dreams?
> BELLBOY: I'd like to do some travelling, maybe go to sea. And Alaska. I've had the strangest notion to go see Alaska.
> SAM CLEMENS: That's a great idea, son. That's exactly what

I would do if I were your age. Alaska, the Klondike, the Aurora Borealis. That's it. Follow your dreams and write about 'em.
BELLBOY: Thank you, Mister Clemens. You know, that is exactly what I'm going to do.
SAM CLEMENS: You do that, son.
BELLBOY: You'll see my name in print, too.
CLEMENS: I'm sure I will.
BELLBOY: Don't forget. The name's London. Jack London.
SAM CLEMENS: Goodbye now. Bye bye.
(*Star Trek, the Next Generation*, "Time's Arrow," part 2. Original air date: Sept. 21, 1992)

Though highly unlikely that that conversation ever took place in reality, I love this fictional conversation between two of the most renowned writers of the nineteenth century, Mark Twain and Jack London. But fictional or not, the truth in the exchange holds. You should know your own story and you should be responsible for telling your story.

In the movie, *I Am Somebody's Child: The Regina Louise Story*, there is a scene where Regina Louise is talking with the counselor at the psychiatric facility where she is being housed. She notices that he is taking notes and asks him the question, "What are you doing?" "Writing your story," he responds.

Then comes one of the most powerful parts of the movie, when Regina says, "Suppose I don't like the way you tell my story."

This idea is repeated later on in this movie during the scene where Regina is leaving the facility and is told she cannot be given her files. It is a heartbreaking scene when Regina, in defiance, demands, "I want my files." Regina says, "Before I sign this, I want my files."

The staff tells her that the files are "confidential." (Such a frustrating head-scratcher; they are her records, it's her story!)

Another wonderful, albeit fictional, reference point for this attitude comes from the British TV series *Doctor Who*. When the doctor decides to "protect" Clara by erasing her memory, there is a heated debate between the two over this and, in the end, Clara delivers a most powerful speech.

> Clara: What are you trying to do to me?
> The Doctor: I'm trying to keep you safe!
> Clara: Why? Nobody's ever safe. I never asked you for that, ever. These have been the best years of my life and they are mine. Tomorrow's promised to no one, Doctor. But I insist upon my past. I am entitled to that. It's mine.
> (*Doctor Who*, Series 9, "Hell Bent")

Soundtrack suggestion:
"Thanksgiving Day"
Ray Davies

Are you going on Thanksgiving Day
To those family celebrations?
Passing on knowledge down through the years
At the gathering of generations
Every year it's the same routine

The folks of Alachua County, Florida, could not just forget A. S. J. Allen. He had lived among them in such a way that these everyday folks showed up to fight back. That makes my great-grandfather a leader in Florida's civil rights movement. The world around him would not allow his killing to be swept away as another justifiable homicide of a Black man.

I use the word "killing" because in the eyes of the law this was never deemed a murder.

> The law states that every killing of a human being, when committed by another human being, is a homicide. However, not every homicide is a crime. In certain situations, the taking of human life is justifiable since the killing is done without fault. Under other circumstances the homicide is said to be excusable, meaning that the slayer is at fault, although he is not punished for this act. Those homicides which are neither excusable nor justifiable are considered

to be felonious. They are either murder or manslaughter. Murder at common law was said to be the unlawful killing of a human being with malice aforethought, express or implied. Today, although some states have by statute retained the common-law definition of murder, (or one similar to it, most jurisdictions within the United States have divided the crime into degrees.

Doctrinally, it is the absence of malice which distinguishes manslaughter from murder. This simple definition, which has been codified by most state statutes, produces difficulties which arise when an attempt is made to apply the definition to a given state of facts. The determination of whether malice was present in the act of homicide resolves itself into the question of "whether the accused was subjected to such provocation by the deceased as to cause sudden hot blood or passion, as a result of which his reason was so disturbed or obscured that he acted rashly, without deliberation or reflection and from passion rather than judgment." In order to answer this question, a determination must be made with regard to three factors implicit in the question itself: (1) was the provocation adequate to produce a state of passion in the mind of the slayer; (2) was there time before the fatal act was committed for the passion to have cooled; (3) did the slayer act because he was governed by that passion or was malice the propelling force in his action? (https://scholarship.law.upenn.edu/cgi/viewcontent.cgi?article=7116&context=penn_law_review)

Alabama After the Civil War

Born in 1865. When he was around eleven years old, A. S. J. Allen moved from the state of Alabama to Florida. I do not know exactly why A. S. J. left Alabama in the mid-1860s. I know very little about the circumstances surrounding A. S. J.'s birth, but I can guess. This was the American Reconstruction Era. Reconstruction is the term used by historians to refer to the time after the Civil War and Emancipation. This was a period of both political and social change in the South. Lasting roughly from 1865 to 1874, the Reconstruction period covered much of the time A. S. J. would have spent in Alabama. When Reconstruction ended, life for African Americans got very tough.

> Published: November 21, 1865
> WASHINGTON, Monday, Nov. 20
> The President to-day received the following telegram from
> Gov. MARTIN, of Florida:
> TALLAHASSEE, Fla., Saturday, Nov. 18.
>
> The convention has annulled the ordinance of secession, abolished slavery, and declared that all the inhabitants of the State, without distinction of color, are free; and that no person shall be incompetent to testify as a witness on account of color, in any matter wherein a colored person is concerned. It has repudiated the State debt, contracted in support of the rebellion, amended the constitution in other respects, and adjourned.
>
> (Signed,) WILLIAM MARVIN,
> Provisional Governor

Differing ways of seeing the 1860s

In the South, the interpretation of the tumultuous 1860s differed sharply depending on your race. Significant moments in American history are often explained in religious terms, too. Historian Wilson Fallin contrasted the interpretation of Civil War and Reconstruction in White versus Black using Baptist sermons in Alabama.

He noted that White preachers held to a view that:

- God had chastised them and given them a special mission—to maintain orthodoxy, strict Biblicism, personal piety, and traditional race relations. Slavery, they insisted, had not been sinful. Rather, emancipation was a historical tragedy, and the end of Reconstruction was a clear sign of God's favor.

In sharp contrast, Black preachers interpreted the Civil War, emancipation, and Reconstruction as:

- God's gift of freedom. They appreciated opportunities to exercise their independence, to worship in their own way, to affirm their worth and dignity, and to proclaim the fatherhood of God and the brotherhood of man. Most of all, they could form their own churches, associations, and conventions. These institutions offered self-help and racial uplift and provided places where the gospel of liberation could be proclaimed. As a result, Black preachers continued to insist that God would protect and help them; God would be their rock in a stormy land.

The Ku Klux Klan (KKK) was founded in 1866. In a later section, we'll talk more about them and the era of racism, bad science, and the negative social messages that sprang up during the 1860s. But during Reconstruction, all Blacks experienced a difficult life. Freedom from legal enslavement was not freedom from racial oppression and terrorism. The Klan committed scores of murders and acts of violence and intimidation against Black folks in Alabama between 1868 and 1871 when A. S. J. was a small child. Living in Alabama and the events of these years most likely influenced his (or his parents') decision to leave the state.

By the end of 1871, the number of reported Klan sightings in Alabama declined sharply as a result of the actions of Ulysses S. Grant. President Grant launched a campaign to eradicate the KKK after many violent incidents occurred across the South. Their terrorist acts convinced Republican leaders that the Klan had significantly impaired any progress toward a peaceful restoration of the Union. Grant's campaigns did manage to diminish some of the Klan's activity in Alabama, but it did not end the senseless bloodshed experienced by African Americans.

Florida's Roots in Racism

Oh, Florida! Can we just talk about the great beaches, the swaying palm trees, and the pretty flowers? Sadly, the answer is "no."

So, let's talk about a land called Florida. "Old Folks at Home" is a minstrel song written by Stephen Foster in 1851. Since 1935 it has been the official state song of Florida.

Soundtrack suggestion:
"Swanee River"
Songwriters: Stephen Collins Foster/Peter Meyer-Bits
Swanee River lyrics © Universal Music Publishing Group

Wo, that's where my heart is yearning ever,
Home where the old folks stay.

It's been almost forty years since I've lived in the state of Florida, but on any given day, when asked "Where are you from?" my instinctive answer is a resounding "Florida." I was born there, my ancestors are buried there, I went to school there, and I cannot explain my feelings of allegiance. It's like family, good, bad, or indifferent—at the end of the day you gotta love 'em. I'll have more to say later about my home state, but for now, let's say my opinion is akin to the feeling most of us have about our kids—they're not perfect—but they're mine.

You know, Florida was named for the day on which it was discovered (six days after Easter on April 2, 1513) by Spanish explorer Ponce de León. He called it *La Florida* in honor of *Pascua Florida*, the Spanish Feast of the Flowers, which is what the Spaniards called the Easter season. The name is the oldest surviving European place name in the U.S. (*Florida Handbook, 1997-1998*, by Allen Morris. See: https://www.ereferencedesk.

com/resources/state-name/florida.html)

A. S. J. Allen's move from Alabama to the land of pretty flowers was indeed a good move for him, but I do not want to imply that this move was a move into some sort of surreal utopian or idyllic "promised land." In today's modern times, my home state projects that kind of image. You know the one I mean—like it is a non-radical, "scarcely part of the South," and certainly more enlightened place than the rest of the geographic South. Some would imagine that Florida was some sort of new progressive Southern state free of the Negrophobia of neighboring Alabama, Georgia, and the Carolinas. Not so. Florida, too, was a slave state with its very own brand of racism.

"The rapid spread of Northern fanaticism has endangered our liberties and institutions, and the election of Abraham Lincoln, a wily abolitionist, to the Presidency of the United States of America destroys all hope for the future," John C. Pelot, a slave owner from Alachua County, said in his opening statement as chairman of the convention January 3, 1861.

Slavery was the central reason Florida would become the third state to secede from the United States that year. The men who met at the Tallahassee Secession Convention said so themselves, according to *Journal of the Proceedings of the Convention of the People of Florida,* written by William S. Harris, the convention's secretary. John C. McGhee, who was elected president of the convention, concurred.

> "At the South, and with our People of course, slavery is the element of all value, and a destruction of that destroys all that is property," McGhee said, following his induction January 5. The same day, Florida began discussions with Alabama, Georgia, and South Carolina—the beginning of the Confederacy. McGhee testified that "the institution of domestic slavery is recognized, and the right of property in slaves is expressly guaranteed" in the U.S. Constitution. If that guarantee were to be stripped, McGhee asserted that "slave

states will withdraw their political connection from the non-slaveholding states" to "establish another Confederation." (https://www.miaminewtimes.com/news/five-insane-facts-about-slavery-and-black-history-in-florida-11308098. Jerry Iannelli is a former staff writer for *Miami New Times* from 2015 to March 2020)

The first enslaved Africans arrived in Spanish *La Florida* in 1526. San Miguel de Gualdape, founded thirty-one years before St. Augustine, was the first failed colony in the continental United States. It was also the site of the nation's first successful slave rebellion.

"Florida Spanish territory was involved in the slave trade, and that influence begins at the beginning of the 16th Century," says Nashid Madyun, Executive Director of the Black Archives and Research Center at Florida Agricultural and Mechanical University (FAMU). "Yes, slavery predates 1619 in America. As history goes on, dates and cornerstones tend to become muffled. The important thing is not the date, but to have a conversation about oppression and how people have elevated themselves above it." (https://www.browardpalmbeach.com/news/florida-black-history-and-the-horrors-of-slavery-not-taught-in-schools-10366207)

I will not, to quote a statement made in the Preface and Acknowledgments by Irvin D. S. Winsboro (editor of *Old South, New South, or Down South? Florida and the Modern Civil Rights Movement*), perpetuate the "fallacy of Florida's often presumed exceptionalism and the possibly misguided view that Yankee immigrant and progressive leaders . . . converted Florida into a more enlightened (i.e., moderate) southern state than its peers."

Black Codes

Within the first two years after the Civil War, White-dominated Southern legislatures passed Black Codes. These "Black Codes" were modeled after the old "slave codes." They were particularly concerned with controlling Black people's movement and labor. The Black Codes varied from state to state but were all intended to secure a steady supply of cheap labor, and all continued to assume the inferiority of African Americans. Although now freed, Black lives were greatly restricted by the Black Codes.

The Black Codes were rooted in the earlier "slave codes." The premise behind chattel slavery in America was that enslaved people were property and, as such, they had few or no legal rights. The slave codes, in their many loosely defined forms, were seen as effective tools against slave unrest, particularly as a hedge against uprisings and self-liberations. Enforcement of slave codes also varied, but corporal punishment was widely and harshly employed.

Perhaps the defining feature of the Black Codes was broad vagrancy law, which allowed local authorities to arrest freed people for minor infractions and commit them to involuntary labor. This was the start of the convict lease system, also described as "slavery by another name" by Douglas Blackmon in his 2008 book by the same name.

Under the Black Codes, all African Americans, convicts or not, were subject to curfews set by their local governments. Even their day-to-day movements were heavily dictated by the state. Black farm workers were required to carry passes from their employers, and meetings Black people took part in were overseen by local officials. This even applied to worship services. In addition, if a Black person wanted to live in town, they had to have a White sponsor. Any African Americans who skirted the Black Codes would be subject to fines and labor.

45

In short, in all areas of life, Black people lived as second-class citizens. They were emancipated on paper, but certainly not in real life. (The Black Codes and Why They Still Matter Today. The Black Codes still impact the 21st century. https://www.thoughtco.com/the-black-codes-4125744)

Reconstruction did away with the Black Codes, but, after Reconstruction ended in 1877, many of their provisions were reenacted in the Jim Crow laws. Jim Crow laws were not finally done away with (legally) until the passage of the Civil Rights Act of 1964.

Post emancipation, it is important to look at how Blacks were treated "under the law." Alabama was a desolate place after four hard years of the Civil War. The social and economic fabric of the state had been torn to shreds. As its folks looked around them all they could see was physical devastation. The toll on their mental health had to have been overwhelming. They were spending their days in mourning over the loss of 70,000 men killed or disabled by the war. The systems of industry and agriculture were destitute. While the state's farming Black Belt was pretty much untouched by the War, the once-rich cotton economy was in shambles as the enslaved men and women, who worked the fields and created the state's wealth, were now freed.

A. S. J. Allen's move from Alabama to Florida is understandable in light of the climate there. During the Civil War, Florida was not ravaged as other southern states were. Florida sent 15,000 men and many supplies, including salt, beef, cotton, pork, and other products, to help the Confederacy. Northern ships patrolling Florida's coast tried to block supplies from coming and going. While Union forces occupied many coastal towns and forts, the interior of the state remained in Confederate hands. Many white and black residents helped the northern cause in quiet ways. Several major battles took place, but Florida did not experience as much damage as its neighbors to the north. (http://www.museumoffloridahistory.com/docs/efactivity/civil.cfm, and https://dos.myflorida.com/florida-facts/florida-history/a-brief-history/civil-war-and-reconstruction/)

An online article about the history of Gainesville, Florida, states that:

> Gainesville, Florida, was a rough town after the Civil War and into the early 20th century. Whites and blacks commonly carried firearms, and gunshots were often heard at night. Killings and serious injuries were frequent. Some of the violence was racial. Young Men's Democratic Clubs (usually a cover name for the Ku Klux Klan), formed in the late 1860s to fight political domination by Republican northerners and blacks, reportedly burned the homes of many Republicans and killed nineteen people, including five blacks.
>
> The city had only a single police officer until well into the 20th century, which was inadequate to deal with the violence. A posse authorized by the city council also did little to stem the violence. Punishments for crime included public executions, the pillory, lashes and fines.

A. S. J. lived in what historian Rayford Logan referred to as the "nadir of American race relations." Generally, this was the period in the history of the Southern United States from the end of Reconstruction in 1877 through the early 20th century. It was a time when racism in America was at its worst. In 1876 federal troops were withdrawn from the South as the result of a deal Andrew Hayes made to win a tight presidential race. For Black folks in the South, this move must have felt like they had been abandoned by the federal government. They were now at the mercy of their former enslavers and surrounded by poor Whites who still felt that Blacks were less than human. Worse than in any other period after the Civil War, during this period, African Americans lost many of the civil rights gains made during the Reconstruction period. Anti-Black violence, lynchings, segregation, legal racial discrimination, and expressions of White supremacy were on the rise.

Rayford Logan coined the word "nadir" in his 1954 book, *The Negro in American Life and Thought: The Nadir, 1877–1901*. Logan tried to determine the year when "the Negro's status in American society" reached its lowest point. He pointed to 1901; just a few years before A. S. J.'s killing.

African American Education

Like so many other African Americans, my ancestors turned to education as a solution to the societal ills they faced. They reasoned that if a lack of knowledge and formal education was the source of their lack of acceptance and being targeted for violence, then they would pursue learning as a "proof" of their humanity. Many African Americans took on this challenge and opportunity to show Whites that they could be the people Whites thought they could not be. But Florida law would make that nearly impossible. "The schools for white children and the schools for Negro children shall be conducted separately" declared the law. Integrated education was prohibited in Florida's Constitution of 1885.

In fact, there were many legal barriers to integration into White society for these previously enslaved people. The following is a list of legislation and penalties dealing with racial relations in Florida, some of which were in effect until the relatively recent passage of Florida's current Constitution in 1967:

- 1873: Barred public accommodation segregation statute—prohibited discrimination on account of race in the full and equal enjoyment of public accommodations such as inns, public transportation, theaters, schools, cemeteries, and places of public amusement. This did not include private schools or cemeteries established exclusively for White or colored persons.

- 1885: Education (constitution)—White and colored children shall not be taught in the same school.

- 1887: Education (constitution)—White and colored children were prohibited from being taught in the same schools.

- 1895: Education (statute)—a Penal offense for any persons to conduct any school, any grade, either public or private, where Whites and Blacks are instructed or boarded in the same building or taught in the same class by the same teachers. Penalty: Between $150 and $500 fine, or imprisonment in the county jail between three and six months.

When A. S. J. Allen moved to Florida (sometime around 1889), Union Academy, the first school for Blacks in Gainesville, was in operation. The school was established in 1866 by the Freedmen's Bureau to educate freed slaves. The White residents of Gainesville were opposed to efforts at educating Blacks and treated the teachers at the school badly. There are documented incidents of boys throwing "missiles" into the classrooms. By 1898 the school served 500 students, and it continued in operation until 1929.

The 1892 Liberty Hill Schoolhouse, a smaller public school for African American children, was located at 7600 Northwest 23rd Avenue. The building replaced an older school that was in use as early as 1869 as a rural elementary school, according to the Liberty Hill Schoolhouse application for the National Register of Historic Places. The one-story, one-room schoolhouse served primary students through grade six. The school had no lights or plumbing. It was in use through approximately 1952 and was added to the National Register in 2003.

By 1900 the state's African Americans numbered more than 200,000, roughly 44 percent of the total population. This was the same proportion as before the Civil War, and they were effectively disenfranchised. Not being able to vote meant they could not sit on juries and were not elected to local, state, or federal offices. They also were not recruited for law enforcement or other government positions. After the end of Reconstruction, the Florida legislature passed Jim Crow laws establishing racial segregation in public facilities and transportation. Separate railroad cars or sections of cars for different races were required beginning in 1887. Separate waiting rooms at railroad stations were required beginning in 1909.

Violent Deaths in Alachua County, Florida

My search for ancestors began by consulting the listings of African Americans lynched between 1865 and 1905.

Interestingly a search of these names on the Alachua County

Name	Age	Ethnicity	City	County or Parish	State	Year	Accusation	Comment
Champion, Tony Kelly, Michael		African-American, White (Irish)	Gainesville	Alachua	Florida	1891	Murder	Taken together from jail by mob and hanged.
Ford, Andrew		African-American	Gainesville	Alachua	Florida	1891	Beating a man, aiding Harmon Murray	Taken from jail by mob and hanged.
Hinson, Henry		African-American	Micanopy	Alachua	Florida	1892	Murder	Hanged.
Unknown	boy	African-American	Waldo	Alachua	Florida	1892	Suspicion of burglary and incendiarism	Hanged.
Willis, Charles		African-American	Rochelle	Alachua	Florida	1894	"Desperado"	Shot and burned in bed.
Rawls, William		African-American	Newnansville	Alachua	Florida	1895	Murder	Hanged and shot.
Daniels, Alfred		African-American	Gainesville	Alachua	Florida	1896	Suspicion of arson (barn burning) (no evidence)	Taken by mob on way to jail, hanged and shot.

Virtual Cemetery search page yields no results. Most likely the local officials disposed of the body in a pauper's graveyard with no ceremony; lest attention be brought to the event.

> *Do you know some awards that your parents received when they were young?*
>
> *y n*

Why me?
Because it is what grownups are supposed to do.
Myth: Somebody else will tell the kids.

For most children today, long gone are the days of baking bread in the kitchen with Grandma or sitting out on the front porch snapping peas. We don't visit Granny's house and help her take the clothes down from the clothesline or sit with our hands held out, holding yarn as she knits a blanket anymore. When I was little, my Grandma would travel from our home on the coast to visit her sister, who still lived up in Gainesville, in the middle of the state.

Growing up as an only child, I looked forward to these trips with Grandma to see my cousins. We played and fed the hogs and cows. Most of all, I remember sitting on my Aunt Ella's front porch going through baskets of string beans and peas. We all talked and listened as stories of days gone by were passed on.

These images from my childhood are completely foreign to my adult children and they may not be very familiar to you, either. Today's grandma lives in senior villages or vibrant "over 55" communities; some still own their own homes. Maybe she's still a high-powered executive with staff, board members, and others to direct. My point is that many of today's grandparents are generally tech-savvy, active seniors who Zoom and FaceTime on school nights and fly into town for a weekend visit with their grandchildren.

According to a report last year by the U.S. Census Bureau, "The number of grandparents in the United States is growing. Its population reached 69.5 million in 2014, up from 65.1 million in 2009. Baby Boomers, the youngest of whom turned 50 in 2014, have a total population of 75.4 million." (https://atlantajewishtimes.timesofisrael.com/are-jewish-grandparents-a-forgotten-population/)

Stories of the past, who we are and where we come from, may not be transferred in the form of casual conversations as household tasks are being done. But still, we must take the time to tell the stories.

Soundtrack suggestion:
"We Shall Overcome"
Pete Seeger

Oh, deep in my heart
I do believe
We shall overcome someday.

Kinfolk

My kinfolk are the descendants of Shed and Phyllis Lembric. Who are we? We are the folks they prayed for. Borrowing from the family matriarch, Myrtle, played by the late Cicely Tyson in the 2006 Tyler Perry movie *Madea's Family Reunion:*

> What happened to the pride and dignity and love and respect we have for one another? Young black men, take your place. We need you. Your sons and daughters need you. . . . Young black women, you are more than your thighs and your hips. You are beautiful, strong, powerful. I want more from you. Take your place. I want every single one of you, young man, young woman, turn to the next person standing alongside of you. Grab them and hug them and tell them that you love 'em. Tell them, "If you need anything, come to me. If you need somebody to talk to, come to me. I'll give you the shoulder, I'll give you the hug. I'll feed you, I'll clothe you if you need it." That's how you start from this moment. When you leave this reunion today, you take that with you.

The Women

At the onset, I must recognize a very important aspect of my kinfolk story. I am writing to pay honor to a man, my great-grandfather, A. S. J. Allen, and to honor the legacy he left behind. In doing so I must say a few words about the importance of the women in my family as storytellers. I do not want it to be lost that the bulk of the history of my family is the result of the efforts of the women of the family. If it were not for the women in my family, I would not have these stories. I am grateful that they passed on the stories, the facts, the emotions, and the "feel" of my family narrative.

My first lesson on family legacy was that we are a frugal bunch. My mom and grandma would tell the story that it was my great-aunt Kitty who first confirmed my identity in the family. The story goes like this: When Mom brought me home from the hospital, Aunt Kitty took one look at me with my clenched fists and exclaimed, "Look at those hands. He's a Lembric all right. He's tight-fisted!" Apparently, the Lembrics had a well-established reputation for tightly managing their property.

I later learned that pediatricians call it the palmar grasp reflex, and it is a thing all babies do. The Talmud tells us, "Man is born with hands clenched but dies with hands open." The idea being that we come into the world trying to grab on to all of life, but we leave this life empty-handed. I chose not to argue with either Scripture or Aunt Kitty. I arrived with a tight fist. Every day I strive to open my hands and give more than I take from this world.

Aunt Kitty gave me my first narrative story, but there would be many more to come. Kitty had a son, Major, and two daughters, Bertha and Bessie. The three women lived on the same block right next to each other; Bessie lived in a two-story house on the corner, then Bertha, and then Kitty in the next house. From my house on 31st Street, the walk to their block on 22nd Street took me about thirty minutes. Mom and I would spend hours at my cousins Bertha and Bessie's house, and I would listen as they sat

Katie (Kitty) Lembric Williams
Born: 1871
Died: January 27, 1978

smoking cigarettes, drinking beer, talking about and reliving good times of music, and parties with family and friends.

Jane Baldwin, in her work, *Kara Women Speak: Stories from Women*, makes the observation that "Oral tradition conveys the narratives of their ancestry and family histories, and women are the keepers of this oral tradition through their storytelling of myth, proverb, and song." (https://www.globalonenessproject.org/library/photo-essays/kara-women-speak?metanid=3733&canonical=photo-essay/3717/3733#photo=16)

Other researchers who study family narratives also have found that family information is typically held by and passed on to the next generation by the women. Marshal P. Duke notes:

> "Who is passing this information?" and "When is this information transmitted?" In our study of family stories at the Emory University Family Narratives Project, funded by the Sloan Foundation, we found that family stories seem to be transferred by mothers and grandmothers more often than not and that the information was typically passed during family dinners, family vacations, family holidays, and the like. Other data indicated that these very same regular family dinners, yearly vacations, and holiday celebrations occur more frequently in families that have high levels of cohesiveness and that they contribute to the development of a strong sense of what we have called the intergenerational self. It is this intergenerational self and the personal strength and moral guidance that seem to derive from it that are associated with increased resilience, better adjustment, and improved chances of good clinical and educational outcomes."

Source: Duke, M. P., Lazarus, A., and Fivush, R. (2008). "Knowledge of family history as a clinically useful index of psychological well-being and prognosis: A brief report." *Psychotherapy Theory, Research, Practice, Training* 45: 268-272.

Do you know where your mother grew up?

y n

Ella Allen Doby and her husband John Doby

As I remember her, no longer the little girl in the field with A. S. J. Allen, Ella was an old woman; her once-black hair, now completely white, was still worn piled into a bun on top of her head, just as she had worn it as a teen. When I was a young boy, my grandma and I would take a Greyhound bus from our home on the coast to visit Ella, who still lived up in Gainesville, in the middle of the state.

Farm life was hard, and you could tell by the way she carried herself that this was a woman accustomed to hard work. Yet I've never met such a kind and gentle soul. I looked forward to these trips with Grandma to Aunt Ella and Uncle John's place in the country. They would spend hours talking about "the old days" and catching up on the news of folks who still lived in the area. When not working the land or tending to the animals, Aunt Ella made quilts. Big, heavy quilts. As she worked, she talked. This was one method by which stories of days gone by were passed on.

Some family stories came to me from my mom. I've listened intently as Mom told me stories of her youth and playtimes with her cousins, Edna, Sam, and Charlie. She told me of her days as a child being in the house I grew up in, as it was being built. She gave me stories of her visits to the insane asylum at Tuskegee to visit her dad. Her times dating my dad and going to concerts by BB King. Each day on her return from work, I would hear about the happenings of the day as she worked as a house cleaner and elevator girl at the Serena and Vinoy hotels in St. Petersburg, Florida.

So much of the foundational teachings of family and place in the world came to me via my mom. Mom possessed a very "matter of fact" temperament. One of her frequent mantras to me was, "I say what I mean, and I mean what I say." Rarely did she repeat herself. So she was not a great storyteller, but when she did speak, I learned to stop and listen because there might not be a second chance. When it came to my place in the world, Grandma and Mom taught me that I was good.

The first time I remember an encounter where the message could have been taken that I was "not good" came at a five and dime store in Central Plaza in St. Petersburg, Florida. My favorite dessert is a banana split. Hold that image in mind—we will come back to that at the end. I was about five years old or so and Mom was browsing through a table of head scarfs. I jumped up on a bar stool at the soda fountain and announced to the woman behind the counter that I wanted a banana split. The woman quickly turned around and told me to get down because "We don't serve niggers here." Without a flinch I quickly turned around on the stool and yelled across the store, "Mommy, what's a nigger?"

My mom looked up briefly from the brightly colored scarves, and said "Oh, honey, that just what ignorant White folks call colored people." I looked at the woman behind the counter with a sense of pity. I jumped down off the stool, knowing all along that I was loved and okay. But now I understood that there were "ignorant" people in the world. So, like I said, she was not a prolific storyteller, but she did deliver powerful messages. Throughout her life, Mom would tell me stories of encounters with other folks that somehow always ended with, "Be strong, be confident, and forgive them 'cause they don't know any better." Thank you, Momma, for building up self-esteem and a sense of family pride in me.

There were certain days of my youth that were filled with family stories. Thanksgiving Day dinners were typically at my Aunt Gussie and Uncle John's house. Gussie was another of Grandma's sisters. Which is to say, another source of family stories. The "white house with the golden fence," as Mom called it. Dinners with Aunt Gussie were always formal affairs. My job was to polish the silver before the table was set. Aunt Gussie insisted on a proper table setting for our holiday meals. That meant utensils placed in the order of use: farthest from the plate, utensils that are used first, closest to the plate, utensils used last, in an "outside-in" order. Forks go to the left of the plate while knives and spoons go to the right. And she expected to be able to see her reflection clearly in every silver fork, knife, and spoon. Oh, the stories I would hear, as I sat for hours polishing silverware in the kitchen. Mom, Grandma, and Aunt Gussie would get so involved in the food prep, I honestly think they would forget I was there. That

Areather, with her children; Rose, Dot, and Becky. The dog was called Sukay.

kind of invisibility is a benefit of being an only child. On many occasions, you are just the help, there to serve food and pick up after the guest, but not really engage. Nobody knows more about a family than "the help."

Christmas dinners were usually at our house. This was another great day filled with family stories. These gatherings also included my grandmother's other sister, Cora, and her children, Sam and Edna, and Edna's children, Lynda, Terry, and Lynette. When everyone would gather, I could always escape from the children's table with my cousins to the house—again in the role of the help. After a while, the adults would forget I was there and I could soak up the stories from the grownups' table.

Later on, during my time at University of Florida, I would spend my weekends out in the country with Aunt Ella's daughter and her husband, Cousins Essie and Sam. Essie made the most wonderful pickles every year. After all her pickling was done and the fields were picked, she would call me out to glean the fields. I would show up with guys from my fraternity, and we would go through the melon fields and leave to go back to the campus with cars loaded with cantaloupes, honeydews, and watermelons. I would leave with stories of farm life and her growing up in the house with Aunt Ella and her sister, Melvina.

So many family stories came to me when, as a college student at the University of Florida, weekends were spent outside of the Gainesville city limits in Alachua County. Right down the road from Essie and Sam lived my cousins, Sarah and Roger. My cousin Sarah and I would talk about the family, and I would learn more about the dynamics of my Alachua County kin from her and Roger.

More family lore and stories came to life when, as an adult, I sat in the kitchen of my cousin Minnie. She was always a treasure trove of stories. Not just stories; Minnie had pictures, too. Since she was older than her sisters (Dot, Rose, and Ruth) and me, but not as old as Mom and Essie, from Minnie I would get a different perspective on familiar stories about the family.

But my best family stories came from my grandmother's family photo album. A big black book with tan pages on which she had glued photos and newspaper clippings about all our family members. Most of the photos had handwritten captions identifying the names of the folks in the photos and sometimes the year in which the photo was taken.

In 1991 my cousin, Joyce White Mills, published *Two trees standing: A collection of family stories and a biographical dictionary of two Black families: the Browns of West Georgia and the Whites of East Georgia, 1806-1990.*

In the Acknowledgments section of her work, Joyce states that

"One primary giver of tales was Ozie Belle Brown, a person who at age 77 in 1971 gave several hours of taped stories and information from her past."

I owe so much to these and other women in my family who took the time to capture and share photos, stories, and family history with me.

> *Do you know some things about what happened when your brothers or sisters were being born?*
>
> *Y N*

Why do I care? Because it's *my* story.
Myth: Others will tell the story right.

Soundtrack suggestion:
"Family Affair"
Sly and the Family Stone

It's a family affair
Mom loves the both of them
You see, it's in the blood
Both kids are good to Mom
Blood's thicker than the mud

Soundtrack suggestion:
"That ain't right"
Fats Waller and Ada Brown: "That Ain't Right" (portrayed by Nat "King" Cole and Irving Mills), with Lena Horne; dancer, Bill "Bojangles" Robinson; drummer, Zutty Singleton; bassist, Slam Stewart; trumpeter, Benny Carter in the film "Stormy Weather" (1943) by Andrew L. Stone, for Twentieth Century Fox Film Corporation.

I went to a fortune teller and had my fortune told
She said, you didn't love me, all you wanted was my gold
That ain't right, that ain't right at all
And you're takin' all my money and goin' out havin' yourself a ball

Sometimes things aren't right. The narrative is all wrong. The story is twisted. And in the case of a violent and public death, the feeling can be confusing. On a day in March 2007, I sat in front of my computer screen and read the following words on page 112 of *Emancipation Betrayed: The Hidden History of Black Organizing and White Violence in Florida from Reconstruction to the Bloody Election of 1920* by Paul Ortiz.

In a section on Civic Fraternalism and Resistance, Ortiz states that, "In 1904, a white Alachua County man shot and killed Rev. J. L. Shaw, a neighboring Black farmer, over a fence boundary dispute." He went on to identify the White neighbor as A. S. J. Allen. I had to pen the letter below:

March 24, 2007

Paul Ortiz
Associate Professor

Dear Professor Ortiz,

My name is Alonzo Felder. For the last few years, I have been researching my family history and in so doing recently discovered your book, *Emancipation Betrayed*. While reading the book, I discovered a factual error and thought that in the interest of truth I should bring it to your attention.

I am the great-grandson of the Rev. A. S. J. Allen. In the book there is a reference to a 1904 incident in which my great-grandfather was murdered. On the bottom of page 112 it states:

"In 1904, a white Alachua County man shot and killed Rev. JL Shaw, a neighboring black farmer, over a fence boundary dispute. . . ."

Factually, it was JL Shaw, a white farmer, who killed my great-grandfather, Albert Sidney James Allen and he is also responsible for the "justifiable homicide" of another family member, Stephen Doby. Tensions still exist between the families because of these events, so I can imagine that other relatives of mine who read this error will feel as disturbed as I and just as eager to see the error corrected. Since JL Shaw committed these acts, then it is also inaccurate to write that the African American community of Alachua "mobilized to seek justice for JL Shaw."

Attached is a copy of the newspaper clipping, "Negro Preacher Killed Near Alachua," from the *Florida Times-Union* in Jacksonville, FL, dated Saturday, April 23, 1904, page 3, and it describes the facts of the event. You can also read more about my great-grandfather on my website at http://www. duke.edu/~felde001/family/.

As an aside, when you visit the site you will see reference in the condolence letter from the Florida United Methodist Church to A. S. J.'s death in "San Pulaski, FL." I believe this is a misprint on their part in reference to the Black Seminole town of Pilaklikaha (variously spelled), where I believe there is a family connection and possibly was a Methodist church outreach at the time.

In closing, I feel sure that your intentions were honorable in researching and writing the book, and with that assumption in mind, I am hoping that you will gratefully receive my letter and correct the account. I would suggest that an erratum be added to all new copies of the book that are shipped and that changes be made in any future editions. I would also offer that you and the publisher allow me to pen the erratum. In the erratum, I would first state how the facts should have been presented and then say something about the present-day implications, if you think this is noteworthy in making your point. I would also ask for a reference to my website either in the erratum itself or an additional endnote. I look forward to corresponding with you in the future. Thank you for your time.

Sincerely yours,
Alonzo Felder

I have a relative, Philoron A. Wright Sr., who authored *Night Riders: An African American Family in Peril in St. Augustine, Florida*" to relay the story of his immediate family being forced to flee one Florida city for another by the KKK. In his book's Dedication section, Cousin Phil writes:

"To our rising generations, you should learn of the sacrifices of the 'heros and heroines' of your past. You should educate yourselves so that the path of our forefathers/mothers will not repeat itself in human history. Someday history will

J. L. Shaw, of Alachua, one of the most widely known citizens of that section, was arrested in this city Friday upon a charge of murder of Rev. A. S. J. Allen, a negro minister, which occurred on the place of Mr. Shaw, near Alachua, in February of the present year, and the details of which are yet familiar in the minds of many readers of the Sun

Mr. Shaw was arrested by Sheriff Fennell while conversing with a friend on the street. He submitted coolly to his arrest and accompanied the sheriff to prison willingly, probably feeling that there would nothing serious result from the arrest.

At the time of the killing a coroner's jury was impaneled and held an inquest, the jury entirely exonerating Mr. Shaw of the charge.

Walter M. Davis of Jacksonville, and W. E. Baker of this city will be employed to assist the State in the prosecution of Shaw.

Mr. Shaw experienced no trouble in giving bond, which was fixed at $2,500. Jesse I. Griffin, of Jonesville, and J. L. Mathews, of Alachua, are sureties. Evans Halle will represent the defendant in this matter.—Gainesville Sun.

Miami News, Wednesday, October 12, 1904, page 7.

https://newscomwc. newspapers.com/ image/297543717. Downloaded on June 8, 2019.

tell all of our stories. What will it say about you?"

I echo these words of my kinsman. The stories of our people are tales worthy of telling because the people who lived them were heroes!

But sometimes those stories are missed. No one in the family told me the story of Grandpa and Mr. Shaw. Likewise with the story of my cousin Phil; I never knew his story. Sometimes the stories are not told at all. Other times the stories are told, but they are told wrongly, or they are told from a wrong point of view. "History is written by the victors." This quote is often attributed to Winston Churchill, but in all honesty its origins are unknown. The quote implies that history is not grounded in facts. Rather, history is the battle winners' interpretation of the facts—it's "His Story." This means that the ones in power, the victors, control the narrative that the people hear.

But take a look at 99 percent of books in print today. Are they telling your story? Do they tell the story of your ancestors? Your culture? Your people? If we cannot tell our own stories, we lose a huge part of who we are! This can mean that future generations are left with the stories other people tell about us.

From the "other" point of view:

Power converses coolly with power, power assumes that nothing serious will result from its actions. The story from my powerless family's perspective is different.

My family must now cope with the violent dying of a loved one. This is not done coolly but is deeply painful. Grief is a common experience. People experience grief when someone they love dies. But grief for families of killing victims is different. A killing is a violent and abnormal event. A killing is a violent death; and a violent death is more than just someone dying. It is more intense, it lasts longer, and is more complicated. The violent and unexpected death of a loved one leaves deep wounds and scars in the family members and community of friends.

Most of the time, when there is a violent dying of a family member, the death itself is rarely seen; it is either never spoken of, or it is retold as a "story." Earlier I mentioned my cousins, Sarah and Roger, and the times we spent together while I was in college. The one story I do not remember hearing retold was the story of Sara's dad's and brother's deaths. I think it was too painful for her to give voice to. But the story—the event—was out there. It was public knowledge. It was in the newspaper. The father and son pair, Themester Mack Senior and Junior, were killed in a train wreck when I was a freshman college student. All we had were the news reports, so the story took on a life of its own as I, along with other family members, tried to imagine the events of that day.

> What were they talking about?
> What were they doing?
> Were they distracted?
> Did they see the train?
> Did they try to escape from the car?
> Were there screams?
> Why were they there?
> Why couldn't they have taken a different route?
> How could this have happened?
> How can we find retribution for this dying?

Having to rethink this persistent sort of questioning, and then retelling, of a violent dying event as a story to find an "answer" is empty and exhausting. Which is probably another reason no one talks about it.

An unwanted aspect of a violent death can be that the dying becomes a public story. Whether the dying is by accident or a crime, often the event hits the news and, once the reporting is out, the survivors must deal with newfound and often unwanted publicity.

The publicity about a loved one's death only adds to the grief. Many adults who have lost a loved one to a violent death, such as an accident or a killing, suffer from depression, post-traumatic stress disorder (PTSD), and complicated grief.

Photos from Mt. Nebo Cemetery
http://www.wizardofar.org/CFDocs/common/StoneTemp.
cfm?ID=130&Cemetery=MtNebo&CemName=Mt%20
Nebo&SCount=315&org=ACHC

After the violent dying of a family member, the story of the dying may become preoccupying. The sustained replay of this dying story becomes unbearable because it always ends the same, often leaving you with a powerless sense of horror, terror, and fear.

Knowing of an ancestor's killing changes you. A killing is caused by an external force or action. It is not at all like the quiet, internal, impersonal, and invisible dying of old age or the wasting away of sickness or disease. A killing involves the drama of a fatal human act—someone dies by the hand of some other person. Those who study this kind of grief tell us that stories of violent dying often have a lasting negative impact on the family and friends left behind. In fact, studies show that such traumas are often carried on from one generation to another: transgenerational trauma.

What is true of individuals is also true of communities. I've heard it said that "You are as sick as your secrets." A violent killing shows that when we experience trauma, often we try to hide it. Either we hide it from ourselves or, most often, from others. We don't talk about it. We don't let folks know. Instead, we carry the trauma around in our souls. Doing so makes us sick.

Well, if a person is as sick as their traumas; then a family, likewise, is as sick as its secrets or traumas. As families we hide racism, incest, rape, murder, abuse, addiction, and so many other "sins." When we do, then we as a community, as a family, make sure that each generation knows the importance of continuing to hide that trauma. A violent death like A. S. J.'s was a family secret. It was so well guarded that it took me until I was an adult, with grown children of my own, to discover the truth of his race-based killing. His lynching was a taboo subject among the old, and an untold history for the young. The details had been long forgotten, but the family all knew to leave White folks (especially White men) alone. The trauma was there, but no one could explain why. By contrast with natural dying, the story of the death and the feelings around it are focused more on the deceased person and his or her living interactions with the storyteller rather than on the drama of the deceased person's dying episode.

Like the deaths of my cousins due to the train wreck, A. S. J.'s death was public knowledge. There were newspaper reports accompanied with many of the same questionings about the events leading up to his final moments on earth. In the following pages, I attempt to piece together what I can of his life and times.

> *Do you know some of the illnesses and injuries that your parents experienced when they were younger?*
>
> *Y N*

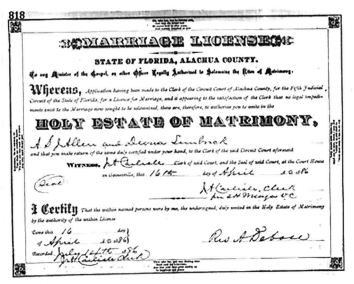

A. S. J. and Dinah's marriage license
Source: https://duke.app.box.com/file/322907718236

1880 United States Census

Census Place **Precinct 9, Alachua, Florida**
Source FHL Film **1254125** National Archives Film **T9-0125** Page **52D**

	Relation	Sex	Mar	Race	Age	Birthplace
Shed LIMERICK	Self	M	M	B	46	SC
Phillis LIMERICK	Wife	F	M	B	35	SC
Shed LIMERICK	Son	M	S	B	20	SC
Milly LIMERICK	Dau	F	S	B	17	FL
Diana LIMERICK	Dau	F	S	B	15	FL
Jack LIMERICK	Son	M	S	B	10	FL
Rose LIMERICK	Dau	F	S	B	7	FL
Louis LIMERICK	Son	M	S	B	5	FL
Tilly LIMERICK	Dau	F	S	B	2	FL
Sally LIMERICK	Dau	F	S	B	6M	FL

1880 census record showing Dinah and her family.

The Lembrics

"Now the Lord said to Abram,
'Go forth from your country,
And from your relatives
And from your father's house,
To the land which I will show you.'" (Gen. 12.1)

For much of America, genealogical research is heavily dependent on knowing your ancestor's last name. This is not always the case in African American research, as most noted by the civil rights activist, El-Hajj Malik El-Shabazz, born Malcolm Little, but better known as Malcolm X.

Malcom and numerous others used the "X" as a way of representing their real names that were now lost to history. The last names of most Black folks in America were not their original names, but rather the names of the families that enslaved their ancestors.

The origins of my family surname of Lembric are unclear. In fact, the historical documents vary greatly concerning the spelling of the surname. My research has uncovered findings with the spellings of Limbric, Limbrick, Lembric, Limbrie, Lembrick, Limberic, Lanbrice, Limerick, and Timberick. At the end of the book, we will discuss more on surname spellings and variations in the chapter on "Your Folks."

A. S. J. Allen left Alabama and grew to manhood in Florida. There he saw the efforts of the nation to heal from a terrible chapter in its history. By age twenty, A. S. J. had found the love of his life and in 1886 he married Dinah Lembric. Dinah was the youngest child of Shed (a.k.a. Shedrick or Shadrack) and Phyllis Lembric. The Lembric family (however you chose to spell it) was a well-established family in Alachua and Duval Counties.

Prior to his marriage to Dinah Lembric, I have no paper record for A. S. J. Allen. I know nothing of his father or mother or if he had siblings. Nothing. In many ways, his life began when he married

Zachariah David (aka "ZD") Lembric

Dinah Limbric and became the "extra" son of Shed and Phyllis. In addition to the union with Dinah, he is active in preaching with her brother, Zachariah David (aka "ZD") Lembric; and by 1890 is an ordained deacon in the Methodist Episcopal Church. The closeness of these two men is evident by their names often appearing together in the conference minutes of the Methodist Church. In oral interviews with Wilbert Allen (A. S. J.'s youngest son) my uncle Wilbert tells of how he was told growing up of his dad and Uncle ZD spending lots of time together traveling around Florida preaching and ministering to the folks of central Florida. Note that on the 1880 census record, ZD appears as Jack. My assumption is that the census enumerator mistook "Zack" for "Jack" when recording the name. Interviews with Uncle Wilbert also revealed that he knew his grandparents (Phyllis and Shed) and Phyllis's parents (Lewis and Milly Harris).

In the 1900 United States Federal Census I find the following record.

Name:	Milly Harris
Age:	18
Birth Date:	1881
Birthplace:	South Carolina
Home in 1900:	Archer, Alachua, Florida
Sheet Number:	13B
Number of Dwelling in Order of Visitation:	24
Family Number:	244
Race:	Black
Gender:	Female
Relation to Head of House:	Wife
Marital Status:	Married
Spouse's Name:	Lewis Harris
Marriage Year:	1896
Years Married:	4
Father's Birthplace:	South Carolina
Mother's Birthplace:	South Carolina
Mother: Number of living children:	1
Mother: How many children:	1
Can Read:	Yes
Can Write:	Yes
Can Speak English:	Yes
Household Members:	Name / Age Lewis Harris / 25 Milly Harris / 18 Flora Harris / 3

> *Do you know where your father grew up?*
>
> *Y N*

Why such large families?

Because no birth control.

Myth: No need to know our neighbors.

The two most popular answers to why our ancestors had large families are:

- If you wanted to eat after you were too old to work, the only option was to have enough children to make it likely that one of them would survive and be wealthy enough to support you.

- The popular culture of most of our ancestors dictated that a woman's place was in the home, and her fulfillment was found there, where she served her husband and raised her children.

1900 United States Federal Census

Name:	**Dianah Allen**
Age:	34
Birth Date:	Sep 1865
Birthplace:	Florida
Home in 1900:	Alachua, Alachua, Florida [Alachua]
Race:	Black
Gender:	Female
Relation to Head of House:	Wife
Marital Status:	Married
Spouse's Name:	A J Allen
Marriage Year:	1886
Years Married:	14
Father's Birthplace:	South Carolina
Mother's Birthplace:	South Carolina
Mother: number of living children:	8
Mother: How many children:	8
Occupation:	

Household Members: Name	Age
A J Allen	37
Dianah Allen	34
John Limbrick	15
Cora Lee Allen	14
Ella D Allen	12
Gustava Allen	10
Alonzo R Allen	8
Oliver W H Allen	6
Phillis Allen	5
Ethea M Allen	3
Wilber H Allen	2
Christina Allen	3/12

Source Citation: Year: *1900*; Census Place: *Alachua, Alachua, Florida*; Roll: *165*; Page: *33A*; Enumeration District: *3*; FHL microfilm: *1240165*.

The A. S. J. Allen Family

"For this reason, a man will leave his father and mother and be joined to his wife" (Gen. 2:24).

Dinah had a son, John Lembric, when she and A. S. J. married. As he traveled and preached, more children arrived in the Allen family. In looking at the 1900 census record, John was fifteen in 1900, so he must have been about one year old in 1886 when the couple married. Note in the census image also that Dinah's name is misspelled as "Dianah." In my exploration of the family, I have come across spellings of "Diona," "Dye," (an apparent nickname) and "Diane." Later, we will discuss the name spellings and variations that we encounter on the journey to family history discovery. In this same record below, we see A. S. J. listed as "AJ Allen." Such variations are bothersome, but as we will see later, they can be understood and dismissed as minor as we look at other pieces of the document to confirm the family unit identity.

In June of 1886, two months after their wedding, Dinah gave birth to the couple's first child: a girl they named Cora. The next year, another baby girl arrived, his dear Ella. That same year (1890) a third daughter was born. This child they named Gustava. Everyone called her Gussie.

In 1890 A. S. J., Dinah, and the two girls were living in the struggling town of Newnansville, Florida. Newnansville had been the county seat of Alachua County but back in the winter of 1886, a major freeze ruined the citrus crops. This was a major blow to the local economy. The freeze plus lack of any railway connections led businesses and residents to move to the growing communities of Alachua and Gainesville. Most folks went to Gainesville, where the county seat was now located. By the turn of the twentieth century, the town of Newnansville was a ghost town.

In 1891 A. S. J. would find himself at the historic Mt. Pleasant Methodist Church. Back in 1867, Republicans had summoned Black citizens in town to attend a meeting at Mt. Pleasant. It was here that formerly enslaved people learned of their right to vote. That year, 1,265 African Americans registered and 979 of them cast a ballot. This surge in Black voters contributed to the Republican victories that took place during the Reconstruction.

In 1892 a boy, Alonzo, was born into the family. Within two more years another girl, Phyllis, had arrived. That year, 1894, A. S. J. began preaching in Hague and Stanley and Jonesville.

In 1895 A. S. J. was assigned a church in Palatka. A year later, he was preaching in Arrendo and Union Lake. There, Minnie was born. By 1889 A. S. J. was preaching in Cedar Key and Rosewood.

As 1899 rolled in, the couple welcomed their second son, Wilbert Albert, into the family. Then A. S. J. began preaching in Mikesville and High Springs. In February of 1900 their last child, another girl, Fannie, was born. At least I believe this to be their last child. My grandmother, Fannie, always told the story that her mom had died during childbirth. In hearing this story, I believed that Grandma was saying that Dinah died giving birth to her. I began to question this interpretation of the story when I found a land sale signed by Dinah that was dated 1901. So it is possible that sometime between 1901 and 1904, Dinah gave birth and passed away, and A. S. J. went on to teach and preach in Liberty Hill and Union Lake.

My research shows that "Liberty Hill Schoolhouse in Gainesville, Florida, is a one-room schoolhouse that was built in 1892 to serve African-American children. It replaced a previous Liberty Hill School that was in operation by about 1869, and it operated until the 1950s. It is 24.5 feet by 30.5 feet." This building is just outside the city limits of Gainesville. In 1892 the school provided the first six years of education for Black children from Alachua County.

Sources: "National Register Information System," *National Register of Historic Places*, National Park Service, March 13, 2009.
Murray D. Laurie and Gary V. Goodwin (2003), *National Register of Historic Places* Registration: Liberty Hill Schoolhouse, Natl. Park Service, Ret. September 29, 2016.

The Reverend Albert Sydney James (A. S. J.) Allen, MG

Around age twenty-five, A. S. J. was ordained as a deacon in the Methodist Church. Various ME Church records document his ministry career under the names of A.S.J. Allen or Albert S. J. Allen.

A. S. J. Allen and ZD Lembric traveled between distant churches in small communities. Preachers like them came out of a Methodist tradition of "circuit riders" or "saddlebag preachers," although their official role was "*traveling* clergy." These ministers typically traveled on horseback, or sometimes in a wagon if the roads permitted. There was no interstate road system and few paved roads in Alachua County during the end of the eighteenth century. Travel was hard and the segregated Black communities were spread far apart. Methodist circuit preachers were an efficient way of reaching the people.

Table of A. S. J.'s children and movements

Year	A. S. J.'s Age	Births	Preaching Assignments
1885	20	John L	
1886	21	Cora	
1887	22	Ella	
1888	23		
1889	24		
1890	25	Gussie	Newnansville
1891	26		Newnansville
1892	27	Alonzo	Newnansville
1893	28	Oliver	Hague and Stanley
1894	29	Phyllis	Jonesville
1895	30		Palatka
1896	31	Minnie	Arrendondo and Union Lake

1897	32		Arrendondo and Union Lake
1898	33		Cedar Key and Rosewood
1899	34	Wilbert	Mikesville and High Springs
1900	35	Fannie	Mikesville and High Springs
1901	36		Liberty Hill and Union Lake
1902	37		Liberty Hill and Union Lake
1903	38		Liberty Hill
1904	39		Alachua

Map of A. S. J.'s travels around Alachua County

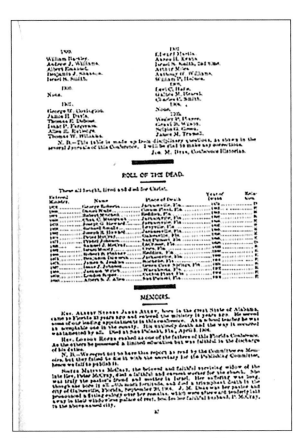

Memoir from the conference journal for 1905.

Source: Nell Thrift, Archivist, Florida United Methodist Heritage Center, McKay Archives Center, Florida Southern College.

A. S. J. Allen at Hague

He Was Rebuilding Lives

"... like a shelter from the wind
    and a refuge from the storm,
like streams of water in the desert
    and the shadow of a great rock in a thirsty land."
(Isa. 32.2)

Every year since 1890 more and more duties were assigned to A. S. J. as he rose in the ranks of the Methodist Church. He had a clear devotion to building family and community.

In "Letters from Conferences," published in the *Southwestern Christian Advocate*, May 11, 1893, we find A. S. J. working hard to build up the church at his new post in Hague, Florida.

The Methodist Church records his involvement in auditing the finances of a church in New York, chairing a committee involved in the education of young people, and chairing a committee that provided education and aid to freed people to get education and housing. He also worked to build Florida's first school for "colored" children (Cookman Institute).

As a part of his work, from 1891 to 1903 he performed thirty known marriages. These are listed below.

Groom Surname	Groom Given Name	Bride Surname	Bride Given Name	Year	Official recorded name and signature	Possible location
Bell	John	Bradley	Janie	1891	A.S. J. Allen	Newnansville
Brown	John	Brooks	Josephine	1891	A.S. J. Allen	
Robinson	William	White	Mary	1891	A.S.J. Allen	
Williams	John	Williams	Mollie	1892	A.S.J. Allen	Newnansville

Alonzo Felder

Mims	S. M.	Williams	Anna E.	1893	A. S. J. Allen	Hague and Stanley
Rutledge	James S	Richardson	Rebecca	1893	A. S. Allen	
Brockington	George	Baks	Lula	1894	Albert L. Allen	Jonesville
Broom	John	Johnson	Ann	1894	A. S. J. Allen	
Cooper	James	McDonald	Mattie	1894	A. S. J. Allen	
Furgerson	Isaah	Smith	Fannie	1894	A. S. J. Allen	
Lumpkin	Isaiah	Cooper	Lilla	1894	A. S. J. Allen	
Ross	Thomas	Johnson	Josephine	1894	Albert Allen	
Singleton	J H	Brockington	Alice	1894	A. S. J. Allen	
Spicer	Thomas M	Smith	Caroline	1894	A. S. J. Allen	
Richeddi	W A	Wright	Lucie C	1896	A. S. J. Allen	Arrendondo/ Union Lake
Childs	David	Lang	Lottie	1896	A.S.J. Allen	
Hendricks	Elbert	George	Betsey	1896	A. S. J. Allen	
Watts	D.J.	Brooks	Phoebe A.	1896	A.S.J. Allen	
Whitaker	W.M.	Lang	M.L.	1896	A.S.J. Allen	
Williams	Lewis	Baker	Alice	1896	A.S.J Allen	

					A.S.J. Allen (signature)	
Anderson	Lee	Cooper	Letitia	1897	A.S.J. Allen	
Davis	William	Haile	Mattie	1897	Albert S.J. Allen	
Doby	Purdy	Johnson	Alice	1898	A.S.J. Allen	Cedar Key / Rosewood
George	Moses	Hollin	Rosa	1898	Albert S.J. Allen	
Lunday	Charley	Anderson	Lula Essie	1898	A.S.J. Allen	
Childs	David	Anderson	Mary	1899	A.S.J. Allen M.G	Mikesville/ High Springs
Limbrick	Louis	Hamilton	Elizabeth	1899	A.S.J. Allen	
Battle	Lonnie	Thomas	Hattie	1900	A.S.J.Allen	Mikesville/ High Springs
Ross	Willie A	Rochelle	Sallie E	1901	A. S. J. Allen	Liberty Hill/ Union Lake
Fisher	Chatham	Neal	Amelia	1902	A. S. J. Allen M.G.	
Hawkins	William	Bullard	Lilla	1902	H. S. Allen	
Hawkins	William H.	B	Lilla	1902	A.S.J. Allen, M.G.	
Hawkins	William H.	Bullard	Lillie	1902	A. S. J. Allen, M.G.	

Note: the "M.G." behind A. S. J.'s signature indicates "Minister of the Gospel."

A. S. J. was not only helping to rebuild lives torn apart by war, slavery, and the racial terror of the KKK, he also worked as a schoolteacher and a farmer. A. S. J. was helping to build a future for the poor White and Black communities of north-central Florida.

As an advocate of the adage "charity starts at home," we find evidence that A. S. J. worked to provide for his own family. In 1895 he secured funds for a relative, Bro. Doby.

Records of the "Third day afternoon session, of Minutes of the Twenty Third Session of the Florida Annual Conference of the Methodist Episcopal Church, convened at Ebenezer ME church, Jacksonville, Florida (Jan 24th, 25th, 26th, and 27th, 1895. Pg. 11," reveal that "On motion of A. S. J. Allan a collection was taken amounting to $3 78 for Bro. Doby, an aged Local Preacher on the Gainesville District, also one by J. Grant involving a collection of $1 74 for the Sexton. Bro. J. M. Deas was appointed to preach the missionary sermon, and A. S. J. Allan."

A. S. J. also actively secured land for his family in Alachua County. Land records show that from 1899 to 1903 he was involved in several land transactions of the same parcel of land:

> Fairbanks to A. S. J.: Deed record 1899 $200
> sw quarter of nw quarter sec 11 township 9 range 18
> Arredondo grant
> Watson to A. S. J.: Deed record 59—1900 $50
> no half of nw quarter sw quarter of section 11 township 9 range 18 of Arredondo
> A. S. J. & Diana to Williams: Deed record 55 --- 1901 $100 and ???
> SW quarter of NW quarter of Sec 11 township 11 range 18 Arredondo grant.
> Williams to A. S. J. (grantee/buyer): Deed record 60---1903 $100
> sw quarter of nw quarter of sec 11 township 9 range 18 in Arredondo grant.

> *Do you know where some of your grandparents grew up?*
>
> *y n*

Why are the family and community important?
Because our society thrives on strong families.
Myth: No need to know our neighbors.

The land record, dated 1901, is the last record I can find on
Dinah Allen.

The only research that has given any data on Alonzo Reed (sometimes spelled "Reid") Allen is via education and the census records.

Essie remembers him as a dapper, kind man. "He always brought us something when he came to visit," she recalled.

A. S. J. fled Alabama, found a wife and a career, and was growing both a family and a community. He was rising in experience and leadership in the Methodist Episcopal Church. His family was growing. From the time that A. S. J. was a small child up into the early 1900s, the Ku Klux Klan opposed many of the social changes in Alabama and Florida that resulted from emancipation, including the development of independent Black schools and churches.

A. S. J. was a Black man living through the post-Civil War Reconstruction era of the American South. The Civil War had ended a relatively short time ago. This means that just about every Black adult A. S. J. encountered who was older than he, had known slavery. He was of that first generation of American Blacks born into freedom. It is not difficult to see why his heart turned toward the betterment of his people. The older mentors in his life were freedmen of color and northern Whites.

The care and provision for the family is a theme that runs throughout A. S. J.'s life story. The theme continues even after his death. The Lembric family was close to the Allen couple, and with A. S. J.'s death in 1904, Dinah's sister, Phyllis Limbric, and her husband, Charlie Hamilton, stepped forward to care for the two toddlers, Wilbert and Fannie. They eventually won approval to take the children into their home in St. Petersburg, Florida. (See the guardianship document on page 104.)

Note: Since Fannie had both a sister and an aunt named Phyllis, she would refer to her aunt as "Momma Phyllis," and her sister as "Sister Phyllis."

Interesting side note here:

Census record for Alonzo Allen (eight years old) in 1900 in Alachua, line 51

I found him again in the Bookman Institute at Daytona school census records of 1910. Apparently, Alonzo left home and lived at school. See line 8; Alonzo at 18.

In 1920 he is on the Tampa census on page 102 (27 years old).

Alonzo Allen

Momma Phyllis eventually remarried a man named Willie Mitchell. Grandma never had any good things to tell me about my uncle Willie. In 1956, when she passed away, her will was revealed (see next page).

Phyllis left wealth to my grandmother (Fannie Felder) and my mom (Willie Mae Felder) in the form of houses. These houses provided rental income for us when I was growing up. The washing machine was crucial also, as we took in laundry from others. I find it interesting that she had the foresight to leave her husband, Willie, $1.00. Had she not, he could have contested the will as her legal spouse, potentially won, and taken control of everything. The Lembric reputation for managing their property well seems to have some grounding in truth.

With a single gunshot, nine children became orphans in 1904. I honor them. Knowing their stories makes me strong. Their lives influence my future. I spent my school years going to family funerals and talking with my grandmother and mother about the latest family passing. Before I graduated from college in 1980, forty-eight members of our family had passed away. The Mt. Nebo Methodist Church cemetery in Alachua, Florida, is where many of them now rest. I did not personally know all these folks, but my grandmother and others close by shared many of their stories with me, and for this I am grateful. I want to make sure their stories survive.

If a consequence of knowing a family narrative is well-being, then the converse must be that not knowing is a root of depression, loneliness, discontent, dysfunction, and low self-esteem. Now I am not saying that if you dive headlong into DNA testing, and build your family tree back to Noah, you will flourish into the most stable and well-adjusted person on the planet. As it turns out, it is not just the knowing, but more importantly how we arrive at the knowing, that produces the good benefits.

Now, I did not understand this early on. I remember being a bit bored at listening to my grand talk about "poor old so and so"

3 PAGE 92

15 PAGE 211

WILL—Short Form. Printed and For Sale by K-B Printing Co., 350 Central Ave., St. Petersburg, Form No. 25

23,492

In the Name of God. Amen

I, Phillis Hamilton Mitchell

being of sound mind and memory, and considering the uncertainty of this frail and transitory life, do therefore make, ordain publish and declare this to be my last WILL AND TESTAMENT, that is to say:

FIRST—After all my lawful debts are paid and discharged, I give and bequeath to my daughter Fannie Allen Felder, Lot Seven (7), Blk. 1-Grand Central Subdivision according to record-recorded in the Court House, Pinellas County, Fla. And to my son Wilbert A. Allen- Lots Nineteen and Twenty (19-20) of Grand Cetral Subdivision No.1. To my niece Bertha Williams Lot eighteen (18), Grand Central Subdivision No.1. To my niece Addie Mavins-Lot Thirteen (13), Grand Central Subdivision No.1. To my niece Phillis A. White, Lot Fourteen (14), Grand Central Subdivision No.1. And I further request that Lot Twenty One (21)-Grand Central Subdivision No.L- be sold by my Executrix and the proceeds be equally devided by my brother L.C.Lumbric and my sister-inlaw Nacy Benjamin. And my further request is that all my my property situated and lying in Alachua County, Florida, described as follows; Lots 4,13,14,15,16 of Block Five (5), and Lot Thirteen (13) of Guinn Williams and Reeves Addition, Lots 1,2,3 Block Eight (8). Alachua, Fla. And the NE¼ of the NE¼ Sec 15-Twsp 8 Range 18 8 acres more or lest. All of this property I give and bequeath to my daughter Fannie A. Felder and my son Wilbert A. Allen. And to my grand niece Willie Mae Felder I give my washingt machine. To my friend Rosa Lee Moore I give and equal share of what ever amount of money that I may leave after my death. And I further give to my husband Willie Mitchell, One (1), dollar. And it is my further request that after my death I want McRae Funeral Home to take my remains to my home and deposit same in the cemetery with the rest of my relatives .

Likewise I make, constitute and appoint Fannie A. Felder, and in the event of her death before this will is probated I appoint my son Wilbert A. Allen as my executor

to be my executrix of this my last Will and Testament, hereby revoking all former Wills by me made.

IN WITNESS WHEREOF, I have hereunto subscribed my name and affixed my seal the 17th, day of June , in the year of our Lord one thousand nine hundred and fifty two

Phillis H Mitchel (Seal)

Phyllis's will

who had recently passed away. However, even though I was "not listening," apparently I was, because I remember the stories and can retell them.

I sat in my living room a while back and processed that much of my family was dead. The four of us were all that was left of the family, or so it seemed. Now I was an adult, and my children had no grandparents. There were no "old folks back home." My wife and I had become the old folks.

Sign in front of Mt. Nebo church and cemetery.

The Return to Dust

"You turn people back to dust,
    saying, 'Return to dust, you mortals.'
A thousand years in your sight
    are like a day that has just gone by,
    or like a watch in the night.
Yet you sweep people away in the sleep of death—

94

they are like the new grass of the morning:
  In the morning it springs up new,
    but by evening it is dry and withered." (Ps. 90:3-6)

A. S. J. did not know that Thursday, April 21, 1904, would be his last day alive. He would never return to the house to see his babies. By four o'clock that evening, this promising young man, five months shy of his thirty-ninth birthday, would be dead.

His babies would be the subject of a custody battle waged by Dinah's sister, Phyllis, and the state of Florida. Phyllis would eventually prevail and take Wilbert and Fannie to live with her in St. Petersburg. Fannie Allen would complete the Daytona Normal and Industrial Institute for Negro Girls and eventually leave Bethune College at seventeen years old to care for her baby girl, Willie Mae.

Five years later, Fannie would marry a man named Ned Felder. Ned would adopt her baby girl and change her name from Willie Mae Allen to Willie Mae Felder. Then, at the age of thirty-nine, Willie Mae would give birth to a baby boy whom she would name Alonzo Albert—me.

It all began with this larger-than-life teacher, preacher, and farmer, A. S. J., who was murdered on a warm Thursday evening in Florida. I believe that for all of us, the best of our forefathers lives in us. A. S. J. left behind nine orphaned children.

Phyllis guardianship document

Remembering the orphans of A. S. J. and Dinah Allen
(ages at the time of his death)

John (19 years old), Died: May 1965

Cora (18 years old)
Died: December 25, 1971

Ella (17 years old),
Died: May 22, 1980

Gussie (14 years old),
Died: March 28,1976

Alonzo (12 years old),
Died: unknown

Phyllis (10 years old),
Died: January 20, 1955

Minnie (8 years old),
Died: June 14, 1964

Wilbert (4 years old),
Died: 1992

Fannie (2 years old),
Died: November 21, 1975

In 1990 my great-uncle, Wilbert A. Allen, gave an interview with a group of high school students at Mount Vernon High School. The interview was a part of the class's "Seniors on Seniors" program, where senior citizens from the area were invited by the school's senior class to come in and be interviewed about their lives.

Perhaps the most moving part of watching the video of that interview was seeing my uncle (A. S. J.'s baby boy who was four years old at the time of his dad's killing) choke back and wipe away tears during the discussion of his being raised as a motherless and fatherless child.

Gannett Westchester Newspapers/Thursday, February 15, 1990

J. Gregory Raymond

Wilbert Allen, who will celebrate his 92nd birthday Feb. 24, spent yesterday fielding questions about his life and times from a class of news media students at Mount Vernon High School. At right is a 1963 photo of Allen that appeared in the newspaper and Mount Vernon High School student Eddie Vichaidith.

Mount Vernon man relives history

By Kathy Moore
Staff Writer

When Wilbert Allen was born on a farm in Alachua, Fla., the ninth of 10 children, William McKinley was president, America was at war with Spain and the Klondike Gold Rush was sweeping the Yukon.

The Mount Vernon resident, who will celebrate his 92nd birthday Feb. 24, reminisced yesterday with a group that will reach retirement age in 2038.

"I never thought I would live so long to see the day when they would ask me to do this," Allen said.

Wilbert Allen spent the morning fielding questions about his life and times from a class of news media students at Mount Vernon High School. The interview between students and senior citizen was preserved for history on videotape.

It was sponsored by the city's Office of the Aging and was meant to foster better understanding between the old and the young.

From all indications, yesterday's session accomplished its goal. The students described Allen as inspirational, interesting and even relevant to their own teen-age existence.

"He came through a lot, and we might have to come through the same things in our time," said Marshall Regin, a 17-year-old senior.

Some of the events that Allen lived through were the two world wars, the Depression, and the technological revolution. He recalled that blacks weren't allowed to serve in the military at the beginning of World War I, but that when World War II came around, he joined the Army Air Corps.

He said he ended up "serving" nine officers at a base in Victorville, Calif. On the weekends, the officers would take off for Los Angeles, leaving Allen an envelope with cash.

"It was so helpful and so joyful (to receive the extra money) that I often went to Los Angeles myself," he said.

When asked what the greatest invention of his lifetime has been, Allen answered, "The airplane, which I wasn't too excited about because I didn't understand what it was all about."

He said he didn't have a car, but had "some nice horses." When asked about his courting days, Allen said that working two jobs didn't leave much time for romance but then astonished the students when he said that he had been married four times.

"I was 10 years with the first wife, 10 years with the second wife, 43 years with the third wife and about six years with the fourth wife and doing well," he said.

A messenger and clerical worker with the New York City Transit Authority for 44 years, Allen seemed equally proud that he was always self-supporting and that he still had his own teeth.

His recollections about life were heavily laced with references to God, the work ethic and the value of helping others. Allen has volunteered for the past 16 years at Mount Vernon Hospital, where he said he supplies the sick with reading material, prayers and jokes.

"I know quite a few jokes," he said.

A Legacy to Be Proud Of

"Make us glad for as many days as you have afflicted us,
    for as many years as we have seen trouble.
May your deeds be shown to your servants,
    your splendor to their children.
May the favor of the Lord our God rest on us;
    establish the work of our hands for us—
    yes, establish the work of our hands." (Ps. 90:15-17)

The death of someone close to us has pervasive consequences in many areas of our lives. Many good and wonderful folks fill the roles as descendants of the Lembrics and Allens of Florida. Strong, hard-working men and women. The descendants of these poor Black farmers became successful crafts workers and professionals.

But far more important to me than their occupations was the transformation and skillsets they cultivated to become men and women of good character, wisdom, and judgment.

"Brothers, consider the time of your calling: Not many of you were wise by human standards; not many were powerful; not many were of noble birth. But God chose the foolish things of the world to shame the wise; God chose the weak things of the world to shame the strong. He chose the lowly and despised things of the world, and the things that are not, to nullify the things that are." (1 Cor. 1: 26-28)

"John Adams was a farmer. Abraham Lincoln was a small-town lawyer. Plato, Socrates were teachers. Jesus was a carpenter. To equate judgment and wisdom with occupation is at best ... insulting." (Benedict Valda, from the television series *Warehouse 13*, "Breakdown" [1.10])

In a later chapter, we'll discuss how you can use your ancestors' occupations to further your research and learn more about them.

Do you know where some of your grandparents met?

Y N

Why tell the story about my "horrible" folks?
Because they are family.
Myth: You should tell of family successes but hide the darker side of family stories.

Soundtrack suggestion.
"Mrs. Robinson"
Songwriter: Paul Simon

Hide it in the hiding place where no one ever goes
Put it in your pantry with your cupcakes
It's a little secret, just the Robinsons' affair
Most of all you've got to hide it from the kids.

In 1870 an African American man born into slavery, Josiah T. Walls, was the nominee of the Republican Party for Florida's only seat in the U.S. House of Representatives. Walls became the state of Florida's first Black congressman. He was re-elected in 1872.

Walls ran for office and was elected again to the Florida Senate in 1876. He was the first African American to serve in the U.S. Congress from Florida, and it was nearly one hundred years before he was succeeded (https://themasonicobserver.wordpress.com/josiah-t-walls/ and https://themasonicobserver.wordpress.com/).

Josiah Walls paved the way for future generations of Blacks to occupy seats of power in the Florida government. In the late 1890s, A. S. J. would seek a government post but not receive it. Generations later one of Dinah Limbric Allen's descendants, Arnett Girardeau, would rise to the Florida Senate. His rise was historic, in that he was one of the first African Americans to serve in the Florida Senate since Reconstruction. My cousin served in the Florida House from 1976 through 1982.

Soundtrack suggestion:
"Family Tree"
Loretta Lynn

Bring out the babies' daddy, that's who they've come to see
Not the woman that's burnin' down our family tree.

You should always tell the truth, the whole truth, and try to set the record straight.

A. S. J. was a leader, not because someone elected him to a position, but because the people around him felt they knew him. "Your people will follow you because," as leadership guru, Noel Tichy, said, "leadership is autobiographical: If I don't know you as a person, how do I know you as a leader?"

What I do know is that, as I interviewed my one-hundred-year-old cousin Essie, she stammered and her eyes filled with tears as she related to me how, as a child, she had to pass the Shaw house on her way to school.

I watched as this elderly woman choked up trying to tell me how scared she was just to walk by the Shaw house. That memory still haunted her eighty years later and caused an emotional response.

"May the LORD judge between you and me. And may the LORD avenge the wrongs you have done to me, but my hand will not touch you" (1 Sam. 24:12).

The "Outsider" Story

In the article "How children benefit from learning their family history," A. J. Jacobs said: "I mean, we all have horrible, horrible relatives. My family has its share of criminals: con artists, thieves, murderers, and a whole assortment of other sinners. Yep, they are all there. However, my grandma taught me to believe that 'the best of your forefathers lives in you,'

and that is the TRUTH." (https://myrootsfoundation.com/
wdykya-who-do-you-know-you-are/)

Most families have a "tainted" past. Welcome to the human
race. Nobody's perfect. And nobody's family is perfect. It took
all of those folks to create you and me. That is why the stories
of family members accomplishments like Arnetts' walk onto the
Florida Senate floor, and the stories of family fears, like Essies'
walk past the Shaw house, must both be told.

The Importance of Offering Children an Intergenerational Identity

The Importance of the Narrative

A motive for keeping the family's history quiet might have been to protect the kids from the hurt and confusion of death and divorce, or it might have been to avoid sharing personal mistakes and missteps from the past.

Researchers agree that children need to know that they have a place in a bigger story than their own. Children who have what is called an intergenerational identity feel more in control of their lives, according to research by Dr. Marshall Duke and Dr. Robyn Fivush from Emory University. Dr. Duke works with a foundation to ensure Jewish heritage stories are passed on to grandchildren. Knowing where they fit in a story also seems to paint a rosier view of the family overall, since children in the study who knew the most about their families viewed their family units in a more positive light.

Telling our kids' family stories may even lower the chances of anxiety and depression, even when world events stand to trigger a negative response. After the September 11 terrorist attacks, Dr. Duke and Dr. Fivush followed up with the kids who had participated in their study only months before. Those who knew they had a place in a larger family story were more resilient than those who scored low on what they knew about their families. An intergenerational identity helped serve as a shield between these kids and the catastrophe.

There's also the benefit of having kids who are less likely to become narcissists. Being a part of a bigger story means not being the center of the universe, a fact we want to instill in our children. We can give them both self-confidence and humility by sharing family stories, helping them develop a sense of self-worth and resilience without losing empathy, and becoming solely self-focused.

In the Ten Commandments, God gave Moses a command to "honor our father and mother." This is a call to honor those who got us here. The stories of those who came before us must be told and retold—this is one way we honor our ancestors. When the stories are told they offer us an oscillating story that transforms us. Oscillating, in that our stories will include highs and lows. Great victories and crushing defeats of our family members. As we hear of their defeats, we also learn of our family's coping actions and of resilience, and of determination, and of grit, and of strength. When these stories are told we can see clearer that there is hope. For if they made it through all that, then surely I can make it through the mess I am confronted with now.

Author A. J. Jacobs, the organizer of the Global Family Reunion, points out another advantage of children knowing their family history: they may become interested in going even further back, looking deeper into genealogy. Their interests can create opportunities for them to find out that we live on a very interconnected planet. "It's eye-opening," Jacobs said during an interview. "It's much harder to be racist and narrow-minded when you see how closely linked all the races are."

Robin Fivush article from *Psychology Today*:

> There is little debate that the American Indian Movement helped to transform American Indians who were stuck on Indian reservations or in ghettos of large cities across America during the 1970s. The American Indian Movement allowed American Indians to feel good about being who we are.

> The events of his life come alive in *Where White Men Fear to Tread*, his autobiography that was released by St. Martin's Press in the fall of 1995. Means co-authored *Where White Men Fear to Tread* with Marvin J. Wolf.

> Autobiographies are great tools for students of history to discover and understand the "whys" behind the "whats" of those writing their own stories. *Where White Men Fear to*

Tread accomplishes just that because Means is very open about the reasons why he did certain things along the way in his life.

This is important because American Indians should tell their own stories. I am glad Means wrote this book and shed light on his involvement in the American Indian Movement. Given the prejudicial treatment against the American Indian Movement by the Nixon-led federal government, many lies were perpetrated about the Movement. History, particularly American Indian history, told by non-Indians has become suspect.

Source: Editor Russell Means Autobiography Important for History, web post by Levi Rickert/28 Dec 2013. (Levi Rickert, a tribal citizen of the Prairie Band Potawatomi Nation, is the publisher and editor of Native News Online. Previously, he served as editor of the Native News Network. He is a resident of Grand Rapids, Michigan.

Soundtrack suggestion:
"Here We Are"
Jimmy Buffett

But here we are, for a family reunion, costume barbeque
All the black sheep, family outcasts, and a freak or two

How we tell the story is important also. In "Ode to Billie Joe," the story is told about a family's unfeeling, nonchalant, cold telling of a suicide of a local boy. I hope that we tell the stories but never relegate them to such cruelty. These are the stories of real people's lives.

Soundtrack suggestion:
"Ode to Billie Joe"
Bobbie Gentry

Seems like nothin' ever comes to no good up on Choctaw Ridge
And now Billy Joe MacAllister's jumped off the Tallahatchie Bridge

Skinfolk

On April 23, 1904, an article in the *Ocala Evening Star* described A. S. J. Allen as a "Negro." In the April 26, 1904, edition of the *Gainesville Sun*, A. S. J. Allen is described as "col.," an abbreviation for "colored."

I share the hope for the world MLK spoke of, where "my four little children will one day live in a nation where they will not be judged by the color of their skin, but by the content of their character."

That day has not yet arrived. This type of bias still does exist. The world tends to want to lump like things into one easy-to-digest portion. This is easier and faster than getting to know a person and their character. People you do not know make assumptions about you based on your skin color.

Less quoted, but to this point, King said in a speech called "The Other America," given at Grosse Pointe High School, March 14, 1968:

> ... a reporter asked me some time ago when I first took a strong stand against the war didn't I feel that I would have to reverse my position because so many people disagreed, and

people who once had respect for me wouldn't have respect, and he went on to say that I hear that it's hurt the budget of your organization and don't you think that you have to get in line more with the administration's policy ... and of course those were very lonely days when I first started speaking out and not many people were speaking out but now I have a lot of company and it's not as lonesome now. But anyway, I had to say to the reporter, I'm sorry sir but you don't know me.

For public figures this mistaken familiarity is not uncommon. For people of color, it is often an exposure of racial bias. So here we see that among the "non-celebrity," or common man, White people you do not know will make assumptions about you based on your skin.

The Problem of Identity

Not only is this problem of identity a problem for African Americans from the perspective of others looking in at the race, the perception of "who we are" is exacerbated by the changing verbal landscape or words used to identify people of color. This changing "namescape" based on skin must be dealt with as we research ancestors of color.

Redd Foxx, in one of his stand-up routines, said that the colors of Black folks could range from "black walnut, burnt almond, chocolate, chocolate mocha, pecan, vanilla, yellow, mellow, light, bright, and damn near white."

With such variety, maybe it should come as no surprise that the language of my skinfolk has changed so much over time. Indeed, the language of race has always been a moving target.

Black People

Black people is a skin color-based classification for specific people with a mid- to dark brown complexion. Not all Black people have dark skin; in certain countries, often in socially based systems of racial classification in the Western world, the term "Black" is used to describe persons who are perceived as dark-skinned compared to other populations. It is mostly used for people of sub-Saharan African descent and the indigenous peoples of Oceania, Southeast Asia, and the Indian subcontinent.

In the United Kingdom, "Black" was historically equivalent with "person of color," a general term for non-European peoples.

For many other individuals, communities, and countries, "Black" is perceived as a derogatory, outdated, reductive, or otherwise unrepresentative label, and as a result is neither used nor defined, especially in African countries with little to no history of colonial racial segregation. Some have commented that labeling people "Black" is erroneous, as the people described as "Black" are seen by some to have a brown skin color. However, the reasoning for the "Black" label is due to the person's primary ancestry being seen as sub-Saharan African, a part of the world where there are, in fact, people with black skin.

Here in the USA, the language of race has taken many forms and, as a researcher, I have needed to be aware of them all. The U.S. press, census, and other historical documents have called Black folks Niggers, Negroes, Colored, Afro-American, Black, and African American, and let's not forget Mulattos, Octaroons, and Maroons (and these do not include the many racial slurs that have appeared throughout the decades, but fortunately not frequently found in relevant historical records).

America is not alone in its quest to name people of color. In the early 2000s I was traveling in South Africa and came upon the curator of the District Six Museum; a structure that was an old Methodist church in Cape Town, South Africa. As we viewed the many signs of apartheid racism, we came upon a bench that translated "Europeans only." Ibrahim (M. N. Ibrahim; see https://1000 fights.com/observations-race-south-africa/) shared a story of a time when he and a friend were in a public park and his friend decided to rest by sitting on one of the park benches. It did not take long for a law officer to approach and point out the words painted on the bench: "Europeans Only."

The friend looked at the officer with confusion and replied, "Yes, I know, I'm from Europe." It was not long before all the park benches were repainted to read "Net Blankes," and "Slegs vir blankes," which translate from Afrikaans to English as "whites only."

As I have searched historical record sources for data on A. S. J., I've had to use most of these terms, and indeed found information I may not have discovered as I only looked for "colored"—the term most widely used during his lifetime.

Soundtrack suggestion:
"You Don't Know Me"
Ray Charles
Songwriters: Walker, Cindy/Arnold, Eddy
You Don't Know Me lyrics © Mijac Music, Sony/atv Songs Llc Obo
Mijac Music

And anyone can tell
You think you know me well
But you don't know me, no

All skinfolk ain't kinfolk, but there is strength and power when skinfolk embrace one another. There is solidarity in Blackness—speaking as one voice, acting for the good of all. But this is tricky, as Joe Biden found out in his 2020 presidential run. He made the statement to a panel of journalists at the National Association of Black Journalists–National Association of Hispanic Journalists 2020 virtual convention:

> And by the way, what you all know but most people don't know, unlike the African American community with notable exceptions, the Latino community is an incredibly diverse community with incredibly different attitudes about different things. You go to Florida, you find a very different attitude about immigration in certain places than you do when you're in Arizona. So it's a very different, a very diverse community.

"African Americans are all the same," was the twist the Trump campaign put on Biden's words. He later tweeted:

> In no way did I mean to suggest the African American community is a monolith—not by identity, not on issues, not at all. Throughout my career I've witnessed the diversity of thought, background, and sentiment within the African American community. It's this diversity that makes our workplaces, communities, and country a better place.

People are messy. Add race into the mix and you find race is messy. I understood exactly what he meant, but the Trump campaign jumped on this and tried to say that Biden was being racist. Sometimes the need of a moment is for solidarity; at other times, the need is for differentiation. This should not be a hard thing. We all have times when our family identity is primary. And other times when we stand alone, singular, apart from our families. Same principle.

One of my treasured mementos from my college days is an autographed name tag from Angela Davis. I stood with her as an usher on stage as she gave a speech in 1974 at the University of Florida. The badge is autographed "In Solidarity."

Coming out of enslavement, the Black population of America had to cope with issues of devaluation placed upon the entire race. Nowhere was this devaluation seen more painfully than in the separation of families caused by slavery. While under slavery, children were torn from the arms of mothers. Black babies and children had little value. The resulting fatherless and motherless children were especially vulnerable in White society.

A. S. J. Raised his "Voice" to Help SkinFolks During the Nadir of American Race Relations

As I began my research into my family history, the bulk of what I knew about my family story came from my grandmother, A. S. J. Allen's baby girl, Fannie. With Grandmother now gone, and Mom, too, the most precious items I have of theirs are their phonograph record collections. Grandmother had a large collection of 78s. I've spent (and still do) many a Saturday moving around the house to the sounds of Ma Rainey, Bessie Smith, Fats Waller, and Mamie Smith.

When doing family history research, everybody hopes for a great find. That is, finding discoveries that give us reason to either personally identify with or be proud of the folks who came before us. This was certainly the case with me as I researched A. S. J. Knowing that he was a preacher, I wanted to connect with his voice.

I knew the likelihood that there would be a voice recording of a Black preacher from the turn of the century was small. The soundtrack of history is silent until the late nineteenth century. For figures of great historical importance, we have no voice recordings. Thomas Edison created the first phonograph recording in 1877. In 2012 sound historians, Patrick Feaster and Stephan Puille, revealed the discovery of a wax cylinder recording from 1889 of the voice of Otto von Bismarck, the first chancellor of the German Empire.

Chronologically, the next important voice recording we find comes in 1890 when the singer, George W. Johnson, became the first African American to record commercially. Mainstream records during the 1890s, and the first two decades of the 1900s, were mainly made by and for White, middle class, and urban Americans.

As much as I have come to admire A. S. J. Allen, he was not a world leader nor a famous entertainer; so I had little actual expectation of actually hearing his voice. Then I got a call from the Divinity Archivist at Duke University, Rebecca Bowers. She found "new" information on A. S. J.—an 1899 *Journal of the Florida Annual Conference of the Methodist Episcopal Church* that had yet to be digitized for public consumption. This new discovery included written reports given by A. S. J. at the conference. Now, for the first time, I held in my hands words composed by A. S. J. As I read, it was like hearing his voice.

The reports told me of two causes A. S. J. held dear to his heart. One was the education and spiritual development of Black children. The other was the Methodist Church's care for the poor. He chaired a committee for the educating of Black children and poor White kids (Freedmen's Aid and Southern Educational Society). It seems he did feel a "special burden" to care not only for his kinfolk but to supply the needs of his skinfolk as well. Here is a transcription from that 1899 document:

ON THE STATE OF THE CHURCH.

After a careful study of the rise of the Methodist Episcopal Church in Florida, commencing in the year 1873, with 1,670 communicants and one Presiding Elder, the church was destined to win her way in defiance of prejudice, race pride and ignorance, to the position in rank where history now credits the Methodist Episcopal Church as being the first to provide an institution of learning for the youth of her colored members in the State. It is impossible to describe all of the benefits that have come to our people through the agency of the church. Notwithstanding that the old church has a wide spread over this State, still there are places where she must yet go to do a work that no other church can do. We, your committee, regard the state of the church far in advance of any years of the past along all lines, hence bind ourselves to do all in our power to further this great and good cause for Christ.

Faithfully submitted,
A. S. J. Allen, Chairman.
F. M. Spicer, Secretary

In high school history class, I read about the creation of schools and the focus on education for both Blacks and Whites in the South after the Civil War. It is inspiring to know that Florida education history includes my great-grandfather.

JOURNAL

—OF THE—

Florida Annual Conference,

—OF THE—

Methodist Episcopal Church.

THE TWENTY-SEVENTH SESSION,

Convened January 12, 1899, in

TRINITY M. E. CHURCH,

AT FERNANDINA, FLORIDA.

PUBLISHED BY THE AUTHORITY OF THE
CONFERENCE AND APPROVED AS
ITS OFFICIAL RECORD.

...ED AND PUBLISHED BY THE SECRETARY

J. M. DEAS. ASSISTED BY S. A. HUGER.

Seat of the next Conference Gainesville. Florida.
1899

A Preacher's Job, the Gospel, Education, and Announcements

Soundtrack suggestion:
"All Around the World"
Lisa Stansfield
Produced by Ian Devaney and Andy Morris
Album "Affection"

I don't know where my baby is
But I'll find him, somewhere, somehow
I've got to let him know how much I care
I'll never give up looking for my baby

I sometimes think that Black preachers of the last century had a better understanding of the church's mission than we do today. Bible commands on how to treat people were easy to understand. The book of Deuteronomy says: "The alien, the orphan and the widow who are in your town, shall come and eat and be satisfied, in order that the Lord your God may bless you." The words of Isaiah are pretty straightforward: "Learn to do good; seek justice, reprove the ruthless. Defend the orphan, plead for the widow." The Psalmist echoes the same sentiment: "The Lord protects the strangers; God supports the orphan and the widow, but thwarts the way of the wicked."

The role of the Black preacher in the late 1860s to early 1900s was far more nuanced than just standing in a pulpit on Sunday morning and preaching a sermon. He used his voice to proclaim the "Good News," but also to be a voice for those who either had no voice or needed an amplifier. These Ministers of the Gospel understood the commitment to care for the vulnerable people of their day. Traditionally Black preachers have always been spiritual, social, political, and community leaders. This was the life of A. S. J. During his lifetime, the effects of slavery and family separation were still very real. Enslaved African American people were forbidden "normal" families. When a man and a woman are owned as property by someone else (the enslaver) the couple has no ability to "love, honor, and protect" each other. They could not

119

Source:http://afrotexan.com/AfroPress/Papers/
Denominations/christian_advocate.htm

FRANK HAMILTON.

MR. EDITOR: I want to inquire for my people. My father's name is Jack Silas and mother's Julian, my oldest brother's Billie, Silas. Sisters Francis and Cilvil Grace. I had two uncles by the names, of Somerset and Leboy. Our owner's name was Mack Ledell. I left them in East Florida, Alachua County, I was seventeen years old when I left them. I came to Texas with Mrs. Mary Doer. Address me at Spring, Harris county, Texas, in care of Rev. James R. Price.

Source: https://www.hnoc.org/database/lost-friends/search-results.php

I want to inquire for the following brothers and sisters: Vina Gatewood belonged to a widow named Juda Gatewood, she lived in Anson county, North Carolina, seven miles from Wadesborough. Vina was sold to William Hill who took her to Florida, —I think Jacksonville. One brother's name was Gibson Gatewood; he was sold at the same time to a man named McCalpin. He took him to Alabama. My brother's wife's name was Anna. I belonged at that time to Henry May; I was called Ned. I lived in Anson county, North Carolina, at that time. I had also two brothers, James and Jack Gatewood, also another sister by the name of Harriet who belonged to Griffin Gatewood. I was sold by Henry May to Shala Arnold. I now go by the name of Edward Arnold. Any one knowing of any of the above parties write to Edward Arnold, Brenham, Washington county, Texas.

ED. ARNOLD.

Lost Friends.

We make no charge for publishing these letters from subscribers. All others will be charged fifty cents. Pastors will please read the requests published below from their pulpits, and report any case where friends are brought together by means of letters in the SOUTHWESTERN.

MR. EDITOR—I wish to inquire for my people. I have two sisters and brothers, whose names are Malinda, Sallie, Aaron, Alfred and James Bailey. Our master, John Bailey, brought us from Florida to Texas. I have not seen my people since we were set free. Address James Bailey, Dewese Woods, Liberty county, Texas.

pledge to do this and be as one "until God, by death shall separate" them. The enslaver at any time could separate the couple and sell off any and all of their children at will. Also, the enslaver was free to treat them harmfully and the man, woman, or parent were completely helpless to intervene and help or comfort, much less protect them from the enslaver. This did not stop enslaved folks

Information wanted of John Mc Eachern, aged about 35. He left Homer, S. C., Marion county, ten years ago and went to Florida, and I received unreliable information that he had been killed in Florida. Ministers in Georgia, Florida and Alabama please read to their congregations. Any information of him will be liberally rewarded by his brother, W. D. McEachern, Homer, Marion county, S. C.

"W. D. McEachern," Information Wanted Ad, *The Christian Recorder* (Philadelphia, PA), September 28, 1899, *Last Seen: Finding Family After Slavery*, accessed February 26, 2020, https://informationwanted.org/items/show/189.

Do You Know Them.

I desire to know the whereabouts of my mother, Frances Woodson, who sometimes went by Frances Bowles, which was her owner's name. She was born in and sold from Goochland County, Va. into Florida, at which place she was when last heard of. She then had two daughters with her. Any information will be gladly received.

Address, Mrs. MELINDA ROBINSON,
14½ W. Jackson St.,
Richmond, Va.

Florida papers please copy.

"Melinda Robinson searching for her mother," Do You Know Them Ad, Richmond Planet (Richmond, VA), *April 19, 1902, Last Seen: Finding Family After Slavery*, accessed February 26, 2020, https://informationwanted.org/items/show/2813.

Do You Know Them.

I desire to know the whereabouts of my mother, Frances Woodson, who sometimes went by Frances Bowles, which was her owner's name· She was born in and sold from Goochland County, Va. into Florida, at which place she was when last heard of. She then had two daughters with her. Any information will be gladly received.

Address, Mrs. MELINDA ROBINSON,
14½ W. Jackson St..
Richmond, Va.

Florida papers please copy.

"Joe Hawless," Information Wanted Ad, The Christian Recorder (Philadelphia, PA), February 9, 1899, Last Seen: Finding Family After Slavery, accessed February 26, 2020, https://informationwanted.org/items/show/103.

MR. EDITOR: I want to inquire for my people. My father's name is Jack Silas and mother's Julian, my oldest brother's Billie, Silas. Sisters Francis and Chivil Grace. I had two uncles by the names of Somerset and Leroy. Our owner's name was Mack Lodell. I left them in East Florida, Alachua County, I was seventeen years old when I left them. I came to Texas with Mrs. Mary Doer. Address me at Spring, Harris county, Texas, in care of Rev. James R Price.

"Unknown searching for family," Lost Friends Ad, Southwestern Christian Advocate (New Orleans, LA), June 8, 1882, Last Seen: Finding Family After Slavery, accessed February 26, 2020, https://informationwanted.org/items/show/1653.

MR. EDITOR.—I desire to inquire for my people. I left them in Quincy, Florida in 1861, in Gadson county. My oldest brother went by the name of George Wilder; my younger brother belonged to Foreman and Muse; two sisters, the oldest named Jane, she belonged to William and Jessie Wilder, and she was brought from Florida to New Orleans, La., in the year 1851; my youngest sister was named Hanna Williford; she and my mother, Sarah Williford, her real name was Sarah Wilder, I left in Leon county, below Talahassee, in 1858. My daughter, Sarah Forbes, her mother named Nancy Forbes, I left at Quincy, Florida in 1861. While I was in Florida I went by the name of Amos Philgore, but since the emancipation I go by my father's name, Amos Wilder. The last time I heard from my daughter she was married to a man by the name of Thomas; I never learned his given name. Any information as to their whereabouts will be thankfully received. Address, Amos Wilder, Orange, Orange county, Texas.

"Amos Wilder," Lost Friends Ad, *The Southwestern Christian Advocate* (New Orleans, LA), March 25, 1886, *Last Seen: Finding Family After Slavery*, accessed February 26, 2020, https://informationwanted.org/items/show/1745.

from loving one another and building families. These families had no legal authority or recognition. However, they were established anyway; they were "real" family.

After slavery was abolished, there was a nation of folks now longing to reunite with long-lost loved ones. One way they did this was by placing ads in newspapers. Back then there was no Internet and phone communication was limited (Alexander Graham Bell did not get the U.S. patent for the telephone until 1876). However, many newspapers accepted advertisements from folks looking for their family. Generally, a newspaper would charge to run an ad. This, in fact, was the way papers made their money, via ads and subscriptions. Nevertheless, these were hard times, and some allowed these "Lost Friends" ads to be published free of charge. One such paper was the *Southwestern Christian Advocate*. It was widely distributed for the African American community in the southern United States.

Since most could not afford to buy the paper, the way folks heard about the ads was through the church. Those who could afford the $2 per year subscription fee could post a Lost Friends advertisement free of charge. Non-subscribers had to pay fifty cents to publish an ad. To give an idea of what that meant, consider that in 1880, $2 would be about $12.65 in today's money. Just as now, most church services included the "announcements." In addition to the reading of such ads, Lost Friends advertisements were tacked on the walls of church buildings. Here are some samples of the announcements preachers like A. S. J. would read to a congregation on a typical Sunday morning. While African Americans left the thought of slavery behind, they made a priority to reunite with their family and friends. Many Lost Friends advertisements appeared in the Methodist *Southwestern Christian Advocate* newspaper beginning in 1879. This newspaper billed itself as "the official organ of the Methodist Episcopal Church," and A. S. J. Allen had numerous mentions in the newspaper.

The newspapers published a Lost Friends section for folks searching for loved ones lost to slavery, and these ads were regularly read by preachers like Rev. Allen in Black churches throughout the late 1800s.

Conference Notices

GAINESVILLE DISTRICT.

Commenced in Bethlehem (Fla.) Methodist Episcopal church on the 7th of September, 1900. Promptly at 9:30 o'clock a. m. the presiding elder, J. P. Patterson, opened the conference with the usual religious exercises, together with the administration of the Sacrament of the Lord's Supper, assisted by Revs. S. Welch and J. Wilson. The former secretary was requested to call the roll, and nearly all of the brothers answered. Brother A. S. J. Allen was elected secretary, Rev. A. Emanuel was chosen assistant. The presiding elder, though feeble, read the best report we have ever witnessed. Showing marked success along all lines, and made strong suggestions for the securing of subscriptions for our church periodicals, especially the SOUTHWESTERN CHRISTIAN ADVOCATE. The conference took immediate action to the effect to renew no brother's license of the classes, nor grant license to any applicant, unless the applicant subscribe for the S. W. C. A. for at least six months, which I am sure will be helpful. The session was a grand one. It must be known "*that it was in the woods.*" Of course, this made us a little fearful of a long walk but to the joy of the brothers, on the arrival of the cars, Capt. A. S. J Allen and his guard came up with vehicles enough to convey fifty delegates to their homes, where they never before met a sweeter welcome. Among the heroes and heroines should be mentioned Rev. O. F. Niblack. Brother Reason, Brother Anderson, Brother Sallet, Brother Harrass, Bother Henderson Olridge, Brother Sullivan, Mr. H. Gregg, Mr. Grant, Mrs. Singleton, Mrs. Smith, Mother Singleton, Brother McNish and others who rendered splendid help in making the conference happy. It must be mentioned also that the pastor and his committees made no request of our, white friends that were not freely granted, for which we are very grateful. The district, the Old Banner, is alive. Nearly all the charges have had revivals with a number of conversions and accessions. Benevolent collections are in the advance of previous years, together with renewed efforts to secure subscriptions for the S. W. C. A. All honor to the grand old paper. Among the many distinguished visitors was Prof. H. R. Bankard, president of the Cookman Institute, Jacksonville, Fla., who represented the F. A. & S. E. society to our encouragement. The brothers are willing to have another conference in the sticks. The collections were unusually good; total, $84. All of the brothers left with one eye to guide them, for the other was looking back requesting the pastor to send for them when he needed help, which was accepted. We left the presiding elder there enjoying himself with Dr. Niblack. God bless him; he is the right man in the right place.

A. S. J. ALLEN, Sec.

Sent $1.00 for 25 copies.

Source: *Southwestern Christian Advocate*, November 1, 1900
https://search.ebscohost.com/login.aspx?direct=true&db=h7
i&AN=84263565&site=ehost-live&scope=site&kw=true&acc=
false&lpId=divlo94&ppId=divp0014&twPV=&xOff=0&yOff=
0&zm=fit&fs=&rot=0&docMapOpen=true&pageMapOpen=tr
ue

A. S. J. Allen's life shows God's love for folks and challenges me to be like him

> "I rescued the poor who cried for help, and the fatherless who had none to assist them. The one who was dying blessed me; I made the widow's heart sing. I put on righteousness as my clothing; justice was my robe and my turban. I was eyes to the blind and feet to the lame. I was a father to the needy; I took up the case of the stranger. I broke the fangs of the wicked and snatched the victims from their teeth." (Job 29:12-17 [NIV])

Soundtrack suggestion:
"Sometimes I feel like a motherless child"
Traditional Negro Spiritual

Sometimes I feel like a motherless child
A long ways from home

Numerous Bible verses deliver this same message. God has consistently identified the fatherless, orphan, widow, the alien, and stranger as people who need to be our focus for love and support. These groups represent folks who are marginalized in our own society: those most likely to be lonely, vulnerable, economically in need, and often cut off from their biological families. Many times, they are unaware of their own biological families and the folks who made them. The fatherless or orphan is the child who is not tied into healthy adult relationships. As a result of poor or no mentorship, they may suffer from low self-esteem. The widow or widower is the woman or man who has lost their spouse and is facing old age with little family support or interaction. Yet these are the folks who possess a wealth of family history and story. The alien or stranger is the person who has limited healthy connections with a community. Often the minority within the mainstream of society, they are pioneers of a new generation in a new land; the cornerstone of future generations—if their story can survive.

As a Minister of the Gospel, A. S. J. Allen cared for these folks and was active in offering the love, attention, and benevolence they needed. Passing on these ads to the congregations was a way for preachers like A. S. J. to give hope to a marginalized population; making the church gathering a time of hope and hopefulness in the midst of the despair of separation. There is no evidence that these ads led to a great number of reunions. In *Help Me to Find My People: The African American Search for Family Lost in Slavery*, author Heather Andrea Williams says, "I think reunification did not happen very often—at least we don't have evidence of it happening very often—but when it did, there were complications." (https://www.wbur.org/npr/156843097/piecing-together-stories-of-families-lost-in-slavery)

We can admire men like A. S. J., as he stood up for his people. In his short life, A. S. J. Allen showed us what it meant to live out Isaiah 32:2 and be there for people.

> "Each one will be like a shelter from the wind
>   and a refuge from the storm,
> like streams of water in the desert
>   and the shadow of a great rock in a thirsty land."
> (Isa. 32:2)

Whether he was advocating for educating poor children, finding lost family, or caring for the marginalized communities he served, A. S. J. was keen to see the needs of those around him and look for practical solutions.

An Era of Racism, Bad Science, and Negative Social Messages

All Blacks experienced a difficult life after slavery. Freedom did not mean freedom from oppression and terrorism. The KKK committed more than one hundred murders and thousands of acts of violence and intimidation against Black folks in A. S. J. Allen's home state of Alabama between 1868 and 1871. In July 1870, when little A. S. J. would have been about five years old, Alabama Klansmen killed six people, including a schoolteacher, at Cross Plains, Calhoun County. Local freed people identified the murderers by name during a grand jury hearing, but the all-White jury refused to indict the killers.

Bad Science: Eugenics

During the early 1900s, there was a wave of bad science sweeping the nation. Not only was a sentiment of White supremacy rampant, but this was a time of suspicion and segregation even among Whites. This was the beginning of the age of eugenics.

To be fair, eugenics was supported by some African American intellectuals, such as W.E.B. Du Bois, Thomas Wyatt Turner, and other academics at Tuskegee University, Howard University, and Hampton University. They believed the best Blacks were as good as the best Whites and "The Talented Tenth" of all races should mix. W.E.B. Du Bois believed that "Only fit blacks should procreate to eradicate the race's heritage of moral iniquity."

Eugenics was a movement aimed at improving the genetic composition of the human race, and eugenicists advocated selective breeding to achieve these goals. It is no surprise that America used this "science" to promote negative views towards Blacks.

About twenty years after the freeing of African American slaves, in 1883, Sir Francis Galton, a respected British scholar and a cousin of Charles Darwin, first used the term eugenics, meaning "well-born." Galton believed that the human race could help direct its future by selectively breeding individuals who have "desired" traits. This idea was based on Galton's study of upper-class Britain. Following these studies, Galton concluded that an elite position in society was due to superior genetic makeup. While Galton's plans to improve the human race through selective breeding never came to fruition in Britain, they did take sinister turns in other countries.

The eugenics movement began in the U.S. in the late nineteenth century, right around the time when A. S. J. Allen was a young adult. Unlike in Britain, eugenicists here in America focused on efforts to stop the transmission of "undesirable" traits from generation to generation. This focus resulted in thirty-three states creating sterilization programs. All told, Alabama sterilized 224 people in the early 1900s. Florida did not have a eugenic sterilization law. (https://www.uvm.edu/~lkaelber/eugenics/) At first sterilization efforts targeted mentally ill people exclusively; later the traits deemed serious enough to warrant sterilization included alcoholism, criminality, chronic poverty, blindness, deafness, feeble-mindedness, and promiscuity. It was not uncommon for African American women to be sterilized during other medical procedures without consent. Most folks subjected to these sterilizations had no choice, and because the program was run by the government, they had little chance of escaping the procedure. It is thought that around 65,000 Americans were sterilized due to America's obsession with eugenics.

Soundtrack suggestion:
"A Change Is Gonna Come"
Sam Cooke
Songwriter: Sam Cooke

It's been too hard living and I'm afraid to die
I don't know what's out there, beyond the sky
It's been a long time coming

But I know a change is gonna come
Oh yes it will

Black Lives Matter, or Fighting a History of Being Dispensable and Negative Press Coverage

It boggles my mind to make sense of the headlines involving the senseless killing of Black men. It is important to write these things to young America. Our young will learn history in school, and I encourage them to listen to the teachers. Nevertheless, know that the history that is taught is from a biased viewpoint. You must learn your history from the vantage point of your people. This is what I call teaching "hard history." Studying the history of A. S. J. focused my attention on certain patterns. One of the patterns I see is that Black lives matter only within the Black community.

"Anyone who claims to be in the light but hates his brother is still in the darkness" (1 John 2:9).

Throughout his 2016 presidential campaign, Donald J. Trump continually reached out to African-American voters, presenting the question: "What the hell do you have to lose?" His platform spoke to Black folks across America, and said, "You're living in poverty, your schools are no good, you have no jobs, 58 percent of your youth is unemployed—what the hell do you have to lose?" (https://www.cnn.com/2016/08/19/politics/donald-trump-african-american-voters/index.html)

At the time I wondered to whom, and about whom, he was speaking. I certainly do not experience any of that. This calls back to my earlier statements of stereotyping and bias. In his view, and possibly the view of many Whites, this is the image of Black America.

Suggesting that Black communities are hardly worth fighting for, and that whatever it is you think you have, it is nothing, is a common tactic used by White America over the years. This dismissal of the positive and good of Black communities and Black lives is dangerous and highlights two important facts:

- Black lives have been considered dispensable a long time

- Black images have been portrayed negatively for a long time

The motivation behind W.E.B. Du Bois's 1900 Paris World's Fair exhibit was to attack these notions and to show the world the advancement of the Negro race and commemorate the progress made since slavery. The Exhibit of American Negroes was a photographic display within the Palace of Social Economy at the 1900 World's Fair in Paris.

DuBois wanted a media experience to combat the existing stereotypes that so much of the world held. I cannot say enough on this subject of the relationship between the print/news media and Blacks. For centuries, Black folks have been demonized and misrepresented by mainstream news reporting.

This photo, circa 1915, from the Library of Congress, shows Ota Benga. In 2020 the organization that runs New York's Bronx Zoo apologized for racist episodes in the zoo's past, including putting Ota Benga on display in the Monkey House in 1906.

Black Men as Demons

Some of my initial shock and confusion over A. S. J. Allen's murder is taken away when I look at how Black folks were viewed back in 1904. One of the hardest things to do—yet an essential thing to do when studying history—is to put yourself in the mindset and context of the time period you are investigating.

I had to ask myself what it meant to be Black in the late 1800s and early 1900s. Except for exploitation and entertainment, the Negro life was of little value. The perception then was dismal. In the early 1800s, Sara Baartman was the most well-known of at least two South African Khoikhoi women who, due to their large buttocks, were exhibited all over Europe. She was displayed as a freak show attraction under the name Hottentot Venus. "Hottentot" was the then-current name for the Khoi people of

Africa. Today the term is considered offensive.

Four decades after the time the Civil War had been fought and won there was still the spectacle of the Negro. Consider the curious and sad story of Ota Benga (c.1883–March 20, 1916). Benga was a Mbuti (Congo pygmy) man. At the time of my great-grandfather's violent dying in 1904, Benga was featured in an exhibit at the Louisiana Purchase Exposition in St. Louis, Missouri. Two years later he was displayed in a human zoo exhibit at the Bronx Zoo. Benga had been purchased from African slave traders by South Carolina missionary and anthropologist, Samuel Phillips Verner. He traveled with Verner to the United States. At the Bronx Zoo, Benga had free run of the grounds before and after he was exhibited in the zoo's Monkey House.

There's a report that as many as 400,000 people a day went up to the zoo just to see Ota Benga. Benga was moved to the Howard Colored Orphan Asylum in Brooklyn, and he ended up in Lynchburg, Virginia, at the Lynchburg Theological Seminary and College. There he committed suicide by firing a single bullet through his own heart. Eugenics theory was on the rise and the theory of evolution was still being hotly debated. People were led to believe that Benga was a missing link, a sort of bridge between animals and humans.

"We deeply regret that many people and generations have been hurt by these actions or by our failure previously to publicly condemn and denounce them," the zoo officials said in a statement which was first reported in the *New York Times*. (Library of Congress via AP).

The Big, Bad, Black, Magical, Superman

PARENTAL ADVISORY EXPLICIT CONTENT

Important Note: Before I begin the discussion, I think it is important to express my opinion concerning some language you are about to see. Two things:

- "Nigger" is not now, nor has it ever been, an endearing positive term of affection.

- Adding "big black" in front of nigger only serves to dehumanize and intensify the demonized image of a Black man.

Even though both Black men and women were seen as not fully human, Black men were especially demonized and seen as a threat. The newspapers of A. S. J. Allen's times (and news reports today), depict folks with brown and black skin as somehow supernatural, and thus scary. This is the insidious "magical negro" stereotype.

The *Journal of Social Psychology and Personality Science* recently released a study that suggested White people hold a "superhumanization bias" against Black people. As Jesse Singal of *Science of Us* explained, "The researchers showed that whites are quicker to associate blacks than whites with superhuman words like *ghost, paranormal*, and *spirit*; are more likely to think a Black person as opposed to a white person has certain superhuman abilities; and that the more they think Blacks are superhuman, the less they view Black people as having a capacity to feel pain."

Soundtrack suggestion:
"(What Did I Do to Be So) Black and Blue?"
Louis Armstrong
Songwriters: Harry Brooks/Andy Razaf/Fats Waller

They laugh at you, and scorn you too
What did I do to be so black and blue?
I'm white inside, but that don't help my case
'Cause I can't hide what is in my face

The post highlighted newspapers'—particularly the *New York Times*'s—obsession with "giant negroes," superhuman in strength and impervious to normal law enforcement methods, who terrorized police and civilians. From the turn of the twentieth century until the 1930s, terrifying tales of giant or big and bad Negroes popped up regularly.

Here's a sample of how this played out in the media:

- In 1897, the paper exclaimed, "Giant negro disables 4 policemen in fight." He was eventually felled by a baton blow to the head.

- The September 24, 1900, edition included a double whammy: back-to-back stories about criminally insane Negroes of "gigantic build," headlined "Giant Negro Attacks Police" and "Big Negro Spreads Terror."

- A "ghost-haunted darkey" went nuts at sea in 1916, according to a story titled "Armed Negro giant goes mad on liner." He was rather tall, the reporter makes sure to note.

And so on. Florida newspapers in the early 1900s reference "a bad negro" and "a bad nigger" in articles about individual police encounters (https://www.vox.com/2014/11/25/7283327/michael-brown-racist-stereotypes).

Most Whites seemed to have embraced this mythical concept of Black men as dangerous and brute-like after slavery. Black men were perceived as innately savage, animalistic, destructive, and criminal—deserving punishment, even death. This bad brute is a fiend, a sociopath, an antisocial menace; he is a hideous, terrifying predator who targets helpless victims, especially White women. The myth of cruelty and vicious attacks directed toward White women grew in popularity during the 1890s. As the myth grew and stories spread about the savage Black brute, so did the occurrences of lynching. Charles H. Smith, writing in the 1890s, claimed, "A bad negro is the most horrible creature upon the earth, the most brutal and merciless."

In addition to the mythical concept of Black men as dangerous and brute-like, there was also the "coon."

> The coon caricature was one of the stock characters among minstrel performers. Minstrel show audiences laughed at the slow-talking fool who avoided work and all adult responsibilities. This transformed the coon into a comic figure, a source of bitter and vulgar comic relief. He was sometimes renamed "Zip Coon" or "Urban Coon." If the minstrel skit had an ante-bellum setting, the coon was portrayed as a free black; if the skit's setting postdated slavery, he was portrayed as an urban black. He remained lazy and good-for-little, but the minstrel shows depicted him as a gaudy dressed "Dandy" who "put on airs." Unlike Mammy and Sambo, Coon did not know his place. He thought he was as smart as white people; however, his frequent malapropisms and distorted logic suggested that his attempt to compete intellectually with whites was pathetic. His use of bastardized English delighted white audiences and reaffirmed the then commonly held beliefs that blacks were inherently less intelligent. The minstrel coon's goal was leisure, and his leisure was spent strutting, styling, fighting, avoiding real work, eating watermelons, and making a fool of himself. If he was married, his wife dominated him. If he was single, he sought to please the flesh without entanglements. (Dr. David Pilgrim, Professor of Sociology at https://www.ferris.edu/jimcrow/coon/)

Unfortunately, these attitudes of fear and anxiety are not just anecdotal today. A recent experiment by John Wilson, a psychologist at Montclair University, found consistent racial biases in participants. The group included multiple races and asked several questions related to race and perceptions. All of the respondents believed that Black men were larger and more powerful than same-sized white men. They also believed that the Black men were more likely to cause harm in an altercation and that police would be justified in using force against them. Black respondents also believed Black men were stronger and larger, but they did not believe they were capable of causing more harm or were deserving of more police force. Wilson concluded that these findings could explain why Black men are more likely than White men to be shot and killed by police, explaining, "this research suggests that misperceptions of black men's size might be one contributor to police decisions to shoot." (https://www. motherjones.com/coronavirus-updates/2020/04/the-dangers- of-covering-your-face/)

The History of Whites Charged With Killing Negroes is Rare

By the 1904 killing of A. S. J. Allen, there was already a rich history of "Black lives do *not* matter." That history began around 1669 with the Casual Killing Act. This Act declared it legal to kill a slave while correcting him or her because malice could not be presumed.

In "An act about the casual killing of slaves," passed by the Virginia General Assembly in 1669, enslavers who kill the people they enslaved in the act of punishing them are held not to be responsible for murder.

Transcription from Original:

WHEREAS the only law in force for the punishment of refractory servants resisting their master, mistress or overseer cannot be inflicted upon negroes, nor the obstinacy of many of them by other then violent meanes supprest, *Be it enacted and declared by this grand assembly,* if any slave resist his master (or another by his masters order correcting him) and by the extremity of the correction should chance to die, that his death shall not be accompted a felony, but the master (or that other person appointed by the master to punish him) be acquit from molestation, since it cannot be presumed that prepensed malice (which alone makes murder a felony) should induce any man to destroy his own estate. (https://www.encyclopediavirginia.org/_An_act_about_the_casuall_killing_of_slaves_1669. The author has made transcript spelling corrections.)

The simple fact here is that during the time A. S. J. lived, (and unfortunately in our present day) there was great violence and injustice done to Black folks by "policing" White people and it was rarely punished by law or seen as a crime. The idea of White supremacy over Black lives was accepted and rarely challenged.

Help for the Poor and Uneducated

About the Freedmen's Aid and Southern Educational Society:

> Eric Foner: Freedom had many meanings to people coming right out of slavery. But one of the things that it critically involved was access to education. Most of the Southern states, before the Civil War, made it illegal to teach a slave to read and write. Now, some African Americans did learn to read and write secretly. Some ... their master or mistress actually taught them to read and write. But the vast majority had had no access to education at all. And they realized that education was critical to advancement as free people in this society. As well as, many of them, being deeply religious, wanted to be able to read the Bible. (https://www.pbs. org/wgbh/americanexperience/features/reconstruction-schools-and-education-during-reconstruction/)

The Freedmen's Aid and Southern Educational Society organized teachers from the North and provided them with housing. They came into the South to set up schools for freedmen and their children.

About the Epworth League:

> "Above all, love each other deeply, because love covers over a multitude of sins. Offer hospitality to one another without grumbling. Each of you should use whatever gift you have received to serve others, as faithful stewards of God's grace in its various forms." (1 Pet. 4:8-10)

The Epworth League was founded in 1889, as a Methodist young adult association. The purpose of the League was "the promotion of intelligent and vital piety among the young people of the Methodist Church. Their mission was to encourage and cultivate Christ-centered character in young adults around the world through community building, missions, and spiritual growth."

The name Epworth comes from the village of Epworth in

Lincolnshire, England, the birthplace of John Wesley and Charles Wesley, founders of the Methodist denomination.

Transcript below of 1898 REPORT ON EPWORTH LEAGUE, co-authored by A. S. J. Allen:

> The organization of the Epworth League is one of the greatest forward movements in church work of this 19th century. It meets a demand and responds to a long and much-felt need in the Church. The question which has so often confronted us—"How shall we hold our young people in the Church"— is fully answered in the purpose and work of the Epworth League. Just at the point of life where our young people are most inclined to turn away from the work and influence of the Sunday School and drift out into worldliness the Epworth League comes in, and with its attractive features, entertaining programs, enlightening literature and departments of work gathers them in and conserves and develops their usefulness for the Master's service.
>
> As an organization the Epworth League is a wonderful developer of latent powers in our young people, which otherwise would lie dormant and undeveloped. In its several departments of work are given wide and large opportunities for the use and improvement of such talent as our young people may possess. It strives to bring out the best possibilities in our young on social, benevolent, moral, literary and religious lines. It aims at the formation and building up of the best type of moral, intellectual and religious character in our young people. It endeavors to increase their Spiritual growth and activity, to deepen and strengthen their piety and to bring them into more immediate contact and relation to the Spiritual life and work of the Church. No movement in the Church looking toward the interest and care of our young people has been more marked and significant in success or grander and more inspiring in its results. We hail with gladness the hopeful outlook for the most glorious and gratifying achievements to be wrought by our young people

in the Church and the world through their concerted action and united work in the Epworth League.

We hail with a high sense of appreciation and honor the appointment of Prof. I. Garland Penn to the position of Asst. Secretary of the Epworth League, and we congratulate ourselves that his ability, efficiency and enthusiasm is making and inspiring Epworth Leaguers throughout all our work. Therefore, we resolved, that as a Conference we pledge ourselves to diligence and earnestness in organizing Chapters in all and every charge throughout our Conference; that we will procure Epworth League literature for our *young* people and put them in the way of acquiring all the needed information for becoming thorough and active Epworth Leaguers.

Respectfully,
J. B. L. WILLIAMS,
A. S. J. ALLEN,
W. H. AUSTIN,
Committee.

Source: Florida/Annual Conference of the Methodist Episcopal church. JOURNAL OF THE TWENTY-SIXTH SESSION, JACKSONVILLE, FLORIDA, January 13, 14, 15, and 17th, 1898.
PUBLISHED BY THE AUTHORITY OF THE CONFERENCE AND APPROVED AS ITS OFFICIAL RECORD.
PUBLISHED BY J. M. DEAS. F. ELLIOTT and S. BARTLY, COMMITTEE.

Another transcript below of the "1898 COMMITTEE ON STATE OF THE CHURCH" co-authored by A. S. J. Allen:

COMMITTEE ON STATE OF THE CHURCH.

A careful study of the rise and progress of the Methodist Episcopal Church in Florida, dating the start from the year 1878, it was with 1670 communicants and one Presiding Elder that the church was destined to win her way, in defiance of prejudice, race pride and ignorance, to the position in rank where history now credits the Methodist Episcopal Church as being the first to provide an institution of learning for the youth of her colored members in the State. And now as an inducement to ambition, aspiration, and the maintenance of zeal for the aspiring young ministers, though not thought advisable by some; we "your committee," believe the expansion of the Conference boundary essential, inevitable and indispensable for the future growth of our church in the State, and we recommend that the delegate elect ask for and show cause why the Florida Conference should include all the State of Florida.

On behalf of the committee,
F. M. Spicer, Sec.
A. S. J. Allen, Ch'm.

Do you know some of the lessons that your parents learned from good or bad experiences?

Y N

Why should leaders care?
Because bad decisions are made in vacuums.
Myth: I can live in a world and be oblivious to the history around me. I can make progress without looking back.

Soundtrack suggestion:
"Nobody Knows the Trouble I've Seen"
Louis Armstrong
Songwriter: Louis Armstrong

Nobody knows but Jesus
Glory, Hallelujah

Sometimes I'm up, sometimes

Alonzo Felder

I'm down, oh, yes Lord
Sometimes I'm almost
To the ground, oh yes, Lord

(http://upload.
wikimedia.
org/wikipedia/
commons/5/5e/
BLAKE10.JPG)

A New and Uninformed King Resulted in Israelite Slavery in Egypt

The Society for the Abolition of the Slave Trade was founded in 1787 by Granville Sharp and Thomas Clarkson. The other nine founding members were William Dillwyn, John Barton, George Harrison, Samuel Hoare Jr., Joseph Hooper, John Lloyd, Joseph Woods, James Phillips, and Richard Phillip, and later Josiah Wedgwood. It was Josiah Wedgewood who created the engraving shown above of a kneeling, chained, and supplicant slave, with the powerful words below: "Am I not a friend and a brother?"

This image didn't come out of the blue; it was made specifically to move hearts and minds. There's a lot of talk in the news now about inalienable, civil, and constitutional rights. We can agree or disagree on any number of such stances. What we cannot afford to disagree on is the value of a human being to be seen, heard, and treated as human. Today we must consider and answer in the affirmative the question "Am I not a man?" To answer in the negative is to devalue a soul. Devaluation comes in many forms. All of them should be fought against. A. S. J. Allen stood up for folks who had no voice because of their race and/or economic status. He believed Blacks and poor Whites deserved a chance at education and salvation. He was also a voice for the fatherless in his personal life, as is evidenced by his marrying a single mom and bringing her child into their home. Neither her social nor legal status interfered with his ability to love Dinah.

> "These are the names of the sons of Israel who went to Egypt with Jacob, each with his family. Reuben, Simeon, Levi and Judah; Issachar, Zebulun and Benjamin; Dan and Naphtali; Gad and Asher. The descendants of Jacob numbered seventy in all; Joseph was already in Egypt.

> "Now Joseph and all his brothers and all that generation died, but the Israelites were exceedingly fruitful; they multiplied greatly, increased in numbers and became so numerous that the land was filled with them.

"Then a new king, to whom Joseph meant nothing, came to power in Egypt. 'Look,' he said to his people, 'the Israelites have become far too numerous for us. Come, we must deal shrewdly with them or they will become even more numerous and, if war breaks out, will join our enemies, fight against us and leave the country.'

"So they put slave masters over them to oppress them with forced labor... But the more they were oppressed, the more they multiplied and spread; so the Egyptians came to dread the Israelites and worked them ruthlessly. They made their lives bitter with harsh labor in brick and mortar and with all kinds of work in the fields; in all their harsh labor the Egyptians worked them ruthlessly." (Exod. 1:1-14)

The Bible verses above are poignant examples in lessons on the dangers of forgetting, and especially the danger of uninformed leadership. When the Egyptian leadership forgot about Joseph, the Bible teaches us that this resulted in four hundred years of slavery for the Jews.

We make the world a better place by bringing a sense of history to the present world. People often say, forget the past and move forward. While that may be true, I like a line from one of my favorite *Doctor Who* TV episodes, where Clara says "The future is not promised, but the past is mine, and I am entitled to that."

The Law

A White historian once wrote: "It was almost impossible to convict a White man of a crime against a Black person." In one Louisiana town, two White men were convicted of murdering a Black man. After they were convicted, they rose and walked out of court after the verdict was announced and no effort was made to stop them. Just think about that. In 1890, a White man was convicted for the murder of a Black man and was fined $5 for the crime—and the judge let it be known that he would not press for collection. That is how little Black lives meant in this society. White people will pick a dog up on the highway and have the dog sit down at the dinner table, but a Black human being will be sent to prison for mistreating dogs, while White people mistreat Blacks every day and there is no penalty. (http://www. finalcall.com/artman/publish/Minister_Louis_Farrakhan_9/ article_8679.shtml)

A. S. J. Allen helped to show me that Black lives do matter, and my family story tells the story of how being considered dispensable and negative by others does not make it true. The pushback by the Alachua County, Florida, community came because A. S. J. had built up a lot of "social capital." Teaching, preaching, working the farm, and raising two babies by himself was a big job, but A. S. J. was up to the task. He was a hard worker and was well known and thought of by the community. I'll talk more about social capital and cultural agility in the section *Village Folks*.

The laws of the land during and immediately after slavery that restricted the lives of formerly enslaved people generally addressed the former owners and penalized them for breaking the law. Laws governing enslaved people allowed enslavers to beat or kill them under certain circumstances. The law did not allow freed people to go to court to seek redress for any "wrongs" done to them. A person of color was not permitted to testify against a White Christian, as illustrated by the 1717 Maryland law:

II. Be it Therefore Enacted, by the right honourable the

Lord Proprietary, by and with the advice and consent of his Lordship's Governor, and the Upper and Lower Houses of Assembly, and by the authority of the same, That from and after the end of this present session of assembly, no Negro or mulatto slave, free Negro, or mulatto born of a white woman, during his time of servitude by law, or any Indian slave, or free Indian natives, of this or the neighbouring provinces, be admitted and received as good and valid evidence in law, in any matter or thing whatsoever depending before any court of record, or before any magistrate within this province, wherein any christian white person is concerned.

As I mentioned earlier,

. . . with the end of the Civil War came the rise of the Ku Klux Klan and accompanying racial tensions. Public violence and general lawlessness were on the rise as well. Shootings and other crimes had become such everyday occurrences that the people became desensitized to much of the violence in their small community. Deputies were often killed in the line of duty because they rode out alone on horseback on their calls, with no backup and no method of communication or assistance.

This continued until Lewis Washington Fennell was brought in as interim Sheriff in 1890. Sheriff L. W. Fennell was born in Melrose, Florida, in 1855, the son of an orange grower and the youngest out of seven children. He started his adulthood as a farmer in Hawthorne, but sold the ranch in 1885 and entered politics. He held office on the County Board of Supervisors and was also a deputy tax assessor before being appointed to fill in as a Sheriff for two years, finishing out Sheriff S. C. Tucker's term. He was then elected in his own right in 1896, 1900, and 1904 on the Democratic Party ticket. He also served on the Alachua County Commission, the State Democratic Committee, and at one time, was President of the State Sheriffs' Association.

Sheriff Fennell, also known as Uncle Wash, was an avid outdoorsman and a well-known fox-hunter. As Sheriff he struggled to maintain staff at the agency because at that time, deputies worked strictly off commission instead of salary. JL Shaw worked at times as a deputy. The Sheriff's Office was responsible for most criminal investigations and the physical apprehensions of suspects, including fugitives from other counties. In those days, a fugitive chase meant talking to witnesses, tracking footprints, and using hounds—all from horseback and usually alone since the county was larger than it is now and the agency had only a few full-time deputies. Alachua County was still very much rural frontier land. Authority did not rest with the rule of law, but with whoever chose to take it by force. (https://www.alachuasheriff.org/pdfs/ACSO%20History%20Project%20Word%20version.pdf)

Image of Fennell from https://heritage.aclib.us/1051-1100/1089.html

Why are Jews and Blacks in solidarity? Because in the early 1900s, Jewish newspapers drew parallels between the Black movement out of the South and the Jews' escape from Egypt.

Below is a screenshot showing A. S. J. Allen on the official death index record.

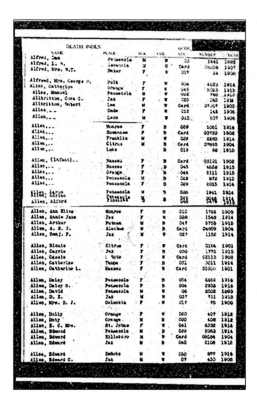

Myth: Racial Purity

My great-grandfather was a Methodist preacher and he left behind a legacy in which spirituality is important. Throughout this book I will expose you to Bible scriptures and midrash stories from my Christian heritage—a heritage that has never forgotten its Jewish roots. I will not seek to untangle these roots; on the contrary, it is my desire to show the history of connection in these two communities. There are many "theories" afloat on the Jew/Black racial connection. I cannot tell you why the two groups tend to seek solidarity, I just know that in my life experience, the bond seems deep-rooted.

Jewish immigrants entered northeastern and midwestern American cities at the same period Black folks were migrating by the hundreds of thousands from the rural South. This period is known as the Great Migration.

In the early 1900s, Jewish newspapers drew parallels between the Black movement out of the South and the Jews' escape from ancient Egypt, pointing out that both Blacks and Jews lived on the margins, in ghettos, and calling anti-Black riots in the South "pogroms." Stressing the similarities rather than the differences between the Jewish and Black experience in America, Jewish leaders emphasized the idea that both groups would benefit the more America moved toward a society of merit, free of religious, ethnic, and racial restrictions.

Jews made substantial financial contributions to many civil rights organizations, including the NAACP, the Urban League, the Congress of Racial Equality (CORE), and the Student Nonviolent Coordinating Committee (SNCC). About 50 percent of the civil rights attorneys in the South during the 1960s were Jews, as were over 50 percent of the Whites who went to Mississippi in 1964 to challenge Jim Crow Laws. ("From Swastika to Jim Crow: Black-Jewish Relations," ITVS. Archived from the original on October 2, 2002. Retrieved February 17, 2017.)

"You shall not hate the stranger in your heart for you know the soul of a stranger for you were strangers in the land of Egypt" (Ex. 23:9).

Why does the Torah warn against wronging "the stranger" thirty-six times? Because mankind has a strong inclination toward that particular evil (see Bava Metzia 59b). Hatred of the stranger or foreigner is an ancient affliction. Jewish tradition teaches that man's inclination to fear those "not like us" is so strong that the care of the stranger needs cultivating. It is a value that requires intentional attention and vigilance. I don't know how or when, but somewhere along my family's journey, lessons of taking care of "others" were deposited into our family culture on a Biblical scale.

> I am a Jew. Hath not a Jew eyes? hath not a Jew hands, organs,
> dimensions, senses, affections, passions? fed with
> the same food, hurt with the same weapons, subject
> to the same diseases, healed by the same means,
> warmed and cooled by the same winter and summer, as
> a Christian is? If you prick us, do we not bleed?
> if you tickle us, do we not laugh? if you poison|
> us, do we not die? and if you wrong us, shall we not
> revenge? (Shylock, from *The Merchant of Venice*, William Shakespeare)

Shylock seems to be justifying the revenge he has planned for Antonio in advance, as he seems to be desperately excusing himself by asking if Jews are any different from Christians in a series of rhetorical questions which query their parallel experiences.

Connected Communities: Methodist, Jews, the Poor, and the Orphaned

In the next chapter on "villagefolk," we will discuss the components of the village or communities that we are a part of. But as we prepare for that discussion, I want to introduce you to a small part of that villagefolk concept. For starters, you should understand that sometimes skinfolk and village folk can be the same folk. Sometimes they are not, and your village folk are just folks you decide to include and accept in your life as family. What I'm talking about here is the idea of "my brother from another mother" when the two mothers are of different races. Or as we are about to see—different ethnicities and religions. This was the case of my meeting my "other brothers" in a Jewish fraternity at the University of Florida. As I said earlier, later on we will explore the "village folks" and fictive kinship bonds, but I think it important to insert this perspective here.

Ella, Wilbert, and Fannie's story did not end in that bloody field in Alachua, Florida. Wilbert and Fannie moved to St. Petersburg, Florida, and grew up under the care of their aunt Phyllis. Fannie Allen Felder was one of the first faces I saw when I was born. My grandma was my hero. We spent so much time together, but as I look back now, I realize that we did not talk enough about her childhood. What was it like growing up as an orphan? Knowing her history now, I understand more fully the decision to keep me and not send Mom off to a home for unwed mothers, as was common during this time. Grandma was always very protective of me, and I understand that a bit more now.

As a Black child growing up in the South during the late 1950s and 1960s, it was obvious to me that the world was broken. My family was one with deep religious roots. Early teachings found within the first five books of the Bible reveal a concept familiar to Jews and Christians alike. In Hebrew the term is "Tikkun Olam" (pronounced tee-KOON oh-LUHM) and it refers to and can be translated as "Repairing the World." God's intent from earliest times was that his people would care for the marginalized.

"He hath shewed thee, O man, what is good; and what doth the Lord require of thee, but to do justly, and to love mercy, and to walk humbly with thy God?" (Mic. 6:8)

As I viewed the broken world around me, I wanted to find a community of folks to "sanctify God's name," to *kiddush hashem*. Folks who were looking to associate loving deeds with God's reputation.

As a college student, I encountered a Christian group on campus that offered me great hope. They were teaching about the God and Jesus that I knew of but did not really know. During the course of Bible studies, the man studying with me asked a curious question: "Alonzo, why are you a Methodist?"

Mom, Grandma and Me

In nineteen years, no one had ever asked me that question. It struck me as odd that I had never considered the question on my own. I was Methodist because that's what Mom and Grandmother were. I'd been exposed to years of Catholicism at school, my best friend was Baptist, and I'd attended church frequently with him (despite the protests of his preacher, who chastised us for our long hair and playing of the "git-fiddle" [guitar]). Our next-door neighbors were Presbyterian. My grandfather on my dad's side was a Pentecostal preacher.

I could hardly wait for a break to go back home and talk to my grandmother. "Why are we Methodist?" I can still remember standing in front of my grandmother as she sat in her chair by the front door. Her answer was oddly mysterious and poignant. "Honey, there are two groups of people who have been very good to us: the Jews and the Methodists. Always do right by them."

> *Do you know the names of the schools that your dad went to?*
>
> *y n*

During the Nashville lunch counter sit-in in 1960, when John Lewis and other Black students decided to go down to the Woolworth store for a sit-in, Dale Schwartz remembers "several of my AEPi brothers and I thought it would be good to be there. So, on a Saturday just before noon, about ten of our brothers and new members showed up at Woolworth in downtown Nashville."

He describes how the Whites in the store "mocked me and my Brothers and called us "Ni**er Lovers."

The resulting evening fight between the AEPi brothers and the Whites was brutal. Just Google "Nashville sit-ins video" and you'll see it. Note that while the Black student protesters were committed to a nonviolent stance, my fraternity brothers were not. Just saying . . .

As Dale tells the story, "My mother and father got to see me being beaten on the national network news that evening, as photographed by the local TV stations, which arrived shortly after the rednecks. The university threatened to kick us AEPi brothers

My AEPi Big brother, Marty, and me

out of school for 'inciting a riot.' We dared them to do that, and they backed down."

In 1964 a group of civil rights workers had gone into Meridian, Mississippi, to register Black folks to vote and to begin a "freedom school." Among them were two young Jewish New Yorkers, Michael Schwerner and Andrew Goodman. Michael Henry "Mickey" Schwerner was described by many as a friendly, good-natured, gentle kid. Sadly, Mickey gained national attention when he and his two companions were reported missing.

These young civil rights workers were murdered by a lynch mob while traveling around the South attempting to prepare and register African Americans to vote. The three were found murdered and buried in a shallow grave in Neshoba County, Mississippi, in June of 1964.

AEPi brothers around the world continue to stand strong in the face of hate and intolerance to sustain Schwerner's legacy.

I was nine years old, and in the fourth grade, that year Mickey and his friends were murdered. The sense was very real in my house that I had just lost some brothers from a different mother. The "us" and "them" thinking that divided most of America along racial lines was not center stage in my home. Sure, I knew about race and the differences in treatment it achieved. But no one at home cared that a kid was Black, a Jew, or anything else. The previous year I had witnessed my teachers, my mom and grandmother, and other adults around me weeping over the murder of a young White Catholic man—President John F. Kennedy. I was young, but not so young as to not recognize heroes and men of honor; and to recognize that they came in all religions, colors, and ethnicities.

Mickey Schwerner was a student at Cornell University and later Columbia. When I went off to the University of Florida years later, a friend prompted that we should rush a frat house. We found the Florida chapter of Alpha Epsilon Pi fraternity and pledged. To be associated with the same fraternity as guys like Dale and Mickey was meaningful for me.

The "history" of Blacks and Jews was somewhat known to me historically. The specific allies our family found in the Jewish community have gone to the grave with A. S. J., Grandma, and other relatives. I wish I had asked more questions. During the 1960s it was hard not to notice that whenever civil rights leader MLK showed up, Rabbi Abraham Heschel was there too. He and other members of the Jewish community showed us what it meant to pray with our feet. In this community I saw a real desire to make the world right again.

History teaches that American Jews played a significant role in the founding and funding of some of the most important civil rights organizations, including the Leadership Conference on Civil and Human Rights, the Southern Christian Leadership Conference (SCLC), and Student Non-Violent Coordinating Committee (SNCC). But that is not all. In 1909 a Jew, Henry Moscowitz, joined W.E.B. Du Bois and other civil rights leaders to found the NAACP. Another Jewish ally, Kivie Kaplan, a vice-chairman of the Union of American Hebrew Congregations (now the Union for Reform Judaism), served as the national president of the NAACP from 1966 to 1975. Arnie Aronson worked with A. Philip Randolph and Roy Wilkins to found the Leadership Conference.

From 1910 to 1940, more than 2,000 elementary and high schools, and twenty Historically Black Colleges, including Howard, Dillard, and Fisk Universities, were established by contributions from Jewish philanthropist, Julius Rosenwald. At the height of the so-called Rosenwald Schools, nearly 40 percent of southern Blacks were educated at one of these institutions.

During the Civil Rights Movement, Jewish activists represented a disproportionate number of Whites involved in the struggle. Jews made up half of the young people who participated in the Mississippi Freedom Summer in 1964. Leaders of the Reform Movement were arrested with Rev. Dr. Martin Luther King Jr. in St. Augustine, Florida, in 1964 after a challenge to racial segregation in public accommodations. Most famously, Rabbi Abraham Joshua Heschel marched arm-in-arm with Dr. King in his 1965 March on Selma. (Jews and the Civil Rights Movement, https://rac.org/jews-and-civil-rights-movement)

Jews similarly made up at least 30 percent of the White volunteers who rode freedom buses to the South, registered Blacks, and picketed segregated establishments. (Jews in the Civil Rights Movement https://www.myjewishlearning.com/article/jews-in-the-civil-rights-movement/)

In my youth, I was drawn to the teachings of both Judaism and the Methodist Church. I walked away from the conversation with my grandmother knowing that I had her approval to join a Jewish fraternity, and that I should make an effort to be mindful of my relationship with Methodist people.

In January of 1937 a New York Jewish teacher, poet, and songwriter named Abel Meeropol published a poem he'd penned, titled "Bitter Fruit." He published it under his pseudonym, Lewis Allan, as a protest against the racial killings, lynchings, of the day.

Later, in 1939, the African American singer, Billie Holiday, would sing that song to the world, so that no longer could the men and women of America say, "I didn't know." My family tree, like that of many other BIPOC (Black, Indigenous, and People of Color) people, has blood at its roots. The poem, now a song, "Strange Fruit," stands as just another example and tribute to the collaboration of Jews and Blacks against White Supremacy. That collaboration and connection continued to be exemplified well into the 1960s in the stories of folks like Dale Schwartz and John Lewis in Tennessee; Goodman, Schwerner, and Chaney in Mississipi; and Rabbi Heschel and MLK, and AEPi brothers in Indianola.

I pledged AEPi because I sought a group of men to do justly, and to love mercy, and to walk humbly with God. Shortly after my initiation into AEPi, I ushered civil rights activist, Angela Davis, onto a stage along with Michael Snyder, the chair of Accent '74 and Sentinel officer of AEPi. We stood with Davis as she gave a moving speech on our community need to look out for the bullies of the world and speak out for the marginalized.

Research into A. S. J. Allen has helped me understand Grandmother's feelings toward the Methodist Episcopal Church, too. Indeed, they had been very good to us.

Care for the Children Orphaned by the Tragedy

Another call from Rebecca Bowers at the Duke Archives revealed more about the Methodist Church and the aftermath of A. S. J. Allen's killing. Rebecca had found journals that recounted money disbursements to "the orphans of A. S. J. Allen."

> Now, not forgetting our friend and brother in the person of Rev. A. S. J. Allen, who was appointed to the Jacksonville charge, and went to his work with great earnestness and there labored faithfully until April 21, 1904, when he fell a victim to the power of death, leaving nine children without mother or father to care for them, we trust that our loss is heaven's gain, and we can but say:
>
>> Rest from thy labor, rest, soul of the just set free,
>> Blest be thy memory and blest thy bright example be.
>> Now, toil and conflict o'er, go take with saints thy place,
>> But go, as each has gone before, a sinner saved by grace.
>
> Humbly submitted, OSCAR F. NIBLACK

> (From page 15 of *Journal and Yearbook of the Florida Annual Conference, Methodist Episcopal Church, Thirty-Third Session.* Held In Zion Church, Ocala, Florida, February 2, 1905. Published by the Authority of the Conference and Approved as the Official Record.
> Edited by the Secretary, Jos. M. Deas, D. D.)

Rebecca also discovered a "STEWARDS' REPORT FOR 1904." Page 18 of the document shows that disbursements to A. S. J. Allen's children of $41 were made by T. E. Debose.

Further scanning of church documents showed a close association between O. F. Niblack and A. S. J. We also found that Niblack was personally delivering funds to the orphans as noted by: this entry into "Committees and Board Reports. Stewards' Report" of February 3, 1906. 'We have received the following amounts: Orphans A. S. J. Allen paid to O. F. Niblack ... 46 00.'"

Further reporting shows the disbursement.

"The Official Journal and Year-Book of the Florida Annual Conference of the Methodist Episcopal Church Thirty-Sixth Session." Held in Jacksonville, Florida, January 30 to February 3, 1908. A. S. J. Allen's Orphans-20 00. O. F. Niblack.

A. S. J. Allen's children 30 00

From: *The Official Journal and Year-Book of the Florida Annual Conference of the Methodist Episcopal Church Thirty-seventh Session.* Held in Fernandina, Florida, January 28 to 31, 1909.

Edited and Published by
Stephen A. Huger, Secretary
Gainesville, Fla. Pepper Pub. & Ptg. 1909

OUR WIDOWS AND ORPHANS.

Sisters Georgiana, Small Precilla Welch, and the four orphan children of Rev. A. S. J. Allen are blessed with reasonable health.

CLASS C—ORPHAN CHILDREN.

A. S. J. Allen's children $25.00

J. E. DeBose's children 21.75

B. J. Shannon's daughter........................... 5.00

Total $51.75

A. S. J. Allen's orphans 20 00

A. S. J. Allen's children 30 00

Florida African American Education and Lynching

"A violent person entices their neighbor and leads them down a path that is not good" (Prov. 16:29).

The records of the Methodist Church from the years after A. S. J.'s death showed that the children were cared for. The Allen children were educated at Cookman Institute, the first high school of African Americans.

Coming out of slavery, A. S. J. Allen and other Blacks of the time realized that the care and education of Black youth were of paramount importance. Being a Black orphan child was not a good thing in the early 1900s in Florida.

The combination of being orphaned and Black frequently meant a fast track to a life of crime. Besides, in the early 1900s, everybody knew that "uneducated, wild, ignorant negroes" were dangerous.

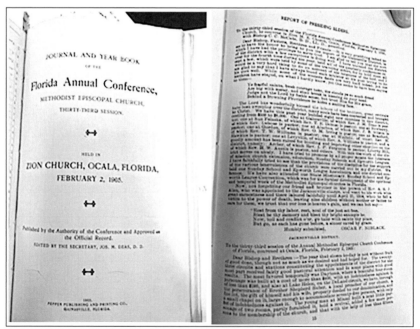

Records of the Methodist Church from the years after A. S. J.'s death

18-year-old Alonzo on line 8 of 1910 census

Six years after A. S. J.'s death (1910) we find eighteen-year-old
Alonzo Allen at Cookman Institute.

"Dangerous negroes" were an easy target for lynching. Between
1877 and 1950, the report, *Lynching in America: Confronting
the Legacy of Racial Terror*, counts 3,959 examples of "racial
terror lynchings," which Equal Justice Initiative (EJI) describes
as violent, public acts of torture that were tolerated by public

officials and designed to intimidate Black victims. Of the twelve states analyzed, Florida ranked fifth, with 331 terror lynchings within its borders. Per capita, however, Florida ranks first, with 0.594 lynchings for every 100,000 residents.

Table 1: African American Lynching Victims by State, 1877-1950	
Alabama	326
Arkansas	503
Florida	331
Georgia	586
Kentucky	154
Louisiana	540
Mississippi	576
North Carolina	102
South Carolina	164
Tennessee	225
Texas	376
Virginia	76
Total	3959

Table 2: Number of African Americans Lynched Annually Per 100,000 Residents in Southern States, 1880 to 1940	
State	Per capita rate
Florida	0.594
Mississippi	0.556
Arkansas	0.545
Louisiana	0.475
Georgia	0.378
Alabama	0.256
South Carolina	0.180
Tennessee	0.165
Texas	0.154
Kentucky	0.111
Virginia	0.072
North Carolina	0.068

Early reporting of the 25 counties across the South with the most lynchings. Florida has six: Orange (34), Marion (30), Alachua (19), Polk (19), Columbia (17), and Taylor (17). *Source:*   https://www.browardpalmbeach.com/news/ florida-lynched-more-black-people-per-capita-than-any-other-state-according-to-report-6470940.

The National Memorial for Peace and Justice in Alabama honors victims of mob lynchings between 1877 and 1950. The six-foot-tall monoliths contain multiple names on each. Pictured above is the Alachua County, Florida, memorial with the names of forty-three documented lynchings.

Updated data concerning that count of nineteen Alachua lynchings increased to forty-three at the time of this writing. EJI's original list only included post-Reconstruction murders. Currently, researchers expect that number to rise as more examples of lynchings during Reconstruction are being discovered.

Why are so many people starting to get into genealogy?
Because it adds to wellness.
Myth: My well-being is not linked to my ancestry.

Linking Your Knowledge of Your Forefathers to Your Wellness

It is important to honor those who came before us. Twenty-three world religions contain an admonition to honor the folks who got you here. The Christian Bible goes a step further and offers not only a command to "honor your father and mother," but it also makes a promise: "so that it will go well with you." Over 2,000 years later behavioral scientists have confirmed this Biblical truth that honoring your elders leads to well-being. In a 2008 study by Marshall Duke and Robyn Fivush, the authors found that children and adolescents who knew their family narratives performed better on wellness tests that those who did not know stories of their parents and grandparents.

Source: M. P. Duke, A. Lazarus, and R. Fivush, "Knowledge of family history as a clinically useful index of psychological well-being and prognosis: A brief report," *Psychotherapy Theory, Research, Practice, Training* 45 (2008): 268-272.

Just as I write this book to honor the memory and legacy of A. S. J. Allen, I want you to honor your family. They are the men and women who helped make you who you are. They are the giants upon whose shoulders you stand today. Learning your family narrative takes time. Often it involves long hours of hanging out with Mom or Grandmother. It is well worth the time.

As interest in family connections, genealogy, and ancestry grows, one of the lessons we are learning is that we are connected more than we previously thought. Instead of a planet of distinct individuals with varying races, we are a single family—one giant human race. DNA testing is revealing far more connections than we previously realized.

Your family, both past and present, consists of imperfect people that you should get to know. They are, as Martin Luther described it, "*simul justus et peccator*" or "simultaneously saint and sinner."

I believe you will find that the best of your ancestors lives on in you.

Unlike science, history is told with bias. As Winston Churchill famously said, "History is written by the victors." If your folks won the battle, then the history that is told is great generals and glorious victory over the cruel enemy. If your folks lost the battle, then you learn the same story in school—not the story of the invading horde that slaughtered your people. When it comes to learning the stories of any non-dominant culture, the public-school history book does not tell the whole story.

According to Edmund Burke, "People will not look forward to posterity, who never look backward to their ancestors."

The world tends to make us feel that we just are. We exist. We are here. It comes across almost as if we magically dropped down onto this planet from nowhere. And now that we are here, we have to follow our instincts and decide what makes us happy and sad, and define success and find fulfillment on our own. Don't believe it.

Newton explained in a letter that, if he had seen further than other men, "It is by standing on the shoulders of giants." He modestly attributed his discoveries to the work done by his predecessors. Think of yourself as standing on the shoulders of those who came before you.

My message to the youth is that you are made up of bits and pieces of your parents, grandparents, and other relatives. The stuff that makes you, you, did not just magically appear out of thin air. As you grow there will be pressure for you to conform and be like others. When I was a kid, I spent way too much time being embarrassed by my big ears, red hair, pink lips, and dark eyes. I did not look like the other kids. What took me years to realize was that I did look like my family. You are an individual. There is not now nor has there ever been another like you.

You are unique. However, never overlook that you are made of parts that come from outside of you. There are limits but also powers that you have because of who your parents and grandparents are. Remember when Daniel Tiger wanted to fly. He had to come to realize that, though Owl is his friend, he is not gifted with wings and bones that would allow him to fly like his friend.

Use the past to impact the present and the future. In life, stand up to the bullies and remember your family did the same before you.

> Knowing our own history, or the history of our culture, is important because it helps us to know who we are while molding the future. Being familiar with past events gives us the ability not only to learn from past mistakes but also from the successes. (Helena Cain)

We are different in our love languages. We are different in our expectations. We are different in where we look for recharging, vacations, relaxation, and energizing. Many of us experience a sense of inspiration and pride when we learn about those who came before us. Our past tends to influence our present-day lives and, inevitably, our futures.

When I was a student at Immaculate Conception Elementary School, I had a poster in my bedroom. It was a photo of a thin, brown boy, standing in a doorway. There was a dirt road in front of the doorway and there were flies all around the child's face. The words on the poster read:

> The best way to understand,
> Is to stand under;
> Which is the best way
> To understand.

To this day, that image is with me. You see the message was clear that I could never understand the life of the little boy in the poster or anyone else, as long as I was standing on top, looking down on him. I needed to be beneath him. To truly know someone else's story demands that I attempt to walk in their shoes. I must empathize with other people and see them more than mere bit players in my show. Jesus said it this way, "Truly I tell you, whatever you did for one of the least of these brothers and sisters of mine, you did for me" (Matt. 25:40, 45, NIV).

Why do parents of Black kids care?
Because lessons of the past hold value for the present and the future.
Myth: My child will be fine navigating a White culture without knowledge of Black history.

Soundtrack suggestion:
"Fortunate Son"
Creedence Clearwater Revival
Songwriter: John C. Fogerty
Fortunate Son lyrics © The Bicycle Music Company
cost of being AWB (accused while black)

Some folks are born made to wave the flag
Ooh, they're red, white and blue
And when the band plays "Hail to the chief"
Ooh, they point the cannon at you, Lord
It ain't me, it ain't me, I ain't no senator's son, son
It ain't me, it ain't me, I ain't no fortunate one, no

It has been over one hundred years, but it seems that a White man still has the "right" to stop and hold a Black man for the police just because he *suspects* the Black man might be doing or saying something illegal. The cost, if he's "lucky," is a stiff fine, incarceration, kicking, and a roughing up. $15 in 1918 equates to about $275 today.

When a Black man encounters a White man with power, it can cost a life—still, even after a hundred years. My struggle for a godly heart is real. It is especially real because I am a dad and a granddad. If you are a person of color in America, or you are raising one, at some point you will come across "the talk."

Black man's code, or the talk—how to behave—lessons every Black child learns from their parents

There are no formal studies that quantify the differences in how these talks are delivered among people with different racial backgrounds. But we know anecdotally that Black parents are much more likely to have the talk with their children. The reason is simple: Black parents are more likely to fear for the safety of their children.

My mom gave me the talk. She impressed on me that, because I was a Black male, I had a burden of proof to go "above and beyond" to show strangers what type of person I am.

I was taught to be polite and never argue with the police. When confronted by someone with a badge or a gun, do not flee, fight, or put your hands anywhere other than up. Family history offered the object lesson. Her dad demonstrates how understanding the talk can leave you free and alive to create the future. Grandpa went along with the police. My mom was his legacy.

> before at this time of the year.
>
> But for the timely arrival of the police, Ned Felder, a negro, would have been roughly handled last night on Central avenue for expressing the hope that the Germans would kill every American soldier now in France. The negro's remark was overheard by a white man, who promptly grabbed Felder and kicked him a few times, and then, as the crowd was gathering and the information regarding the offense was spreading, turned the negro over to the police. Felder was fined $15 and costs in municipal court this morning. He denied making the statement attributed to him.
>
> R. G. McEwen was selected deputy grand chancellor by the local Knights of

Source: *Tampa Tribune*, Wednesday, January 16, 1918.

DISLOYAL TALK LANDS A NEGRO IN CITY'S JAIL

Expressions that were hostile to the the United States army landed Ned Felder, a negro, in the city jail and he had reason to congratulate himself that he was in jail as he narrowly missed being roughly handled. Fortunately for the negro only one white man heard the negro express the hope that the Germans would kill every American soldier in France. The one white man who heard the remark, made as the County guard marched up Central avenue Monday night, promptly caught Felder by the nape of the neck and kicked him several times. He then turned the negro over to the police.

In municipal court Felder was fined $15 and costs. He claimed he had not said anything against the army and protested that he is registered for army service and is loyal but the testimony of the white man who heard the statements was convincing. The negro realized that he was in danger, as he said to Judge Maurer:

"That white man would sure have killed me last night if he had had a gun. They hustled me about so I did not know what was happening."

Felder came here from Gainesville and is a waiter in a restaurant.

The clipping is from a St. Petersburg, Florida, newspaper.

These two newspapers reporting on Grandfather's event draw attention to the unique history of African Americans in America. This happened on January 16, 1918; my mom was born on November 26, 1918, so she wasn't even conceived at this point. If this encounter had not gone "well," then this would have been the end of the "Felder" line, and no beginnings for me.

In closing out this chapter on Skinfolk, let me say that A. S. J. looked out for his skinfolk by being a voice. A voice that proclaimed opportunity for education and betterment. A voice that sought to make connections for families. A voice that sought to keep skinfolk alive and thriving.

If my great-grandfather were here today, I believe his voice would be heard giving the talk. I would imagine that it would go something like this. . . .

Driving While Black

This is not a question of if someone who is Black is pulled over by the police, but when. The goal is to get back home—to survive. Follow some basic rules to increase your chances for survival during a traffic stop:

- Turn off the ignition

- Roll down your window

- Explain where your license, registration, and insurance documents are before reaching for them

- Do what the police officer says

- Do not argue, be polite and respectful, stay calm, do not make any sudden moves

- If, as a teen, you feel things are not going well, say, "I would feel more comfortable if my parents were here. I would like to call my parents, and I would like to have my lawyer present."

Shopping While Black

Before you enter a store to shop:

- Be prepared to always buy something

- Be well-groomed. Dress so that you "don't shame the family," as a friend's mom used to say

- Make a shopping list and carry it with you as you shop

- Use the main entrance/exit even if a secondary exit is more convenient
- Take your hood off outside the store; let the store clerks see your face

While shopping:

- Don't put your hands in your pockets
- Don't wear headphones. Be aware of your surroundings
- Don't wear sunglasses
- Use a shopping cart or basket
- Be courteous; greet the store staff with a smile
- Don't sample fruits or veggies or any other goods until you pay

After your purchase:

- Place your items in a store bag and get a receipt

Before you exit the store:

- Be sure to have your purchases in a store bag and a receipt

Soundtrack suggestion:
"Mama Said"
The Shirelles

Mama said there'll be days like this
There'll be days like this, Mama said
(Mama said, Mama said)
Mama said there'll be days like this
There'll be days like this, my Mama said
(Mama said, Mama said)

Village Folk

What do you think of when you hear the term "village folks?" I know some of you are trying to *not* think about the disco era group of guys dressed as a cop, a sailor, a construction worker, a cowboy, a biker, and an Indian. If this reference makes no sense to you, go ask a "Boomer" about the "Village People."

For some, village folk will bring up an image of an African or a European village with rather homogeneous looking folks going about their daily tasks as children play in the streets. And there is nothing wrong with that image. In this chapter, I'd like to look at the folks in that picture, but I'd also like to expand the scene a bit; because in today's global economy and world, the concept of the village has to include the village next door, and the one next to it, and the next one, and so on.

This expanded village view is very present in my family story. So, village folk will include fictive kin, non-biological kindred, BFFs, communities in which you identify as a member.

Village folk will include just about everybody except those you intentionally chose to exclude from your village. The true stranger, or outsider. So, one way of talking about this is to say—village folk is *us*, which ultimately makes "the others" *them*. The way my mother would explain this to me was simply that the world is made up of friends you just haven't met yet. "Them" or "the others" are folks who don't want to be your friends. In the next few pages, I will talk about the friends who showed up with love and support after the killing of A. S. J. Allen. I also will comment on the others. The shooter, JL Shaw, the media, the grand jury, and others who chose to not be friends.

My position is that any discussion of the village folk must include all of us and them. Let's begin this discussion with a focus on unity.

Soundtrack suggestion:
"We Are Family"
Sister Sledge
Songwriters: Nile Rodgers and Bernard Edwards
We Are Family lyrics © Sony/ATV Music Publishing LLC, Warner Chappell Music, Inc.

We are family
I got all my sisters with me
We are family
Get up everybody and sing
We are family
I got all my sisters with me

We are family
Get up everybody and sing
Everyone can see we're together
As we walk on by

(And) and we fly just like birds of a feather
I won't tell no lie
All of the people around us they say
Can they be that close

Just let me state for the record
We're giving love in a family dose

While the community significantly shapes our self-understanding, it can also influence the perception of the other, or the stranger, as a person who is not a member of our family, kinship, or chosen community.

> *Source:* Patrick D. Miller, "Israel as Host to Strangers," in *Israelite Religion and Biblical Theology: Collected Essays* (JSOT SS 267; Sheffield: Sheffield Academic Press, 2000), 548. Miller says terms of kinship such as "brother" or "sister" imply familiarity and a positive relationship, while the categories of the "stranger" or the "alien" imply uncertainty and the possibility of danger.

A world view that sees "us and them" can lead to disunity. Disunity is a threat to and an enemy of us all.

Knowledge informs decision-making. Many descendants of Black heroes of Reconstruction have lost the memory of their ancestors' heroic achievements. During an episode of *African American Lives 2*, comedian Chris Rock discovers that his great-great-grandfather, Julius Caesar Tingman, had fought for the Union with the United States Colored Troops during the Civil War. After the war, he then served in the South Carolina legislature under its Reconstruction government. The revelation brought the typically glib Rock to tears.

"How in the world could I not know this?" Rock asked the host, Henry Louis Gates. He then goes on to speculate that, had he known of this past, he might have chosen a different path for his life. (https://www.csmonitor.com/Books/2019/0524/Stony-the-Road-lays-bare-the-failure-of-Reconstruction)

The story of A. S. J. Allen's murder is by no means unique in American history. Unfortunately, there are many accounts of African Americans being murdered by Whites and the murder being legally sanctioned as a justifiable homicide. Many such murders were reported by the local news media with little or no explanation other than a simple one-line statement of "negro shot." Or he was "a bad nigger." (See http://chroniclingamerica.loc.gov/lccn/sn95026977/1905-02-15/ed-1/seq-3/under heading Florida

News Items, paragraph 7)

What is unusual about the story of A. S. J. Allen is not the murder but rather the response. In 1904 the African American community did not just accept this murder but rose in defiance of the act and sought to get justice for him.

The killing of A. S. J. Allen seems to fit the definition of a lynching. It was a killing where a White man exercised his "supremacy" over a Black man's body and land.

"Love does no harm to a neighbor. Therefore, love is the fulfillment of the law" (Rom. 13:10, [NIV]).

"Do not plot harm against your neighbor, who lives trustfully near you" (Prov. 3:29).

What were the final thoughts racing through my great-grandfather's mind as he sees his neighbor shoot him? This was not some stranger in a hood and robe or a mask. This was the man next door, whom he saw every day.

"Do not let any unwholesome talk come out of your mouths, but only what is helpful for building others up according to their needs, that it may benefit those who listen" (Eph. 4: 29).

And what words were spoken? The newspapers reveal no clear details. One reports that the men argued over something about a fence; my family has suspected that the argument was over something far more intimate. In 2021 a jury in Glynn County, Georgia, found three White men accused of killing a Black jogger, Ahmaud Arbery, guilty of murder. In the day-long hearing, it was asserted that the shooter uttered the words, "f---ing n-----," as the Black man lay dying in the road.

Did JL Shaw use a racial slur before the sheriff arrived at the scene of my great-grandfather's killing? Did the sheriff? Was the air filled with hateful speech as A. S. J. lay dying on the ground? One report tells that a crowd at the scene heard Grandpa use foul language toward Mr. Shaw. The initial problem with this account is that there was no crowd during the argument. There was Shaw, A. S. J., Ella, and two babies in or near the house. Some things are easy to imagine. Some are inconceivable. In all my dealings with my family over sixty-plus years, I've never heard a single family member utter foul or obscene language. Not saying that it could not have happened, but nothing in the oral or written history of my family suggests that A. S. J., the preacher, within earshot of two daughters and a baby boy, would use foul language.

Did these babies hear foul words from the mouth of the killer? A. S. J., bleeding and dying on the hot Florida dirt, could not shield them from this experience.

Today, we have been given a gift: the radio. Although invented in 1895, the first broadcast of music over radio occurred in 1906; two years after the killing of my great-grandfather. But even then, it would be well into the 1920s before American families would bring this music box into their homes as a source of entertainment. It is difficult for me to imagine his life without radio. The soundtrack of his life was Negro Spirituals and a cappella singing, and the sounds of farm work —hoeing and chopping.

His world was filled with the sounds of farm animals, horses' hooves, horseless carriages, trains, and the predictable Florida evening lightning storms.

And then there was the final sound he heard—a gunshot.

The actual experiences of A. S. J. and Ella and the village folks surrounding him cannot be fully known. History does not record these events. We can only speculate based on what we know of the period then, and what we know of our own experiences today. Even then, the experiences of the villagefolk can vary.

We were visiting with my wife's uncle and aunt who lived in St. Petersburg, Florida. Since I was the family outsider here, they wanted me to talk so they could get to know this new addition to the family. As I talked about growing up in this coastal community, I noticed that Uncle Johnny was oddly quiet, and at times seemed puzzled as I spoke about my childhood growing up in St. Pete. Then it seemed he could take it no more. He abruptly stopped me and asked, "Where did you grow up? That is not the St. Pete I knew!" He explained that he had grown up in this city, too, and although he was slightly older than me, he could not relate to any of the rosy images I had painted.

For him, living in St. Pete in the '50s and '60s was hard. It was racist. It was wrought with barriers. He talked about how his movements were limited to the "colored sections" of town. Now the tables were turned, and I sat there in shock and bewildered.

I had no idea what he was talking about. The explanation, however, was about to be revealed. It came in the form of a question. He asked, "Tell me the names of the boys you played ball with." I gave him the surnames of some of my classmates and friends.

He calmly sat back in his easy chair and, with a rather condescending grin, said "Oh, I see now, you're one of them."

He went on to explain that, while he and his kin lived in the hood, my people lived among and around it but did not fit in. He spoke of how "my people" (the parents of the boys I played with) were doctors, dentists, nurses, lawyers, city councilmen and -women, teachers, shop owners, and the like. His folks were not professionals but were the everyday folks who eked out a living at the bottom of the social strata.

The "it" of "us and them" thinking was real and could work as a threat to the unity of any community.

So even within the skinfolk community, there were divisions. Us and them thinking was real. For whatever reason, my family never talked this way or promoted these ideas of class.

Yet nothing in our interconnected world is a long way away. Everything that could go global does go global, from terror to religious extremism to websites preaching paranoia and hate.

Never before have John Donne's words rung truer: "Any man's death diminishes me, because I am involved in mankind." Therefore, "Send not to know for whom the bell tolls; it tolls for thee."

I guess another way of saying this is, that we are all in this mess (life) together; so be sensitive to each other. A basic reality of the human experience is that we see one another as either kin or strangers. We relate to others as members of our family, kin, community, and nation or as strangers who do not share our worldview.

My upbringing instilled in me a sense of "connectedness" to the world around me. My wife's uncle did not experience the same sense of connectedness. My Uncle Wilbert would travel frequently to the African continent to visit the family. He had an adopted son who lived in the Caribbean. There were friends of my mom and grandma who were Jews and who were regular visitors in our home. The legacy of A. S. J. Allen to me was that the world was made up of "us"—just folks I had not met yet. Once we met—we'd be family.

> *Source:* Love the Stranger for You Were Strangers
> e-Publications, J. Ramirez Kidd, https://epublications.
> marquette.edu/cgi/viewcontent.cgi?article=1687&context=di
> ssertations_mu

The Hebrew Sages noted the repeated emphasis on the stranger in biblical law. According to Rabbi Eliezer, the Torah "warns against the wronging of anger in thirty-six places; others say, in forty-six places."

תהילים ל"ט:י"ג

(יג) שִׁמְעָה־תְפִלָּתִי | יי וְשַׁוְעָתִי | הַאֲזִינָהֿ אֶל־דִּמְעָתִי אַל־תֶּחֱרַשׁ
כִּי גֵר אָנֹכִי עִמָּךְ תּוֹשָׁב כְּכָל־אֲבוֹתָי:

Psalms 39:13

(13) Hear my prayer, O LORD; give ear to my cry; do not
disregard my tears; for like all my forebears I am an **immigrant**,
resident with You.

(Ps. 39:13) "Hear my prayer, O LORD; give ear to my cry;
do not disregard my tears; for like all my forebears I am an
immigrant, resident with You" (https://www.sefaria.org/shee
ts/55299.23?lang=bi&with=all&lang2=en).

As proud as I am of my family and its view of the planet as a
village, the reality is this country was built on a foundation of
racism and White supremacy. The demonization of Black folks in
America is just one of a line of racial attitudes that history records.
And if "us" equals "White" it is only in recent history that Italians,
Norwegians, and others became "White." As seen in the following
letter by Benjamin Franklin, there was a time when people of
German ancestry were not considered "us."

I agree that these people are a matter of great concern to
us. I fear that one day, through their mistakes or ours, great
troubles may occur. The ones who come here are usually the
most stupid of their nation. Few understand our language, so
we cannot communicate with them through our newspapers.
Their priests and religious leaders seem to have little
influence over them. They are not used to freedom and do
not know how to use it properly. It has been reported that
young men do not believe they are true men until they have
shown their manhood by beating their mothers. They do not
believe they are truly free unless they also abuse and insult
their teachers. And now they are coming to our country in
great numbers. Few of their children know English. They

bring in much of their own reading from their homeland and print newspapers in their own language. In some parts of our state, ads, street signs, and even some legal documents are in their own language and allowed in courts. In some areas, there is a need for interpreters. I suppose in a few years, interpreters will also be necessary in the state government to tell one half of the lawmakers what the other half is saying. Unless the stream of these people can be turned away from this country to other countries, they will soon outnumber us so that we will not be able to save our language or our government. However, I am not in favor of keeping them out entirely. All that seems necessary is to distribute them more evenly among us and set up more schools that teach English. In this way we will preserve the true heritage of our country.

Source: The complete text of Franklin's letter, "The German Problem in Pennsylvania," (May 9, 1753) can be found in *The Complete Works of Benjamin Franklin*, vol. 2, edited by John Bigelow, Harcourt Brace and Company, 1887, p. 291. From a Speech by a Famous American.

Very often, we toss around the terms "black, "Hispanic" and "white" as if we all agree on what they mean. Yet a look at history shows that ideas about our nation's racial categories—what they are and who fits into them—are always changing. And in particular, answers to the question "who's white?" have never been simple. In the early 20th century, for example, many of the country's new immigrants to the U.S. were from Finland. They had blonde hair, blue eyes and light skin. But the Finns, who some today might consider the epitome of whiteness, were not considered "white" at the time. (Duke University Ways & Means Podcast: Who Is White? From October 25, 2016)

"Have we not all one Father? Has not one God created us? Why then are we faithless to one another, profaning the covenant of our fathers?" (Mal. 2:10)

Who Were the "Us" in the Life of A. S. J. Allen?

As I researched A. S. J., I had an interesting encounter with a librarian-archivist. After numerous failed attempts to find my great-grandfather's name on any of the church and cemetery records at their disposal, I suggested that we look at a certain resource that itemized most of the Black members of the town. That's when she exclaimed, "Oh, was he colored?" Important note to self: Always anticipate the biases of the times in which our ancestors lived. There may be segregated records.

If you view the world as places for us and them, then it is important how you think of *them*. A fundamental reality of human experience is that we encounter one another either as kindred or strangers. My grandma had delivered a message about who I was and who we were as a family. And a part of her message was to take care and be good in my treatment toward Jews and Methodist folks; we were strangers, and they were very good to us.

> "Then the King will say to those on his right, 'Come, you who are blessed by my Father; take your inheritance, the kingdom prepared for you since the creation of the world. For I was hungry and you gave me something to eat, I was thirsty and you gave me something to drink, I was a stranger and you invited me in, I needed clothes and you clothed me, I was sick and you looked after me, I was in prison and you came to visit me.'" (Matt. 25:34-36)

> *Do you know the national background of your family (such as English, German, Russian, etc.)?*
>
> *y n*

Why do non-history buffs care?
Because romanticized versions of history get created.
Myth: There's no harm in "colorizing" or "Disneying up" history.
A real and accurate view of history *must* be from the viewpoint of the people involved.

Soundtrack suggestion:
"The Way We Were"
Barbra Streisand

Memories
May be beautiful and yet
What's too painful to remember
We simply choose to forget

I sat one afternoon with a researcher I'd just met. We talked about the importance of family history in developing our sense of self. He related a story to me that helped me see how important family stories are to all of us.

He received a letter from one of his children. The young man was very excited to share a photo with him. It was a lovely view of a city with a bridge in the background. The son's message revealed that via census records he'd located the place where his grandparents had lived decades ago. Although the house is no longer standing, the young man stood where he imagined the front door might have been and took the picture, showing what his grandparents might have seen as they walked out of their home each day.

It was a lovely shot and a wonderful sentiment to try and imagine that this was the scene that greeted his grandma and grandpa each new morning. What was especially poignant was that the

187

photo and message were from the man's adopted son. His family narrative, though not biological, was just as real as if it had been written into his DNA. Family stories can make us who we are!

Soundtrack suggestion:
"Walk a Mile in My Shoes"
Joe South
Songwriter: Joe South
Walk a Mile in My Shoes lyrics © The Bicycle Music Company

Walk a mile in my shoes
Just walk a mile in my shoes
Before you abuse, criticize and accuse
Then walk a mile in my shoes

Understanding Cousins

As we enter this discussion of village folk, I'd like to take a closer look at cousins. Cousins are true relatives. In simplest terms, a cousin is a child of one's uncle or aunt. But the term is also applied to "play cousins," varying degrees of cousins, and even, as we will soon see, fictive kin. Again, we'll talk more about them later, but this is where a cousin chart can come in handy for examining "blood" cousins.

A cousin chart, or table of consanguinity, is helpful in identifying the degree of cousin relationship between two individuals. The degree of relationship is determined using the most recent common ancestor as the reference point.

Instructions for using a cousin chart in 3 easy steps:

- Determine who your common ancestor is. This happens as you discuss the common family members between you. Let me give an example.

Let's take my cousin, Jacqueline. We talked about who our parents, grandparents, great-grands, and other relatives were. We searched for the common ancestor and quickly found that A. S. J.'s wife, Dinah, and her grandmother, Fannie, were sisters.

Here's how that looks:

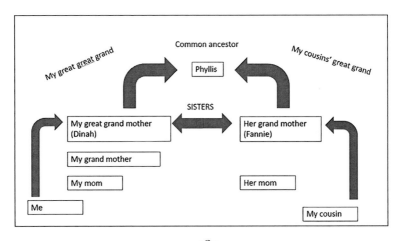

- Now, using the cousin chart below, across the top row, find the common ancestors' relationship to you. So, let's go across the top to find the box labeled great 2x grandparent; as Phyliss would be my great-great-grandparent.

- Next, on the left-hand column going down, find the common ancestors' relationship to the other individual. For my cousin Phyllis, it would be her great-grandparent. See where the lines meet? We can now determine that my cousin is actually my second cousin once removed.

1st run your finger across the top row to find your common ancestor title. Note the column. Next, run your finger down the column to find your 'cousins' title for the same ancestor. Note the row. The cell the column and row meet in is your relationship to your cousin.

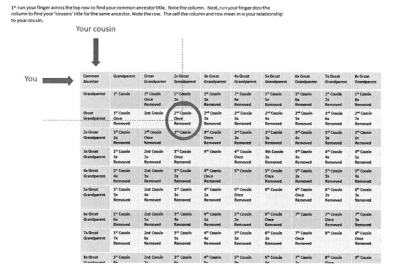

Give it a try for yourself using the chart below. Remember, locate your relationship to the ancestor on the top row (when you find it, draw a line down); and then your "cousin's" relationship to the same ancestor on the far-left column (when you find that relationship draw a line to the right). Where the two lines you've drawn meet will reveal your cousin relationship.

1st run your finger across the top row to find your common ancestor title. Note the column. Next, run your finger down the column to find your 'cousins' title for the same ancestor. Note the row. The cell the column and row meet in is your relationship to your cousin.

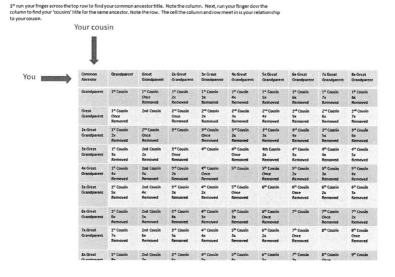

191

Fictive Kin, the Fraternities, Lawyers, and the Media

Roughly two years earlier, A. S. J.'s wife, Dinah, had died. He was a single dad with nine children. The village folk showed up! The newspapers said that the lawyers hired to fight this battle were hired by the Masons and Odd Fellows of the community. His community was behind him.

Fictive Kinship

A type of village folk that I'd like to discuss now is fictive kin. In the sociology of the family, this idea is referred to as chosen kin, fictive kin, or voluntary kin. Sociologists define the concept as extended family members who are not related by either blood or marriage.

So there is no true kinship tie but, rather, a fictitious bond not built on consanguineous and affinal kinship ties as described by most anthropologists and ethnographers. However, in many family communities, relationships with fictive kin can be as real as, or more so than, true kinship relatives.

The ties that allow for this type of kinship may include religious associations, close friendship ties, or other essential reciprocal social or economic relationships. Growing up, I had my Aunt Rose, who functioned very much as an "other mother" to me. It was not until I was an adult with a family of my own that I learned that Aunt Rose had been a boarder in my grandparents' house during the 1920s and '30s. During the 1950s Mom and Aunt Rose worked together. I have many stories of their adventures as domestic laborers in Florida and Maine. Her kinship was based on years of living and working with my family, not blood.

The Italian scholar, Lorenzo Caratti di Valfrei, whose work covered heraldry, genealogy, and historical studies, acknowledged this kinship bond. He wrote in his manual of genealogy that "Genealogy is the science that verifies and studies the relations of consanguinity, affinity and fictive kinship, that exist among different people."

In an article called "Fictive Kinship in the Dying Age of Obama," Imani Thornton explains that "Fictive kinship is the anthropological idea that someone not "blood-related" to an individual can be considered that person's "mother," "father," "brother," "sister," or other "relative."

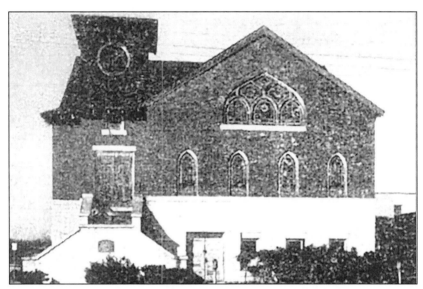

Photo of McCabe M.E. Church building from the book *St. Petersburg Florida* by Sandra W. Rooks

"Within the Black community, black people have historically considered fellow Blacks their 'brother' or 'sister,' especially when that fellow Black person has similar political views or is fighting with them in the good fight" (https://thestripes.princeton. edu/2017/02/fictive-kinship-in-the-dying-age-of-obama/).

Especially within African American families, we see that play-cousins, non-biological family members, fictive kin, and other mothers tend to play a major role in the transmission of culture, health promotion, and decision-making. Members of the Allen's fictive kin family seem to have come mainly from the church.

Looking back on the Alachua County area that A. S. J. knew, there was some religious diversity. In those communities of faith, two names stand out as village folk with A. S. J.: his brother-in-law, ZD Limbric, and another man, Pearl Daniels. Pearl would prove to be fictive kin; that "uncle" my grandmother and her siblings would need after A. S. J. was gone.

There was no dedicated church building in Gainesville in the first years of the town's existence. A church building erected in 1859 by the Presbyterians was shared by itinerant preachers of several denominations until 1874. The Methodist mission to Gainesville lapsed during the Civil War, and a church they had built was used by a black congregation after the war. Several White Protestant denominations organized congregations and built churches in the 1870s. Catholics, who had been holding services in private homes for twenty-five years, built a church in 1887. Jewish families began moving to Gainesville in the late 1860s. Although a Jewish cemetery was established in 1872, there was no synagogue in Gainesville until 1924.

We find A. S. J., his wife's brother, ZD Limbric, and another man, Pearl Daniels, as a documented part of the Methodist mission to Gainesville. In researching the movements of my great-grandfather, I find that his name in the Methodist church records frequently appears next to Pearl Daniels. Pearl was ordained in 1890, just like A. S. J. They were both appointed to the same congregational areas and appear on the rosters in Alachua County, Florida, from 1890 to 1894.

I pulled a program created for the church I grew up in, McCabe Methodist Church in St. Petersburg, Florida. The program was for the celebration of the new church building in 1972. At the opening of the publication, there is a short history of the congregation. To my surprise, they list the first pastor of the congregation in 1905 as—you guessed it—Pearl Daniels!

A. S. J.'s wife, Dinah, died around 1901. After his killing in 1904, four-year-old Fannie and six-year-old Wilbert were taken in and raised by Dinah's sister, Phyllis, in St. Petersburg. The year after A. S. J.'s murder, Pearl and his wife moved to St. Petersburg from Gainesville and founded the McCabe M.E. Church there. Now called McCabe United Methodist Church, McCabe is the oldest African American congregation in St. Petersburg. Fannie worshiped there from its founding in 1905 until she died in 1975.

I lost the trail of Pearl for a while, and then discovered Pearl was really Peorl, a name you do not see very often anymore. His name was frequently misspelled as Pearl. Apparently, the name was so popularly misspelled that he started to use the spelling of Pearl. Pearl died in 1917 in Tampa, the year before my mom was born.

Beyond "the other," the fictive kin, and the church folk in great-grandfather's life circle, there was the village of the African American community.

> *Do you know about a relative whose face "froze" in a grumpy position because he or she did not smile enough?*
>
> *U. N.*

Why This Story Matters.
Because every story matters.
Myth: Your story is not important. Everybody's got the same story.
Those people from your past do not affect you.

Soundtrack Suggestion:
"Take Time to Be Holy"
Songwriter: John Longhurst

Take time to be holy, let Him be thy Guide;
And run not before Him, whatever betide.
In joy or in sorrow, still follow the Lord,
And, looking to Jesus, still trust in His Word.

Agency, or self-agency, also known as "personal agency" in psychology, is a term that describes the power that an individual has over their own life. When people talk about a sense of agency, they are talking about the sense of control someone has over some specific event or action.

The story of A. S. J.'s murder is by no means unique in African American history. Unfortunately, there are many accounts of African Americans being murdered by Whites and the murder being legally sanctioned as a justifiable homicide. Many such murders were reported by the local news media with little or no explanation. Often a simple one-line statement of "negro shot." When these killings have been perpetrated by two or more persons, the killing is usually termed a lynching.

What is unusual about the story of A. S. J. Allen is not the killing, but rather the response. In 1904 the African American community did not just accept this murder but rose in defiance of the act and sought to get justice for the actions of the White perpetrator. They demonstrated a show of agency not typically seen in Black communities. Why? This book looks into the recorded events around 1904 Florida to seek out the catalyst for what the *Daily Sun* newspaper reported as "Negro push."

Daily Sun (Gainesville), October 13, 1904, article titled "Shaw Not Guilty Said Grand Jury. Negroes Pushed the Case."

"It was thought this matter was ended until a few days ago, when it is said a number of prominent colored Odd Fellows and Masons, together with the aid of churches agitated the matter of prosecution."

I want to dive deeper into the question, "What was special about A. S. J.?" Was it because he was a minister, a teacher, a leader in the community? What did A. S. J. do to build the social capital of the African American community to a point that "The negroes hire 2 attorneys?"

As we begin this exploration, I first want to discuss the concepts of social capital in Black agency. A common understanding of democracy is "a political system in which the supreme power lies in a body of citizens who can elect people to represent them." Democratic principles are reflected in all citizens being equal before the law and having equal access to power. This concept was by no means reality to the millions of Free Negroes or emancipated slave descendants of the southern 1900s. Participation in the democratic process was extremely limited and the topic of equality was, as of yet, not a topic of discussion in any serious debate of the day. Yet in the community response to A. S. J.'s murder, we see both an exercise of democratic principle and agency on the part of the community.

In *Making Democracy Work: Civic Traditions in Modern Italy*, written in 1993 by Robert Putnam (with Robert Leonardi and Raffaella Y. Nanetti), the central thesis is that social capital is key to high institutional performance and the maintenance of democracy. Putnam argues that the success of democracies depends in large part on the horizontal bonds that make up social capital.

A closely related idea is that of "cultural agility." This refers to the ability of an individual to work within different cultures; to take on behavioral cues and adapt to them in their own behavior. Another related term is "code switching." Social capital is a sociological concept used in business, economics, organizational behavior, political science, public health, and the social sciences in general, to refer to connections within and between social networks.

Although there are a variety of related definitions, they all tend to share the core idea "that social networks have value. Just as a screwdriver (physical capital) or a college education (human capital) can increase productivity (both individual and collective), so do social contacts affect the productivity of individuals and groups."

I do not refer to real estate, or to personal property or to cold cash, but rather to that in life which tends to make these tangible substances count for most in the daily lives of people, namely, goodwill, fellowship, mutual sympathy and social intercourse among a group of individuals and families who make up a social unit.... If he may come into contact with his neighbor, and they with other neighbors, there will be an accumulation of social capital, which may immediately satisfy his social needs and which may bear a social potentiality sufficient to the substantial improvement of living conditions in the whole community. The community as a whole will benefit by the cooperation of all its parts, while the individual will find in his associations the advantages of the help, the sympathy, and the fellowship of his neighbors. (pp. 130-131)

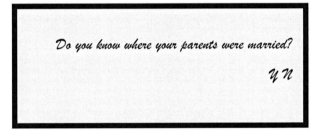

The extent to which citizens are embedded in networks of civic engagement is thought to determine the level of political activity in which a citizen engages (Putnam 1993, 2000). Membership in organizations and associations is thought to facilitate the development of critical thinking skills necessary for political engagement.

Source: African Americans growing or expanding their social capital to the broader community of white America.
Social Capital Patterns in the African American Community
View the whole article online at http://www.allacademic. com//meta/p_mla_apa_research_citation/0/8/7/5/5/ pages87553/p87553-1.php

Earlier in the chapter on KinFolks, we talked about the social capital A. S. J. Allen built in the community as a Minister of the Gospel. We see his involvement in thirty or so marriages of folks within the Alachua County community. A chart documenting some of those marriages he performed is shown in the earlier section.

This was the currency that A. S. J. sowed that reaped the harvest of a community of African American citizens in 1904 Alachua County, Florida, standing up to the White establishment after his killing.

At first glance, the "logical" places to look would be the secret societies and the churches of the Black community as mentioned in the previously quoted article. This article gives us this clue to the origins of this social capital. The folks felt they had a voice via the Masons and Odd Fellows. Also, the Methodist Church offered help for the bereaved family. Other sources of Black agency and social capital would be Black insurance companies and burial fund clubs.

I also believe A. S. J.'s involvement with the Negro press was critical to his building of social capital or worth in the community. In the Thursday, March 17, 1898, edition of the *Southwestern Christian Advocate* (New Orleans, Louisiana), Volume 33, Issue [11] below, we see how great-grandfather did not hesitate to involve himself in the communities he was assigned to.

A. S. J. Allen, P. C., Bethlehem M. E. Church, Cedar Key, Fla. —This is my first year here. I arrived here early after the conference which you so much graced, held in the city of Jacksonville. I found the people ready to take hold of the work with an unusual amount of interest. Our membership is greatly reduced by the running down of the business of this town, but somehow we are encouraged to

the extent to make greater sacrifices for all causes of Christ and the Church. Our presiding elder, J. P. Patterson, was with us on the 17th and 20th, which resulted in a great spiritual blessing. The Lord was with us. The writer sends along one subscriber, E. Martin, but don't want to send one man that far alone any more; so get ready, members and friends, for I shall call on you for your susbcription for the grand old paper. You will hear from us again soon.

Article from the Thursday, March 17, 1898, edition of the *Southwestern Christian Advocate* (New Orleans, Louisiana), Volume 33, Issue [11]

In my work, I want to look at the origins and sources of the social capital built by African Americans in Alachua County before A. S. J. Allen's shooting. My premise is that there had to be a considerable amount of social capital within the community for the community to react and act as it did in this shooting. I want to explore the mechanisms that created this capital that gave the community the freedom, impetus, and courage to push back. Examine the newspaper text, social club minutes, and other sources for evidence of strong social capital in Alachua. Look for reports of fence or boundary disputes between races. Look at other reports of violence (shooting, lynching, murder, KKK activity) against Negroes in 1900 through 1904. Examine the recorded land transactions involving A. S. J. (and family) and neighbors.

Was there another source of tension between A. S. J. and Shaw? Investigate any news, business, court, or city government contact between them.

One report by A. S. J.'s granddaughter, Essie, is that the argument had nothing to do with the fence, but rather that Shaw was bothering one of A. S. J.'s daughters. Check census records to see which of the girls would have been living there at the time. Is there any other evidence that there is a hidden source of conflict?

Agency, synonymous with mediation, is illustrated in the case of the attorneys, who represent the leaders of the Black community in dealings with the White community. I'd like to consider the two attorneys, W. E. Baker of Jacksonville, and Walter M. Davis of Gainesville. Who were they? Were they African American? Had they a track record; a history of success? Why were they chosen?

The Lawyers

Since a major part of my story involves the community response to my great-grandfather's shooting, then let's look at the legal team.

Who were Davis and Baker?

Information on U.S. lawyers is in the *Martindale's American Law Directory.* The professional rating of A. S. J. Allen's lawyers from the 1905 Martindale's American Law Directory (January 1905) follows:

	W. E. Baker		Walter M. Davis	
Born	1880	25 yrs old	1873	32 yrs old
Admitted to Practice	1902	3 yrs experience	1891	14 yrs experience
Estimate of Legal Ability	B	Good	E	Declined to rate
Recommendations	V	Very high	Z	Declined to rate
Estimated Worth	7	$2,000-$5,000		Declined to rate
Promptness in Paying Bills	FI	Fair	FF	Fair

W. M. Davis was considered "one of the foremost lawyers of Florida" and W. E. Baker was a member of the first graduating class (class of 1902) of Stetson Law School.

Below are the names of ministers (not listed in the order in which they were appointed) who pastor New Mt. Zion and Pleasant Plain United Methodist Churches and names of the district superintendent who served the Gainesville district. Note the "Sidney Allen" listed here is Rev. A. S. J. Allen.

Ministers	District Superintendents
Tony Mayes	D S Selmore
L G Scott	Pickens
G S Cameron	T W Wilimas
L Zimmerman	J B Cook
A J Anderson	F E Welch Sr
Ministers	District Superintendents
Ashely	H J Blunt
Robert James	William Murray
H H Hawkins	J B F Williams
Rs Tyre	S S Robinson
H M Trapp	W M Ferguson
Zack Smart	D C Mcdonald
H C Green	W M Roughton
W P Pickens	D C McDonald
Wooten	H E Huel
H J Blunt	M Gibbs
Grant Niblack	J Jones
Lee Foster	Joe Smith
Sidney Allen	Geraldine Mcclellen
Frank Cambridge	
Essex James	

Alonzo Felder

J J Truel

F E Welch Sr

Oscar Niblack

E B Young

Arthur Miles

Chatman Haile

Simon Welch Sr

Ministers

David Edwards

C L Huggins

Willie Session Jr

Clarence Desue Jr

Source: personal communications with Sherry DuPree,
http://cisit.sfcc.edu/~sdupree

Something New-Black Communities Fighting Back

They thought they could kill him and bury him—they did not realize he was a seed.

Fraternal organizations

Freemasonry is a fraternal "voluntary association" organization. They describe themselves as a religious brotherhood of man. They are involved in charitable work in the community and among its membership. Freemasonry is a voluntary association in that no one is invited to become a member. The wives and daughters of Masons have their own fraternal organization, the Order of the Eastern Star.

Freemasonry is not a "secret society." It does not keep its existence a secret. Members do make known their affiliation with the group both in life and in death. It engraves the words "Masonic Temple" or "Masonic Lodge" on many of its buildings, and numerous tombstones display masonic markings to identify the deceased as Freemasons.

My grandmother, Fannie Allen Felder, was an Eastern Star. And according to their official website:

> Any Female relatives who are related by birth, marriage, or adoption to an affiliated Master Mason in good standing, or if deceased in good standing at the time of their death; as well as members – either active for three (3) years or majority – in the International Order of the Rainbow for Girls or in Job's Daughters International, each of whom having attained at least the age of eighteen (18) years, are eligible to membership in the Order of the Eastern Star.

So, was A. S. J. Allen a Freemason? I believe he was. My messages to this society have thus far gone unanswered. I remember Sunday evenings when Grandmother would leave the house in her white dress to go to her meetings of the Eastern Star. This was the one place Grandmother went that I could not follow. This was a fraternity that I could not be a part of. As I searched for clues to my heritage, it was Grandmother's hundred-year-old Bible that offered up the "official" genealogy. And who do you think gave her that Bible? The Queen Esther Circle of the Eastern Star.

Image of Grandmother's dedication page: from the Eastern Star to Fannie Allen in her Bible.

Soundtrack suggestion:
"Joshua Fit the Battle of Jericho"
Songwriters: Roger Wagner/Pd Traditional

Joshua fit the battle of Jericho
And the walls came tumblin' down
Up to the walls of Jericho
With sword drawn in his hand
Go blow them horns, cried Joshua
The battle is in my hands

The Civil Rights Act of 1964 (Pub.L. 88–352, 78 Stat. 241, enacted July 2, 1964) is a landmark piece of civil rights and U.S. labor law legislation in the United States that outlawed discrimination based on race, color, religion, sex, or national origin.

In the *Daily Sun* (Gainesville), October 13, 1904, the headline read: "Shaw Not Guilty Said Grand Jury - Man Arraigned for Murder of Rev. Allen Was Not Indicted. - Negroes Pushed the Case."

Did you catch that last part? "Negroes Pushed the Case." For the first time since the end of Black codes, a group of African Americans in Florida banded together to legally push back against the once-legal practice of the "casual killing" of Negroes, now commonly deemed "justifiable homicide." They took action against the unfair treatment of folks based on race. They did not believe that this murder and the way it was handled would have happened if my great-grandfather had been White. This premise is supported by the newspapers announcing that the "Negroes" pushed back.

Power concedes nothing without a demand. It never did and it never will. Find out just what any people will quietly submit to and you have found out the exact measure of injustice and wrong which will be imposed upon them, and these will continue till they are resisted with either words or blows, or with both. The limits of tyrants are prescribed by the endurance of those whom they oppress. (Frederick Douglass)

Like so many, A. S. J. Allen died the victim of gun violence, "standing his ground" in Florida. Thank you, A. S. J., for standing up to the status quo. A. S. J. had a long history in central Florida; he had lived and worked long enough in the community that even in life, folks noticed him. A. S. J. built social capital in his community. He gave of himself as a teacher and minister and served the community (he even ran for postmaster with local Republican backing). Gave more than he took.

Soundtrack suggestion:
"Ain't Gonna Let Nobody Turn Me Around"
"Aint Gonna Let Nobody Turn Me Around" is a traditional American song. It has been performed by Joan Baez, Rachel Tucker, the Freedom Singers, and Sweet Honey in the Rock. In the version performed by Joan Baez, each verse ends with "Gonna build a brand-new world."

Ain't gonna let nobody turn me around
Turn me around, turn me around
Ain't gonna let nobody turn me around
I'm gonna keep on a-walkin', keep on a-talkin'
Marchin' up to freedom land.

"Defend the weak and the fatherless;
    uphold the cause of the poor and the oppressed.
Rescue the weak and the needy;
    deliver them from the hand of the wicked." (Ps. 82:3,4)

The Media

Quotes below are taken from the newspaper reports on the A. S. J. murder:

- a colored minister and teacher well known in this city
- well known in Gainesville, and was considered a rather inoffensive Negro
- a Negro preacher and politician
- He was an educated Negro and for several years was employed as a school teacher in this county
- he seemed to gain prominence by his affable tongue
- applicant for the postmastership of Alachua
- He had the independent endorsement of many prominent Republicans
- a pastor
- a minister

And then, later on, the papers reported:

- regarded as a troublesome Negro and had few friends even among his own race

It is hard to read this and understand that these are all talking about the same individual. This list leaves me scratching my head, asking, "Which ones of these descriptions are true? How can they describe the same man?" Here's what's going on.

As you read the newspaper reports, a few things stand out. Note that the October 10 report says Shaw was arrested later as he was hanging out with friends, but then the story changes in the October 13 report that now says Shaw surrendered immediately.

After the initial report, the media then began to create a negative image, to demonize A. S. J. Allen. In the April 22 article, he was described as a "rather inoffensive negro." By the next day, the media reports him as being "a troublesome Negro."

One line that stands out for me in reading about A. S. J. is where it says: "It was thought the matter was over." This line speaks volumes about the attitude of the times. It also cuts directly to a reason I am so proud of my great-grandfather. He lived the kind of life that empowered those around him. The community he was a part of and served for many years did not think the matter was over.

The narrative of 1904 in the southern United States was that a Black man was to be silent and unseen. When a decision was made by White America, the Negro was to quietly accept it. It was virtually unheard of for any decision to be questioned. To do so would get you labeled as a "troublemaker" at best; killed, at worst. This unwritten code of behavior was all a part of the Jim Crow system.

Stetson Kennedy, the author of *Jim Crow Guide* (1990), offered the following examples that Blacks were supposed to observe in conversing with Whites:

- Never assert or even intimate that a white person is lying.

- Never impute dishonorable intentions to a white person.

- Never suggest that a white person is from an inferior class.

- Never lay claim to, or overly demonstrate, superior knowledge or intelligence.

- Never curse a white person.

- Never laugh derisively at a white person.

- Never comment upon the appearance of a white female.

As you can see, Jim Crow Laws were numerous and nuanced. More Jim Crow rules can be found on the web at https://www.ferris.edu/jimcrow/what.htm

The village folks of A. S. J. would have been very familiar with all of these rules, yet the community came together and hired two attorneys. To see a community of nineteenth-century Blacks take such action has a few implications worth noting. First, it means that they thought that they could win. The small communities around Alachua where A. S. J. Allen preached were poor and easily disenfranchised by the Whites in the larger towns of Alachua and Gainesville. Nevertheless, A. S. J. must have been worth fighting for in their eyes. I have come to see him as possessing what we would term today as cultural agility. He had the ability to work within the Black and White cultures of his day by adapting behaviors that caused the conflict of attitude described in the newspapers. The press of the time could not pigeonhole him and thus struggled to adequately portray him in their reporting. This man was a family man, an educator, a preacher, and a landowner. He embodied everything his world told him he could not be.

> *Do you know what went on when you were being born?*
>
> *Y N*

Three Consequences of Telling a True Story

The process of telling this story leads into multiple discussions. This kind of dying messes with your head and the heads of future generations. First is a discussion of transgenerational trauma, second the experience of a violent death, and third, a discussion concerning family bias.

First, transgenerational trauma and transfer

My telling the story of A. S. J. Allen comes with a sense of overwhelming and uncomfortable pain. His untimely, violent, and traumatic killing was a horrible event in my family. For most of my childhood and young adult life, A. S. J.'s children were a part of my life. His baby girl raised me. I spent summers visiting and living in Ella's house. Minnie was a frequent guest in our house. Most weekends were spent at Cora's house. Holiday dinners were always at Gussie's house. Wilbert drove from New York to Florida every year for as long as I can remember to spend time with his little sister. He was even there to walk my mom down the aisle at my wedding. His children surrounded me for years and not one of them ever told me the story of his killing. This was our family's unspeakable pain. No one would tell the story. It simply hurt too much.

Soundtrack suggestion:
"The Beat Goes On"
Sonny and Cher
Songwriter: Sonny Bono

Charleston was once the rage, uh huh
History has turned the page, uh huh
The miniskirt's the current thing, uh huh
Teenybopper is our newborn king, uh huh

And the beat goes on, the beat goes on
Drums keep pounding a rhythm to the brain
La de da de de, la de da de da

Grandmas sit in chairs and reminisce
Boys keep chasing girls to get a kiss
The cars keep going faster all the time
Bums still cry, "Hey buddy, have you got a dime?"

Transgenerational Trauma Transfer

Transgenerational trauma, or intergenerational trauma, is a psychological theory that suggests that trauma can be transferred between generations. After the first generation of survivors experiences trauma, they can transfer their trauma to their children and further generations of offspring via complex post-traumatic stress disorder mechanisms. This field of research is relatively young but has expanded in recent years.

To my knowledge, the trauma as described above was not transmitted within the family. None of my cousins seem to have picked up this trauma. None of them carry it as their own burden. For this, I am grateful, as this would be a burdensome and wearing task.

> Transmission is the giving of a task. The next generation must grapple with the trauma, find ways of representing it and spare transmitting the experience of hell back to one's parents. A main task of transmission is to resist disassociating from the family heritage and "bring its full, tragic story into social discourse." (Fromm, xxi)

> Often one child within a family is nominated to both carry and communicate the grief of their predecessors. There was a man who entered a Holocaust Museum requesting that the institution keep the remains of the tattooed serial number taken from his arm. The chosen child is analogously charged with the mission of keeping the family heritage, being a "holding environment."

Historical trauma

Intergenerational trauma was first recognized in the children of Holocaust survivors. In 1966, psychologists began to observe large numbers of children of Holocaust survivors seeking mental help in clinics in Canada. The grandchildren of Holocaust survivors were overrepresented by 300% among the referrals to a psychiatry clinic in comparison with their representation in the general population. Since then, transgenerational trauma has been documented in descendants of slaves, Native Americans, war survivors, refugees, survivors of interpersonal abuse, and many other groups.

Instances of Transgenerational trauma where the trauma is a shared experience amongst a group of people and their role in society are often referred to as historical trauma. This form of trauma is specific as it affects a large population and is typically more complex than individual trauma. Historical trauma can result in a greater loss of identity and meaning, which in turn may affect generations upon generations until the trauma is ingrained into society.

My introduction to this theory came when I moved to North Carolina. My wife and I had returned to the states after a few years living and working as missionaries in the USVI. We'd left STX and moved back to St. Pete, Florida, when a close friend invited us up to North Carolina for a two-week vacation. Thirty-plus years later, we're still here.

The first few weeks in North Carolina, I accepted a job with the Duke Medical Center Sickle Cell Clinic. In the clinic was a young African American physician named George Phillips. George and I spent many hours working together in the clinic, and after the clinic closed would often walk together to the parking lot to get our cars and go home.

One particular topic seemed to dominate many of our conversations. "What's wrong with Black people?" With 90 percent of the patient population of the clinic being Black folks from rural North Carolina, George and I had a front-row seat to many of the ill effects that Southern segregation, Jim Crow, and White supremacy had brought upon our Black brothers and sisters.

So as far back as 1984, Dr. Phillips had a concept that the problem with Black folks is historical transgenerational trauma.

He would often (and quite seriously) propose that he wished that at the birth of every Black male baby at Duke, he could write a refillable-for-life prescription for antidepressants. Our collective racial problem: trauma and its subsequent depression and C-PTSD symptoms.

> "He has shown you, O mortal, what is good.
>> And what does the Lord require of you?
> To act justly and to love mercy
>> and to walk humbly[a] with your God." (Mic. 6.8)

So, this has implications for the question "Does slavery affect Black people today?" How far down the family tree does the trauma reach? And might this explain some of the dysfunction we see today? While the intergenerational trauma of my great-grandfather's killing does not seem to have been transferred, there is a noticeable sense of despair that I observe in my family and, in many ways, in most Black people. I describe this despair with a definition I picked up from the writings of Rob Bell, who says despair is "The belief that tomorrow will be just like today."

Descendants of slaves

In recent years, symptoms of transgenerational trauma have been identified among Black Americans, in relation to the effects of slavery and racial discrimination. This passing of trauma can be rooted from the family unit itself or found in society via current discrimination and oppression. The traumatic event does not need to be individually experienced by all members of a family; the lasting effects can remain and impact descendants from external factors....

In general, Black Americans who suffer from any mental illness are resistant to receiving treatment due to stigma, negative conceptions, and fear of discrimination. This reduces the number of those affected to seek help. Lack of treatment causes the symptoms to compound leading to further internalization of distress and a worsening of mental health in the individual. Those affected by race-based trauma oftentimes do not seek treatment not only because of stigma but because of fear that the medical professional will not understand their perspective of a disenfranchised minority.

Sources: Franks, J. (2007-08-29), "Slow recovery goes on in crime-weary New Orleans," Reuters, Retrieved 22 September 2018.

Haag, A.M. (2007), "The Indian Boarding School Era and Its Continuing Impact on Tribal Families and the Provision of Government Services," Tulsa L. Rev. 43:149.

Researchers at the University of Zurich and ETH Zurich found the changes are so powerful they can even influence a man's grandchildren. (http://www.dailymail.co.uk/health/article-2611317/How-trauma-life-passed-SPERM-affecting-mental-health-future-generations.html?ito=email_share_article-bottom)

Second, a violent death

JL Shaw pulled the trigger. His role is essential in this tale of A. S. J.'s violent death. A closer look at him reveals that after the Civil War, the Shaws moved down to Alachua, Florida, from Georgia, and the family still lives and farms there. (https://www.findagrave.com/user/profile/49131460)

Shaw's descendants and those of my great-grandfather continue to live and work in Alachua County today. The impact of Shaw's actions has also rippled down through the ages.

It has been said that history is written by the victors. That might be true for the "official" and commonly published history. But the story of a violent death is retold by the victims. In a blog post, "After the murder, a family grapples with generations of trauma," and forthcoming book, *Nobody's Slave: How Uncovering My Family's History Set Me Free* (HarperCollins), Lee Hawkins, news editor and on-camera reporter for the *Wall Street Journal*, tells the story of how his grandfather's first cousin was found dead after rifle bullets pierced his heart. This shooting, like that of A. S. J. Allen, was ruled a homicide by the local coroner, and in eerily similar form, the shooting was thought to be related to a property dispute with a white family. (https://www.centerforhealthjournalism.org/2018/07/19/after-murder-family-grapples-generations-trauma)

The murder and the subsequent fallout became a national story. Folks gathered around the family and community. The shooter(s) were not identified so the NAACP filed a civil lawsuit, charging local authorities with a racially motivated failure to investigate the crime and an attempt or intent to cover up the crime.

Lee writes that "the effects of the murder and the feeling of racial injustice devastated my deceased cousin's children, rippling through the next two generations of his descendants, in the form of post-traumatic stress and other health issues."

This is but another of many seldom-told, or at least seldom-published, stories where a look is given to the intergenerational impact of a violent murder within an African American family.

> For many black families a genealogical line of lethal racial violence can be traced over successive generations of the same family-from chattel slavery in 1600s Jamestown, through the 1800s when ancestors were born into plantation slavery, to the present.

Again, Lee Hawkins says:

> I believe the intergenerational trauma suffered by the survivors in my family was directly tied to fatal tragedies. According to the *American Journal of Preventive Medicine*, about 16.4 million people in the U.S. have been affected by homicide. Five million adults have experienced the murder of an immediate family member; 6.6 million people have experienced the murder of a relative other than a family member, and 4.8 million have experienced the murder of a close friend. "These homicide survivors experience a variety of difficulties, some like post-traumatic stress disorder (PTSD)," the *Journal* reports. (https://www. centerforhealthjournalism.org/2018/07/19/after-murder-family-grapples-generations-trauma)

Soundtrack suggestion:
"Grandpa Told Me So"
Kenny Chesney
Songwriters: Hicks/Springer
Grandpa Told Me So lyrics © Sony/ATV Music Publishing LLC, BMG
Rights Management

If you don't get in the water you're never gonna learn to swim
He said a snake is just as scared of you as you are of him
He could tell by the moon when the fish would bite
Seems there was nothing that he didn't know

As I do some serious soul searching and examination of the data, not only do I find my great-grandfather a man worthy of honor; I find that this is an honorable family with outstanding traits that I am proud to have embraced. I will by nature want to place a positive spin on anything I write related to my family.

"Do not conform to the pattern of this world but be transformed by the renewing of your mind" (Rom. 12:2).

"Do not say, 'I'll pay you back for this wrong!' Wait for the LORD, and he will deliver you" (Prov. 20:22).

One indicator of my family's attitude toward the Shaw family seems to be a lack of negative discussion about them. No one I've spoken to in the family has ever expressed any resentments over the killing of A. S. J. Allen.

I know I'm repeating myself here, but to be very clear, I have never heard a family member say a disparaging word about the shooter, his family, his property, or his anything! I've never heard his name or family mentioned in any gathering. One legacy of A. S. J. is that of being true to the text of God's word. Primary among the teachings of the Bible is what we commonly refer to as the Golden Rule, a teaching spoken by Jesus in Luke 6:31 and Matthew 7:12 that instructs us to "do unto others as you would have them do unto you."

James 4:11-12 (ESV)

"Do not speak evil against one another, brothers. The one who speaks against a brother or judges his brother, speaks evil against the law and judges the law. But if you judge the law, you are not a doer of the law but a judge. There is only one lawgiver and judge, he who is able to save and to destroy. But who are you to judge your neighbor?"

James 1:26 (ESV)

"If anyone thinks he is religious and does not bridle his tongue but deceives his heart, this person's religion is worthless."

Ephesians 4:29 (ESV)

"Let no corrupting talk come out of your mouths, but only such as is good for building up, as fits the occasion, that it may give grace to those who hear."

Ephesians 4:31 (ESV)

"Let all bitterness and wrath and anger and clamor and slander be put away from you, along with all malice."

Colossians 3:8 (ESV)

"But now you must put them all away: anger, wrath, malice, slander, and obscene talk from your mouth."

Romans 12:19 (ESV)

"Beloved, never avenge yourselves, but leave it to the wrath of God, for it is written, 'Vengeance is mine, I will repay, says the Lord.'"

To my knowledge there is not now nor has there ever been a feud between the Allens/Dobys and the Shaws. Feuds begin because one party (correctly or incorrectly) perceives itself to have been attacked, insulted, wronged, or otherwise injured by another. Intense feelings of resentment trigger the initial retribution, which causes the other party to feel equally aggrieved and vengeful.

To my knowledge, I've never met a Shaw family member. But if one of Mr. Shaw's direct descendants walked up to me today, I would hope that I would extend an open hand of fellowship and love toward them as I would to anyone else. Why? Because that's what I believe great-grandfather would do. My family, in general, has not taught me or preached a way of hatred, retribution, retaliation, or violence. To "do unto others as you would have them do unto you" has been the guiding principle of my life.

Third-Bias

This book is titled *Discovering A. S. J. Allen: A Story of Skinfolk, Kinfolk, and Village Folk,* and indeed it is about my great-grandfather, the folks in his life, the events of his life, and his legacy. I am writing about my grandpa; you know—papa, grandad, grampy—that quintessential figure in American family life that is often elevated to sainthood, at least by the grandchildren. However, the story is incomplete unless I speak about the shooter. I desire to do so without prejudice or bias. This book is not about Mr. Shaw. It is about A. S. J. Allen, the man who was shot and killed, and about the ripple effects that one incident has had on me, my family, and an entire community.

A. S. J.'s role as a minister of the Gospel is, I'm sure, one of the reasons my family cherishes the teachings of Jesus from Matthew 5:7, commonly known as the Beatitudes, and the teachings of the Sermon on the Mount. Such a legacy leaves no room for a mindset of resentment or retaliation. Resentment is often defined as anger, bitterness, or indignation experienced as a result of unfair treatment.

Now, let's be honest here. I am telling you what I am aware of. The statements within this book reflect my bias. Both bias towards the individual family members I know and bias towards their character as a unit. There could well be individuals in my family who do not hold these views. And if you and your family have been the victims of violent deaths among your ancestors, you may experience a very real struggle with resentment among your own family members.

"Do not gloat when your enemy falls; when he stumbles, do not let your heart rejoice" (Prov. 24:17).

Finding Help and Hope Now That the Story Has Been Told

> *Do you know the source of your name?*
> *Y N*

Why do spiritual folks care?

Because of a command and a promise.

Myth: Genealogies are senseless and hold no value.

Soundtrack suggestion:
"Tell me the old, old story, of unseen things above."
Author: Kate Hankey

Tell me the old, old story,
Of unseen things above,
Of Jesus and His glory,
Of Jesus and His love;

Tell me the story simply,
As to a little child,
For I am weak and weary,
And helpless and defiled.

Tell me the old, old story.

Because of its sense-making function, storytelling is potentially beneficial for individuals' health and well-being (Neimeyer and Levitt, 2000). Research in narrative psychology (e.g., McAdams, 1993; Pennebaker, 1997) and narrative therapy (e.g., Monk, 1997; White, 2007) suggests that the opportunity to tell and/or reframe stories of trauma, difficulty, or stress can have a positive effect on mental and physical health. (Koenig, Kellas et al., 2010)

Remember, earlier on I acknowledged my need to check my

bias. Do I have a bias toward my family? Yes. I am a Southern man writing about my great-grandfather from my point of view. I've been sharing with you my story of a terrible, violent, traumatic death. Do I need help and hope? Yes. If you discover this type of story in your family history, then you are going to need hope and help, too. The best help and path to hope I know is to honor those who came before us. This means honoring them no matter what good or bad things we learn about them. We don't get to pick our ancestors; we don't get to decide to only honor them if they were "good." If you learn your ancestor committed a horrible crime or deed, you don't get to just write them off and dishonor them. Every person is greater than the worst thing they have ever done. You will always find what you look for, so look at your family tree and ask, "What's good about these folks?"

According to Weber, Harvey, and Stanley (1987), telling the story of a stressful or traumatic event can help an individual develop a sense of control and understanding. It provides an opportunity to create a coherent, ordered account of events (Neimeyer and Levitt, 2000), and it enables individuals to make sense of difficult life experiences, which in turn enhances their mental health and well-being (e.g., Kellas and Manusov, 2003).

In other words, knowing what's good about you contributes to good mental health and well-being. Your story is good and the people who made you, you, have added to that goodness.

"Honor your father and your mother so that you may live long in the land that Yahweh your God is giving you" (Exod. 20:12 [NJB]).

In the Torah, keeping this commandment was associated with individual benefit and with the ability of the nation of Israel to remain in the land to which God was leading them. Dishonoring parents by striking or cursing them was punishable by death. In the Talmud, the commandment to honor one's human parents is compared to honoring God. According to the prophet Malachi, God makes the analogy himself:

"'The son honors his father, the slave stands in awe of his master. But if I am indeed father, where is the honor due to me? And if I am indeed master, where is the awe due to me?' says Yahweh Sabaoth to you priests who despise my name." (Mal. 1:6-8 9 [NJB])

Because honoring parents is part of honoring God, the mitzvah does not depend on the worthiness of the parent: "Even if his father is wicked and a sinner, he must fear and revere him.... A convert to Judaism must not curse or despise his non-Jewish father."

It also requires honor to one's stepparents or an older sibling who is raising one, and one's teachers, though one has a greater obligation to honor a parent than a grandparent.

The commandment is repeated eight times throughout the Bible.

Though we may have different religious beliefs and spirituality, there are many ways that folks remember those who have passed on, the contributions their existence has made to our lives, and the ongoing relationships that defy even death. Nearly every religious belief system on the planet has some guiding text to "Honor thy Father and thy Mother." Some examples are listed below.

"Show honor to your parents and pay homage to them. This will cause blessings to descend upon you from the clouds of the bounty of your Lord, the Exalted, the Great."
Baha'i Faith
Baha'u'llah in the Family Life compilation

"Those who wish to be born in [the Pure Land] of Buddha ... should act filially towards their parents and support them and should serve and respect their teachers and elders."
Buddhism
Meditation on Buddha Amitayus 27

"Honor your father and your mother, that your days may be long in the land which the Lord your God gives you."
Christianity and Judaism
Exod. 20:12

"The gentleman works upon the trunk. When that is firmly set up, the Way grows. And surely proper behavior towards parents and elder brothers is the trunk of Goodness."
Confucianism
Analects 1.2

"Now filial piety is the root of all virtue, and the stem out of which grows all moral teaching.... Our bodies–to every hair and bit of skin–are received by us from our parents, and we must not presume to injure or wound them: this is the beginning of filial piety. When we have established our character by the practice of the filial course, so as to make our name famous in future ages, and thereby glorify our parents: this is the end of filial piety. It commences with the service of parents; it proceeds to the service of the ruler; it is completed by the establishment of [good] character."
Confucianism
Confucius, Classic of Filial Piety 1

"Do not neglect the works due to the gods and the fathers! Let your mother be to you like unto a god! Let your father be to you like unto a god!"
Hinduism
Aittiriyaka Upanishad 1.11.2

"Thy Lord has decreed ... that you be kind to parents. Whether one or both of them attain old age in your lifetime, do not say to them a word of contempt, nor repel them, but address them in terms of honor. And, out of kindness, lower to them the wing of humility, and say, 'My Lord! bestow on them Thy mercy even as they cherished me in childhood.'"
Islam
Qur'an 17.23

"One companion asked, 'O Apostle of God! Who is the person worthiest of my consideration?' He replied, 'Your mother.' He asked again, 'And second to my mother?' The Prophet said, 'Your mother.' The companion insisted, 'And then?' The Messenger of God said, 'After your mother, your father.'"
Islam
Hadith of Bukhari and Muslim

"There are three partners in man, God, father, and mother. When a man honors his father and mother, God says, 'I regard it as though I had dwelt among them and they had honored me.'"
Judaism
Talmud, Kiddushin 30b

"Do not despise the breath of your fathers,
But draw it into your body.
That our roads may reach to where the life-giving road of our sun father comes out,
That, clasping one another tight,
Holding one another fast,
We may finish our roads together;
That this may be, I add to your breath now.
To this end:
May my father bless you with life;
May your road reach to Dawn Lake,
May your road be fulfilled."
Native American Zuni Prayer

"Attend strictly to the commands of your parents and the instructions of your teachers. Serve your leader with diligence; be upright of heart; eschew falsehood; and be diligent in study; that you may conform to the wishes of the heavenly spirit."
Shinto
Oracle of Temmangu

"Son, why do you quarrel with your father,
Due to him you have grown to this age?
It is a sin to argue with him."
Sikhism
Adi Granth, Sarang, M.4, p. 1200

Your Folks

A Guide to Finding Your Folks

Soundtrack suggestion:
"Wade in the Water"

Wade in the water, children,
Wade in the water,
God's a-going to trouble the water

There is a fifty-one-year gap between A. S. J. Allen's leaving this world and my arriving into it. A lifetime of events has happened within that space. My biological family is shrinking and there are fewer people alive now who remember much of his story as told in this book. When I began high school, many of the kinfolks I talk about in this book were still alive. The orphan children of A. S. J were a part of my life. His baby girl, Fannie—my beloved grandmother—his darling Ella, Minnie, Cora, Gussie, and Wilbert—these folks and their spouses, children, and other kin were the kinfolk who surrounded me.

By the time I graduated from college, married, and had children of my own, these kinfolk were gone. Not one of A. S. J.'s children ever got to meet my children. In fact, over forty members of my biological family had passed away by the time my children were born. They were gone and, unfortunately, so were many of their stories and memories. Records, photos, paintings, furniture, and other heirlooms get thrown away or destroyed, either on purpose or accidentally. Houses and lands are sold or repurposed. Our histories are important and must be told and retold so that we never forget where we came from and the folks who made us, us!

Now that you've traveled with me through my discovery, it is time for you to "wade in the waters" and discover the folks of your family tree. It is time to get to know and honor the folks who created you.

In the next few pages, I will talk about some of the resources I used in my discovery adventure. I hope that this insight will be useful for you.

About Surnames

Spelling

As we begin our search for ancestors, typically the one piece of information we have is a name. Sometimes only our own surname is the launching point for our journey. At this beginning point we may discover that exploring family history can be impaired due to inconsistencies with surnames. As I began to question who my ancestors were and how to find them, I had to first navigate the issue of the family name spellings. To date, I have found documentation on validated individuals in the family with numerous spellings of the surname "Lembric." Among the variations found within church, census, and cemetery records are Limbric, Limbrick, Lembric, Limbrie, Lembrick, Limberic, Lanbrice, Limerick, Lunerick, and Timberick.

Sometimes the name is misspelled or changed in historical records. There are also legitimate or agreed-upon deliberate changes. Such changes can be motivated by an attempt to make the names "more American," such as a change from Smythe to Smith.

A fact that I had to confront is that when it comes to many older documents, spelling just doesn't count. It did not matter for the recorder of the information, and we must give leniency in this area as the researcher. Today we take spelling for granted, but before Samuel Johnson published *A Dictionary of the English Language* in 1755, there were no commonly acknowledged spelling rules.

So why weren't our ancestors at least consistent? That would have ensured the continuation of the same misspelling throughout history. There are two big reasons: 1) The ancestor may not have been literate, and 2) The record(s) may have been created by another person. If the ancestor was unable to read and write, she may not have known how to spell her own name. Even if she had memorized the spelling, a literate person recording the information may not have asked or may have "corrected" it.

Another reason for spelling variations could be an individual's accent. It is very difficult to know what type of accent or dialect a person may have spoken with. I refer to the story of how the trail for "John Rice" grows cold. Then, as a result of a phone conversation, the researcher alters her search criteria after hearing "John Royce" as pronounced by her Australian relative. Turns out "John Rice" and "John Royce" were the same man—on different continents. Easy to see how an enumerator would have made this mistake based on what he thought he heard.

When researching African American ancestors, another impairment, or "brick wall," can be name changes over the lifetime of a single individual often due to enslavement, transfer of ownership, or emancipation. In an earlier chapter I spoke about how, after emancipation, African Americans would use newspaper advertisements to try to contact their family members. The advertisements below show how enslavers named and renamed the folks they enslaved at will. Also, we see name changes noted in some "Lost Friends" ads that do not give any reference as to why the name, sometimes names, (both first and last) were changed.

Another impediment to your research may be the occurrence

of multiple surnames within a single family unit. Individuals within the same family group (husband, wife, and children) may use different surnames; thus, the method of following a thread of the same name is not useful in determining genealogy. Again, this is especially true among formerly enslaved people. This practice makes it even harder to find and make family connections. In the ad below, notice the phrasings of "I now go by the name of . . ." and "My name at that time was . . ."

Mr. Editor: I want to inquire for my father and brother. My father's name is Carter Bowlding, and my brother's name is Jeams Edwards Tiler. My mother's name was Nancy Coal, she belonged to old Mrs. Ashmore, and at the death of her she belonged to Mr. Alexander Berryman. My name was Fannie Bowlding when I left Virginia. I am now at Harrisburg, Tex. My name is changed to Fanny Burns. Direct your letter to Fanny Burns, care of Wilson Burley, Harrisburg, Tex.

Source: "Children's Day Gleanings." *Southwestern Christian Advocate*, 16 July 1891, p. 3. Nineteenth Century U.S. Newspapers, https://link.gale.com/apps/doc/GT3011662337/NCNP?u=duke_perkins&sid=NCNP&xid=a06942ed. Accessed 26 August 2020.

MR. EDITOR—I desire some information about my mother. The last time I saw her I was in Alexandria, Virginia, about the year 1852 or 1853. Her name was Hannah. She belonged to Lawyer Tibbs who sold her when I was quite young to a trader named Bruthing. Lather Tibbs lived at Leesburg, Va., when he sold mother to Bruthing, and afterwards Tibbs moved to Alexandria, Va., and swapped me to Bruthing for another boy. Bruthing put me in jail and I cried, so he told me if I would hush he would bring my mother there next morning, which he did; but I was so young mother hardly knew me, so Bruthing stood four or five boys in a line and asked her which one of them was her boy. She stood a few moments and then said I was the boy. Mother then brought me some cake and candy, and that was the last time I saw her. I now go by the name of Henry Tibbs. I remember the names of two of Tibbs' sons, Abner and Kennedy. Bruthing brought me to New Orleans, La., and sold me to a man named M. Pickett. If mother is found please address me at Deasonville, Yazoo county, Miss., in care of Rev. James Allen.   HENRY TIBBS.

Southwestern Christian Advocate, Dec. 11, 1879. Historic New Orleans Collection/Hill Memorial Library, Louisiana State University Libraries.

ville, Richland parish, La.

Mr. Editor: I want to inquire for my children, John Russell and Wilson Arley. Before the war I belonged to a man by the name of Mr. Billie George, who lived between Raleigh and Pittsburg, in Wilkerson county, North Carolina, I was sold from North Carolina about forty years ago. I was brought to this State by a Negro trader by the name of John Hooper, and sold to a man by the name of John Ward. My name at that time was Eliza George. Any information as to their whereabouts would be thankfully received. Address Eliza Ward, corner of First and North streets, Vicksburg, Miss.

Source: https://www.hnoc.org/ database/lost-friends/search-results.php

The Ellis Island change of surnames myth

As we've seen, there are cases of intentional name changes that we might encounter as we research our family tree. But I'd like to take a moment to talk about one intentional change idea that is commonly circulated among those doing family research. This intentional change accuses personnel at the immigration inspection station at Ellis Island of changing an ancestor's surname.

Between 1892 and 1954, well over twelve million folks entered the United States via this tiny island located in the bay off the New Jersey coast. The Ellis Island Immigration Records contain information on ship passengers arriving at both Ellis Island and the Port of New York. These immigrants were registered at one end of the Main Hall, U.S. Immigration Station. They were then processed through the building to receiving sponsors and relatives at the other end. There is a myth that persists in many of our family stories, that the family names were changed there. The truth is —they were not. Numerous blogs, essays, and books have proven this. Your family's last name was almost certainly not changed at Ellis Island. That's just not how the island operated when admitting immigrants into the United States of America.

It is always possible that the names of passengers were spelled wrong, perhaps by a clerk when the ticket was bought, or during transliteration, when names were translated from one alphabet to another. But here's the thing: there is good evidence to suggest that the folks actually changed their own names before they migrated to America.

Some immigrants would change their names themselves when they arrived to make them sound more American, to fit in with the local community, or simply because it was good for business. But whether before they left their home country, or after arriving in America, the surname change was most likely a deliberate choice made by your ancestor, and not a mistake made by an Ellis Island clerk.

Surname Origins Linked to Occupation

While we are on the topic of surnames, let's talk about name origins and what a surname might tell us about the family story. In the case of ancestors of African descent, at times, when enslaved folks were freed, they would take their last names from the jobs they did, as opposed to taking an enslaver's last name. Ancestors of European descent also followed this pattern of surnaming in accordance with the family trade. Here are just a few last names used by enslaved folks.

- Turner: a person who would turn wood on a lathe to make spindles or turn a crank to help keep cotton gins operating

- Chiffonnier or Peruker (Perruker, sometimes called Perook, Peroker): folks who made wigs

- Lavendar: a woman who washed clothes

- Hind (Hine, Hines): a farmworker

- Hayward (possibly Haywood): a keeper or repairer of fences

- Tanner: a person who tanned or cured animal hides into leather

- Slater: a person who used shingles to make roofs, a roofer

- Joyner or Joiner: a skilled carpenter

- Fuller: a person who "fulled" cloth; that is, they shrank or stretched woolen cloth by wetting it, heating it, and then pressing it

- Tucker: a person who cleaned cloth goods

- Cooper: a person who made or repaired barrels or wooden tubs

Other occupational names used in England and America include Archer, Baker, Brewer, Butcher, Carter, Clark, Cooper, Cook, Dyer, Farmer, Faulkner, Fisher, Fuller, Gardener, Glover, Head, Hunt or Hunter, Judge, Mason, Page, Parker, Potter, Sawyer, Slater, Smith, Taylor, Thatcher, Turner, Weaver, Woodman, and Wright (or variations such as Cartwright and Wainwright).

In Appendix A: Working Folk, we will explore occupation names from days gone by.

Some surnames are linked to a personal characteristic. They are adjectives based on nicknames that described a person. These surnames may have described a person's size (Short, Long, Little), coloring (Black, White, Green, or Red, which could have evolved into Reed), or another character trait (Stern, Strong, Swift). Someone named Peacock might have been considered vain.

Some surnames are derived from a geographical feature of the landscape, such as Bridge, Brooks, Bush, Camp, Fields, Forest, Greenwood, Grove, Hill, Knolles, Lake, Moore, Perry, Stone, Wold, Wood, and Woodruff.

Useful Tools

Now that you understand a bit more about surnames—spelling variations, and other issues with them — it is time to dig into some useful tools for your actual research.

Newspaper Obituaries and Funeral Programs

Newspaper obituaries are valuable resources into family history. Newspaper obits can give a detailed view of the life accomplishments (and sometimes failures) of a relative. They also reveal close family relationships. Newspaper obituaries were extremely helpful to me in identifying surviving relatives of my ancestors.

If you are lucky enough to have a relative who collects actual funeral programs, these sometimes contain a wealth of information not given in the "public" published obituary. I am referring here to the paper funeral programs that are handed out at the funeral. I have an older relative who has a large box in which she places newspaper clippings and the funeral programs of every family member she knows. This box is indeed a treasure chest for my relatives researching this particular branch of the family. Funeral programs have photos of the relative, and may reveal the pallbearers' names, the speakers at the funeral service, and other details of family members or very close friends who take part in the homegoing ceremonies.

Using Google

Of all the online tools I use for research, let's face it; my Internet searches almost always begin at www.google.com. So, let's talk about some ways Google can make your searches more fruitful. Google lets you use up to thirty-two keywords in any search. Generally, with common names, I only use about four or five keywords to get a reasonable number of site results.

Google is case-insensitive, except for the search operators AND and OR. I like to type in lower-case characters and use the caps as intentional, visual reminders that I am using a search operator. All search terms return the same results, regardless of the combination of upper- and lower-case letters used in your query. Google also ignores most common punctuation, such as commas and periods. Thus, a search for "Albert Sidney James Allen, Methodist, preacher" will return the same results as "albert sidney james allen Methodist preacher."

Google will return results that contain all of your search terms but will give higher priority to the earlier terms in your query. In other words, your word order matters. So, a search for "1904 Rev. A. S. J. Allen killed" will return pages in a different ranked order than "Rev. A. S. J. Allen 1904 killed." This is why you should put your most important terms first and group your search terms in a way that makes sense, to achieve the most relevant results at the top of your results listings.

I mentioned operators earlier. Let's take a closer look at these now. Of the forty-plus Google search operators, the operators (or command words) that I use the most are "AND" and "OR." It's useful to know how to use command words and symbols in Google searches. Notice when I give examples of searches, the exact search words are in bold type. These bold-type words are the words I type into the Google search field.

The AND command word: This command word combines words. When no commands are in the search, Google will assume that AND is the command. AND must be capitalized for Google to recognize it as a command word.

For example, when you type in Shed AND Phyllis Lembric, Google will only show results that contain both the names Shed and Phyllis Lembric. That's about 2,000 results for you to look at instead of the 6,000,000 results you get by searching Shed and Phyllis Lembric.

The OR command word: This command word combines words and asks for results that contain either one item or another. Say I wanted to search for one word/phrase or another, the OR must be capitalized.

Sometimes you may want to search variations of an ancestor's name. In my case, I knew that my great-grandfather signed his name in two different ways. Sometimes he wrote "A. S. J. Allen and other times he used his first name and wrote "Albert SJ Allen." Here is how I searched for one or the other in the same search.

- Searching "A. S. J. Allen" OR "Albert SJ Allen" results in about 300 hits.

- Searching for "A. S. J. Allen" or "Albert SJ Allen" will return about three results and a message of "It looks like there aren't many great matches for your search."

Notice in the search above how I used the quotation marks. If you want to search for an exact phrase, use quotation marks to surround the exact phrase. For example, I performed searches for "Albert Allen" and also "Allen, Albert" to reveal results from sites that may place the last name in front of the first name.

Sometimes you may only have partial information. As a child, I remember asking my mother how to spell a word, and she would respond with, "Look it up in the dictionary." Well, if I don't know how to spell it, how can I look it up? Never did get a good answer from Mom on that one, but Google has an answer for us. How do you search Google for what you don't know? Search for what you know and use a wildcard symbol * to stand in for the unknown. A wildcard is used inside quotes.

One asterisk for one set of characters; two asterisks for two sets; etc. For example, "Albert * Allen" will display about 200,000,000 results, whereas the results of "Albert ** Allen" may result in a more manageable result.

The Minus Sign Command: We talked earlier about issues surrounding the reuse of family names. The minus sign is a potential aid when using Google to parse out individuals with the same or common names. Sometimes my searching for ancestors revealed folks with the same name. What can you do to find useful results when your ancestor had a common name? Your search may repeatedly turn up a certain person you are NOT looking for– frustrating! Well, that is where the minus sign command comes in.

To exclude a word or phrase, type in the name and, with no space between the name, insert a minus sign or hyphen. For example, John Kennedy-president will eliminate the majority of the results for the U.S. President JFK.

Google can also help you with Date Range searching. This is one of the best and most underused Google search tips for genealogists. This method lets you search multiple dates at one time without having to enter them individually. This is helpful if you are looking for, say, an ancestor's birth, marriage, or death records but you don't know the exact date of the event. To search for a range of numbers like a date range, type in the dates with no spaces between the numbers and the periods. Do not use a hyphen, only the two periods between the numbers.

You type DATE..DATE into the search field with two periods in between the dates, like this: 1900..1950. For instance, we know that Albert Allen was most likely born between 1865 and 1870 based on the information we have, so we could search for "Allen, Albert" 1865..1870. This will bring up only pages that include one or all of the dates 1865, 1866, 1867, 1868, 1869, and 1870.

Search for Terms Near Each Other: One of the most frustrating things about searching for ancestors in Google is that, while the search engine will search an entire page for terms, your terms may not have any association with each other. It is entirely possible, for example, to find the exact names, dates, and other details you're looking for—but not in relation to each other in any way. For instance, our searches for Albert Allen and 1890 turned up pages that include Albert Allen and the date 1890, but that date was often associated with other folks or names on the page. However, there is a way to ask Google to find terms near each other.

Introduce the command AROUND(n). Here's how this works. When I enter "A. S. J. Allen" AROUND(10) 1890, that means I want Google to look for pages where the exact name A. S. Allen appears within 10 words of the date 1890.

You can apply AROUND(n) to multiple terms in the same search. For example: "A. S. J. Allen" AROUND(10) Alachua AROUND(5) 1890). This request looks for pages where the exact name A. S. J. Allen appears within ten words of the word Alachua and within five words of the date 1890. I was blown away by how much the use of this little command helped me find more relevant results.

Using Census Records

The last tool I'd like to mention here is census records. Census records are the "lifeblood" of anyone doing family history research. A census record is an important document, but a warning is in order here. The census record is not the Bible. As we research, remember we are looking at manmade records. We are not investigating infallible Scripture. When you behold a census page, it is NOT like looking at an ancient Torah, or the Dead Sea scrolls. These are documents penned by minimum-wage public servants, not Moses, and as such will contain errors.

Sometimes these are honest mistakes. Sometimes they are the result of maliciousness or bias by the census taker. Sometimes the wrong information is given by the person being interviewed. Sometimes the census taker mishears the information being given. Remember our earlier conversation about dialects and accents? These records are the result of human interactions, so there will be flaws.

Earlier, we looked at the 1860 Calhoun County, Florida, census page where the census taker made disparaging comments about my ancestors. He wrote, "The free negroes of this county are ... a lazy, indolent, and worthless race."

This slight was recorded for all times' sake. That, however, does not make it true. Therefore, I encourage you to remember the words of advice from the master of mystery and the macabre, Edgar Allan Poe, "Believe half of what you see and nothing of what you hear."

Brief Word About Race and the Census

The 1790 United States Census was the first census in the history of the United States. When the census began in 1790, the racial categories for the household population were "free white" persons, other "free persons" by color, and "slaves." Census takers did not use standard forms in the early censuses.

From 1850 through 1880, the codes for enumerators were generally white (W), black (B), and mulatto (M). Beginning in 1850, the data item was labeled "color." In 1870, Chinese (C) and Indian (I) were added. In 1880, the data item was not labeled; it was "whether this person is ..." In 1890, "Japanese," "quadroon," and "octoroon" were added.

> *Source*: https://www.pewsocialtrends.org/2010/01/21/
> race-and-the-census-the-negro-controversy/ also see
> https://scholar.harvard.edu/jlhochschild/publications/
> racial-reorganization-and-united-states-census-1850-1930-
> mulattoes-half-br

The 1850 census saw a dramatic shift in the way information about residents was collected. For the first time, free persons were listed individually instead of by family. There were two questionnaires: one for free inhabitants and one for slaves. (https://www.census.gov/history/www/through_the_decades/index_of_questions/1850_1.html)

Research Mindset, Approach, and Methodology

Think like a detective. The similarities between family historians and detectives run deep.

You began with a few choice morsels about an ancestor. After looking in all the places mentioned so far for direct ancestors, you may reach a point where you feel that you've hit a wall. You've examined census records, scanned all of Aunt Bessie's funeral programs, collected obituary clippings, and performed countless Google searches, but you want more. To go deeper, it is time to step up the research and start to pay attention to methodology. How are you approaching the search? It's like when you are presented with a word search puzzle where you are asked to find words hidden in the chart, like the one on the next page.

I start by first glancing at the chart and seeing what pops out for me. After a few minutes of staring at the chart, looking for an obvious word or pattern of letters, I then begin to search row by row, first horizontally, then vertically, then diagonally, then from bottom to top and on it goes. A few words always show up immediately for me as I just glance at the chart, but I really make headway once I begin a systematic study of the chart. This is what I'm recommending we do with our family history research. We need a method to follow. Just as detectives rely on sound information to break a case, genealogists must be able to find and interpret clues to make meaning of the past.

Develop a Genealogy Research Plan

A major goal in developing a genealogy research plan is to identify what you want to know and formulate the questions which will provide the answers you seek. The elements of a good genealogy research plan may include:

1. Objective: What Do I Want to Know?

What specifically do you want to learn about your ancestor? Their marriage date? Spouse's name? Where they lived at a particular point in time? When they died? Be specific in narrowing down to a single question, if possible. This helps keep your research focused and your research plan on track.

2. Known Facts: What Do I Already Know?

My Roots
Word Search

P	A	F	B	I	R	T	H	B	X	C	E	N	S	U	S	R
C	E	Y	L	I	M	A	F	T	U	A	B	O	Q	D	A	N
W	H	N	B	Y	S	E	S	I	R	P	S	G	R	C	M	D
X	V	I	D	E	U	F	D	O	Q	A	T	E	T	O	Z	E
C	S	U	L	O	R	J	R	T	D	Y	H	N	L	J	L	E
K	A	L	Z	D	N	V	O	W	L	T	I	E	D	R	T	D
I	N	E	S	R	A	H	C	J	O	G	K	A	Q	N	I	A
Z	C	M	F	L	M	S	E	M	M	D	Y	L	X	Y	C	L
G	E	H	P	W	E	T	R	T	O	E	S	O	M	K	E	W
B	S	D	I	X	G	U	O	S	G	P	Q	G	Z	H	X	B
Y	T	O	W	S	F	J	R	T	M	S	Y	Y	C	G	U	R
A	R	E	F	T	T	D	E	C	E	N	D	A	N	T	S	E
L	Y	D	I	J	L	O	H	P	A	R	E	N	T	S	A	H
G	E	S	K	H	W	Y	R	N	U	E	C	N	U	S	D	T
C	D	Z	S	E	F	X	M	Y	E	R	O	O	T	S	L	A
B	A	L	R	E	S	E	A	C	H	Z	C	J	C	H	A	F

Ancestry | Birth | Census | Child
Decendants | Deed | Family | Father
Genealogy | History | Mother | Parents
Records | Research | Roots | Surname

7

What have you already learned about your ancestors? This should include identities, relationships, dates, and places that are supported by original records. Search family and home sources for documents, papers, photos, diaries, and family tree charts, and interview your relatives to fill in the gaps. The folks in your family are always the best first source.

3. Working Hypothesis: What Do I Think the Answer Is?

What are the possible or probable conclusions that you hope to prove or possibly disprove through your genealogy research? Say you want to know when your ancestor died? You might start, for example, with the hypothesis that they died in the town or county where they were last known to be living.

4. Identified Sources: Which Records Might Hold the Answer and Do They Exist?

Which records are most likely to provide support for your hypothesis? Census records? Marriage records? Land deeds? Create a list of possible sources, and identify the repositories, including libraries, archives, societies, or published Internet collections where these records and resources can be researched. (Kimberly Powell, "Creating a Genealogy Research Plan Like a Detective," ThoughtCo, Feb. 11, 2020, thoughtco.com/how-to-develop-genealogy-research-plan-1421685)

Once I have a plan of what I want to accomplish, I then turn to how to go about getting to my goal. That is when I lean on the similarities between family historians and TV detectives.

Let me explain. When not searching for ancestors, in my spare time I love crime TV. I spend a lot of time watching detective shows like *Forensic Files*, *NCIS*, and *Law & Order*. What do *Homicide Hunter: Lt. Joe Kenda* and the NYPD homicide investigation team on *Castle* have in common? They are investigators. A crime happens. The cops show up and immediately start to examine the scene of the crime. Then they canvass the neighborhood and talk to the neighbors and witnesses. Then they interview family and known associates of the victim.

This is my crime fighter mode. After I've visited the scene (cemetery or burial records along with census records), now it is time to "canvass the neighborhood and talk to the neighbors and witnesses," to look at nearby places, friends, associates, co-workers, schools, schoolmates, teachers, and others who witnessed the life of the ancestor you are in search of. This part of your plan is the Research Strategy. This is where you determine the best order to consult or visit the various repositories, considering the available records and your research needs.

 Snooping Away from the "Kids' Table"

Growing up the only child of a single mom, I sometimes felt cheated. I wondered what other kids knew about their families. The other boys knew so much about their dads and had wonderful stories about the exploits of their dads when they were young. I had no stories. When a parent reads to their children it has great educational and emotional benefits. But so much more is gained when they tell their own stories of their past.

The way folks are treated in families is different, therefore, folks will have different perspectives and memories of family members (especially ancestors). The recordkeeper may have a strong bias or perception. When seeking answers, record the facts.

My daughter has taken many of those birth order and personality tests. You know the ones that try to tell you that birth order affects who you are. Every time she does one, she comes up strongly as an only child. This is probably my fault. Even when you try to not show favorites, it shows through. My daughter jokingly introduces herself as being an only child, except for her brother. I love them both. Is my love equal? No. They each have a special part of my heart. My brain lights up in different sections and in unique ways as I interact with them because they are unique people.

As you are seeking answers to your family history questions, begin early on by asking the family members around you. Especially helpful are folks who were peers or had firsthand contact with the ancestor you are researching.

Intergenerational Storytelling

In an earlier chapter, we talked about the importance of transgenerational trauma or intergenerational trauma. These are real concerns for any family or family story, but I do not want to imply that "bad" family stories should not be told, just to avoid trauma. Emory University psychologists, Robyn Fivush and Marshall Duke, have done research on family storytelling that reveals that

"(W)hen parents share family stories with their children—especially when they tell those stories in a detailed and responsive way—their children benefit in a host of ways. For instance, experimental studies show that when moms and dads reminisce about everyday events with their preschool children in more detailed ways, their children tell richer, more complete narratives to other adults one to two years later compared to children whose parents didn't tell the stories in great detail.

"In the preteen years, children whose families collaboratively discuss everyday events and family history more often have higher self-esteem and stronger self-concepts. And adolescents with a stronger knowledge of family history have more robust identities, better coping skills, and lower rates of depression and anxiety. Family storytelling can help a child grow into a teen who feels connected to the important people in her life."

These researchers developed a "Do You Know" (DYK) scale to measure how much children knew about family history and intergenerational family stories. The twenty yes/no questions ask the child to report if they know such things as how their parents met, or where they grew up and went to school. Sound familiar? These are the questions you've been seeing in the boxes throughout this book.

Teens who knew more stories about their extended family showed "higher levels of emotional well-being, and also higher levels of identity achievement, even when controlling for general level of family functioning."

"There is something powerful about actually knowing these stories," the study concludes.

The research was funded by the Alfred P. Sloan Foundation. (See abstract at http://www.journaloffamilylife.org/doyouknow; https://www.mother.ly/parenting/330928-2)

Let's Talk to the Coworkers and Other Associates

Church Records

Remember our earlier discussion on occupations? Well, my great-grandfather was a preacher, so let's look at Church sources.

Church records can include documents on:

- Christenings/Baptisms
- Marriages*
- Burials
- Confirmations
- Communions
- Congregation admissions and removals
- Church financial records
- Sunday School lists
- Church censuses
- Church committees
- Church-related newsletters, rolls, and/or contact lists

*As an extra note on marriages, did you know that there are actually multiple kinds of marriage documents?

Church records are kept at local churches, in church archives, at church historical and genealogical societies, and in libraries. Many church records have been published in books and periodicals. Many denominations have an online historical or archival presence and church records are housed there.

There are several different types of marriage documents created before a couple marries. All of these won't exist for any one couple, but genealogical information that can be found in these documents may enhance your search.

Marriage records can be divided into two general categories: those that relate to a couple's intent to marry and those documenting that a marriage actually took place.

Records of Intentions to Marry

Marriage Banns (or Bans). The banns of marriage were the public announcements in a Christian parish church or in the town council of an impending marriage between two specified persons. They are commonly associated with the Catholic Church, the Church of England, and the Church of Sweden, and with other denominations whose traditions are similar. Banns began as a church custom, and later became English common law.

In 1983 the Roman Catholic Church removed the requirement for banns and left it to individual national bishops' conferences to decide whether to continue this practice, but in most Catholic countries the banns are still published. Banns gave advanced notice of a couple's intent to marry over three consecutive Sundays, either in church or a public place. The banns would give the names and the proposed wedding date. The purpose was to give anyone who might have an objection to the marriage time and opportunity to state why the marriage should not take place.

As you will see in other marriage intention-type documents, such documents were intended to protect against any moral or legal reason why the couple should not be married. The couple would be found ineligible for marriage if:

- one or both of the parties was too young or of unlawful age
- one party was already married
- the couple was more closely related than allowed by law
- one or both of the parties was underage without parental approval

Marriage Bond. The use of marriage bonds was especially common in the South and mid-Atlantic United States through the first half of the nineteenth century.

The bond carried a monetary amount to cover financial loss if the marriage did not take place. It affirmed that there was no moral or legal reason why the couple could not be married. It also served to keep the groom from changing his mind.

A bond was posted before the marriage license by the groom and usually the father of the bride or some other close relative. It was usually recorded in the bride's county of residence.

If either party declined to go through with the union, or if one of the parties was found to be ineligible, the bond money was generally forfeit. The bondsman, or surety, was often a brother or uncle of the bride, although he could also be a relative of the groom or even a neighbor or a friend of either of the two parties.

In colonial Texas, where Spanish law required colonists to be Catholic, a marriage bond was used in a slightly different fashion: as a pledge to local authorities in situations where there was no Roman Catholic priest available that the couple agreed to have their civil marriage solemnized by a priest as soon as the opportunity came available.

Marriage License. Perhaps the most commonly found record of a marriage is the marriage license.

These applications to marry usually contain the most genealogical information of all marriage documents. A marriage license will typically contain personal information on both the bride and the groom.

They're most common after the Civil War, when they replaced banns and bonds; but not all states required marriage licenses.

The marriage license is about the couple's eligibility to marry. As in other instruments mentioned here, the intent was to ensure no moral or legal reason existed as to why the couple should not be married.

After confirming the couple was eligible for marriage, a license form was issued by a local public official (usually the county clerk) to the couple intending to marry and granted permission to anyone authorized to solemnize marriages (rabbi, minister, priest, justice of the peace, etc.) to perform the ceremony.

The marriage was usually—but not always—performed within a few days after the granting of the license. In many localities both the marriage license and the marriage return are found recorded together.

Marriage Application. In some jurisdictions and during certain time periods, the law required that a marriage application be filled out before a marriage license could be issued. Marriage applications may be recorded in separate books or might be found with the marriage licenses. The application often required more information than was recorded on the marriage license. This makes the application quite useful for family history research.

Consent Affidavit. In most jurisdictions, individuals under the lawful age could still be married with the consent of a parent or guardian as long as they were still above a certain minimum age. That age varied by locality and time period as well as by gender. So, this might be anyone under the age of twenty-one in one jurisdiction, whereas in another, lawful age might be eighteen, or even as young as thirteen or fourteen for females.

Marriage Contract or Settlement, Prenuptial. While much less common than the other marriage record types discussed here, marriage contracts have been recorded since colonial times. Similar to what we would now call a prenuptial agreement, marriage contracts or settlements were agreements made prior to marriage.

They were most common in the South, when the woman owned property in her own name or wished to ensure that property left by a former husband would pass on to his children and not the new spouse. Marriage contracts might be found filed among the marriage records or recorded in the deed books or records of the local court. "Prenups" can be found by looking in deed books and in other court documents.

The different types of marriage records that might be available for your ancestors, and the amount and kind of information they contain, will vary depending on the location and time period, as well as, sometimes, the parties' religion. In some localities, a marriage license may include the most details, while in a different locality and time period more information might be found in the marriage register. Locating all available marriage record types increases the chance of learning additional information— including confirmation that the marriage actually took place, the names of parents or witnesses, or the religion of one or both parties to the marriage.

Records Documenting that a Marriage Took Place

Marriage licenses, bonds, prenups, and banns all indicate that a marriage was planned, but not that it actually happened. For proof that a marriage actually took place, you'll need to look for any of the following records:

Marriage Certificate. A marriage certificate confirms a marriage took place and is signed by the person officiating. Typically, the information from the marriage certificate, or at least verification that the marriage actually took place, is recorded at the bottom or on the back of the marriage license, or in a separate marriage book (see marriage register below).

It may not have all the personal detail that can be found on a license. Copies of certificates may be recorded in the church or with a town or county clerk. Unfortunately for the family history researcher, the original marriage certificate is not a public document; it is given to the bride and groom, so if it hasn't been passed down in the family, you may not be able to locate it.

Marriage Returns or Registers. Ministers and justices of the peace sent a record of the marriages they performed to the town hall or county courthouse. These were recorded in books called returns or registers. Unfortunately, some marriages were never recorded beyond what the minister or justice of the peace kept in their private journals or ledgers. So, what's the difference between a marriage return and a marriage register?

Marriage Return/Minister's Return. Following the wedding, the minister or officiant would complete a marriage return form, indicating that he had married the couple and on what date. He would later return this paper to the local registrar as proof that the marriage occurred.

In many localities you can find this return recorded at the bottom or on the back of the marriage license. Alternatively, the information may be located in a Marriage Register (see below) or in a separate volume of ministers' returns. The lack of an actual marriage date or marriage return does not always mean the marriage didn't take place, however. In some cases, the minister or officiant may have simply forgotten to drop off the return, or it wasn't recorded for some reason.

Marriage Register. Local clerks generally recorded the marriages they performed in a marriage register or book. Marriages performed by another officiant, such as a minister, priest, or justice of the peace, were also generally recorded following receipt of the marriage return from the officiant. Sometimes marriage registers incorporate information from a variety of marriage documents, so may include the names of the couples, their ages, birthplaces, and current locations, the names of their parents, the names of witnesses, the name of the officiant, and the date of marriage.

Finally, let's look at newspaper announcements. These announcements can fit both the pre- and post-marriage categories. Some are engagement announcements and will announce an upcoming wedding ceremony, while others may report on the wedding gathering in the society section of a newspaper.

Newspaper Announcement. Historical newspapers are a rich source of information on marriages, including those which may predate the recording of marriages in that locality. Search historical newspaper archives for engagement and marriage announcements, paying special attention to clues such as the location of the marriage, the name of the officiant (may indicate religion), the members of the marriage party, the names of guests, and other useful information. Don't overlook religious or ethnic newspapers if you know the ancestor's religion, or if they belong to a specific ethnic group (e.g., the local German language newspaper). (Kimberly Powell, "Marriage Records," ThoughtCo, August 27, 2020, thoughtco.com/marriage-records-types-4077752 and Sharon DeBartolo Carmack, "7 Kinds of Marriage Documents," Family Tree Magazine, June 2000)

In order to locate your ancestor in church records you must know two important things: a place where your ancestor once lived and the religious denomination they were part of.

Major U. S. Religious Denominations

- Anglican

- Baptist

- Buddhist

- Church of the Brethren

- Congregational

- Disciples of Christ

- Dutch Reformed

- Episcopal
- German Reformed
- Greek Orthodox
- Huguenot
- Jehovah's Witnesses
- Jewish
- The Church of Jesus Christ of Latter-day Saints (Mormons)
- Lutheran
- Maronite Catholic
- Melkite Greek Orthodox
- Methodist
- Mennonite
- Moravian
- Muslim
- Pentecostal
- Presbyterian
- Roman Catholic
- Russian Orthodox
- Society of Friends (Quakers)
- Syriac Orthodox
- United Church of Christ

    Source: https://www.familysearch.org/wiki/en/United_
    States_Church_Records

A handy resource for me in my search turned out to be my employer. I work on the campus of Duke University, a private research university in Durham, North Carolina. Founded by the

Methodists and Quakers, the school is home to the Divinity School Library, which provided a wealth of information for me.

Soundtrack suggestion:
"Time in a Bottle"
Songwriter: Jim Croce
Time in a Bottle lyrics © BMG Rights Management

If I could save time in a bottle
The first thing that I'd like to do
Is to save every day
'Til eternity passes away
Just to spend them with you

But there never seems to be enough time
To do the things you want to do
Once you find them

Let's Look Around the Neighborhood.

Location

Another valuable resource of family history is to look into the location(s) your ancestors occupied. Since my ancestral roots are in Alachua County, Florida, I looked throughout the Internet for online historical resources related to Alachua County. In addition to online resources, I wrote letters and emails to local historical societies and history museums within the county. You can easily find these by a Google web search of "[your county] (museum OR "genealogical society")"

Professional Associations

According to the newspaper articles I found, my great-grandfather was somehow connected to the Masons and Odd Fellows. So the next place I looked was for records of these organizations. I started with an online thread on "Grand United Order of Odd Fellows" on the AfriGeneas (www.afrigeneas.com) Genealogy and History Forum.

City and Area Directories

Ancestry is home to an extensive collection of city and area directories. Directories typically contain entries for working family members and include name, occupation, and home and business addresses. You may find street directories, lists of advertisements (which may include your ancestor's business), lists of government officials, charitable organizations, churches, cemeteries, hotels, maps, and much more. Directories typically contain the name of the person, home and business addresses, and their occupation.

These records help place your ancestor in a specific location in a particular year. Use that information to expand your search and seek out other local records that may have been created while your ancestor lived there. (Ancestry/com. https://www.ancestry.com/search/categories/dir_city/)

Let's Check in with Others Who May Be Working on the Same or Similar Cases.

Internet Resources to Help You in Finding your Folks.

The bulk of my ancestors' graves are located in the state of Florida. Fortunately for me, Jim Powell has done a great job of creating an online Search the Virtual Cemetery web application at https://www.wizardofar.org/CFDocs/common/MenuTemp. cfm. Jim and his extended family have done much fieldwork documenting most of the historical cemeteries in Alachua County, Florida. His online search includes the cemeteries that his group has photographed and the transcriptions from the 1966 DAR (Daughters of the American Revolution) books. In addition to the Virtual Web application, Jim Powell also has organized volunteers to document Alachua County's burial grounds. His Facebook page is available at https://www.facebook.com/wizardofar/.

But for those of you looking for ancestors not in Alachua County, take heart! Again, a Google search of "[county] (cemetery OR genealogy)" will yield local resources that might hold information on the burial grounds of your ancestor(s). When I find such resources, I will typically look for others buried in the same cemetery as my known ancestor with the same or similar surname. You may find a lost spouse, child, or another relative. Additionally, as I have searched, I have tried to pay attention to whom my known ancestor is buried beside. Many times, folks like the thought of being buried with someone they love, so both can be at rest together. You may notice that married couples are laid to rest together, or folks are buried next to their parents.

Writing or making a call to a local cemetery to discover the physical resting place of an ancestor is a good idea if you would like to investigate this more. Some cemeteries have an online presence that allows you to virtually walk the grounds and see the tombstone of your ancestor and the headstones adjacent to them. You never know what you may find on such a walk. But before you head out, look at the following websites.

- Ancestry.com is a great place to begin. Search using the names and birth/death dates of the person you are researching, just as you would any other Ancestry search, only instead of pressing the [search] button to get all available data, we want to limit our search to death records.

- Another good starting point is Find a Grave, at findagrave.com, a free resource for finding the final resting places of famous folks, friends, and family members.

- There are also good resources available at MyHeritage.com.

- WorldVitalRecords.com includes free information and grave photos. For cemeteries, it often gives the exact plot location.

- There is also TombFinder. It uses web and mobile technologies to easily pinpoint your loved one's grave and to celebrate their life online.

- See also the Online Cemetery Records and Burial Indexes from DeathIndexes.com.

- If your loved one was a U.S. veteran, there is the National Cemetery Administration's Nationwide Gravesite Locator.

Another helpful resource can be Facebook groups. There are a number of groups that focus on genealogy. Once you join such communities, you can then post to present the family name you are researching or reach out for help if there are others doing similar research.

There are more online genealogy and virtual cemetery websites and state websites to explore. However, online research will only get you so far. You may eventually want to take a real trip to the actual cemetery.

Links for genealogy research:

- AfriGeneas-http://www.afrigeneas.com/

- Ancestry-www.ancestry.com

- Archives.com-http://www.archives.com/

- Billion Graves-http://billiongraves.com/

- Chronicling America Newspapers*-https://chroniclingamerica. loc.gov/

- Cyndi's List-http://www.cyndislist.com

- FamilySearch.org-http://www.familysearch.org/

- FamilyTreeMagazine.com-https://www.familytreemagazine. com/

- Find a Grave.com-http://www.findagrave.com

- FindMyPast.com-http://www.findmypast.com/

- Fold3.com-http://www.fold3.com/

- Genealogy Bank-http://www.genealogybank.com/General Land Office Records-http://www.glorecords.blm.gov/

- Google-http://www.google.com/

- HeritageQuestOnline.com-http://www.heritagequestonline. com/

- Interment.net

- Mapping the Freedman's Bureau-https:// mappingthefreedmensbureau.com/about/

- Mocavo-http://www.mocavo.com/

- MyHeritage-www.myheritage.com

- MyHeritage.com-http://www.myheritage.com/

- National Archives Resources for Genealogists-http://www. archives.gov/research/genealogy

- National Archives*-www.archives.com

- NewspaperArchive-https://newspaperarchive.com/

- Newspapers.com-www.newspapers.com

- RootsWeb*-www.rootsweb.com

- Social Security Death Index*-www.ancestry.com, www.genealogybank.com, or www.familysearch.org

- Soldiers and Sailors Database-https://www.nps.gov/civilwar/soldiers-and-sailors-database.htm

- USGenWeb Project-http://usgenweb.org/

   See https://myrootsfoundation.com/resources-finding-biological-family/ for a listing of online resources specifically related to adoptees.

Other Resources:

- City directories

- County Clerk's office

- Funeral records

- Obituaries

Looking to dig into DNA resources? Then try:

- 23andMe

- Ancestry DNA

- Cyndi's List: DNA, Genetics, and Family Health

- Facebook DNA Groups

- DNA Detectives

- DNA For Genealogy

- DNA Tested Descendants of Angola, Cameroon, the Congos, and Gabon*

- DNA Tested Descendants of Nigeria, Benin, and Togo*

- The African Descendant's Genetic Genealogy

- Family Tree DNA

- GEDmatch

- GPS Origins

- Living DNA

- My Heritage DNA

- Tips for using GEDmatch

- Your DNA Guide

Due diligence: "Leave no stone unturned"

Finally, I would encourage you not to neglect "certain" sources. Do not limit yourself to just census research and collecting birth, death, and marriage records. Do not be afraid to comb through prison records, state execution rolls, and lynching records. Look for records of state hospitals, insane asylums and sanitariums, houses of correction, old folks' homes, orphanages, poorhouses, poor farms, and similar less glamorous institutions and sources. For starters, you might want to check out resources like:

- Cyndi's List-Prisons, Prisoners, and Outlaws

- Criminal records-Ancestry

- Blacksheep Ancestors

- InstitutionalCemeteries.org

Alonzo Felder

> *Do you know some things that happened to your*
> *mom or dad when they were in school?*
>
> *y n*

Why retell the story?
Because retelling cultural stories provides roots for growth.
Myth: No harm is done by not telling.

Do you know how a boatman faces one direction while rowing in another? To move forward, you have to face the past and do the hard work of rowing.

> Why is storytelling such a critical part of every tradition? Why is it important and meaningful to keep these stories alive? Marcus Garvey said, "A people without the knowledge of their past history, origin and culture is like a tree without roots." Our knowledge of our family and group identity gives us nourishment and helps us grow. This is true whether it is a religious identity, or an ethnic or racial group. Who we are as individuals in the world is anchored in our histories, and knowing these histories provides us strength and resilience. Being part of a cultural group and participating in the passing on of stories and rituals that define a group history and a group identity is highly beneficial for adolescents. In our research in The Family Narratives Lab, we have found that adolescents who tell elaborated stories about religious rituals and traditions show higher levels of well-being. And, importantly, not knowing these traditions and rituals can be detrimental. (https://www.psychologytoday.com/us/blog/the-stories-our-lives/201704/cultural-stories-provide-roots-growth\=)

Consider the research done on Jewish heritage here in America. In talking about the way oral tales play a role in sustaining

Jewish traditions and strengthening families, study after study reinforces the findings of Raphael and Hendler: Grandchildren cite the relationship with their grandparents as a major reason they identify as Jewish.

> The Cohen Center for Modern Jewish Studies at Brandeis University reported in a 2015 study ("Millennial Children of Intermarriage"): "Having close ties to Jewish grandparents had a direct effect on a variety of outcomes, including identifying as Jewish by religion, celebrating Jewish holidays, feeling a connection to Israel and the Jewish people, and wanting to marry someone Jewish." (https://atlantajewishtimes.timesofisrael.com/are-jewish-grandparents-a-forgotten-population/)

The Dash and the Mindset List of Fun Facts for A. S. J. Allen's Lifetime

Looking at a tombstone and seeing the birth date hyphen death date laid out beneath the name, you get the idea that life is the dash; it is what happens between the dates. Think about all the days of your life, all that you've been through, all that you've experienced; what's happened to you; secrets shared with siblings; backyard barbeques; family vacations; your first pet, your first car, first date, first kiss; building a career or a business; saving for that first home; raising children, your regrets, your wounds, your pains. The times you spoke and wish you hadn't; the times you were silent and wish you had spoken. The decisions you made that you can't get back. The ones you loved who are now gone. The things you wanted to happen that didn't; the things that happened that you didn't want. All of this takes place in what we call a lifetime.

The Dash, written by Linda Ellis, is a poem that discusses the importance of embracing every day of our lives. We often get asked: What is the meaning of the dash poem? After each of us passes away, we will be remembered by two notable dates: our birth date and our death date, separated by a dash in between. That tiny dash mark represents all the time we lived on this earth.

How will you spend the time you have? How will you make the most of each moment? *The Dash* makes you think about what truly matters in life. The poem concludes by asking the question, "So when your eulogy is being read, with your life's actions to rehash, would you be proud of the things they say about how you lived your dash?" (© 1996-2020, *Southwestern Inspire Kindness, Inc.* by Linda Ellis, Copyright © 2020, Inspire Kindness, thedashpoem. com)

Look closely at the dash. Family is hard; you will need a hard hat to do this work. Some of my highest highs in life have been because of, and in conjunction with, family. Likewise, some of the lowest lows, and most hurtful, disappointing episodes of life, were due to and caused by family. As the old saying goes, "You can pick your nose, you can pick your friends, but you cannot pick your family."

Soundtrack suggestion:

"I'm My Own Grandpa" (sometimes rendered as "I'm My Own Grandpaw") is a novelty song written by Dwight Latham and Moe Jaffe, performed by Lonzo and Oscar in 1947, about a man who, through an unlikely (but legal) combination of marriages, becomes stepfather to his own stepmother—that is, tacitly dropping the "step-" modifiers, he becomes his own grandfather.

In the song, the narrator marries a widow with an adult daughter. Subsequently, his father marries the widow's daughter. This creates a comic tangle of relationships by a mixture of blood and marriage; for example, the narrator's father is now also his stepson-in-law. The situation is complicated further when both couples have children.

As you search, you are bound to discover things previously unknown, or at least buried in your family's past. Let's discuss the experience where you make a family discovery that uncovers a negative finding or a deep, dark, hidden secret, and now a family member (or group of family members) is upset with you. Remember Ben Affleck on PBS's *Finding Your Roots*? Some family stories have been carefully hidden, deliberately not talked about, and some folks will not appreciate the uncovering of those stories.

In the song "I'm My Own Grandpa," the singer/narrator of the tale becomes his own grandpa once his father marries the woman's daughter. A situation many would find uncomfortable, but which onlookers simply view as comic. But what about when you discover real uncomfortable situations in your own family narrative?

What do you do when you discover hard things in your family story? I mentioned earlier that we should not be afraid to explore "insane" asylums, old folks' homes, orphanages, or prisons as we search for ancestors. When discoveries are made in such places, we must learn to be comfortable with what some might find uncomfortable. Understand you are not alone and your discovery, no matter how disturbing, is not unique. We all have uncomfortable truths waiting to be discovered.

I had a quiet conversation this last year with a longtime friend of mine. I had asked him how his Thanksgiving holiday went. He smiled and said, "It was interesting. We had dinner with my brother."

Now I've known this fellow for well over thirty years and I was pretty sure he did not have a brother, so I stood there with the "deer in the headlights" look until he explained. Turns out that before my friend was born, his mom had given birth to a baby and placed the child up for adoption. She later married and had my buddy. Many years have gone by and now both his parents have passed on as well. But thanks to the current popularity of DNA testing, a man in another city decided to submit his DNA and voilà! There was a close relative match. After almost forty years these two have found each other.

I could go on with other stories of pleasant, yet surprising, endings in family history discovery. But what I would like to draw your attention to is the question of what you do when the discovery is uncomfortable. Not like my friend's discovery of a child his mother never told him about. I'm talking about the uncomfortable feeling one gets when you discover an ancestor who was a rapist, or a murderer, or a racist!

There's no end to the uncomfortable stories you may find in family story research. One such uncomfortable storyline involves confusion and often misunderstanding of family ties. Some family ties may, at first glance, appear too close, in that you discover folks who are too closely related. This may be the case; or maybe it's a case of mistaken identity among folks with the same or similar names. Over the years there have been many songs and stories of hidden kinships. There are a number of "head-scratch" moments ahead as you explore your family story. Two that you may experience can either cause you frustration or provide you with comic relief, or both. You decide how to respond. The first situation is when you encounter frequent reuse of a given name.

Here's what this looks like for me . . .

A. S. J. marries a woman named Dinah. Dinah's mother's name is Phyllis. In addition to naming one daughter Dinah, her mother, Phyllis, names another daughter Phyllis. So Dinah has a mother named Phyllis and a sister named Phyllis. In 1894 she names her fourth-born baby girl—you guessed it—Phyllis.

The way my grandmother resolved this in her life was to use titles with the names of her relatives. In other words, she referred to her Grandma Phyllis (Dinah's mother), her Momma Phyllis, (Dinah's sister who raised her as her own after Dinah's death), and her Sister Phyllis (A. S. J. and Dinah's child).

So why do families reuse names? Is this an attempt to thwart future family historians? I don't think so. In my family, I think it is mostly a way to honor someone you think highly of. But I find name reuse, and especially reuse patterns, to be a source of head scratch.

Reuse patterns? Let me explain. This is when folks follow the same naming pattern for generations. My great-aunt (A. S. J.'s daughter, whose sister is Phyllis) Fannie has a daughter, Willie Mae. Just like my grandmother Fannie (A. S. J.'s daughter, whose sister is Phyllis), has a daughter, Willie Mae. So both Willie Maes have mothers named Fannie, with grandmothers and aunts named Phyllis.

Another head scratcher situation is marriages that confuse family relationships. At one extreme of family relations comes incest. In these situations, family titles can be intentionally hidden and misdirected due to bad behavior. At the other end of this spectrum is the complication that occurs, due not to inappropriate sexual behavior, but to marriages that introduce complications.

Going back to the old Ray Stevens song, "I'm My Own Grandpa," no inappropriate scandals in that family. Prior to this comic song was one published in the 1940s by Harry Belafonte, titled "Shame and Scandal." In this situation, the song explores a man's love being smashed with the knowledge (or suspicion) that his love interest may actually be his sister.

Soundtrack suggestion:
"Shame and Scandal"
Harry Belafonte

In Trinidad there was a family
With much confusion as you will see.
There was a Mama and a Papa and a boy who was grown,
He wanted to marry a wife by his own.

He met a young girl, who suited him nice.
He went to his Papa to ask his advice.
His Papa said: Son, I have to say no
That girl is your sister, but your Mama don't know!

While the previous examples are lighthearted, I do acknowledge that there are cases where real family disfunction will be revealed by your research. Real feelings of guilt and/or shame will result. I worked with a woman once who knew nothing about her father's side of the family. He had been shifted around from family member to family member all his childhood, and as soon as he was able, he ran away from home. The family lore was that his dad had been lynched in the Deep South sometime during the Jim Crow era and that his mother had given him away to other family members.

I began my search following the lynching story. There are some records concerning lynching in America, notably the works published in *100 Years of Lynchings* by Ralph Ginzburg and, more recently, the work *Lynching in America: Confronting the Legacy of Racial Terror*. When I found no mention of her relative's name here after looking at all the record sources available for a mob killing and/or lynching, I decided to expand my search to "legal" executions. Turns out her grandfather was charged with multiple horrendous murders, was tried, found guilty, and executed by the state for these murders.

I found newspaper articles about the crime. I contacted the state prison to obtain more information and they responded with his criminal reports. I even got a series of his mugshots. She was so excited. Not only had she never seen a photo of her grandpa (who bore a striking resemblance to her dad, brothers, and other male members of the family) but now she knew his name, his date of birth, where he lived. A treasure trove of information. She was ecstatic. Her first call was to one of her siblings. Eventually, she noticed the silence on the other end of the phone, and then he spoke.

"Why? Why are you telling me this? Grandpa was a serial killer, executed by the state for horrible crimes—and this excites you?"

The feeling was like the scene out of the movie *Hitch* where the Will Smith character reveals to the woman he likes and is trying to impress that he found her ancestor on the rolls at Ellis Island. He takes her there and reveals his discovery of "The Butcher of Cadiz!" only to discover that this was not an occupational title but a news headline concerning her murderous ancestor.

All over the South, especially, Confederate monuments are being torn down. I applaud this action and see it as a step toward healing in our broken nation. But what of the folks related to those men that the statues depict?

Let's be clear. I don't for one second believe that we are our ancestors. They had their stuff, and we have ours. The folks living today were not around and are in no way responsible for the acts of their ancestors. But still, there can be tremendous shame and guilt associated with being related to such people. What do we do about that? What do we do when we discover these uncomfortable truths in an era of BLM, and toppling of Confederate heroes?

Suppose you discover an uncomfortable truth about your ancestor: say, a grandfather or great-grandmother was a member of the KKK? Or suppose you identify a family member in a lynching postcard?

Is that Grandma, the little girl at foot of hanging man?
Source: https://digital.library.cornell.edu/catalog/
ss:1508536

Is that Uncle James looting during the Watts riots?
Source: https://www.ushistory.org/us/54g.asp

Is that Uncle Jimmy holding that sign?
Source: https://www.pbs.org/wgbh/americanexperience/features/
eyesontheprize-responses-coming-civil-rights-movement

DISLOYAL TALK LANDS A NEGRO IN CITY'S JAIL

I still remember the day I discovered this
clipping about my grandfather, Ned Felder, from
a 1918 Florida newspaper.

We all hope to find new and interesting items concerning our ancestors when we set out on our genealogical journeys, but finding out my ancestor made headlines for being jailed was not exactly what I had anticipated.

Bloody Sunday: Cousin Charlie attacking a man with a dog?

On that old photo of your great-uncle standing in front of his shop, you notice a sign in the window: "We serve white clients only."

Again, what do we do with our past? Well, we've already said. First, understand you are not alone and your discovery, no matter how disturbing, is not unique.

Second, do not give in to guilt, but face the facts you find. What I mean is that you should give up all hope of having a better past. You cannot change it. It is what it is. This means that you realize that the sins of the fathers are not the sins of the children.

Third, you must consider the context of your discovered fact. We all live and function as a participant of the times we live in. What we today find offensive may have been beyond the sensibilities of an earlier generation. This is not to excuse them and their behaviors, but it makes no sense to hold folks accountable for things they are unaware of. If you're sixty-plus, or thereabouts, it is not fair to judge your parents and accuse them of child abuse because they did not buckle you up in a car seat and seatbelt as a child. There's no need to forgive them for using that lead-based paint in the nursery when they brought you home from the hospital. I guess what I'm trying to say is, breathe. Do not panic.

History should be discovered, presented, and displayed; taught as it is and from the perspective of how it was lived and in light of any recent or new revelations.

We have to reckon with the history of our country and with the role that our family members have played in creating and perpetuating inequity, racism, and the like.

Gather all the facts. Read books about the context. See the uncomfortable truth of prejudice, crime, trauma, and genocide through the eyes of the ancestors who might have lived it. Also, consider the context of the folks who have kept this secret. What was the reason? What was the benefit? What was the motivation?

Life of a Klansman tells ugly truths about America, past and present. In his book, Edward Ball retraces an ancestor's involvement with the Ku Klux Klan. In Ball's retelling of his family history, the sins and stains of the past are still very much alive today.

"It is not a distortion to say that Constant's rampage 150 years ago helps, in some impossible-to-measure way, to clear space for the authority and comfort of Whites living now—not just for me and for his 50 or 60 descendants, but for Whites in general," Ball writes. "I am an heir to Constant's acts of terror. I do not deny it, and the bitter truth makes me sick at the stomach."

Fourth, take time to process; don't force yourself to process quickly. Explore your emotions: rage, sorrow, disbelief, denial, projection, guilt.

Fifth, don't share information with family right away. Do so, and you might get an earful of criticism when you bring up the "family secret," or your invitation to the next family event is lost in the mail, or worse. Review, reflect, and reconsider that urge to march into the room and confront the family members with your newly discovered fact!

The truth is what it is. You cannot control (or predict) how you or family members will respond to bad news about an ancestor. What you can strive to do is to present the truth as simply and straightforwardly as possible. So how do you go about telling the next generation?

You research your family and discover your ancestor was a serial killer, was arrested for cruelty to animals, perpetrated domestic violence, owned and enslaved people, or any number of things. Don't run from it, but in an age-appropriate way, tell the kids. Some would argue that the lessons children learn when they know both the good and the bad of their family narratives help them to chart their course. These narratives can show them that they don't have to follow the path of what their less-than-stellar ancestors did. They also learn that they are part of something bigger than themselves.

In 2015 an article, "Group of Eighth Graders in Raleigh Uncover Family Secrets, Stories in Classroom," was published. In the article, a thirteen-year-old shares a story she was initially hesitant to talk about.

"My dad went to jail," she says.

For her project she explored her upbringing and, in the process, learned more about her dad's encounters with the law through police records. In the end, she says that she "never understood to the full extent why he was always so hard on me about school, and I found out he didn't go to high school, and he wants me to do better."

In the article, "How children benefit from learning their family history," A. J. Jacobs is quoted as saying "... we all have horrible, horrible relatives. My own family has its share of criminals: con artists, thieves, murderers, and a whole assortment of other 'sinners.' Yep, they are all there. However, my grandma taught me to believe that the best of our forefathers lives in us, and that we must not run away from who (or whose) we are." (CNN.com)

Your Legacy, Your Footprint, Your Stuff—Er, I Mean Your Prized Possessions

Why Save Your Personal History for Future Generations?

Only part of our identity comes from our actions. A part of who we are is revealed in the items we collect and possess. Another part of our identity is found in the stories we tell. Look for ways to preserve the memories in your family. The acts, things, and stories of you and your generation are just as important as those of your ancestors.

Think about the things you have that once belonged to your relatives. It is hard for me to explain to others how much it means to have "things" from my ancestors. Some of the things that I have saved over the years include:

- Aunt Minnie's oil lamp—Aunt Minnie was afraid of the dark and ALWAYS slept with an oil lamp next to her bed.

- Grandma's China Cabinet—It is a beautiful wood and rounded glass piece with claw-and-ball feet (the feet are fashioned to represent a bird's claw gripping a ball). The story is that the piece was originally too tall to fit in Grandma's house, so she sawed off the balls under the claws and now we have a beautifully devalued "claw only" footed piece of furniture. It's priceless to me.

- Mom's Blue Willow dishes—At least part of the set. As a teenager, I gave away a significant number of pieces of those "old dishes" to a Vietnamese refugee family my church was helping to get on their feet after they arrived in America.

The things we own have stories. Seeing and touching your family history is gratifying. My items help me remember my loved ones in very special ways. But just as these items have come into my life, they can easily go away; so it's important to have a plan.

When the "stuff" is gone, a special effort has to be made to not lose the stories, too. You see, most of us can look at our stuff, and we remember who gave it to us, or the day we got it, or where we were, and so on. Our stuff is more than just the things, but a memory point.

Preparedness

Sometimes in life, natural disasters, theft, or other circumstances can rob you of the things that you would want to pass on to future generations. Since 2004 the month of September in the USA is designated as National Preparedness Month. September was chosen as National Preparedness Month as the tragedies of September 11, 2001, highlighted to the nation the importance of being prepared. Also, September has been chosen partly because the peak of the Atlantic hurricane season is in mid-September.

It is good to make a checklist of the things you feel are important to pass on to your future generations and have a plan to keep them safe and make sure they end up in the hands of the folks you want to have them when you have passed on.

If you have old family photos, portraits, letters, a family Bible, heirlooms, or other artifacts, make sure that you have written down the provenance of the items. How did they come into your possession? Who owned them before you did? Having a written provenance can help your descendants understand the significance and value of the items.

Don't forget to label your photos, whether printed or digital. When you're compiling documents and family trees, be sure to cite your sources. Even though this may not be the most interesting part of genealogy research, writing source citations is so important. Make sure future researchers know where you got your information. Include specifics like authors, editions, page numbers, and any other identifying information you (or future researchers) may need if the source ever needs to be located again.

Make sure that the paper documents that you have are stored in a condition that will allow them to last for future generations. If you have a lot of printed photos or photo albums or scrapbooks, make sure that these are kept in a manner that ensures that they will last long-term.

> *Do you know some of the jobs your parents had when they were young?*
>
> *Y N*

Why all this fuss over me and my possessions?
It seems a bit self-centered.
Because you are not doing this for yourself so much as you are doing it for your children, grandchildren, and future generations.

Knowing and remembering you

Let's think about how your descendants will get to know their ancestors. What would you like your descendants to know about you? If you are involved in discovering your family stories, then you know the work that's involved in piecing together the bits of information that have been left behind.

Just as we want to learn about our parents, grandparents, great-grandparents, and other ancestors, our grandchildren, great-grandchildren, nieces, nephews, cousins, and extended family will also want to learn more about us and our lives. Consider what happens to the "documents" that you create during your lifetime that can tell future generations about you? Also consider what types of documents you have and will create and the questions you want them to answer for future generations. Your descendants will have questions like, "What has your spiritual journey been like?" Consider how you have navigated the difficult times. Where do you find strength? Who were the folks who inspired you? Why did you make the life choices you made?

These are the kinds of questions you might address in a legacy letter, a letter you write for your descendants. You can do this in a variety of ways. I heard an account of a woman who was terminally ill, who decided to leave a legacy letter to her grandchildren. She grew tired from the effort and ultimately made a video for them.

"Every time an old person dies, a library burns to the ground" (African Proverb).

How will you store your work? In a computer file, a paper file folder, in a three-ringed binder? Items tossed into a hope chest? Remember, you can always upgrade later.

How To Save Your Personal History for Future Generations

"Carve your name on hearts, not tombstones. A legacy is etched into the minds of others and the stories they share about you." (Shannon L. Alder)

There are four main ways we can do this, using modern technology or using traditional formats, or somewhere in between.

1.   A Traditional Diary or Letter

As we have journeyed through my family discovery, you have seen the kinds of things I've looked for. Perhaps you might consider the following suggestions to help guide you as you write your legacy letter. For each phase of life consider five things to talk about.

Your Childhood

- Your earliest memories

- The house you grew up in

- What you liked to do for fun as a child

- Your favorite toys

- Your earliest best friends from the neighborhood, from school

- An adventure you had with your friends

- Your most memorable birthdays and holidays and stories about what happened

Your Teen Years

- Your first crush, first kiss, and first real boyfriend or girlfriend

- Favorite teachers and why

- What you discovered you were pretty good at doing

- Favorite movies, movie stars, books, or music in those days

- Jobs you had or after school activities

Leaving Home and Being on Your Own

- How you chose a college or a job

- Your favorite or least favorite subjects/jobs

- How you chose your major or a career path

- Your first real, full-time, life-supporting jobs

- Your first on-your-own living space, furnishings, challenges

Your Family—The Child-Raising Years

- A biographical sketch of your partner

- Your first home, favorite memories, furnishings

- Having children—who, when, where, and special stories about their births

- Favorite stories, special times, stories about trips, events, family activities, high moments or crisis times

- The things you did to support your kids or community during these years

The Empty Nest Years

- How you felt about the kids leaving home

- Things you started to do that you couldn't have done before the kids moved on

- Hobbies, collections, jobs, transitions during those years
- Challenges with aging
- Looking back; how you feel about the life you've lived so far

2.   Family Photos and Video

Most of our smartphones, tablets, and computers contain vast libraries of photographs and videos documenting our lives. Organize those digital images and store them.

3.   Social Media

We could view social media as the modern diary, but this time it's not written for personal use, but to communicate with friends, family, and acquaintances. It is immediate and you always have a way of recording in the palm of your hand using your cell phone. Be familiar with your social media platforms and how they handle your data once you have passed. Create a plan for someone to "inherit" your account so that your posts, videos, and pictures can be viewed beyond your lifetime.

4.   Creating Your Memoirs in Books

There is a reason so many memoirs and autobiographies are in printed books. They allow the author to concentrate on capturing their memories and thoughts and the details of their life. They are also the best way of storing these memories—we have books that go back hundreds, if not thousands, of years. If you're considering writing a book, the same outline we talked about for the legacy letter may work for your book.

Some companies will guide you through this and take care of not only the printing of your memoirs but also record your voice onto CDs and electronic audio files. They make it easy; they interview you over the phone or Skype so that it's convenient.

Once you have documented and organized your future legacy items, consider donating your research to a local historical or genealogical society, if they have archival collections. Contact the institution you would like to work with. Institutions vary in their collection policies and the media they will accept and have different access and copyright policies. Your chosen institution will work with you to help you understand these policies before you donate your materials. By placing your research into the hands of an institution, you are both ensuring its long-term preservation, and opening up your research to others who have the same ancestors.

1865-1904–Inventions and World Events He Missed

The dash in my great-grandfather, A. S. J. Allen's, timeline is explored below. I've taken the years of his childhood, teen years, twenties, and his final decade of his thirties and tried to align the calendar with inventions and events that may have been of interest or impact to him.

A. S. J.'s Childhood

The years 1865–1875: A. S. J. was born and lived in Alabama, and sometime around the age of ten or eleven moved to Florida. While in Alabama, he lived out his childhood mostly under the presidency of Andrew Johnson. Around the time of his birth, the 13th Amendment passed, permanently outlawing slavery.

1865

- Vice President Andrew Johnson becomes the 17th president after the April assassination of President Abraham Lincoln.

- April-June–American Civil War ends as the last elements of the Confederacy surrender.

1866

- Civil Rights Act of 1866

- Ku Klux Klan founded

1868

- Impeachment of Andrew Johnson, acquitted by the Senate by one vote.

- Fourteenth Amendment is ratified. Arguably one of the most consequential amendments to this day, it addresses citizenship rights and equal protection under the law and was proposed in response to issues related to former slaves following the American Civil War.

- Ulysses S. Grant is elected eighteenth president, and Schuyler Colfax vice president, of the USA.

- Florida Legislature adopts an official state seal, passing a resolution "that a seal the size of the American silver dollar, having in the center thereof a view of the sun's rays over a high land in the distance, a cocoa tree, a steamboat on water, and an Indian female scattering flowers in the foreground, encircled by the words, 'Great Seal of the State of Florida: In God We Trust,' be and the same is hereby adopted as the Great Seal of the State of Florida."

1870

- 15th Amendment

- Enforcement Acts

1871

- Great Chicago Fire

1872

- Yellowstone National Park created

- Amnesty Act

- Alabama Claims

- U.S. presidential election, 1872: Ulysses S. Grant reelected president; Henry Wilson elected vice president

1873

- Financial crisis known as the Panic of 1873

- President Grant begins his second term; Henry Wilson becomes Vice President

- Influenza epidemic (1873 to 1875)

1875

- Civil Rights Act of 1875

- Vice President Wilson dies

These events happened when A. S. J. was just a boy. I doubt

he was aware of any of these happenings in the world although they may have been in the peripheral vision of his parents and community.

A. S. J.'s Teen Years

From 1875 until 1885 A. S. J. was in his teenage years. This is the period I most associate with the wild, wild west, and stories of cowboys and Indians. Culturally these are the years depicted on TV shows like *Bonanza*, *Little House on the Prairie*, *The Virginian*, and the like. Spending all of this period in Florida, A. S. J. would have witnessed the following events occurring around the country.

1876

- National League of baseball is founded.

- Centennial Exposition in Philadelphia

- Munn v. Illinois establishes public regulation of utilities.

- Battle of Little Bighorn

- Wild Bill Hickok is killed by a shot to the back of his head by Jack McCall while playing poker in Deadwood, South Dakota. He held aces and eights, now known as the dead man's hand.

- U.S. presidential election seemingly elects Samuel J. Tilden president and Thomas A. Hendricks vice president, but the results are disputed with twenty Electoral College votes allegedly in doubt.

- Battle of the Little Bighorn. The 7th Cavalry under the command of Col. George Armstrong Custer is vanquished by Lakota and Northern Cheyenne warriors led by Sitting Bull in the Battle of the Little Bighorn. Although it is a major victory for the Northern Plains folks against U.S. expansionism, the battle marks the beginning of the end of Native American sovereignty over the West.

- Alexander Graham Bell got the first patent for an electric telephone.

1877

- The Electoral Commission awards Rutherford B. Hayes the presidency and William A. Wheeler the vice presidency in return for ending the military occupation of the South.

- Great Railroad Strike of 1877

- After only two days as president-elect, Hayes becomes the nineteenth president and Wheeler the vice president.

- Reconstruction ends.

1878

- Yellow fever epidemic hits. An estimated 74,000 cases result in 15,934 deaths.

- Bland–Allison Act requires the U.S. Treasury to buy a certain amount of silver and put it into circulation as silver dollars.

- Morgan silver dollars are first minted.

1879

- Thomas Edison creates the first commercially viable light bulb.

- Knights of Labor go public.

1880

- University of Southern California is founded.

- U.S. population exceeds 50 million.

- U.S. presidential election. James A. Garfield is elected president and Chester A. Arthur vice president. Their popular vote margin is less than 2,000 votes.

1881

- Garfield becomes the twentieth president. That same year he is shot by a deranged gunman.

- President Garfield dies after ninety-nine days, and Vice President Arthur becomes the twenty-first president.

- Gunfight at the O.K. Corral in Tombstone, Arizona Territory

- Clara Barton creates the American Red Cross.

- Tuskegee Institute is founded. A. S. J.'s yet-to-be-born baby girl, Fannie, would marry a boy who ends up at the home hospital developed here to provide care for African-American veterans of World War I, who complained about difficulties in getting served in other facilities, particularly in the segregated South.

- Billy the Kid is shot and killed by Sheriff Pat Garrett.

- *A Century of Dishonor*, a nonfiction book that chronicles the experiences of Native Americans in the United States, focusing on injustices, is written by Helen Hunt Jackson.

1882

- Chinese Exclusion Act

- Jesse James is shot and killed by Robert and Charlie Ford.

1883

- Buffalo Bill's Wild West show is founded. Participants include: Sitting Bull, Geronimo, Calamity Jane, and Annie Oakley.

- Civil Rights Case 109 US 3 1883 legalizes doctrine of segregation.

- Pendleton Civil Service Reform Act

- Brooklyn Bridge opens.

1884

- U.S. presidential election. Grover Cleveland is elected president and Thomas A. Hendricks is elected vice president.

1885

- Grover Cleveland becomes the twenty-second president and Thomas A. Hendricks the vice president.

- Washington Monument is completed.

- Vice President Hendricks dies.

- The automobile is invented, with special credit going to the German Karl Benz for creating what is considered the first practical motorcar.

The Years of A. S. J.'s Manhood

Leaving the teenage years and entering his twenties, A. S. J. enters the decade between the years 1886 and 1896. In January 1886 a child, Cora, is born. On the 16th of April that same year, A. S. J. marries Cora's mom, Dinah Lembric, and begins life with her, their newborn daughter, and Dinah's son, John Lembric. Four years later, in 1890, probably due to the influences of Dinah's brother, Zachariah David "Z. D." Lembric, A. S. J. is ordained a Minister of the Gospel. Five more children will arrive before he reaches thirty.

Year	A.S. J.'s Age	Births	Preaching Assignments
1885	20	John L	
1886	21	Cora	
1887	22	Ella	
1888	23		
1889	24		
1890	25	Gussie	Newnansville
1891	26		Newnansville
1892	27	Alonzo	Newnansville
1893	28	Oliver	Hague and Stanley
1894	29	Phyllis	Jonesville
1895	30		Palatka
1896	31	Minnie	Arrendondo, Union Lake

1886

- Yellow Fever outbreak in Jacksonville, Florida

- Statue of Liberty (Liberty Enlightening the World) dedicated.

1887

- The United States Congress creates the Interstate Commerce Commission.

- Dawes Act. The nominal purpose of the act was to protect "the property of the natives" as well as to compel "their absorption into the American mainstream." Some native folks who were deemed to be "mixed-blood" were forced to accept U.S. citizenship, while others were "detribalized."

- Hatch Act. The University of Florida was founded in 1853 and is based in Gainesville, Florida. It was then and remains today Florida's premier land-grant university.

1888

- Washington Monument completed.

- U.S. presidential election. Benjamin Harrison is elected president and Levi P. Morton vice president, despite coming in second in the popular vote.

- George Eastman develops the Kodak camera. This is the first handheld camera to incorporate roll film. The Kodak camera could take one hundred pictures. When it was done, the camera would be mailed back to Kodak to have the film developed and new film put in. It weighed just over two pounds.

1889

- Harrison becomes the twenty-third president and Morton becomes vice president.

- Worldwide influenza pandemic

- North Dakota, South Dakota, Montana, and Washington become states.

- December 6. Former Confederate president Jefferson Davis dies.

- During a speech given by Benjamin Harrison, he becomes the first U.S. president in history to have a voice recording.

1890

- Peanut butter is developed by a St. Louis doctor for his patients with bad teeth.

- Idaho and Wyoming become states.

- National American Woman Suffrage Association founded.

- The Sherman Anti-Trust Act became law in the United States.

- Artist Vincent Van Gogh dies in France at the age of thirty-seven after shooting himself two days earlier.

- October 1. At the urging of John Muir, The U.S. Congress designates Yosemite a National Park.

- December 15. Sitting Bull, legendary Sioux leader, dies at the age of fifty-nine in South Dakota. He is killed while being arrested in the federal government's crackdown on the Ghost Dance movement.

- December 29. The Wounded Knee Massacre takes place in South Dakota when U.S. Cavalry troopers fire on Lakota Sioux who had gathered. The killing of hundreds of unarmed men, women, and children essentially marks the end of Native American resistance to White rule in the West.

1891

- James Naismith invents the game of basketball.

- William Tecumseh Sherman, Civil War general, dies in New York City at the age of seventy-one.

- The St. Patrick's Day parade in New York City begins using the traditional route up Fifth Avenue.

- American showman, Phineas T. Barnum, dies in Bridgeport, Connecticut, at the age of eighty.

- Carnegie Hall opens in New York City.

- Sherlock Holmes, created by Arthur Conan Doyle, appears in *The Strand* magazine for the first time.

- Herman Melville, author of *Moby Dick*, dies in New York City at the age of seventy-two. At the time of his death, he is not well remembered for his classic novel about whaling, but more for earlier books set in the South Seas.

- The pastry fork, also known as a pie fork, is invented. It is a fork designed for eating pastries and other desserts while holding a plate. The fork has three or four tines. The three-tine fork has a larger, flattened, and beveled tine on the side, while the four-tine fork has the first and second tine connected or bridged together and beveled. On July 7, 1891, Anna M. Mangin of Queens, a borough of New York City, filed the first patent for the pastry fork. U.S. patent #470,005 was later issued on March 1, 1892.

1892

- General Electric Company is founded.

- U.S. presidential election. Grover Cleveland is elected president and Adlai E. Stevenson, vice president.

- Joshua Pusey invents book matches (he calls them Flexible Matches). He sells the patent to the Diamond Match Company in 1895 or 1896.

- American poet, Walt Whitman, dies in Camden, New Jersey, at the age of seventy-two.

- Writer and naturalist, John Muir, founds the Sierra Club. Muir's campaigning for conservation would exert an influence on American life in the twentieth century.

- August 4. Andrew Borden and his wife are murdered in Fall River, Massachusetts, and his daughter, Lizzie Borden, is accused of the gruesome crime.

- November 8. Grover Cleveland wins the U.S. presidential election, becoming the only president to serve two non-consecutive terms.

1893

- Grover Cleveland becomes the twenty-fourth president; Adlai E. Stevenson becomes vice president.

- Panic of 1893; a serious economic depression.

- Sherman Silver Purchase Act is repealed.

- African American inventor, Thomas W. Stewart, of Detroit, Michigan, receives U.S. patent no. 499,402 for an improved mop with a levered clamp to hold the mop rag in place.

- The song "Happy Birthday to You" is first published.

- January 17. Rutherford B. Hayes, who became president following the disputed election of 1876, dies in Ohio at the age of seventy.

- Thomas A. Edison finishes building his first motion picture studio.

- March 4. Grover Cleveland is inaugurated as president of the United States for the second time.

- May 1. The World's Fair, known as the Columbian Exposition, opens in Chicago.

- A decline in the New York stock market triggers the Panic of 1893, which leads to an economic depression second only to the Great Depression of the 1930s.

- June 20. Lizzie Borden is acquitted of murder.

- The zipper, a popular device for temporarily joining two edges of fabric, is invented. Zippers are found on trousers, jeans, jackets, and luggage. Whitcomb L. Judson was an American mechanical engineer from Chicago who was the first to conceive of the idea, and to construct a workable zipper. Using a hook-and-eye device, Judson intended this earliest form of the zipper to be used on shoes. He also conceived the idea of the slide fastener mechanism in conjunction with the invention of the zipper. Patents were issued to Judson for the zipper in 1891, 1894, and 1905. The zipper came into common use for children's clothing and men's trousers in the 1920s and 1930s, but it was not until World War II that the zipper was widely used in North America and Europe.

1894

- The mousetrap is invented by William C. Hooker of Abingdon, Illinois, exactly three years before James Henry Atkinson developed a prototype called the "Little Nipper." Atkinson probably saw the Hooker trap in shops or in advertisements and copied it as the basis for his own model. Hooker received U.S. patent #528671 for his invention, the mousetrap, in 1894.

- The medical glove/disposal surgical glove is invented. Medical gloves are disposable gloves used during medical examinations and procedures that help prevent contamination between caregivers and patients. Medical gloves are made of different polymers, including latex, nitrile rubber, vinyl, and neoprene; they come unpowdered or powdered with cornstarch to lubricate the gloves, making them easier to put on the hands. In 1894 William Stewart Halsted, the Surgeon-in-Chief of Johns Hopkins Hospital, invented the medical glove to make medical care safer and more sterile for patients and health care workers.

- The Pullman Strike begins and spreads throughout the summer, before being put down by federal troops.

- Wilson–Gorman Tariff Act, including income tax

- Coca Cola was first bottled by Joseph A. Biedenham of Vicksburg, Mississippi. Before that, it was only mixed to order at the soda fountain.

- The U.S. Congress designated the first Monday of September as a legal holiday, Labor Day, to mark the contributions of labor, in part as a peace offering to the labor movement following the crackdown on the Pullman Strike.

- The Winchester Model 1894 rifle, also known as the Winchester 94 or Model 94, is developed. It is a lever-action repeating rifle that becomes one of the most famous and popular hunting rifles of all time. It is designed by John Browning in 1894 and originally chambered to fire two metallic black powder cartridges, the .32-40 Winchester and .38-55 Winchester. It is the first rifle to chamber the smokeless powder round, the .30 WCF (Winchester Center Fire, in time becoming known as the

.30-30) in 1895. In 1901 Winchester creates the new .32WS caliber with the production of rifles starting in 1902. The 1894 was produced by the Winchester Repeating Arms Company. A. S. J. Allen was most likely killed with a Winchester Model 1894 rifle.

1895

- February 20. Abolitionist and author, Frederick Douglass, dies in Washington, D.C., at the age of seventy-seven.

- May 6. Future president, Theodore Roosevelt, becomes president of the New York City police board, effectively becoming the police commissioner. His efforts to reform the police department became legendary and heightened his public profile.

- President Grover Cleveland arranges for a White House Christmas tree lit with Edison electric bulbs.

- Alfred Nobel, the inventor of dynamite, arranges in his will for his estate to fund the Nobel Prize.

- Jell-O is created.

- Lee Shelton shoots Billy Lyons, spawning countless ballads.

His Final Years

The years from 1896 until 1904 represent the final decade of A. S. J. Allen's life. He was thirty-one through thirty-nine years old. In these years he and Dinah are in their thirties and the last three children, Minnie, Wilbert, and Fannie, are added to the young family. Dinah dies, A. S. J. is killed, and nine kids are left orphaned.

Year	A. S. J.'s Age	Births	Preaching Assignments
1896	31	Minnie	Arrendondo, Union Lake
1897	32		Arrendondo, Union Lake
1898	33		Cedar Key and Rosewood

1899	34	Wilbert	Mikesville and High Springs
1900	35	Fannie	Mikesville and High Springs
1901	36		Liberty Hill and Union Lake
1902	37		Liberty Hill and Union Lake
1903	38		Liberty Hill
1904	39		Alachua

This last decade of A. S. J.'s life begins with the passing of legal segregation laws. With the end of Reconstruction in the 1870s, the enactment of Jim Crow Laws enforced racial segregation in the South. In its 7–1 decision in the Plessy v. Ferguson case of May 18, 1896, the U.S. Supreme Court gave constitutional sanction to laws designed to achieve racial segregation by means of "separate but equal" public facilities and services for African Americans and Whites, thus providing a controlling judicial precedent that would endure until the 1950s, legalizing principle of Jim Crow segregation laws in the American South.

1896

- Harriet Beecher Stowe, author of *Uncle Tom's Cabin*, dies in Hartford, Connecticut at the age of 85.

- William McKinley was elected president of the United States, defeating William Jennings Bryan. Garret A. Hobart becomes vice president.

- Alfred Nobel, the inventor of dynamite and creator of the Nobel Prize, dies in Italy at the age of sixty-three.

- Gold is discovered in the Yukon's Klondike.

- Utah becomes a state.

- Miami, Florida, is officially incorporated as a city; population about 300.

1897

- The Klondike Gold Rush begins in Alaska.

- Boston subway is completed.

- Cotton candy is co-invented by William Morrison and John C. Wharton, candy makers from Nashville, Tennessee.

1898

- The USS *Maine* explodes in Havana Harbor, precipitating the Spanish-American War. On April 25, 1898, the United States declares war on Spain.

- The Treaty of Paris (1898) ends the Spanish-American War. The Philippine-American War begins.

- Hawaii is annexed.

- American Anti-Imperialist League is organized.

- At the Battle of San Juan Hill, Col. Theodore Roosevelt and his Rough Riders charge Spanish positions.

- Newsboys in New York City go on strike for several weeks in a significant action related to child labor.

- July 18. Writer Horatio Alger dies in Massachusetts at the age of sixty-seven.

- Teller Amendment, by which the U.S. would help Cuba gain independence and then withdraw all its troops from the country.

- Vice President Hobart dies.

1900

- The fly swatter, a hand-held device for swatting and killing flies and other insects, is invented by Robert R. Montgomery.

1901

- President Theodore Roosevelt invites educator, Booker T. Washington, to dinner at the White House. Other presidents had invited African Americans to meetings at the White House, but Washington was the first African American to dine there.

1902

- The Teddy Bear, a toy bear stuffed with soft cotton and having smooth and soft fur, is invented by Morris Michtom, owner of a Brooklyn toy store. He was inspired by Clifford Berryman's political cartoon "Drawing the Line in Mississippi" that depicted President Theodore "Teddy" Roosevelt on a hunting trip in Mississippi who spared the life of a Louisiana black bear cub. Michtom asked for and received President Roosevelt's permission to use his name for the hand-sewn bears that he invented and his wife helped construct.

1903

- The airplane is invented by the Wright brothers.

- Mary Anderson is credited with inventing the first operational windshield wiper with a motorized arm. In Anderson's patent, she calls her invention a window-cleaning device for electric cars and other vehicles.

1904

- A banana split, an ice cream-based dessert, is developed. In its classic form, it is served in a long dish called a boat. A banana is cut in half lengthwise (hence the split) and laid in the dish. There are many variations, but the classic banana split is made with scoops of vanilla, chocolate, and strawberry ice cream served in a row between the split banana. Although the banana as an exotic fruit was introduced to the American public in the 1880s, it was later, in 1904, that the banana split was invented in the town of Latrobe, Pennsylvania, by twenty-year-old pharmacy apprentice, David Strickler, who was inspired to create a new sundae after seeing a soda jerk during a visit to Atlantic City.

A simple dessert that I grew up with that my great-grandfather never had the opportunity to experience and that would serve as one of my first lessons in life on self-esteem and knowing my place in this world. Told you, I'd get back to that banana split!

Sources:

https://www.thoughtco.com/timeline-from-1890-to-1900-1774042
Decade-Defining Events in U.S. History https://www.britannica.com/list/25-decade-defining-events-in-us-history
Food history timeline http://www.foodreference.com/html/html/yearonlytimeline1900-1950.html
Winchester Model 1894 https://en.wikipedia.org/wiki/Winchester_Model_1894

Soundtrack suggestion:
"Time"
Pink Floyd
Songwriters: David Jon Gilmour/Nicholas Berkeley Mason/George
Roger Waters/Richard William Wright
Time lyrics © Universal Music Publishing Group, T.R.O. Inc.

Tired of lying in the sunshine staying home to watch the rain.
You are young and life is long and there is time to kill today.
And then one day you find ten years have got behind you
No one told you when to run, you missed the starting gun.

Epilogue

At this point, the story calls for an epilogue: "a final or concluding act or event." Warning: I'm not good at endings, but here goes ...

"Strange Fruit"

Southern trees bear strange fruit
Blood on the leaves and blood at the root
Black bodies swinging in the southern breeze
Strange fruit hanging from the poplar trees.

Like the Biblical origin story of Genesis, this story opens with a question, a plea for acknowledgment, and a call to listen. In the Bible account, an envious Cain murdered his brother, then went on coolly about his business, not anticipating that the very ground that soaked up his brother's blood, would cry "foul" to God.

My story here began with a man and his daughter toiling as drops of sweat dripped from their faces into the hot, dry Florida soil. There was a question about a boundary line. An envious neighbor wanted more land. A plea for the neighbor to acknowledge the wrong was given. Then there were pools of A. S. J.'s blood and Ella's tears pouring into the ground. Again, the ground cried out. A call to no longer let the spilling of Black blood go unnoticed. The spilled blood of A. S. J. Allen and the tears of his kinfolk, skinfolk, and villagefolk cried out. I believe that God still hears and responds to the cry of the blood-soaked earth. God still hears the silent screams of our brothers and sisters who have been slain.

In the Bible narrative, I am encouraged that God says, "Your brother's blood cries out to me from the soil." That tells me that God heard then and is still listening now.

Today, more than a century after A. S. J.'s killing, our American soil is stained with the blood of thousands of BIPOC men, women, and children killed by a system of White supremacy. The nation's soil cries out not just for A. S. J. Allen, but with the blood of Tamir Rice, Trayvon Martin, Emmet Till, George Floyd, Breonna Taylor, Ahmaud Arbery. It cries out with the blood of these and hundreds more whose silent screams we are called to hear. It gives me encouragement that we are in a time of finally listening; we as a nation are beginning to hear and listen to the cry of the blood spilled in racial violence.

I invite you to dig into your own family story. For some of you, it is to discover the cries of your slain ancestors and to honor them. For some of you, it is to take ownership of the narrative that it was your ancestors who caused the spilling of the blood. Such an acknowledgement results in intentional living to correct past wrongs and work for a more just present and future. The work is to make sure that systems that enabled the spilling of innocent blood are not perpetuated. In scripture, God tells Cain, "Listen! Listen! Your brother's blood cries out to me from the soil." God deeply loves Cain and his descendants. He protects and provides for them and their future. God expects him to be strong and brave, and in the face of evil, he says, "You must master it!" The evil of racial hatred and violence is at all of our doorsteps and we must put it in its place.

It is the job of the living to honor the dead. An amazing discovery in doing genealogy and family history work is to identify the struggles our ancestors were engaged in and see life from their perspective. That such brave, resilient, and strong people lived is worthy of our honor. It has been an honor for me to be a voice to speak to you of my ancestor and to honor him and the kin, skin, and village folks who listened to the blood cries of this thirty-eight-year-old Black father of nine from the early twentieth century.

The Final Chapter, of the Book – Not the Story

Someone once told me that in some of life's conversations, we should "accept and expect that there will be a lack of closure" in dealing with the work of family story. I wholeheartedly agree. This is the part of the book where I close out the journey with A. S. J. Allen. Maybe the hardest section to write; mostly because closure is so elusive when talking about family story. We are still here, the story is still going on, evolving, growing, changing. . . .

Instead of closure, I invite you to hold a different goal. Too often folks dive into these waters of exploration and discovery expecting to surface with the full name, eye and hair color, country, state, and numbered street address of their most distant ancestor. In most cases this is an unrealistic expectation. My invitation is for you to embrace a transactional encounter with your story. You can count the number of children, you can note the ages, see the places they lived. These are good things, but these are transactions. I caution you to not be so focused on the transactions of the story that you miss out and do not savor the moments that transformed your ancestors, and perhaps the story itself.

See the census that shows Uncle Joe moving into the neighborhood where Sally lived. Would she be Aunt Sally if he'd found a different apartment?

Set expectations to learn about them. To get a sense of who they were, what they ate, saw, and felt.

I believe family discovery is not just about finding a name and country of origin and then closing the book and moving on to some other task. The telling and discovering of your family story is best treated like a loving relationship you come back to again and again. Each time you meet, you see a little bit more that makes you love them even more. Expect to grow in your discoveries. As you go, there will be markers, events, discoveries for you to take special note of and savor the moment of their discovery.

Such moments may be when you discover a marriage that no one ever told you about. Or a piece of land that a relative owned that you never knew about. Or a newspaper article about a good deed performed by a relative.

These moments should shine and illuminate the person, letting you know just a bit more about their character. Cherish them, mark them, celebrate them, and know that there are possibly more jewels like this to be discovered.

An honoring: 117 years later–Alachua/Newnansville Soil Ceremony for A. S. J. Allen

We are called to remember.

> In this soil, there is the sweat of the enslaved. In the soil there is the blood of victims of racial violence and lynching. There are tears in the soil from all those who labored under the indignation and humiliation of segregation. But in the soil, there is also the opportunity for new life, a chance to grow something hopeful and healing for the future.

EJI Director Bryan Stevenson

As we sit here today many who suffered a violent death due to racial hatred still wait. Their blood still cries out. They cry "Remember Me!" Since 2015 the EJI Community Remembrance Project has worked alongside community partners throughout America who are taking on "the challenging, necessary work of telling the truth about our history and building a future rooted in justice." This work has been focused on commemorating and recognizing the trauma of racial terror by collecting soil from various lynching sites. The Community Soil Collection Project website states that the project "provides a tangible way for community members to confront the legacy of racial terror lynchings and to memorialize the African American victims whose lives were lost and the communities impacted by such violence."

I am grateful for the work of the Alachua County Community Remembrance Project which began its work in January 2020. This community group works in partnership with the Equal Justice Initiative from Montgomery, Alabama, and researched my great-grandfather's killing, along with the more than 4,400 other African Americans who were lynched in America from 1877 to 1950. Their investigation of racial terror involving groups of White people committing "acts of fatal violence" against African Americans to instill a sense of fear and dread in the local Black community concluded that my great-grandfather was killed, not by a mob, but by a sole White neighbor, which resulted in racial trauma to the community.

A. S. J.'s killing cannot be classified as a lynching, however, the EJI approved a local remembrance: a soil collection jar memorial for him in Alachua County. This work of the EJI and the Alachua County Remembrance Committee brought together a community that includes the heirs of victims from Alachua for soil collection ceremonies.

Jars of collected soil are displayed in Montgomery, Alabama, at the Legacy Museum: From Enslavement to Mass Incarceration, the Peace & Justice Memorial Center, and in the EJI office. Alachua County, Florida, and others have permanent, local exhibits with jars of soil.

The collection of soil and the display of these jars is important because in the communities where these violent killings took place, there are monuments recognizing the Civil War and champions of the Confederacy. However, there are few monuments or memorials that address the history and legacy of violent racial killings, and most victims of lynching and racial violence have never been publicly mourned or acknowledged.

The jars serve to create greater awareness and understanding about racial terror killings, and to begin a necessary conversation that advances truth and reconciliation. My great-grandfather's killing traumatized and instilled a sense of fear and dread within the Black community. It also unleashed a backlash never before seen from the African American community toward the system of White supremacy. It was reported at the time that "a number of prominent colored Odd Fellows and Masons, together with the aid of churches agitated the matter of prosecution" over the lack of charges against the White man who killed my great-grandfather. This was the beginning of something new—Black agency. One newspaper account described my great-grandfather as "an inoffensive negro." Maybe so, but his character clearly motivated this community to take a risk to stand up for justice. Such agency on the part of the Black community must have been spurred by a great deal of respect for my great-grandfather.

Back to the scene of the crime: Remembrance and Soil Ceremony

"What Did I Do to Be So Black and Blue"
Louis Armstrong

I'm white inside, but that don't help my case
Cause I can't hide what is on my face
I'm so forlorn. Life's just a thorn
My heart is torn. Why was I born?
What did I do to be so black and blue?

How will it end? Ain't got a friend
My only sin is in my skin
What did I do to be so black and blue?

After years of searching and collecting my family history, I sat with some members of my family as we and A. S. J. Allen were honored on the campus of the University of Florida with a remembrance celebration. The speakers at this event included UF President, Kent Fuchs; Alachua County Commissioner, Charles Chestnut IV; and City of Alachua Vice Mayor and Commissioner,

Shirley Green Brown. They spoke passionately about the importance of knowing history, and of being brave enough to stand up for the truth.

President Fuchs spoke first and welcomed and thanked the family for being there. "This history that brings us here this afternoon is neither long ago nor far off. Thank you for helping us to see," he said. "I pray that we will find hope and healing this weekend."

Chestnut emphasized the awesome presence of A. S. J. Allen within the Alachua County community as a man of God.

"To have truth and reconciliation, first we must acknowledge all of those who have lost their lives to lynching," the commissioner said. "He had to be a courageous man to go and approach someone, a white man, during that time. My hat's off to him."

President Fuchs went on to quote Dr. Phoebe R. Stubblefield, a forensic anthropologist at the University of Florida, who said "By restoring history, we can make history."

As Fuchs commented on the activities of "digging up and collecting the soils," he noted we were "digging up and collecting the stories. It's vital work." He then directed our thoughts toward "what could have been."

"What could have been if Rev. Allen had become postmaster of our county, Alachua County? What could have been if his Black neighbors and friends had been able to achieve their ambitions, their hopes, and their dreams?"

I appreciated that President Fuchs engaged in this bit of speculation. It is something I have often done over the years.

What could have been if my great-grandfather had lived to raise the children he and Dinah loved so much? What could have been if he'd continued to preach and teach throughout north and central Florida?

When Vice Mayor Shirley Green Brown of the City of Alachua took the podium, she spoke of the importance of history. Saying in part, "The who, the what, the when, the where. History, history is so valuable." She also emphasized the importance of human relationships in the process of discovering and transmitting family history as she elaborated on the 5-month long process of contacts with me, my family members, and Dr. Ortiz. Our communication started in February of 2021, first via Zoom, then there was a phone call or two, and finally on June 25th we all met in-person. Vice Mayor Brown invited all to attend the soil ceremony.

The next day was the Soil Ceremony. It was held at A. L. Mebane Middle School in Alachua where many of my family members told me they had attended school. As I sat listening to the stories of lynching victims, the Louis Armstrong song 'What Did I Do to Be So Black and Blue" rang in my head. The lyrics to this song are heartbreaking; especially when Armstrong concludes, "My Only Sin Is in My Skin."

Indeed, the only reason we were sitting under a tent this warm, Saturday morning was to honor folks who were killed because of their skin.

For many of the victims of lynching in Florida, their stories may never be known. The lives of my skinfolk were not considered important enough for anyone to record their stories. The aim of these non-legal executions was to show that Whites could take the law into their own hands, and kill and instill terror in the Black community. Who these Black folks were, was not important. What was important was to send a message of White supremacy. Whatever supposed crime, infraction, or offense they committed was not of primary concern. The human cost of crossing the line of White privilege and authority—that was the issue of primary concern. Black life was the price of such a crossing. These killings were intended to keep Blacks from causing trouble and to show lynching as an acceptable form of punishment.

The eight victims being honored this particular day were: Cooley

Johnson, George Bibbon, Willey Bradley, Caesar Sullivan, Harry Hurl, A. S. J. Allen, William Rawls, and the fifteen-year-old son of Harry Harold (his name is unknown).

This soil ceremony and remembrance of these folks came with numerous reminders that reconciliation begins with a decision to listen.

> "Now Cain said to his brother Abel, 'Let's go out to the field.'
> While they were in the field, Cain attacked his brother Abel and killed him.
> Then the Lord said to Cain, 'Where is your brother Abel?'
> 'I don't know,' he replied. 'Am I my brother's keeper?'
> The Lord said, 'What have you done? Listen! Your brother's blood cries out to me from the ground.'" (Gen. 4:8-10)

We must tell and listen to the truth; truth precedes reconciliation.

William Shakespeare gave us the line; "The evil that men do lives after them; The good is oft interred with their bones." For victims of racial terror, the good memory of the folks killed is oft interred with their bones, and they are publicly memorialized as evil. The stories of the good that they did often go unspoken. Even their burial sites are often unknown or unmarked; unrecorded and considered places to be avoided.

Remembrance of these violent deeds is important so that we do not make the same old mistakes and hopefully do not make new and similar ones. Mark Twain reminds us that "History doesn't repeat itself, but it often rhymes." When memories fail, past evils arise.

> "Then a new king, to whom Joseph meant nothing, came to power in Egypt. 'Look,' he said to his people, 'the Israelites have become far too numerous for us. Come, we must deal shrewdly with them or they will become even more numerous and, if war breaks out, will join our enemies, fight against us and leave the country.'"

"So they put slave masters over them to oppress them with forced labor, and they built Pithom and Rameses as store cities for Pharaoh." (Exod. 1:8-11)

The Hebrew Bible implication is that previous Pharaohs respected Joseph's role in saving their nation; but this new ruler had either no knowledge of, or no concern for, this history. The result was 400 years of enslavement of the Hebrew people.

There can be no reconciliation without truth. To skip the truth-telling renders any apology hollow. It was meaningful for me and my family to have current authorities show up and express that this particular history of Alachua County was shameful, and that the deeds done there were wrong. During the Soil Ceremony, it was encouraging to hear a young Santa Fe High School student, Megan Walls, chair of the City of Alachua's Youth Advisory Council, say that, "One of the best ways we can begin to address these issues is by addressing this within our school system, working these kind of things into our curriculum . . . so we can move on from them or they are just going to continue to be repeated unless it is brought to our attention."

Stay humble. Put your ears on for the after party because time with family is story time.

"My mom will make me walk the dogs or take out the trash when I go home" (Queen Latifah).

The trip to Alachua to honor my great-grandfather was moving. But you know how these things go, right? The private meet and greet conversations among family—now that's where the good stuff happens. And, indeed, it happened to me!!!

Having grown up as an only child, I constantly remind myself of a truth that folks with siblings are normally well aware of. That is, time with family will bring humility (and if you're not careful, humiliation). You cannot escape time with family without someone putting you in your place. For better or for worse, family will always remind you that you are not "all that." I believe Jesus said it best. "Prophets are honored everywhere except in their own hometowns and in their own households."

So, to prepare for this inevitable fact of family life, always make it a point to be humble and to ask questions. Find an elder in the room and ask; "Did I get this right? What stories have you heard?"

Even if you are being hailed as the special guest and keeper of the family history, put on your listening ears. Respect the elders in the room; ask them for their input. It always pays off.

At the conclusion of the public Remembrance event and the Soil Ceremony, some of the family ushered me to the home of an older family member; one I'd never met. He questioned me on who I was and how I came to be a part of the family. After he was convinced of my legitimacy, he began his stories.

The Backwards Church and More Graves

The lullaby effect is when you hear something so many times you just sing along with it and never stop to ask what may later seem like obvious questions. For example, how many of us have sung the lullaby "Rock-a-bye baby" to a sleeping baby. Let's examine that song for a moment.

"Rock-a-bye baby, on the treetops. When the wind blows, the cradle will rock. When the bough breaks, the cradle will fall. And down will come baby, cradle and all."

Upon closer examination, I find the song terrifying. But to my point about conducting a closer examination of the verses and asking different questions...

The baby is in a treetop! Who would do such a thing? Why would someone do this?

When you engage in family history research you must learn to fight the lullaby effect and learn to ask better questions.

The effects of the lullaby effect hit me hard a while ago as I listened intently to a sermon. It was a part of Scripture I had heard hundreds of times. I could quote most of it verbatim. But one day I really heard it. I grew up hearing preachers preach the "Sermon on the Mount." I grew up asking questions about the Beatitudes that focused on what my attitude should be. On this particular occasion, I overcame the lullaby effect and asked a better question. That is, "Why was the sermon on the mount? Would the normal place for a Rabbi to teach and preach be inside the Temple or synagogue?"

When I asked this question, a deeper understanding resulted. Look at the people who approached him afterwards: his audience. These were unclean people who would not have been allowed in the Temple. Maybe he preached on the mount to deliver a message that God's favor (blessed are ...) was available for *all*.

This is the difference between transactional thinking and transformative thinking. And this difference in thinking is important. Transactional thinking is easy for most of us here in Western culture and it allows the lullaby effect to go unchallenged. We see a situation and we accept it by making it fit into our world view with no questions.

Transformational thinking takes a different approach. It looks for problems. It asks, "What is wrong with this picture?" and leads us to ask better questions, which in turn will give us better answers that transform us.

My lullaby

As a storyteller it is important for me to get the story right. Though I sometimes have a hard time remembering what I had for breakfast on any given day, I do tend to remember vivid details of events from long ago. One such memory has always disturbed me. As a child I attended a funeral at Mt. Nebo. Sometime during the service nature called, and I desperately needed to answer. My grandmother instructed a male relative to take me to the bathroom.

Now, here is where my lullaby occurs. I remember walking out of the church building and taking a left turn, going back toward the back of the building to an outhouse. I was visiting my country cousins. In St. Pete we had indoor plumbing. There were burial sites with tombstones on the other side of the building; that is the right side. In my memory of events, I remember I had turned to the left where there were trees, tables and chairs, and the outhouse.

My visits to Mt. Nebo over the last decade have always caused me trouble when I look at the building and recall that outhouse event. Something was off but I tried to force myself to rethink the story. If you walk out of the front of the church building and turn left, you end up in the cemetery.

My most recent visit has resolved the mystery. The family explained that the church building is not the original structure.

As one of my cousins put it when I asked what happened to the original building, "The white people blew it up!"

When the structure was rebuilt, the builders chose to rebuild on the same foundation (thus the mystery of why the cornerstone has two dates is solved). But they also elected to turn the building around. The new building faces the opposite direction. This discovery explains why my memory of going to the outhouse as a child would today result in me pooping in the graveyard!

As my cousins and I revisit the Mt. Nebo Cemetery, my cousin tells me of his months' earlier explorations in what was the front of the property. He recants seeing much older tombstones with earlier dates near what originally was the front of the property. Perhaps a cleanup crew could discover more. Perhaps we might even find the burial sites of A. S. J. and Dinah Allen. I'm gearing up for another family adventure, and all because I challenged the lullaby effect of my story and questioned the direction a small boy turned to find an outhouse.

The Rest of the Story with the Train

Earlier I mentioned the story of the violent dying of the father and son pair, "Mac" (Themester Mack Sr.) and "Slim" (Themester Mack Jr.).

Unlike a natural dying, a violent dying can become a public story. Their deaths caused family members to suffer from depression, posttraumatic stress disorder (PTSD), and complicated grief. Driving back from dinner, I learned the extent of that grief in my family and, for the first time, the back story surrounding the violent dying of my two cousins.

The story I was told was that the weekend entertainment for my cousins was a regular gathering for a *Soul Train* line dance. Slim, especially, loved to dance. On this particular weekend, the car needed attention. Florida had a vehicle inspection process which required all vehicles to have an inspection sticker displayed on the windshield in order to prove the vehicle was safe to operate. The nearest inspection station was in the nearby town of Trenton. Mac and Slim drove by the house where my cousins lived. Everyone was excited about that evening's *Soul Train* line. The two men just needed to run this quick errand to the inspection shop. It would be the last time they would be seen alive.

Speculation is that the car radio was loud and that the train did not blow its horn. There was no gate to drop down and block traffic from the approaching train. The car and the train collided.

When word reached the family back at the house, Rose fainted. Ruthie wailed. Dot described her sister's wail as intense. "She cried, she screamed, she convulsed. I thought she would never stop sobbing" said Dot, as she relived the moment. Even now (almost fifty years later) she was visibly shaken as she recounted the events.

Another Story on Why A. S. J. Was Killed

Throughout much of U.S. history, the sexual advances of White men toward Black women were both widespread and institutionalized. The legal system offered Black women no protection. To make matters worse, stereotypes about Black women's hypersexuality were used to justify limited social support for Black rape victims.

To maintain the economic power and political dominance they had enjoyed during slavery, Southern White men were slow to relinquish their freedom to violate Black women with impunity.

In 1855 a nineteen-year-old enslaved Black woman named Celia killed the White man who owned her and was trying to rape her. Missouri law allowed a woman to use force when in imminent danger of forced sexual intercourse, but the judge ruled an enslaved woman had no right to refuse her "master." Celia was convicted of murder, sentenced to death, and hanged on December 21, 1855.

In 1952 Ruby McCollum was a wealthy married African-American woman in Live Oak, Florida, known for being arrested, tried, and convicted for killing Dr. C. Leroy Adams. Dr. Adams was a prominent White doctor. Mrs. McCollum testified in court to Adams's sexual exploitation, which led to her shooting and killing him. She was sentenced to death by an all-White jury.

To date, I have been told two similar stories of sexual advances that purport to be the "real" reason behind A. S. J. Allen's killing. The first time I heard the story was during a nursing home visit with my cousin, Essie Mae Singleton. Essie was the daughter of Ella Allen, the teenage daughter with A. S. J. at the time of his killing. After a recorded interview with Essie, when the cameras had stopped rolling and I was packing up to leave, Essie motioned me over, and in a quiet whisper, told me that the fence wasn't the real reason A. S. J. got shot. She explained that that fence story was only part of the story. The primary cause of the argument between the two men was that the neighbor wanted to "mess around" with the girls. It had been a long and tiring day, and I dismissed the story as the failing memory of an old woman.

Now, twenty years later, I sit with another relative, who asks me, "Now you do know the real reason he got shot, don't you?" I respond with a humble and curious "no."

According to this older relative, Ella was a daddy's girl. Wherever A. S. J. went, Ella went. They were inseparable. As they worked the fields that hot April day in 1904, they did go out to investigate the fence construction on their land, but of greater disturbance than the fence was the White neighbor's insistence that A. S. J. give him his daughter for sport. My family member stated that A. S. J. was killed for denying a White man a Black girl's body. He was convinced that to deny a White man this desire would certainly end in death. And he believes this is what fueled A. S. J.'s killing. This, he and a few other family members tell me, is the hidden story that has been circulating privately among the family for the last hundred years.

This new revelation leaves me feeling much like one of the characters in the parable of the blind men with the elephant. The story is of a group of blind men who have never come across an elephant before. They learn and conceptualize what the elephant is like by touching it. Each one tells a different story because each has come in touch with a different part of the animal. I now have two parts (collaborated now by multiple voices) of the same story.

"For now we see only a reflection as in a mirror; then we shall see face to face. Now I know in part; then I shall know fully, even as I am fully known" (1 Cor.13:12).

History is a journey. There is no "stopping point" with family history. Expect twists and turns. The parable of the blind men and the elephant illustrates how our individual perceptions can lead to miscommunication and conflict. So, follow all the clues. Verify all you can; the rest can live on as family folklore until one day perhaps one of your descendants may piece together the story.

I am at home now. The events of the past weekend are still unsettled in my mind and heart. I went to Florida to thank some folks for honoring my grandfather; I have returned with so much more gratitude and more questions. I've grown closer to my family and to a community in Alachua that I hardly knew a month ago.

I got a text from a cousin that helped me see that this sense of "wellness" I am now basking in was not confined to me alone. The text message told of her depression and feelings of being alone. Then a weekend with family helped her to feel the love that can only come from family. From being a part of something bigger than yourself. It was true; honoring the folks who got us here does indeed bring wellness to our souls!

I sit here and reflect on my childhood. I see Grandmother. She's sitting in her big chair in the living room, right beside the front door. As I approach the door to leave, she smiles and reveals a big gold tooth. She clears her throat and says, "Remember who you are out there."

I close my eyes and smile as a tear finds its way down my face and rolls off my chin. "I remembered, Grandma." I did not shame the family. I feel I made Grandma proud as I showed the world her daddy, not the man portrayed in the press as:

...a colored minister and teacher

...well known in Gainesville

...considered a rather inoffensive Negro

...a Negro preacher and politician

...prominent by his affable tongue

...regarded as a troublesome Negro and had few friends even among his own race

but the honorable, courageous, loving father, and community builder, the Reverend Albert Sidney James Allen. His photo hanging on the wall in Grandma's bedroom, clearly visible from our front door.

The story of this "troublesome Negro" now lives in the Joel Buchanan Archive of African American Oral History at the University of Florida; and is, as of this writing, headed for publication by the Florida Historical Society Press. This story has been heard and told throughout the nation in books, magazine articles, classrooms, workshops, and seminars.

I can imagine my great-grandfather and his baby girl (my grandmother) smiling as this history unfolds and spreads throughout the land. It is my honor to make the family proud.

Thank you for reading. It is my sincere desire that you are motivated to see your family now that you've journeyed with me in the telling of my story. You now have some tools (and hopefully inspiration) to see yourself, your kinfolk, skinfolks, and your village folks.

"Killing Me Softly"
Roberta Flack
Songwriters: Norman Gimbel, Charles Fox
Killing Me Softly lyrics © Warner Chappell Music, Inc.

And there he was this young boy, a stranger to my eyes
Strumming my pain with his fingers
Singing my life with his words
Killing me softly with his song
Killing me softly with his song
Telling my whole life with his words
Killing me softly with his song

Alonzo Felder

As you walk away from this book, I hope that you walk away with a feeling of "I've found my folks. Now, I can honor the folks who made me, me."

In genealogical solidarity,

Alonzo

Acknowledgments

I'm head over heels in love with these folks!

Like my great-grandfather, A. S. J. Allen, there has been a community of folks who "showed up" for me. I am deeply grateful for the following kinfolk and villagefolk; for their expertise, love, encouragement, and motivation for me to put this work together. Thank you for being on this journey with me to honor my beloved kin.

My Kinfolk:

Dorothy O'Neal–My dear cousin, providing me with stories, names, and data on the folks in Alachua County. We have come a long way from shelling peas on Aunt Ella's front porch!

Essie Mae Singleton–Offered me shelter from the wind and a refuge from the storms of college life during my years at UF. So grateful for her offering me a place to "be" while I was away from home.

Francine Felder–My wife and best friend. She left her family to cleave to me and embraced my folks as her own. Her mom and dad embraced me not as a son-in-law but as a son. Could not have made this journey without her warm embrace and that of the whole Phillips clan.

Joyce Mills—My cousin who quite literally "wrote the book" on our family. Thank you for collecting the stories and publishing them. You gave me tremendous inspiration.

Jenna Felder—My daughter-in-law. Thank you for the reading and rereading of this manuscript and for all your editorial help. Most of all, thank you for the complete embrace of our family. You didn't just marry my son, you became family.

Mia Felder Rowe—"My heart," my baby girl. Stood by me as a tireless worker, cheerleader, organizer, marketer. It is no understatement that without you, "My Roots Foundation" would not exist and my journey would be far less interesting, rewarding, or successful.

Seth Felder—My "happy thought" son. For AV and tech support. Traveling with me to interview family members and tell their stories.

Phil Wright—My newly discovered kin. Thank you for your love and support. So glad we finally met.

Sarah and Roger King—Thank you for feeding me and caring for me, especially during those early college years in Gainesville. I will always treasure those days sitting at your feet and hearing stories of our family.

Essie Singleton—My dear cousin; Ella's little girl. You loved me, fed me, welcomed me into your life with open arms. You taught me so much about our family. You were a model of hospitality and showed me what being family should look like. I miss you so much.

My Village Folk:

Aldreka J. Everett–SPOHP/UF Alumni

Ben Weast (aka "Cousin Ben")–He started this ball rolling by offering to go on a road trip with me to Alachua County to find my folks at the Mt. Nebo Cemetery.

Cassandra Davis–Former My Roots Foundation board member, Righteous Response Workshop team leader, and lover of all things historical. Thank you for your sense of mercy and justice and your eagerness to bring the marginalized folks of the world into the conversation.

Claudine Woods–My Roots Foundation board member. A model of "do your own work," you inspire me so much by the work you have put into your own family history and the way you share it with your family and friends.

Corbie Hill–Thank you for befriending me and making me a better writer. You have my gratitude for your encouragement as I struggled to finish this book.

Frances Lyons-Bristol–Archivist over the collection maintained by the United Methodist General Commission on Archives and History

Francine Clarke–Collection Services Associate, Duke School of Law

George Digsby–My "brother from another mother," My Roots Foundation board member, my friend.

Janeen Gammage–Collection Services Associate, Duke School of Law

Jennifer Behrens–Duke School of Law Librarian

Jennifer Carpenter–"Sista girl" who helped me with web design and organization. Thank you for listening to my stories and sharing so many of your own.

Jim Powell Jr.–Ancient Records Coordinator, Alachua County Clerk of Court. Thank you, Jim, for all the emails over the years and for letting me into the "secret vault" warehouse to see actual documents related to my great-grandfather.

John Weistart–Duke School of Law professor and friend who shared his ancestry.com account with me and encouraged my curiosity.

Justin Dunnavant–UC-Santa Cruz/Vanderbilt SPOHP/UF Alumni

Kevin Stewman–My Roots Foundation board member, legal advisor, and friend

Laine Staton and Gerard Staton–Thank you for the Helius Foundation classes and mentorship. Thank you for helping me see how to use "my mess to bless."

Larry Wood–Proofreader, friend, My Roots Foundation board member

Lee Cloninger–Duke School of Law library staffer

Lewis Beale–Thank you for rekindling in me the desire to write and the confidence that I could do this.

Mike Hannon–Duke University School of Law staffer

Miriam Gan Spalding–State Archives of Florida

Mitchell Schane–oral history interviewer, SPOHP/UF Alumni

Patricia Hilliard-Nunn–University of Florida

Paul Ortiz–Director, Samuel Proctor Oral History Program. One of my biggest fans. Paul, you have believed in me, even at a time when I did not believe in myself. Thank you for showing me what a real academic looks like. You do not just teach you model the lessons of history so that it comes alive (or, rather, never dies).

Randi Gill-Sadler–Lafayette College; Justin Hosbey–Emory University, SPOHP/UF Alumni

Rebecca Bower-Duke–received BA with Honors in Studio Art from Wake Forest University and a MSLS from the University of North Carolina at Chapel Hill. She worked for Special Collections at North Carolina State University and for the National Digital Newspaper Project at UNC-Chapel Hill. Rebecca's areas of interest include photography, microfilm digitization, and preserving records for underrepresented groups. Thank you for finding the Rev. A. S. J. Allen records from the UMC on his work with kids and the poor.

Ryan Morini–SPOHP graduate research coordinator for the African American History Project (AAHP)

Sarah Blanc–SPOHP/UF Alumni

Shanee Murrain–MDiv MLS, Reference and Public Services Librarian, Duke University, Divinity School Library

Sherry DuPree–Director, UNESCO-Transatlantic Slave Trade

Tina Moore–Duke School of Law Library staffer

Appendix A – Working Folk

By the sweat of your brow, you will eat your food until you return to the ground, since from it you were taken; for dust you are and to dust you will return" (Gen. 3:19).

"All their days their work is grief and pain; even at night their minds do not rest. This too is meaningless. A person can do nothing better than to eat and drink and find satisfaction in their own toil. This too, I see, is from the hand of God, for without him, who can eat or find enjoyment?" (Eccles. 2:23-25)

"You shall eat the fruit of the labor of your hands; you shall be blessed, and it shall be well with you" (Ps. 128:2).

"And to aspire to live quietly, and to mind your own affairs, and to work with your hands, as we instructed you" (1 Thess. 4:11).

"Success is to be measured not so much by the position that one has reached in life as by the obstacles which [one] has overcome while trying to succeed" (Booker T. Washington).

"My father used to have an expression. He'd say, 'Joey, a job is about a lot more than a paycheck. It's about your dignity. It's about respect. It's about your place in your community'" (Joe Biden).

Within the Ten Commandments, we find two prominent ideas. Right in the center, unfolding as a centerpiece in this great work, are the Fifth and Sixth Commandments:

Honor thy father and thy mother.
Thou shalt not kill.

I cannot help but think that the point being made by such a placement is that we ought to honor those who give life and never take it upon ourselves to take life. Life matters.

Those who create life are doing something divine. They are creating. And we will spend the rest of our lives following that example of being creators; being creative. We all have within us the power and the will to create. We find fulfillment, purpose, joy in creating. At times we allow ourselves to be defined by our work.

The sixth great commandment is about killing someone else's work.

We are all the product—the endpoint—of two other people's work. Their lives mattered. Their work matters. Our life matters. Our ancestors were hard-working folks. To understand them (and ourselves) it is helpful to understand the ways they created; to understand the work they did.

Census data should prompt you to ask questions. What kinds of questions? Well, for most Americans, the usual question we ask upon meeting a new person is "What kind of work do you do?" This question is typically one of the first items we gravitate toward when trying to get to know someone.

> *Do you know which person in the family you act most like?*
>
> *YN*

Why does it matter what they did?

Because leanings toward certain occupations and vocations seem to flow in families. Knowing what they did builds personal and institutional self-esteem and intergenerational identity.

Myth: Family patterns do not matter. I can be my own person and choose to be whoever or whatever I want, regardless of my roots.

You don't have to inherit the family craft, but it may be useful to know what it is. There is a sense of family continuity, both comic and tragic in this idea of the "family business."

I'm reminded of the scene from *Forrest Gump* where Forrest recounts the generations of women in Bubba's family involved in the "shrimpin' business."

> Bubba Blue: I'm talkin' about a shrimp-catchin' boat. I've been workin' on shrimp boats all my life. I started out on my uncle's boat, that's my mother's brother, when I was maybe about nine. I was just lookin' into buyin' a boat of my own and got drafted. My given name is Benjamin Buford Blue, but people call me "Bubba." Just like one o' them ol' redneck boys; can you believe that?

> Forrest Gump: My name's Forrest Gump. People call me Forrest Gump.

> Forrest Gump [narrating]: So Bubba was from Bayou La Batre, Alabama, and his momma cooked shrimp. And her momma before her cooked shrimp. And her momma before her momma cooked shrimp, too. Bubba's family knew everything there is to know about the shrimpin' business.

> Bubba Blue: I know ever'thing there is to know about the shrimpin' business. Matter of fact, I'm goin' into the shrimpin' business for myself after I get out o' the Army.

> Forrest Gump: Okay.

In days past a job or trade actually did define your ancestors.

So defining were trades, that many common English names are derived from trades; surnames such as Carpenter, Weaver, Smith, and Taylor.

It is important to note that attitudes toward work have changed. In the past your trade, your work, defined who you were. Today more and more people see their work as "it's a job, it does not define me." This change reflects a view of self that was not as much focused on who you were, but what you did.

To gain insight into our ancestors it's useful to look at what they did. In this Appendix, I'd like to explore how to use our ancestors' occupations to find out more about them and possibly more about their character.

But where to look to find their jobs? Historical records tended to treat employment with much less privacy than we associate with it today. In days past a person's position or title within a workplace was readily available in such places as City Directories, census records, andorganization records (like Methodist annual reports).

Also, there were occupation-sponsored entities like workplace or company cemeteries. Housing units were at times limited to members of a particular occupation.

As an example of the wealth of data found in something as mundane as a City Directory, my great-great-grandmother (A. S. J. Allen's wife, Dinah) had a sister, Kitty, living in St. Pete along with her two daughters. In the listings for the two daughters, Bessie Harden and Bertha Williams, in the 1949 St. Petersburg, Florida, phone book, their race was noted. Back then you could tell if the person was considered Black by the "c" next to their name, which stood for "colored."

Speaking of race . . . our historical research has to be aware of the pervasive racial segregation of former days. If an ancestor was Black, you will need to ask for and search the segregated institutions to find them. Segregation limited options on where folks could work and live. I mentioned earlier the days I spent with an archivist, searching for an ancestor among the records of the Methodist Church. Our frequent communications had been by email and telephone, and we were coming up empty at every turn, it seemed. Then, in the course of the conversation, I made mention of a noted Black preacher from the area and suggested a resource that might list other associated clergies. With much sighing and frustration, she exclaimed "Oh, you mean your ancestor was colored? We'll have to look in the colored books to find anything about him." I had no idea that the church directories and records would be segregated.

As I've researched my family, I've been encouraged to find many good and wonderful folks on the rolls of my Lembric and Allen family lines of Florida. Strong, hard-working men and women, who became:

Artists	Dental technicians	Journalists
Athletes	Domestic workers	Landowners
Beauticians	Educators	Librarians
Building contractors	Farmers	Physicians
Chauffeurs/drivers	Fashion models	Radio and record DJs
Civil rights activists	Freemasons	Scientists
Coaches	Gospel preachers	Equipment Operators
Cooks	Government Officials	Shop Owners
	IT professionals	Soldiers

Far more important to me than their titles and occupations were the transformations and the skill sets they cultivated to become men and women of character; people of wisdom and judgment. As to those family members who did not achieve greatness in a profession or who chose more humble creative work endeavors, they are no less valuable in my family history discovery. Honor is due them whatever their occupational labors.

By now, I'm sure you understand what I am about to say. But a point I always like to emphasize when discussing family history is that you have people, you have history. You did not just drop out of the sky. In fact, the biology it took to create you is amazing. Biologically, we all have two parents, four grandparents, eight great-grandparents, sixteen great-great-grandparents, and thirty-two great-great-great-grandparents. In just five generations, you have thirty-two direct ancestors who had lives, aspirations, loves, and, yes, jobs. Knowing the jobs they performed can help you know them better. Along the way, you may also learn a thing or two about yourself. You have a past, and you have a destiny. Follow your roots. Connect with what's been trending in your family—don't fight it.

There is a wonderful episode of TV's *Long Lost Family* where the woman discovers that a co-worker is her birth mother. The show "proves" a theory I've been seeing for a while. I refer to a theory of personality types, where personality types run in families and result in similar careers and vocations showing up frequently in one's family tree. The Holland Codes, or the Holland Occupational Themes (RIASEC), lists six types:

- R = Doers (Realistic)

- I = Thinkers (Investigative)

- A = Creators (Artistic)

- S = Helpers (Social)

- E = Persuaders (Enterprising)

- C = Organizers (Conventional)

In the episode titled "Your Mom's Been Here the Whole Time," forty-year-old Jenny Thomas spent fifteen years trying to find her birth mother. She signed up for help with the TV reality show and discovered that a coworker, Nita Valdez, was her birth mother. But here's the thing. When the two women were told (independently) that their family member had been found, they both had the same reaction. They used the same words "Is she happy?" Both are hospital workers. Both caring and nurturing women who, by the way, actually liked each other as coworkers.

For some time now, in my work tracing family histories I've noticed something interesting in the occupations and vocations of the folks I've researched. That is, there are trends and patterns of vocational interests and personality traits within most family groupings.

I first picked up on this with my own family. I was born out of wedlock and did not have any significant contact with my biological father until I was an adult. Yet, growing up, I was constantly chastised by my mother for the things I did that were "just like your father," in her words. I held my head like him, had similar reactions to him. Even dressed like him. But all the time, I never spent any time with him to learn these behaviors.

As I dug deeper, I discovered that we both worked in similar industries. He had worked as a mortician; I, too, had spent a lot of time around funeral homes. In fact, two of my longtime friends are morticians. I worked in a hospital for the criminally insane. One day, while going through some decades-old records in an office that I was setting up to use, I discovered the records were from my father, who had worked in the very same building years before I was born.

He had worked with deaf, mute, and blind children as a young adult. One of my first college jobs was in a hospital ward, caring for children with autism. My point is my father was a nurturing soul, and, though I did not grow up in his house, so am I. And our vocational paths have crisscrossed at various points.

"History doesn't repeat itself, but it does rhyme" (Mark Twain).

Back to the movie, *Forrest Gump*, that I mentioned earlier. While that scene of Forrest recounting Bubba's family involvement in preparing shrimp is comic, the plight of Lt. Dan's keeping in step with the family business of soldering is, shall we say, tragic. . . .

Dan "was from a long, great military tradition; someone in his family had fought and died in every single American War." The film shows relatives of Lt. Dan dying in the Revolutionary War (1778), the Civil War (1863), World War I (1918), and World War II (1944). In the movie we find a despondent Lt. Dan saddened by the fact that he would live through the Vietnam War.

So I'd like to leave you with two takeaways here. First, children should grow up with the encouragement that they can do and become anything they want to. The world is theirs for the taking. The hard part is deciding what direction to move in.

Second, as descendants of folks who may have tended to be involved in a particular trade or occupation, there is no science to suggest that we must follow the family business.

Knowing the family story inspires. When we study the biographies of relatives (no matter how distant) and learn that they did it, then we are more apt to believe that we can, too.

When considering topics of occupations, vocations, and lifestyles of our ancestors, we would be wise to always remember who is speaking through the documents we find. Your ancestor's work, and what others may have thought of that work, is highly subjective. Remember, prior to 2020 folks who worked in housekeeping, or fast foods, and some other "unskilled," below-minimum-wage workers were invisible to society at large. Now, since the outbreak of COVID-19, these same jobs and folks are considered essential.

Again, I pull an example from my own family history. On a page from the 1860 census of Calhoun County, Florida, the census taker felt compelled to write a note at the bottom of the page. It reads:

> "The free negroes in this county are mixed blooded almost white and have intermarried with a low class of whites - Have no trade or occupation or profession. They live in a settlement or town of their own. Their personal property consists of cattle hogs. They make no produce except corn

peas & potatoes & and very little of that. They are a lazy indolent & worthless race."

These folks were considered unimportant; but history would later show scientists, doctors, and writers as the descendants of these "lazy indolent & worthless" folks.

The history of labor is filled with fascinating stories. Butchers and bakers to DIY makers—we all have relatives who made monumental contributions to our labor force in unique ways. In honor of their hard work, we've compiled some of the best sources on Ancestry for learning about trades and occupations. These details can help add to the portrait of a person's life and even inspire you with your own pursuits. Your ancestors' occupations can provide you with intriguing insights into both who they were, and the manner in which they lived.

The fact that we had a civil rights movement and the ability to protest was due to folks who went to work every day, sometimes in low-paying, overlooked jobs. Some folks did the visible and now honored work of protest. We remember and honor folks like John Lewis, MLK, and Rosa Parks. But not everyone marched . . . in an article, "The Long Road to Angela Davis's Library," December 26, 2014, in the *New Yorker*, Davis, an icon of the Black Power movement, political activist, philosopher, academic, and author, said of her mother, Sallye Bell Davis, "When asked what she did during the earlier Civil Rights marches and protests, she said: 'I was at work.'"

Hollywood picked up on this notion in the 2013 movie, *Lee Daniels' The Butler. The Butler* is loosely based on the real life of Eugene Allen, who worked in the White House for decades. The film stars Forest Whitaker as Cecil Gaines, an African American who is a firsthand witness of notable political and social events of the twentieth century during longtime service as a White House butler.

The movie stars Oprah Winfrey as Gloria Gaines, Cecil's wife, and David Oyelowo as Louis Gaines, the Gaines's oldest son. In one dramatic scene from the movie, Cecil tells his rebellious son that he needs to leave the house. Louis disrespects his father with the line; "Oh, I'm sorry, Mr. Butler. I didn't mean to make fun of your hero!"

At this point, he is slapped by his mother, and she delivers the wonderful line; "Everything you are and everything you have, is because of that butler." You see, the whole reason young Louis could go out and march and protest, was because his dad was working to provide for the family.

> "Brothers, consider the time of your calling: Not many of you were wise by human standards; not many were powerful; not many were of noble birth. But God chose the foolish things of the world to shame the wise; God chose the weak things of the world to shame the strong. He chose the lowly and despised things of the world, and the things that are not, to nullify the things that are." (1 Cor. 1: 26-28)

"John Adams was a farmer. Abraham Lincoln was a small-town lawyer. Plato, Socrates were teachers. Jesus was a carpenter. To equate judgment and wisdom with occupation is at best . . . insulting." (Valda: *Warehouse 13* "Breakdown" [1.10])

In a previous chapter (Yourfolks), we discussed how you can use your ancestors' occupations to further your research and learn more about them. Since we have four grandparents, eight great-grandparents, sixteen great-great-grandparents, and so on, the odds are good that we all descend from someone "famous." On the other hand, this means that less than one percent of your DNA comes from that famous great-great-great-great-great-grandfather. The other ninety-nine percent comes from ordinary and hard-working folks you have never heard of. These other ancestors have stories of their own—stories that will be told only if you tell them. (https://freedomcenter.org/_media/pdf/genealogy/19.%20Famous%20Ancestors.pdf)

Soundtrack suggestion:
"A Hard Day's Night"
The Beatles
Songwriters: John Lennon and Paul McCartney
A Hard Day's Night lyrics © Sony/ATV Music Publishing LLC

It's been a hard day's night, and I've been working like a dog
It's been a hard day's night, I should be sleeping like a log
But when I get home to you, I'll find the things that you do
Will make me feel all right

You know I work all day to get you money to buy you things
And it's worth it just to hear you say you're going to give me
everything
So why on earth should I moan, 'cause when I get you alone
You know I feel okay

Our ancestors were ordinary folks, but they did extraordinary work. When things became difficult, they didn't wallow in their sadness or self-pity. They rolled up their sleeves and did something for those around them, and for those who would live long after them. In short, they lived good lives, and they gave something to the future. Our ancestors were working folks!

A great way to gain insight into our ancestors is to look into their work lives. Searching publications associated with their field might reveal information on them in their workspaces, and maybe even how they were perceived.

Starting off in his life as a Minister of the Gospel, the *Southwestern Christian Advocate* newspaper revealed that my great-grandfather showed great potential. The following positive job review appeared in 1891.

> creeC a ClOOO cHurcH.
> ## Newnansville, Rev. A. S. J. Allen—His revival resulted in 7 converts. This brother is a young man, and is making splendid progress in general.
> Hagne Station. Rev. J. Jenkins

Source: Letters from the Districts
Author: J. L. Witten, Date: Thursday, Dec. 10, 1891

In a later issue of the same newspaper, under the column "Doings of the Workmen," the paper reports of Great-grandfather entering an environment where church membership was down due to economic factors in the city but prepared to make "greater sacrifices for all causes of Christ and the Church."

Source: "F. E. Wynn, P. C., Sheffield, Ala." *Southwestern Christian Advocate*, 17 Mar. 1898, p. 10. Nineteenth Century U.S. Newspapers, https://link.gale.com/apps/doc/GT3011745375/NCNP?u=duke_perkins&sid=NCNP&xid=c6a5908a. Accessed 26 Aug. 2020.

https://go-gale-com.proxy.lib.duke.edu/ps/i.do?p=NCNP&u=duke_perkins&id=GALE|GT3011745375&v=2.1&it=r&sid=NCNP&asid=c6a5908a

The Job Options Available to Our Ancestors

In these next pages, I would like to show what it took to perform those jobs. I would also like to take special note of how race and gender played a part in who did what work.

Over time, language changes, and with it the meaning and usage of certain words. Some of the occupations listed may not appear on an actual Census record, but you may run across an unfamiliar job title in stories of your ancestors or in documents related to your ancestor's livelihood.

What follows here is a table of old job names and either their current new name or, in most cases, a description of the old job.

The 1850 census was the first to ask United States respondents their occupation. The following list contains mostly U.S.-based and some British English job terms; there are also included a few French, German, and Scottish origin occupations. Note that the U.S. census does not contain references to all the occupations listed here, but the glossary is good to have in hand as you research non-U.S.-based census records. The source of many jobs and descriptions in my chart below is http://rmhh.co.uk/occup/index.html, where a far more extensive list may be found.

Old Job Names List

Old Job Name	New Name or Meaning
Abactor	Cattle thief
Acater	Supplied food, provisions, e.g., Ship's Chandler. French: Achateur (buyer)
Accipitary	Falcone
Accomptant	Accountant
Accoucheur	Assisted women in childbirth (midwife)
Accoutrement Maker/ Accoutre	Supplier or maker of Military Clothing and Accessories
Ackerman/Acreman	Ploughman or Oxherd
Actuary	Accountant-public business account keeper

Administrator	Court appointee who settled affairs of the estate of the deceased
Advertisement Conveyancer	Sandwich Board Man
Advowee	Usually a nobleman who had the right to present a clergyman to a benefice
Aeronaut	Balloonist or Trapeze Artist in circus or music hall
Affeeror/Assessor	Also Assessor. Manorial Court Official. Assessed monetary penalties and collected taxes and dues
Alabasterer	One who worked with alabaster
Alblastere	Crossbowman
Alderman	Senior Councilor immediately below Mayor in local Councils. (Still extant today.)
Ale-Conner/Ale Founder	Official who tested quality and measure served in Public Houses (pubs)
Ale Draper	Seller of Ale
Ale Tunner	Filled the Ale casks (tuns) in Breweries
Alewife	Woman who kept an Alehouse or Tavern
All Spice	A Grocer
Almoner	In charge of an Almshouse Giver of charity to the needy Hospital employee who assists patients with personal matters arising from their stay in hospital
Almsman	Receiver of Alms
Alnager/Aulnager	Official - examined quality of woolen goods and stamped them with the town seal of approval
Amanuensis	Secretary or stenographer
Amber Cutter	Cut and polished Amber for jewelry
Amen Man	Parish Clerk
Anchor Smith	One who made Anchors
Anchoress	Female hermit or religious recluse
Anchorite	Male hermit or religious recluse
Angle Smith	A blacksmith skilled in forging angle irons, beams, etc., into various forms used in shipbuilding
Ankle Beater	Young person who helped to drive cattle to market
Annatto Maker	Made dyes for paint or printing trades

Annuitant	Receiver of an Annuity - An annuity is income paid to a beneficiary at regular intervals, for a fixed period or ascertainable period (usually the lifetime of a nominee) in return for a lump sum payment having been previously made into the scheme by a subscriber - i.e., a spouse, benefactor, or employer.
Antigropelos Maker	Made waterproof leggings
Anvil Smith	Maker of anvils and hammers for the smithy trade
Apiarian	Beekeeper
Apothecary	Prepared and sold medicines and drugs. Pharmacist
Apparitor	Official who summoned witnesses to the ecclesiastical courts
Apposer	Examiner; officer of the Court of Exchequer
Apprentice	Trainee bound to a skilled (Master) worker or Company for a specified time to learn the Trade
Apronman	Engineer or mechanic
Aquarius Ewar	Waterman
Aquavita Seller	Seller of Alcohol
Arbiter	Arbitrated in disputes
Archiator	Physician
Archil Maker	Made a purple dye from lichens - used in the textile industry
Arkwright	Skilled craftsman making "Arks" (wooden chests or coffers)
Armourer	Made armor for wear or for buildings, ships etc. and now used to include armaments generally
Arrowsmith	Forged arrowheads
Artificer	A military mechanic who does repairs
Artisan	One who is employed in any of the industrial arts; a mechanic, handicraftsman, artificer
Ashman	Dustman - today called a "Cleansing Operative/ Engineer"
Assayer	Determined the proportions of minerals in ore
Assay Master	Determined the amount of gold or silver in coins
Assisor	Scottish juror
Auger Maker	Made carpenters' augers, used for boring holes in wood
Aulnager	See Alnager
Aurifaber	Goldsmith
Avenator (Plantifene)	Hay and forage Merchant

Avowry	Lord of the Manor
Axel Tree Maker / Turner	Made axles for coaches and wagons
Backmaker	Made "Backs" - vats, tubs - a Cooper
Backsmann / Backster / Beck / Becker	Baker
Back-Boy	Kitchen servant - from Back House Boy
Back Tenter	Employed at the back of the weaving looms, clearing away debris. Tenting was a term for watching items or a process. Small children were commonly employed in this dangerous job as they were small enough to work underneath the working loom machinery.
Back Washer	Cleaned wool in worsted manufacture
Badger	Licensed pauper - wore a badge with "P" on it and was restricted to working a defined area (origin of "Badgering") Corn Miller or Dealer Itinerant food trader
Badgy Fiddler	Military boy trumpeter
Bagman	Travelling salesman
Bailie / Bailie / Baillee / Bailiff	Bailiff - Sheriff's Officer, land steward acting for the landowner/landlord. In Scotland, a magistrate of the Burgh - also looked after fishing rights on some rivers
Bairman / Bareman	Pauper or beggar
Bal Maiden	Female mine worker employed on the surface (Pit Brow Lass)
Balancer	Employed in coal mines to operate a system of hauling coal tubs (Balance)
Baler	Baled hay In the mills, one who baled wool or cotton goods
Balister	Archer. Most commonly, a crossbowman
Ballad Monger	Street seller of printed ballad sheets
Ballard Master	In charge of ballasting vessels
Ballast Heaver	Loaded ballast in ships - commonly stone. Necessary when ships were not carrying cargo
Baller / Baller Up	Potter's assistant - measuring out the balls of clay. Also see Cotton Baller
Bandsman	Worked on the ropes and pulleys (bands) in coal pit hoisting arrangements

Bandsmith	Made the bands for barrels
Band Filer	Metalworker in gun making
Bandster	Bound wheat sheaves after harvesting
Bang Beggar	Parish Officer who controlled how long strangers could stay in the Parish
Banker	Dug drainage trenches/ditches, banking up the diggings along the edges General surface worker in coal mining
Banksman / Bank Manager / Browman	In charge of the cages at mine pitheads - sometimes known as a Bank Manager
Bar Collecter	Collected the tolls (road, bridge, etc.) at a Toll Bar
Barber, Barber/ Surgeon	One who cut hair and also served as a surgeon. FYI: In the 18th Century, an Act was passed, limiting Barbers to hair cutting, shaving, dentistry and bloodletting. It should be noted that in the 18th century Barbering was hard work. High-end barbers labored long hours and mastered a range of skills from shaving, cutting, and styling to making and marketing hair and body products. Barbers also typically made and repaired wigs. Even after elites abandoned the powdered wigs of the colonial era around 1800, barbers continued to do a healthy business in toupees as well as false whiskers, although they now fitted these in discreet side rooms. They even groomed the dead. https://www.theatlantic.com/national/archive/2014/01/the-racially-fraught-history-of-the-american-beard/283180/
Bard	Poet or Minstrel
Bareman	Beggar or Pauper
Bargee / Bargeman	Owned or worked on canal barges
Barilla Manufacturer	Made Banilla, obtained from burning saltwort, the resulting sodium salt used in glass & ceramics
Barkeeper	Toll keeper - on toll roads
Barker / Barkman	Tanner of leather using tree bark Fairground cryer
Barleyman / Bylawman	Manorial Court official who enforced the court orders
Barm Brewer	Made yeast
Barmaster	Lead Mine arbiter. In charge of the standard measure for the lead ore
Barrel Filer	Employed in gun making
Barrow Man	Pushed barrows of coal from pit face to the shaft

Bartoner / Barton	In charge of a monastery farm or barton
Basil Worker	Worked with skins of sheep and goats
Basketman	Make wicker baskets & furniture
	Emptied coal baskets into barges
Bass / Bast Dresser	Dressed fiber for matting
Bathing Machine Proprietor	Owned and hired out changing huts used by bathers at the seaside
Batman	Army officers' servant - still current
Batt Maker	Made the wadding (batts) used in quilt and mattress making
Battledore Maker	Made the wicker beaters used on clothes & carpets to beat out the dust. Later made the paddles used in early washing machines
Battery Man	The term 'Battery' is derived from the latin 'Battere', meaning to beat (Old French – 'Batteria'). A 'Brass Battery Mill' is therefore a mill adapted for the manufacture of brass products (hollow-ware) by the beating of brass slabs (naps) using water-driven hammers
Bauer	A Farmer
Baven Maker	Made bavens - split and curled wood pieces used for kindling
Baxter	Baker
Bayweaver	Wove "Bay" (baize) a fine woolen felt like fabric
Bead Piercer	Made the holes in bead making
Beadle / Bedel / Bedell	Town crier and parish officer who kept order
Beadman / Beadsman / Bedesman	Manorial tenant employed for a specific purpose
	Inhabitant of a Poorhouse, Almshouse or Hospital
	Employed to pray for his employer
Beamer	Drew the warp yarn through and onto the long heavy beam of a loom for weaving textiles
Bearer	Carried coal to the pit shaft and placed it in containers for lifting to the surface
Beater / Fuller	Cleaned and thickened cloth by treading it in water with Fuller's Earth
Beatster	Made or mended drift nets used in fishing
Beaver	Made felt for hat making
Bedman	Sexton
Bedwevere	Made webbing for bed frames and also wove quilts

Beer Seller	Sold Beer and Cider in Beerhouses under the 1830 Beerhouse Act
Beeskep Maker	Made beehives
Beetler	Operated the Beetling Machine, used for embossing textiles. The Beetling Machine was also used to give a Shiny effect to cloth as the pressure of the wooden rollers during the squeezing (mangling) of the Cotton Cloth added luster
Belhoste	Tavern keeper
Bell Hanger	Hung bells in church towers
Belleyetere / Belter / Billiter	Bellfounder - bell maker
Bellman	Watchman or town crier Worked for the Post Office, collecting mail by walking the streets ringing a bell Coaches then transported the mail
Bellowfarmer	Maintained the church organ (which was bellows operated)
Belly Builder	Built and fitted piano bellies or interiors
Belly Roller	Operated a machine which rolled and compacted fibers on the belly of cattle hides
Beltman	Changed and maintained the drive belts used in factory machinery
Benchman	In chairmaking, cut out the seat portion
Bender	Leather cutter Bent wooden chair parts
Besom Maker	Broom maker, usually of birch twigs
Besswarden	Appointed by a parish to look after its animals
Biddy	Female servant - usually Irish
Billier / Billyman	Operated a Billy Roller, used to prepare cotton for spinning
Billy Boy	In the '50s and '60s, Billy boys were young apprentices in training that would make tea for the other men at work.
Bill Poster	As today, put up notices, signs and posters
Binder	Bound books, hats, etc.
Bird Boy	Scared away birds from crops
Bird Catcher	Caught birds for sale
Birlyman	Scottish ground officer or parish arbiter

Black Borderer	Made black edged funerary stationery
Black Saddler	Maker of cart and carriage saddlery and harness, and generally work with black leather
Black Tray Maker	Made black (Japanned) trays
Blacksmith	Worked (still does) iron with forge and hammer
Blackworker	Embroidered "blackwork" using black silks on, commonly, white fabric
Blacking Maker	Made boot polish (usually using soot)
Bladesmith	Made swords, knives, etc.
Blaxter / Bleacher / Bleacherer	Bleached cloth or wood pulp for paper in a "Bleachery"
Blemmere	Plumber
Blentonist	Water diviner
Blindsman	Dealt with incorrectly addressed mail for the Post Office
Block Cutter / Blocker	1) Made wooden blocks for hat making
	2)Laid the blocks for laying of a ship's keel in shipbuilding
	3)Cut designs into wooden blocks for printing fabrics
	4)Quarryman, whose job was to cut stone into useable blocks
Block Maker	1) Engraved or set up the blocks used in block printing
	2)Made pulley blocks
	3) Made hatmakers' blocks.
Block Printer	Printed paper or fabrics by the use of inked and carved or engraved wooden blocks
Bloodman / Bloodletter	Used leeches to let blood, thought to be the cure for many ailments. Now being looked at again!
Bloomer / Bloom Smith	Produced iron from iron ore
Blower	1) Glass blower;
	2) Operated a "blowing machine" to clean and separate textile fibres
	3) Operated the blacksmith's bellows
Blowfeeder	Fed the fibers into a blowing machine
Blue Dyer/Maker	Used/made blue dye for whitening fabrics in manufacture or washing
Blue Slater	Split blue roofing slates from rock from the Welsh hills
Bluestocking	Female writer. From the Blue Stocking Society, formed in the 1750s and who wore blue stockings
Bluffer	Innkeeper or pub landlord

Boarder	Term used for a Lodger - usually dined with the family, whilst a Lodger did not
Boarding Officer	Port official who inspects ship's papers on port entry - still exists
Boardman	1) Truant officer for checking school attendance
	2) Manorial tenant who paid rent by maintaining the manor house table
Boardwright	Carpenter. Made tables and chairs
Boatman	1) Worked on river and canal boats
	2) Boat repairer
Boatswain / 'Bosun'	Petty officer in charge of the ship's crew, also the ship's rigging and deck maintenance, responsible to the Chief Officer. Still in use today
Bobber	1) Metal polisher
	2) Unloaded fishing boats
Bobbin Carrier / Bobbiner	Supplied the looms with bobbins in spinning and weaving
Bobbin Ligger	Placed the spools for spinning
Bobbin Turner	Made (lathe turned) the wooden bobbins used in the textile mills
Bobby	Police constable - still used today. (Colloquial)
Bodeys / Body Maker	Made the bodices for women's garments
Bodger	A skilled craftsman who made wooden chair legs and spars using a lathe set up in homemade workshops in deep woodlands. His work was often produced for chair factories
Boilermaker	Industrial metalworker
Boiler Plater	Made rolled steel/iron plate for steam engine boilers, etc.
Boll	Power loom attendant
Bolter	Sifted meal
Bondager	Bonded female farm worker
Bondman	As for Apprentice - bonded to his Master to learn a skill or trade
Bondsman	Stood the bond or surety for a bonded person
Bone Lace Maker	Made pillow lace
Bone Mould Turner	Made the molds for button making
Bone Picker	Rag & Bone Man. Collected rags and bones (originally) later any discarded articles / metal
Bonesetter	Set broken bones

Boniface	Innkeeper
Book Gilder	Gilded book bindings with gold leaf
Bookholder	Theatre prompter
Book Edge Marbler	Decorated the edges of pages in bound books
Book Keeper	As today, looked after business accounts
Bookman	Student
Boonmaster	Surveyed, maintained and repaired roads
Bootbinder	Operated machines in shoemaking, binding uppers to soles
Boot Catcher	Servant at an Inn who pulled off travelers' boots
Boot Clicker	See Clicker
Boot Closer	Stitched the shoe uppers to the soles
boot polisher	Other synonyms are bootblack and shoeblack. See Shoeshiner
Boothman	Corn Merchant
Borler / Boreler	Maker of borel - cheap coarse woolen cloth
Borsholder	Kent regional name for a police constable
Botcher	Tailor or cobbler
Bottiler / Bottler	1) A person who made leather containers for holding liquids, e.g., wine flasks or water bottles. From the turn of the 17th century it would more likely refer to a worker in a bottling factory for beer, soft drinks, water, etc.
	2) In Punch & Judy shows that travelled from town to town in England, the person who collected money from the watching public. They called them "Bottlers" as they used a glass bottle with a narrow neck so that the bottle could not be tipped upside down to take money out easily.
Bottle Boy	Pharmacist's assistant
Bottomer	Adzed out the finished seat from the rough shape in wooden chair making
Bottom Knocker	Sagger Maker's assistant - See Sagger Maker's Bottom Knocker
Bottom Maker	Moulded the bottoms for Saggers in the pottery industry
Boundary Setters / Layers	Employed by the Board of Ordnance (Ordnance Survey) for setting out and plotting important boundaries used in map-making
Bowdler	Worked with iron ore
Bowler	Maker of bowls and dishes
	Made the bowls of spoons before casting

Bowlman/woman	Crockery dealer
Bowlminder	In charge of vats in which raw wool were washed before processing
Bow Maker	Made bows for use around Oxens' neck - used to adjoin two Oxen during farming Made string bows for musical instruments
Bowyer / Bower	Made archery bows
Box Shook Maker	See Shook Maker
Bozzler	Parish constable
Brabener	Weaver
Brachygrapher	Shorthand writer
Bradish Man	A carpenter working in mines; the Bradish Man was responsible for ensuring a steady flow of clean air is cycled past the working face (especially of coal). He achieved this by closing off old shafts with well-sealed wooden doors.
Braider	Made cord by twisting cords or leather
Brailler	Made girdles
Brakeman / Brakesman	Operated pithead winding gear Operated brakes on trains or trams
Brancher	Colliery worker who cuts at the coal face, particularly a new seam or 'branch' from the road
Brasiater	Brewed Ale
Brasiler	Dyer
Bratman	Made rough garments
Brazier	Worked with brass
Breakman / Brickman	Bricklayer
Breech Maker	Made the breeches for guns
Brewster	Brewer
Bricksetter	Worked in a brick works. He worked in the kilns, stacking or 'setting' the bricks ready for firing
Brick Burner	Maintained the firing temperature in a brick kiln
Bridewell Keeper	In charge of a lock-up or jail
Bridgeman / Bridger	Toll bridge keeper
Brightsmith	Metal worker
Brimstone Refiner	Refined sulphur, one of the components of gunpowder
Broadcloth Weaver	Wide(broad)loom operator

Broad Cooper	Go-between for breweries and innkeepers
Brogger	Wool merchant
Broker	Essentially a salesman or middleman to a supplier for arranging sales
Broom Dasher	Broom dealer
Broom Squire	Broom Maker
Brotherer/Broiderer/ Broderer/Browderer	Embroiderer
Brow Girl	Female employed at the pithead
Brown Saddler	Maker of riding saddles
Brownsmith	Worked with copper or brass
Brush Drawer	Fixed the bristles into the stock or handle of a brush
Brush Stock / Stale Maker	Made the handles for brushes
Buckler / Bucklesmith	Made belt buckles
Buckle Tongue Maker	Made the pointed part of a belt buckle
Buckram Maker	Made buckram - used for stiffening lapels, collars, cloth belts, etc.
Buck Washer	Laundress
Buddleboy	Used and maintained ore-washing vats in lead and tin mining
Buddler	Women and children employed washing ore
Bullwhacker	Oxen driver
Bum Bailiff	An officer of the court who went to a convicted person's home or business premises and seized goods in lieu of payment of a fine, in default
Bumboat Man	Seller of goods and foodstuffs from boats to ships at anchor (Typically Suez Canal)
Bummaree	Fish market middlemen - between wholesalers and retailers
Bummer	Army deserter
Bunter	Female rag & bone collector
Bureler	Maker of Borel, a rough woolen cloth
Burgess	Represented a borough official at functions
Burler	Clothing quality inspector
Burleyman / Byelawman	Manorial court official who enforced the court orders
Burmaiden	Chambermaid or lady in waiting
Burneman	Carrier of barm or water for brewers

Burye Man	Grave digger - (bury man)
Bushel Maker	Cooper
Busheler	Tailor's helper
Busker	Hair Dresser
Buss Maker	Gunsmith
Butner	Button maker
Butter Carver	Prepared butter for sale
Butty	Supplied labor to mines and negotiated contracts
Cab Driver / Cabbie / Cabman	Driver of a horse-drawn passenger vehicle for hire. The first two are still in current use for a taxi driver
Cad	Fed and watered horses at coaching inns
Caddie	Messenger or errand boy
Caddy Butcher	Butcher dealing in horse meat
Cafender	Carpenter
Caffeler / Caffler	Rag & Bone man
Cainer	Walking stick maker
Caird	Tinker
Calciner	Made powdered lime from burning bones
Calculator	18th century term for a mathematician engaged in computing tables, such as the annual Nautical Alamanac used by navigators in the calculation of astronomical observations. An extremely laborious occupation!
Calender	A person who listed documents (filing?)
Calenderer / Calenderman	"Calender" operator. A machine used to press and finish fabrics or paper between rollers.
Calico Printer	Dyed, colored and printed calico
Calker	Person who caulks or seals buildings or ships.
Caller Off / Caller Out	Loads and unloads trucks in a goods depot; calls out particulars of incoming and outgoing consignments, from labels on goods, to goods checkers in preparation for their removal from platform or wagon by goods porters
Cambist / Cambrist	Dealer in bills of exchange - financial expert Banker
Cambric Maker	Made cambric, a fine cotton or linen fabric
Camister	Minister of the cloth
Camlet Merchant	Sold "camlet" - cloth used in making petticoats and cloaks
Canal Porter	Loaded and unloaded canal barges

Canal Puddler	During canal construction, 'puddled' layers of clay on the sides and bottom of the canal to waterproof it
Cannaller	Canal boat worker
Cancellarius	Chancellor - from Latin
Candler	Candle maker
Caner / Chair Bottomer	Made woven cane chair seats
Canter / Cantor	Beggar Religious speaker, chanter
Canting Caller	Auctioneer
Canvaser	Canvas maker
Caper / Capper	Cap maker
Capillaire Maker	Made orange flavored syrup
Capitalist	Investor, providing capital for commerce
Cardroomer	Worker in the carding room of cotton/woolen mills
Carder	Person who cards or separates the fibers of raw wool to prepare it for spinning Carded (combed - a skilled job) wool or cotton
Card Maker	1) Made the combs and implements for carding (combing) wool
	2) Made the loom-cards used by Jacquard looms in the weaving of figured fabrics
Card Master	In charge of the carding room in a cotton/woolen mill
Card Sharp	Someone who is skillful at playing or manipulating cards, an expert card gambler who takes advantage of less-skilled players
Carman/Charman/ Carrier/ Carter/ Cartman	Driver of (horse-drawn) vehicles for transporting goods. Carmen were often employed by railway companies for local deliveries and collections of goods and parcels. Modern day van driver. A Carter typically drove a light two wheeled carriage. Also sometimes someone who drove horse-drawn trams was called a Carman.
Card Nailer / Nailorer	Maintained the teeth (nails) on the carding machine used on wool & cotton before weaving
Carnifex	Butcher
Carpentarius	Carpenter - from Latin
Carter	Carrier of goods by wagon
Cart Wheeler	Cart wheel maker
Cartographer	Mapmaker - as today

Cartomancer	Fortune teller using cards
Cartwright	Made carts and wagons
Case Hardener	Heat treats steel to harden its surface
Cashmarie	Fish seller - usually in inland markets
Caster / Castorer	Made small bottles for sprinkling salt, pepper, sugar, etc.
Castrator / Gelder	Castrated farm animals
Catagman	Cottager (phonetic)
Catchpole / Catchpoller	Bailiff or Sheriff's assistant
Catechist	Religious teacher - from catechism
Cats Meat Man	Sold meat from a barrow for cats and dogs
Cattle Jobber	Bought and sold cattle
Caulker	Filled up cracks in ships, casks, windows or seams to make them watertight by using tar or oakum hemp fiber produced by taking old ropes apart
Causey Dresser	"Dressed" or shaped cobbles used in cobbled streets
Ceiler	Installed ceilings
Cellarman	As today, looked after beer & spirits & its dispensing equipment in pubs or warehouses
Cemmer	Hand combed yarn prior to weaving
Ceramist	A craftsman who shapes pottery on a potter's wheel and bakes it in a kiln
Chaff Cutter	Cut straw to make chaff
Chafferer	Dealer in chaff
Chairman	One of two persons who carried a sedan chair
Chair bodger	Travelling chair repairer
Chair Turner	Turned the legs and spindles used in chair making often turned on rough "bodgers" - lathes - as a cottage industry- common in Buckinghamshire
Chaise Driver	Drove a chaise - a two-wheeled open horse-drawn carriage for one or two persons
Chaisemaker	Carriage or cart maker
Chamberlain	Steward in charge of administration of the household of royalty or nobility. One of the four main officers of the court, he controlled access to the King
Chamber Master	Shoemaker working from home or selling to the public

Chandler	Dealer or trader
	Maker or seller of candles
	Retailer of groceries - esp. to ships
Chanty Man	The leader in singing sea shanties aboard ship
Chapeler	Hat maker and seller - from French "chapeau"
Chapman / Copeman / Ceapman	13th century – 16th century Itinerate Trader/Peddler
	Merchant - in the 17/18th century, before the advent of factories, a Chapman would invest in the raw materials of the cotton, woolen or silk trade, put out the work to spinners and weavers at home on piece-rates, and sell the product for profit - the term later became used for an itinerant peddler of goods in the 19th century
Charcoal Burner	Made charcoal from burning, usually on the site of felling the trees
Chartmaster	Negotiated mining contracts and supplied the labor
Charwoman	A woman hired by the day to do odd jobs, usually cleaning, in a house - as still used today and in use as early as 1596. The word "chare" or "char" was used to describe an odd job
Chaser	An engraver
Chaunter	Street entertainer (singer)
Cheese Factor / Monger Cheeseman	Cheese dealer
Check Weaver	A weaver who used a loom that used more than one shuttle, each of which had a different colored bobbin in order to produce checked cloth
Chevener	Embroidered fine silk stockings, popular with the Victorians
Chiffonnier	Wig maker
Chimney Sweep	Chimney cleaner
Chinglor	Tiled roofs with wooden shingles (shingler)
Chippy	Carpenter - esp. Ship's carpenter or shipwright
Chirugeon / Chirurgeon	Apothecary or surgeon
Chowder	Fishmonger
Chronologist	Recorder of important historical events
Cinder Wench	Female who collected cinders from factories for sale door to door

City Meter	Weights and Measures inspector's assistant, checking both the weights of goods as sold and the accuracy of the metal weights used. Some specialized - such as in Coal Meters, etc.
Claker	Magician / Astrologer
Clapman	Town Crier
Clay carrier	Assistant to the shot firer in the pits
Clay Puddler	Made the waterproof clay lining used on canals and dams. Mixing water with clay, they worked it with their feet until it became smooth and waterproof
Clayman / Cleyman	Prepared clay for brick making Rendered buildings with clay to waterproof them
Clergyman without cure of Souls	A clergyman without his own parish (without cure - care - of souls). Getting a Parish with sufficient income when there were more Clergy than Parishes wasn't always possible
Clicker	Foreman printer who looked after the typography and layout; Shoe-maker who cut out the leather for making the uppers The servant of a salesman who stood at the door to invite in customers
Clipper/ on/off	Attached coal carts to the line hauling them from the coal face to the lifts
Clod Hopper	Ploughman
Cloth Dresser / Cropper	Worked in the woolen industry, cutting the cloth surface after it had left the fulling mill
Cloth Lapper	Moved the yarn from the carding machine to the next process in weaving
Cloth Layer	In garment manufacturing, laid out cloth in layers on a long table, checking for evenness and for defects
Cloth Linter or Picker	Removed surplus thread and lint from the finished woven cloth
Cloth Looker	An inspector of finished woven cloth. Also remedied slight defects and applied 'padding' to remove oil spots
Clothier / Clothesman / Clothman	person who makes or sells clothing or cloth Made or sold clothing
Clouter / Clower	Nail maker Shoe maker

Club Collector	The "Club Man" called door to door on a weekly basis to collect payments for clothing, burial or Christmas Clubs
Coachstand Waterman	Watered horses at a coach or cab stand and looked after them in the absence of the drivers
Coach Trimmer	Finished of the building of a coach with painting, upholstery, etc.
Coal Backer	Carried coal from barges to the coal wagons - on their backs.
Coal Burner	Charcoal maker
Coal Dealer / Merchant	Dealer and seller of coal - mainly to domestic customers. Still used today
Coal Drawer	Moved coal carts in the mine
Coal Heaver	Unloaded coalmine carts on the surface
Coalman / Coal Higgler	Sold coal to householders, usually by horse & cart
Coalmeter	Measured the coal
Coal Runner	Attended coal carts in the mines
Coal Whipper	Unloaded coal from ships using baskets
Coast Waiter/Surveyor	Customs Official attending unloading of ships
Cobbler	Shoemaker/repairer - as today
Cobbleman	Fisherman using a cobble - flat bottom boat
Cockfeeder	Looked after fighting cocks
Cocus	A name for someone who worked as a cook, a seller of cooked meats, or a keeper of an eating-house
Cod Placer	Placed fireproof containers, holding pottery being fired, into the kiln
Cohen	Priest
Coiner	Mint employee making coins
Collegeman	Works on 'colleges' - flat bottomed barges
Collier	Coal mine worker or coal barge worker. Term still used today
Colliery Doorkeeper	Doorkeepers or "trappers", opened and closed the ventilation doors to let coal pass. Often young boys were employed in this position
Colonus	Farmer or husbandman - from Latin
Colour Man	Mixed textile dyes
	House painter's assistant
Colourator / Colorator	Worked with dyes
Colporteur	Peddler of religious books

Colt	Worker who has not served an apprenticeship. Particularly applied to women and children in the knitting trade during the 1811-1812 Luddite troubles
Comber / Combere	Combed wool or cotton
Comb Maker	Comb maker for: textile industry hair
Commissionaire	Uniformed doorman at a hotel, theatre, etc. Member of the Corps of Commissionaires, a 3,500 strong team of professionals including many drawn from the military, police and emergency services - still in use (in 2002)
Commission Agent	Salesman who derives his income solely from commission on sales
Compositor	Set type for printing - as today, but now giving way to the computer
Computor / Computer	A person employed in computation of accounts, data etc. During World War II, so-called human computers were used to perform complex mathematical equations. Human computers were also used by NASA in the mid-1900s.
Conder / Conner	1) Gave steering instructions to helmsman Directed inshore fisherman towards fish shoals from ashore Conner - Inspector or tester
Coney Catcher	Rabbit catcher
Confectioner	Person who makes and sells candy
Confinement Nurse	An attending woman during the first month after childbirth. Also known as 'Monthly Nurse'. May also have the initials S.M.S. (Subsidiary Medical Services. i.e., not a doctor, but trained in some way)
Cooper / Cuper	Made or repaired vessels made of wooden staves & hoops, such as casks, barrels, tubs, etc.
Cop Fitter	Fitted "cops" to the looms. A cop is a cone onto which the yarn is wound after spinning, ready for weaving on the loom
Coppice Dealer	Woodsman supplying coppice wood to local craftsmen
Coprolite Digger	Coprolite is fossilised animal dung and was found in Cambridgeshire, between Soham and Royston, and mined out between 1850 and 1890. Ground down and treated with acid, it made an excellent fertiliser

Coracle Maker	Made small round wicker and fabric inshore boats called Coracles
Core Maker	Formed sand molds and cores for the production of metal castings
Cordwainer / Cordiner / Corviner / Corvisor	Shoemaker. Originally, a leather worker using high quality Cordovan leather from Spain for such things as harness, gloves and riding boots. By the 19th century it had reduced to a shoemaker - as distinct from a cobbler, who repaired shoes
Cork Cutter	Worked with cork; mainly stoppers for bottles - in England from the 17th to 19th Century
Corn Chandler	Corn Merchant
Corn Factor	Middleman in corn dealing
Core Maker	Used 'greensand', a mix of clay and wet sand, to form basic molds for brass casting
Corn Meter	Official who weighed and weighed the corn at market
Cornet	The lowest commissioned rank in a cavalry regiment, who carried the colors
Corporation Sworn Weigher	Checked and counted sacks of grain on the docks
Corver	Made baskets, known as Corves, used in coal mining
Costermonger / Coster Wife	Peddler of fruits and vegetables Ditto, female
Cotiler / Coteler / Cotyler	Cutler - maker or dealer in cutlery
Cottager / Cottar / Cotter / Cottier	Agricultural laborer, living in a landowner's farm cottage
Cotton Baller	Wound cotton thread into balls on a special balling machine. These were used in 'Ball Warping', the oldest system of warping, not much used today
Cotton Dresser	Operator who assembled the yarns or threads prior to weaving of cloth
Cotton Feeder	Was employed feeding the cotton into a carding machine, which roughly straightened the fibers prior to spinning
Cotton Piecer	Re-connected the yarns which broke on the spinning mule
Cotton Rover	Loaded cotton yarn onto bobbins, giving the yarn a twist, (Roving) after the Carding and Combing processes
Cotton Singer	(Meaning singe-er) Tends a machine that singes the nap or lint from cloth

Cotton Yarn Gasser	A person who worked in the "gas-room" where raw cotton was de-fumigated
	A person who applied gas to finished cotton threads to smooth them
Coucher	Worker in the paper mills
Countour	Collected rates
Couper	Buyer and seller, usually of livestock
Couranteer	Journalist - from French
Court Factor	Dealer in Courts - small carts
Court Roller	In charge of the rolls and records of the court
Court Toolmaker	Made the tools for making Courts - small carts
Courtier	Owner/driver of Courts - small carts
Cow Leech	Animal Doctor
Coxwain	Helmsman of a ship or boat - still in use
Crate Maker	In the S Derbyshire potteries - wove crates from hazel and willow saplings for the transport of pottery
Crepe Weaver	Wove a cloth called Crepe a light, thin fabric with a wrinkled surface - in the Victorian era, crepe was worn by ladies in mourning and there was a big demand for it
Crier	Town Crier
	Auctioneer
	Law court officer
Crimper	Member of a Navy press gang
Crocker	Potter
Crofter	Tenant farmer of a croft - small piece of land - still in use
	Also connected with bleaching of textiles - see Crofters
Croft Bleacher	Worked bleaching cloth prior to dyeing and spreading it out in enclosed fields, or "crofts." See Crofters
Cropper	Tenant farmer who was paid with a share of the crop
	Also known as a shearman, a skilled textile worker who sheared the nap from the cloth
Crossing Sweeper	Swept ahead of people crossing dirty urban streets in exchange for a gratuity, creating a path that was referred to as a "broom walk." This was an informal 19th century occupation amongst the urban poor.

	The predominance of horse-drawn vehicles—and the general uncleanliness of urban streets entailed certain difficulties in crossing intersections. For example, the long dresses of many elite women might easily be soiled by horse droppings, amongst other forms of refuse.
Crowner	Coroner- an official who investigates violent, sudden, or suspicious deaths
Cupper	Worked in the potteries, making cups
Curer	Tobacco Curer
Curretter	Broker
Currier	Dressed the coat of a horse with a curry comb

Tanned leather by incorporating oil or grease |
Customer	Customs tax collector
Cutterman	Operated coal face cutting machinery
Cutler	Knife maker/seller/sharpener
Cutlooker/Clothlooker	One who inspects the weaver's cut or piece of cloth as it comes from the loom
Cycle	Various occupations in the Bicycle Making Trade
Daguerreotype Artist	Early photographer - derived from Daguerre's method
Damster	Dam builder - for logging
Danter	Female overseer in silk winding room
Dateler/Dataller/Day Man/ Daytaleman/Day Labourer	Casual worker, employed on a daily basis
Dauber/Dawber	Made Wattle & Daub walls using "Lute", a tenacious clay
Day-maid	Dairymaid
Deathsman	An executioner
Decoyman	Decoyed wild fowl, animals, into a trap or within shooting range
Decretist	Knowledgeable in decrees (decretals)
Deemer/Deemster/ Dempster/Demster	Judge
Delfsman / Delphman	Worker in quarries or open pits, usually quarrying stone
Delver	Ditch digger - also a worker in a stone quarry
Dental Mechanic	Made false teeth - a very skilled job. (Mechanic meant a craftsman or artisan)
Depater	Refined precious metals
Deputy	Pit workers' safety officer

Devil	Printer's errand boy
Deviller	Operated a "devil" - a machine that tore rags in the textile industry
Dexter	Dyer
Dey Wife	Female dairy worker
Die Sinker	When forging metals, lays out, machines, and finishes impression cavities in die blocks to produce forging dies, following blueprints and applying knowledge of die sinking
Digger	Coal face worker Day laborer in slate of stone quarries
Dikeman / Dykeman	Ditch digger or hedger
Dipper	Glazed goods in the pottery
Disher / Dish Thrower	Made bowls and dishes from clay
Dish Turner	Made wooden bowls and dishes on a lathe
Distributor	Parish official who attended to the secular needs of inmates of the poorhouse / workhouse
Docker / Dock Walloper	Stevedore, dock worker who loads and unloads cargo
Dock Foyboatman	A shore-based seaman who worked a "foy" to give assistance to vessels entering port - running lines from the ship to shore, towing small vessels, etc. Foy is a corruption of fee, which was what the boatman charged
Docket Room Hand	Employed in a print works, processing the dockets which contain all the details, copy and pictures for a print job
Dockmaster	In charge of a dockyard
Doffer	Worked in the spinning mills, replacing the full yarn bobbins with empties on the looms
Dog Breaker	Dog trainer
Dog Killer	Employed by the parish to round up and kill stray dogs
Dog Leech	Veterinarian
Dog-Whipper	Drove dogs away from the church. The dogs would be attracted by the custom of nailing fox tails to the church door as proof for collecting bounty on them
Domesman	Judge
Dominie	Cleric or schoolmaster
Donkey Man/Boy	Passenger carriage driver
Dorcas	Seamstress

Doubler	Operated a machine twisting yarn in cotton/woolen mills. The yarn on different bobbins is combined onto another bobbin
Dowser / Diviner	Finds water using a rod or witching stick
Dragman	Fisherman who dragged a net along the seabed (trawling)
Dragoman	Interpreter for Turkish or Arabic
Dragoon	Cavalryman
Dragsman	Public transport/hire coach/carriage driver
Drainer	Dug drains
Draper	Dealer in fabrics and sewing goods - in use today. From the French "drap-de-Berry", a woolen cloth coming from Berry in France
Drapery Painter	Second-rate painters employed painting the clothes (drapery) onto a painter's subject
Draughtsmen	drafts·man a person who makes detailed technical plans or drawings an artist skilled in drawing. a person who drafts legal documents
Drawboy	Weaver's assistant - sat on the looms to lift the heavy warps
Drawer	Made wire by drawing the metal through a die Raised the coal up the mineshaft
Drawer In	Draws the warp yarn through loom parts to arrange warp for weaving specified pattern
Drayman	Drove a long strong cart without fixed sides for carrying heavy loads, such as beer kegs
Dresser	A surgeon's assistant in a hospital Operator who assembled the yarns or threads prior to weaving of cloth Assistant to a noble person, preparing clothes, etc. In an Iron Foundry, the person who removed the flash and unwanted bits from castings
Dressing Machine Maker	Sewing machine maker
Drift Maker	Made fishermen's drift nets

Drillman	Agricultural worker who operated a seed drill
Dripping Man	Dealer in dripping - fat from cooking meat
Driver	Literally, a slave driver
	On large plantations, the person who directed the daily work of the slaves was the overseer, usually a white man but occasionally an enslaved black man—a "driver"
Drover	Drove cattle, sheep, etc., to market; a dealer in cattle
Drowner	A Waterman who understood the secrets of irrigation
Drugger	Pharmacist
Drum Battledore Maker	Made galvanized drums with battledores (bat-shaped paddles), used as washing machines
Drummer	Travelling salesman (drumming up business)
Dry Salter	Dealt in dried meat, sauces, pickles
	Dealt in dyes for fabrics, etc.
Dry Stone Waller / Dry Stane Dyker (Scottish)	Builds walls with stones from the fields. The art involves no mortar or cutting, but the ability to see where the stones should fit. Served the dual purpose of disposing of the stones from the fields and building the boundary walls
Dubber	Cloth dubber - raised the nap of cloth
Duffer	Peddler of cheap goods
Dunner	Debt collector
Dyer	Fabric dyer
Dykeman	Hedger or Ditcher
Dyker	(Scottish) Stonemason
Earer	Ploughman
Earth stopper	Stopped up animal burrows - i.e., a fox's earth before the hunt
East India Man	Employee of the East India Company - either commercially or militarily
Edge Toolmaker	Maker of knives, scythes - cutting tools
Eggler / Egg Factor	Egg / poultry dealer
Elevator Operator	Elevators didn't always move with the simple push of a button. In the US prior to the 1960s, elevator operators were in charge of controlling everything from the doors and direction to the speed and capacity of the elevator car.
Elephants Teeth Dealer	Ivory dealer
Ellerman / Ellyman	Sold lamp oil (oilman)

Elymaker	Oil maker
Empresario	Showman
	Land broker
	Settlement scheme promoter
Engineman	In charge of colliery winding machinery under the direction of the Bankman
Engine Smith	Made parts for and repaired engines using the tools of a Smith - similar work to that of a Blacksmith.
Engine Tenter	Oversaw the operation of the steam engine driving factory machinery
	Operated woolen mill machinery stretching cloth whilst drying
Engine Turner	Engraver who produced overlapping geometric (engine turned) patterns on such items as cigarette cases, ladies' compacts, etc.
Enumerator	Collected and recorded census data from households
Esquire	Knight's companion - the term later referred to a gentleman of standing
Estafette	Mounted courier - from French
Eweherd	Shepherd
Exchequer	Revenue collector - Chancellor of the Exchequer is an important English Government post today, setting the National budget
Exciseman	Tax collector
Expressman	A Messenger. He would collect and deliver letters, packages or parcels that needed quick service
Eyer	Made the holes in sewing needles. Also called a Holer
Faber	Workman or Artisan
Factor	Agent transacting business for merchants
	Sold goods on commission
	(Scottish) Steward collecting land rents
Fagetter	Firewood seller - made bundles of faggots
Faker	Photographer's assistant - added hand coloring to monochrome photographs before color film was invented
Fakir / Faker	Street salesman, seller, hawker, vendor or peddler
Fancy Man	A pimp
Fancy Woman	A prostitute

Fancy-pearl Worker	Made items, such as buttons, from mother-of-pearl
Fanner	Grain winnower
Fanwright	Made or repaired fans or winnowing baskets
Farandman	Travelling merchant
Farm Bailiff	Made sure a tenant farmer ran the farm properly and was paying the rent on time. If not the bailiff had the authority to evict
Farrier	A blacksmith who shoes horses Horse Doctor Cavalry NCO responsible for horses
Fawkner/Faulkner	Falconer
Faunist	Naturalist
Fear-Nought Maker	Made thick woolen material called fear-nought for protective clothing and lining insides the powder magazines of warships
Feather Beater/Driver/ Dresser	Cleaned feathers for sale
Feather Mason	Split stone using curved metal 'feathers' with wedges hammered between them.
Feather Wife	Woman who cleaned feathers for sale
Featherman	Dealer in feathers
Feeder	Herdsman
Feller	Woodcutter
Fellmonger	Dealer in hides and skins , also recycled inedible animal parts for glue, fertilizer, offal, horn, bone, gut, etc. Basically, he ran the "knacker's yard." Tree cutter / woodsman
Felter	Worked with felt - normally in the hat trade
Fender Smith	Made and maintained fenders surrounding fires
Fent Dealer	Dealer in "Fents" - cloth remnants, ends of bolts of cloth, etc.
Feroner	Ironmonger or a person who sells hardware such as tools and household implements
Ferreter	Made or dealt in "ferret" - silk tape
Ferur / Ferator	Blacksmith / Farrier
Festitian	Physician

Fettler	Cleaned mill machinery, removing accumulations of fibers, grease, etc. and sharpened fustian cutters' knives
	Needle maker who filed the points
Fever	Blacksmith
Fewster	Made wooden saddle trees – the "chassis" upon which a leather saddle is constructed
Fewterer	Looked after the hounds used in hunting or hare coursing
Feydur (Feather) Beater	Feather beater
Fictor	Modeller
Fiddler	Used a fiddle (small knife) to remove the flashing from cast clay forms such as bowls, creamers, cups or pitchers
Field Master	Inspected hedges and fences of a parish and also impounded stray animals
	Tended fields set aside to produce hay. Also, Hayward
File Cutter	Made files by cutting rows of sharp teeth into a metal blank
Filler	Filled bobbins in textile mills
Fine Drawer	Invisible mender (clothing)
Firemen (Salt Industry)	The men responsible for stoking the furnaces so as to maintain the brine at the correct temperature during the salt making period, which might be a few hours at high temperature for fine salt or several days at lower temperatures for the coarser types. Highly skilled work.
Fireman (Train, Ship)	The person (almost always a man) shoveling fuel (coal or wood) into the engine's firebox. On US steamships and stationary steam engines, such as those driving sawmills, the term was usually a 'stoker' (the British Merchant Navy used fireman).
Fireworker	18th century. Maker of fireworks. A very dangerous occupation - they often actually smoked when working with gunpowder!
Fire Beater	A factory worker who tended fires related to factory boilers. May also be referred to as a Fireman.
First Hand	Silk weaver who owned his own loom. Early silk weaving was largely done in the home
Fiscere	Fisherman - Anglo-Saxon term
Fish Bobber	Landed the fish from trawlers to the quay side
Fish Fag	Female fish seller

Fitter	Coal broker
	Early term for a Joiner
	From 19th century a skilled mechanic
Flagger	Lays paving stones, etc. also called a Paver or Paviour
Flagger & Tiler	Laid roofing tiles and the rectangular stone flags used in some parts of the country for roofing
Flasher	Specialist worker in glass making
Flatman / Floatman	Boatman on a flat bottom boat (a flat) used in shallow waters (mainly rivers and canals) for transport. The term also came to refer to shallow-draft coastal sailing vessels.
Flauner	Confectioner
Flax Dresser	Person who breaks and swingles flax or prepares it for the spinner.
Flax Scutcher	Separated the husk from the flax fibers by holding it against rotating paddles
Flesher / Fleshmonger	Tannery worker
	Butcher
Fleshewer	Butcher
Fletcher	Made arrows - from French, flèche
Floater	Vagrant
Flowering Muslin	Embroidery
Flusherman	Cleaned out water pipes
Fly Coachman / Flyman / Fly Proprietor/Master	Drove a "fly" a one horse, two wheeled light carriage
	Flyman also a term for a theatre stage hand
	A Fly Proprietor/Master employed fly drivers for hire and usually owned the flys
Fly Forger / Maker	A drop forger who stamped out parts of 'flyers' for textile spinning machinery.
Flying Stationer	Street broadsheet (newspaper) seller
Fogger / Pettifogger	Peddler
	Middleman in the nail and chain trade
	Agricultural laborer who fed cattle
	Low class lawyer or "Pettifogger"
Foister / Foisterer / Fuyster	Joiner
Foot-Post	Mail carrier (on foot)

Foot Straightener	Made watch and clock dials
Forester	Looked after woods, normally on gentleman's estate, or major local forest
Forgeman / Forger	Blacksmith or his assistant In 18th century Derbyshire - Coachsmith
Forkner	Falconer (phonetic)
Form Fitter	Fitted "forms" for building, i.e., formwork for arch building.
Fossetmaker	Made (wooden) taps for ale casks
Founder	Foundryman - casts metal i.e., iron, brass
Fower	Sweeper, street cleaner
Foyboatman	A shore-based seaman who worked a "foy" to give assistance to vessels entering port - running lines from the ship to shore, towing small vessels etc. Foy is a corruption of fee, which was what the boatman charged
Frame Spinner	Tended a machine for spinning cotton threads - a Spinning Frame
Framer	Constructed the wooden frames of buildings, also in chair making
Framework Knitter (FWK)	Operated a hosiery making loom (Abbreviated FWK in census returns)
Freedman	A freed slave
Freeholder	Land owner
Freeman	Held the full rights of citizenship, such as voting and engaging in business, free of feudal service - a man who had served his apprenticeship and who could then work at his trade in his own right
Freemason	Stone mason
Freshwaterman	Sailed on inland or coastal waters
Friezer	Friezed cloth (i.e., embroidery with silver or gold)
Frieser	Made rough plaster known as friese, also any strip pattern which repeats itself in some way and used in castings such as are used in decorative gates, railings, etc.
Fringemaker	Made ornamental borders or fringes in cloth making
Fripperer	Bought and sold old clothes and fripperies
Friseur	Hairdresser
Frobisher / Furbisher	Cleaned and polished metal – i.e., armor
Fruitestere	Female fruit seller
Fulker	Pawnbroker

Fuller / Tucker / Walker	One who "fulls" cloth; the process of cleaning (removing the natural oils and lanolin) wool in preparation for spinning and weaving, using fuller's earth. In medieval times, this involved treading the cloth in stale urine for some 8 hours.
Fulling Miller	Milled Fuller's Earth for fulling woolen cloth (above)
Fumigator	During the great plague, Fumigators were employed to disinfect houses by burning sulphur, saltpeter and urine. Presumably the smell would kill the germs!
Funambulist	Tightrope walker
Furner	Baker
Fustian Cutter / Weaver	A person who lifted and cut the threads in the making of Fustian, formerly a kind of coarse cloth made of cotton and flax. Now a thick, twilled cotton cloth with a short pile or nap, a kind of cotton velvet. A long thin knife was inserted into the loops and the threads cut as it was pulled through, stretched between rollers. The cloth was then brushed to raise the pile. Fustian is the old name for corduroy / A weaver of Fustian
Fustian Loom Jobber	Otherwise known as a Tackler, he serviced and maintained the Fustian looms
Gabeler	Tax collector
Gaffer	Foreman
Gaffman	Bailiff
Gager / Gauger	Collector of alcohol taxes. Measured capacity of barrels to calculate the duty
Galloon Maker	Made a decorative woven trim commonly made of metallic gold or silver thread, lace, or embroidery. Galloon is used in the trim of military and police uniforms, ecclesiastical dress, and as trim on textiles, drapery, and upholstery.
Gamester	Gambler
Gandy Dancer	A Gandy Dancer actually has nothing to do with movin' your hips. The title is slang for a railroad worker who maintained the tracks years before the work was done by machines. However, you can still find some of these workers alive and well at major railroads. https://www.goodhousekeeping.com/life/g4530/odd-obsolete-jobs/?slide=5
Ganger / Gangsman	Overseer / foreman - from mid-18th century.
Ganneker	Innkeeper
Gaoler	A keeper of the gaol, a jailer

Garthman	Fisherman using fish traps Yardman or herdsman Maintained a "garth" or dam on the river for catching fish
Gas Maker	Made gas by heating coal to produce gas, which was purified to remove the tar. The coal would be turned into coke. The gas could be used for lighting, heating or powering a gas engine. The tar was used in road surfacing.
Gas Manager	In charge of detecting dangerous gases in mines
Gasser	See Cotton Yarn Gasser
Gater	Watchman
Gatherer	Glassworker. Inserted the blow iron into molten glass ready for the blower
Gatherer's Boy	Assistant who shielded the gatherer's face from the furnace with a shovel
Gatward	Goatkeeper
Gaunter	Glove maker
Gaveller	In the Forest of Dean - Crown officer granting "gales" - the right to work a mine In Suffolk - Female (usually) harvest worker Usurer
Gelder	Animal castrator
GP / General Practitioner	Local medical doctor, a term used today
Gentleman	Believe it or not; this job title actually had an occupation code in the 1880 US census. Gentry; Aristocrat, whose income came from his land
Gentry	Families of hereditary rank - the baronets and knights in England
Geometer	Person skilled in geometry
George	See Porter
Gerund Grinder	Latin Tutor
Gigger	Operated a gigging machine - a machine for dressing woolen cloth by subjecting it to the action of teasels
Gilder	Applied gold leaf for decoration
Gimler	Made gimp - a kind of card
Ginour	Engineer

Ginny / Jenny/ Jenney Tenter	Minded a Ginny - a stationary engine used in coal mining to haul coal to the surface
Girdler	Made leather belts & girdles, mainly for the army
Glass Coachman	Drove a two-horse carriage for hire
Glazier / Glassman	Window glass man / glass cutter Seller of glassware
Glover	Glove maker / seller
Goat Carriageman	Driver of a small carriage
Goldsmith	Banker Worker in gold
Gong Farmer / Gong Scourer	Emptied cesspits, ashpits and outside toilets – "middins" - usually required to work from 9 pm to 5 am. See also Night Soilman
Gooseherd	Tended geese
Gorseman	Sold gorse and broom, largely for making brooms
Gossoon	Servant boy
Gozzard	Herder of geese
Grace Wife	Midwife
Graffer	Notary or scrivener
Grainer	Painted wood grain effect
Granger	Farmer
Grassman/woman	Seller of grease – from Old French graisse, greisse, gresse, "grease."
Graver	Engraver Carver or Sculptor Worker in a ship graving dock, cleaning and repairing ships hulls
Grazier	A person who pastures and raises cattle
Grieve / Greave	Bailiff, Sheriff, Foreman
Greengrocer	Sells fresh fruit and vegetables
Greensmith	Worker in copper - coppersmith
Grey Cloth Dealer	Dealer in Grey Cloth - the unfinished product of the looms before bleaching, dyeing or printing. The term is still used in the trade
Grimbribber	Lawyer

Grinder	Used a grinding machine, mainly for knife and scissor sharpening, which was commonly done door-to-door
	Maintained a carding machine in textile mills
	Tutor
Groover	Miner
Groundsel & Chickweed Seller	Street seller of weeds to feed songbirds
Guinea Pig	Roving (freelance) person, whose usual fee was a guinea (One pound, one shilling)
Gummer	Re-cut old saws, sharpening and improving depth of cut
Gun Filer	Removed the casting imperfections on gun barrels
Gun Stocker	Carves gun stocks from wood and fits them to the metal parts of the gun
Gyp	College servant to undergraduates
Haberdasher	Seller of clothing and accoutrements.
	In the US Brooks Brothers was one of the first haberdashery establishments in 1818. The odd title got its name from haberdashery, a.k.a. notions
Hacker	Woodcutter
	Maker and/or user of hoes or other cutting tools
Hackler / Heckler / Hackman / Hatcheler	Combed or "carded" the coarse flax, using a Hackle - a toothed implement - in linen making.
Hackle Setter	Set and maintained the pins in a Hackle
Hacklemaker/ Heckelmaker	Made the Hackles (combs) for combing flax
Hackney Man	Horse drawn Cab/Taxi driver - Taxis were originally called Hackney Cabs
Haft Presser	Employed in the Sheffield cutlery industry pressing bone/horn into knife handles (hafts). 19th century
Hairweaver / Hairman	Weaver of horsehair cloth
Halberd Carrier / Halberdier	Soldier who was armed with a halberd - a combined spear and axe
Half Timer	Child who spent half the day at school and half in the mills
Hammerman	Smith, hammerman
Handseller	Street Vendor
Handwoman	Midwife or female attendant

Happers	Usually women and children whose job was to square off the drained lumps of salt with wooden implements, ready for drying
Harmer Beck	Constable
Harper	Harp player
Hatter	Hat maker / seller
Hawkshaw	A detective or a police officer who investigates crimes
Hawker / Huckster	Peddler or street seller. Itinerant street dealer who carried his wares with him. Often used as a term of abuse
Haymonger	Dealer in hay
Hayrester	Worker in horsehair
Hayard / Hayward	a keeper or repairer of fences 1) Inspected hedges and fences of a parish and also impounded stray animals 2) Tended fields set aside to produce hay. Also Field Master
Headsman	Executioner
Headswoman	Midwife
Heald Knitter	Made 'healds' - lengths of cord with an eye in the middle through which the warp threads on a loom ran so that they could alternately be raised and lowered for the shuttle to pass through with the weft thread.
Heald/Heddle or Yell Manufacturer	Manufacturer of Healds, used on looms. The warp yarns are passed through loops known as Healds, which raise and lower the yarns after the shuttle has passed the weft across the width of the loom.
Heater	Heated rivets in a charcoal furnace until they were white-hot; he then tossed them in the air for cooling. The catcher would catch them in a metal cone with a handle, then remove them with tongs, place them in predrilled holes in iron or steel plate and the riveter would rivet them in.
Heck Maker	Made spinning machine guides for guiding yarn onto reels
Hedge Looker	Oversaw maintenance of hedges and enclosures. Also see Field Master & Hayward
Hedger	Hedge Trimmer and maker of "grown" hedges - a skilled art
Heelmaker	Made shoe heels
Hellier / Hillier	Roof tiler or Slater
Hempheckler	See Hackler

Hewer	Mine face worker - hewed or cut the coal
Higgler	Itinerant peddler. A lot of the Higgler's trade involved barter, rather than money changing hands and the name derives from the resultant haggling.
Highwayman	Robber, usually mounted, who preyed on travelers on public highways
Hillier	Roof tiler
Hillman / Hillsman	A man who worked at the pithead; a colliery official, late 17th-early 20th century (Scottish)
Hind / Hynd	A domestic servant A skilled farm laborer (Scotland)
Hobbler / Hobler	Towed river or canal boats Casual dock laborer Unlicensed pilot
Hodsman	Mason's assistant - carried the "Hod" in which materials were carried
Hoggard	Pig drover
Holer	Miner Made the holes in sewing needles. Also called an Eyer
Holder up	Rivetter's Mate - whilst the red hot rivet head was formed by the rivetter, he would hold a heavy hammer or dolly against the other end of the rivet Assistant to a forger of chains or shackles by holding up the work Machinist's assistant, holding up work to the various machines
Holloware Turner	Operated a lathe to shape & clean up the inside of metal utensils, teapots, etc. & cooking pots
Hoofer	A dancer
Hooker	16th century Reaper 19th century - Textile mill worker operating machinery which laid out fabric in uniform folds to required length a prostitute or type of sex worker
Hooper / Hoop shaver	Made hoops for casks and barrels
Horner	Made horn cutlery handles, combs
Horseman	Led working horses on a farm

Horse Courser	Owner of racing horses
Horse Knave	Groom
Horse Leech	Farrier, veterinarian
Horse Marine	Towed canal barges where horses could not be used
Horse Capper	Dealer in worthless horses
Horse-hair Curler	Prepared horse hair for upholstery stuffing
Hosier	Retailer of hosiery - socks, stockings, gloves, etc.
Hosteller / Hostelier	Innkeeper
Hostler	Stableman, groom; someone employed in a stable to care for the horse repairer of railway engines
Hotpresser	Worked in textile or paper mills, pressing product between hot glazing sheets to smooth and glaze it
House Joiner	Made the wooden frames of houses
House Wright	House builder
Howdy Wife	Midwife
Hoyman	Used a "hoy" - a small coastal vessel - to transport passengers and goods
Huckster / Huxter / Hookster	Street seller of ale, often a woman Retailer of small wares in shop or booth
Huffler	Worked on the canals assisting boats and barges through the lock.
Huissher	Usher or door attendant
Hurdleman / Hurdler	Made wattle fencing "hurdles"
Hurriers	Usually girls from the age of 5, employed hauling coal underground
Husband-Man / Husbandman	Tenant farmer Farmer dealing with animals (14th century. From the Anglo-Saxon husbonda) - a shepherd
Hush Shopkeeper	Unlicensed beer brewer and seller
Iceman	Ice seller - usually delivered to the door in the early 1800s, ice cutting was the common task of hand-sawing individual ice blocks from lakes and rivers to help store cold food throughout the winter. Then refrigerators were invented and the heavy-lifting job chilled out.
Idleman	Gentleman of leisure
Iggler	See Tinker
Image Maker	A sculptor

Indentured Servant	Was committed to work for a fixed number of years for financial advantage. On completion of the indenture, he became a Freeman. Until that time, had few, if any, rights
Infirmarian	Ran an infirmary
Inspector of Nuisances	A person appointed to look into By-Law offences, such as noisy animals, foul smells, maybe fence disputes, things of that nature
Intelligencer	Spy
Intendent	Director of public or Government business
Iron Charger	Placed the iron ore into the smelting furnace
Iron Founder	Founds or casts iron
Iron Moulder	Made molds for casting iron
Iron Planer	Put flat (plane) surfaces onto, usually, iron castings, required for seatings, etc. where the castings fitted on to other parts of the structure.
Iron Puddler	Made wrought iron using the puddling process; a highly skilled and dangerous occupation which required physical strength, stamina and sustained concentration
Iron Roller	Worked a machine that rolled iron to form and shape it
Iron Turner	Used a lathe to turn items from iron
Ironmonger / Feroner	Hardware merchant
Ironmaster	Foundry owner / manager
Ironsmith	Blacksmith
Ironstone Miner	Mined Ironstone, used to obtain iron and in the making of pottery and also for building material
Jack	Sailor young male assistant
Jack-frame Tenter	A Jack-frame was a complicated machine that twisted textile threads and wound it onto bobbins. "Tenting" meant attending / watching
Jack-smith	Made lifting machinery / equipment
Jagger	Fish peddler 19th century Boy in charge of "jags" or truck trains in a coal mine Man attending pack-horses carrying iron ore to the smelter 20th century Uniformed messenger for London businesses
Jakes Farmer	Cesspool emptier

Japanner	Applied Japanese style black hard varnish – "Japanning"
Javelin Man	Attendant at court who carried a spear or pike
Jenny/ Jenney / Ginny Tenter	Minded a Ginny - a stationary engine used in coal mining to haul coal to the surface
Jerquer	Customs Officer - shipping. Issued "Jerque Note" for clearance of vessel
Jersey Comber	Employed combing Jersey wool before spinning
Job Coachman	Drove a coach hired to nobility or gentry for long periods
Jobber	Dealer in goods Pieceworker - paid by the job In a cotton mill, a Jobber was also known as a Tackler, who maintained machinery
Jobmaster	Supplied horses, carriages and drivers for hire
Jollier	See Potter's Jollier
Jongleur	Travelling minstrel
Journeyman	A tradesman who has served his trade apprenticeship and mastered his craft, not bound to serve a master, but originally hired by the day. The name derives from the French for day - jour. Also Engineer Journeyman.
Jouster	Fishmonger. Female hawker of fish
Jowter	Alternate term for a Jouster, a mounted peddler of fish
Joyner / Joiner	A skilled carpenter, capable of finer work than a plain carpenter. i.e., skilled in making joints for furniture-making. The term is still very much in common usage
Justiciar	Head of the royal judiciary and king's viceroy in his absence abroad
Juvellour	A Jeweler
Kedger	Fisherman
Keeker	Colliery "quality control" man and weighman
Keeler / Keelman	Bargeman on Newcastle Keels - river boats carrying coal down river to ships loading off-shore
Kellerman	A person in charge of the wine-cellars in a great house or castle - of German origin
Kempster	Wool / cotton comber
Kiddier	1) Dealer in young goats and skins
	2) Skinner
Kilner	In charge of pottery kiln/s - limeburner
Kisser	Made cuishes and high armor

Knacker	Harness maker
	Dealer in old and dead animals – "Knacker's yard"
Knappers / Nappers	Dressed and shaped flint as required, mainly for flintlock firearms
Kneller / Knuller	Door to door chimney sweeps
Knocker-up	Man who awoke factory workers with a long stick, knocking on the bedroom windows - often the Lamplighter
Knock Knobbler	Dog Catcher. Knock knobbler had the chore of chasing dogs out of a church during services
	https://www.familytree.com/blog/colonial-occupations-the-common-bizarre/
Knoller	Bell toller
Lace Drawer	Drew out the threads in lace making. Frequently child labor
Laceman	Lace dealer. Commonly bought from the weavers in their homes, normally requiring them to have used his thread, and sold it at the lace markets.
Lace-Master/Mistress	Employed lace workers in factories or at home
Lace Runner	Embroidered on lace
Lace Woman	Lady's maid
Ladle Liner	In ore dressing, smelting, and refining, a person who repairs and re-lines pouring ladles used to transport molten metals, such as iron, steel, and copper.
Lagger	Sailor
Lagraetmen	Constable - contraction of Law Rightman. Term dates back to medieval times, a constable kept the king's armaments, or the weaponry of settlements used for civil defence.
Lairman / Lairsman	Looked after cattle during their brief stops at "lairages", which were the areas where cattle were temporarily housed while in transit to markets.
Lamplighter / Leerie	Employed by the local council to go around the streets and light the (gas) street lamps, using a pole. Also often used to wake people up for work (as a "knocker-up")
Lamptrimmer	In either Royal or Merchant Navy, originally responsible for keeping all oil lamps on the vessel in working order, later became a general assistant to the Boatswain and Storekeeper. A Petty Officer
Lamp Exhauster	Early 20th century. Removed the air from the glass envelope of electric light bulbs. This is necessary to prevent the filament from burning up

Lander	Miner
Landwaiter / Landing Waiter	Customs official overseeing landed goods from ships
Lappett Maker	Made machine embroidered textiles in which the design was worked into the cloth by a series of needles
Lardner	Keeper of the cupboard (larder)
Laster	Shoemaker (from his use of a last)
Lath Render / River	Someone who rends/rives (i.e., splits) wood to form laths
Lattener/Latoner/ Lattensmith	Brass worker. Latten was an alloy similar to brass
Laundress	Woman who provided laundry services to wash, dry, and care for clothes and linens
Lavender	Washerwoman
Layer	Paper mill worker - at a particular process
Leather Currier	Tanned leather by incorporating oil or grease
Leavelooker	Examined market foodstuffs - a sort of quality control
Leech	Physician
Lederer	Leather maker
Legerdemainist	Magician
Legger	Canal boatman. (Barges had to be "legged" through tunnels by men lying flat on deck and "walking" along the roof or sides of the tunnel.)
Leghorn Presser	Pressed a type of straw hat known as a Leghorn
Leightonward	Gardner. Leighton was the term for a garden
Lengthsman	In rural areas, a lengthsman was a man who took pride in keeping his district neat and tidy, well swept and free from litter. On the canals, a lengthsman was responsible for patrolling his length, looking for leaks, seeing to routine maintenance, cutting back vegetation, etc.
Letter Carrier	The 18th century term for a postman, started in 1722
Letter of Apartments	A person who had Apartments to let - (rent)
Licensed Messenger	Licensed couriers who delivered messages and documents
Licensed Victualler	A Tavern or Innkeeper or Publican- term still used today for someone who runs a Pub (Public House)
Lighterman	Works (still) on lighters - flat bottomed barges
Limeburner	Burned limestone (calcium carbonate) in kilns to produce lime for farmers, quicklime for making mortar and for tanneries to remove hair from hides
Limner	1) Illuminator of books

	2) Painter or drawer
Linener / Linen Draper	Sold linens, calicos, flannels, blankets, sheets, sheetings, bed ticks, gloves, ribbons, fancy ties, scarves, etc.
Liner / Lyner	Flax dresser
Linkerboy / man	Carried a "link" or torch to guide folks through the streets at night for hire. (Licensed in early 19th century). Sometimes applied to general manservant
Linman	A wholesale dealer in Flax/Hemp. The name is derived from Linen, which is made from these materials
Lister / Litster	Dyer
Litterman	Horse groom
Loadsman / Lodesman	Ship's pilot. Originally from the man "lodesman" who piloted a ship by heaving the lode (lead) to check the depth of water. Knowledgeable of the local waters, he navigated in this manner
Loblolly Boy	Ship surgeon's assistant
	Errand boy
Locker	Employed in Customs bonded warehouses as a trusted person to keep charge of the elaborate locks [known as the King's - or Queen's] Locks
	Fed a power-driven flat lock machine with knitted fabrics, etc.
	Separated and graded locks of fur in the hat trade
	Cut and folded sheet tin before feeding it into a grooving machine
	Worker in the mining industry
Lock Keeper	(Still) Maintains and operates canal locks
Logwood Grinder	Made a dye from logwood for the textile industry
Log Drivers	Up until the 1970s, log drivers helped move huge tree trunks from the forest to sawmills for construction purposes. The job didn't make the cut as modern transportation progressed. https://www.goodhousekeeping.com/life/g4530/odd-obsolete-jobs/?slide=23
Long Song Seller	Street seller of popular printed song sheets
Loom Sweeper	Child (originally) or small adult employed crawling under weaving looms to clean, whilst in operation. Dangerous work
Loom Winder / Tender	Tended winding units attached to looms that automatically wind yarn onto quills

Looker	Someone employed to look after or inspect something
Looper	Operates a looping machine to close the opening in the toe of seamless hose or to join knitted garment parts
Loriner / Lorner	Maker of horse gear Maker of small ironware Wrought iron worker
Lotseller	Street Seller
Lum Swooper	(Scottish) Chimney sweep
Lumpers / Lumpmen	Lumpers - Dock worker unloading timber for a "Master Lumper" Lumpmen/Lumpers - Makers of table salt or salt for the dairy industry
Lungs	Alchemist's assistant who fanned the fire
Lurryman	Driver of a lurry - lorry or truck. Lurry was the former spelling
Luthier	Made and repaired stringed instruments
Maderer	Garlic seller
Maker-up	Made up garments to order Chemist Agent for paraffin sales
Mail Agent	Government appointed Agent sailing on Royal Mail Ships (RMS) to ensure the mail was "protected and handled in a proper manner"
Malender	Farmer
Maltster / Malster	Brewer, Made or sold malts
Manciple	Steward
Mangler	Worked a mangle for wringing out water from washing. A mangle is a hand-operated device with rollers, for wringing laundry while wringer is a device for drying laundry consisting of two rollers between which the wet laundry is squeezed (or wrung).
Mangle Keeper / Mangle Woman	Woman who hired out her mangle. The possession of a mangle, for the use of which a small sum was charged, was, among the poorer class of English cottagers, a common means of earning money.
Mango	Mango was the term applied to a dealer in slaves, cattle or wares, to which he tried to give an appearance of greater value than they actually possessed.
Mantle Cutter	Cut out the mantles for gas lamps

Mantle Cutter Dress/ Tailor	Cut ladies' Mantles - a cape-like apparel
Mantua Maker	A specific type of Dressmaker A mantua is a loose gown
Marbler	Stained paper or other surfaces to look like marble
Mariken Maker	A dresser & tanner of Moroccan leather
Marine Store Dealer	Proprietor of a store selling equipment to Mariners. There were also those who aspired to that but who were nothing but junk dealers
Mark Maker	Marked steel, silver or gold with the purity/quality of silver - where made, etc.
Marksman	Sharpshooter Marked out land One who makes a mark in place of a signature A grade or degree of the Orange Order (The Loyal Orange Institution, commonly known as the Orange Order, is an international Protestant fraternal order based in Northern Ireland.) One who ranges competitors in a race One who superintended marking New Forest ponies
Marshall	Horse doctor or shoe smith
Marshman	Employed by landowners to tend marshland and the animals grazing there
Mashmaker	Made the mash-vats or "mashels" used in brewing
Mason	Stone cutter or dresser. Bricklayer
Master	One of the three grades of skill recognized by a Crafts Guild. Skilled tradesman, often with his own business
Master Lumper	Contractor employing cheap labor (working on the lump)
Master Mariner	Ship's officer qualified to take command of a ship - not necessarily a Captain. (current term)
Master Writer	Scribe or writer. (In Scotland, a Writer would be a Lawyer)
Matchet Forger	Forged knife blades
Matchet Mounter	Worked in the cutlery industry mounting knife blades to the handles - commonly made of bone then
Mawer / Mather	Mower
Mealman	Dealer in meal or flour

Mechanic	a general term for a craftsman on many census records Machine operator, less skilled than an engineer A journeyman engaged in one of the lower forms of handicraft
Medicus	From the Latin; doctor, physician, also can refer to a homeopath
Melder	Corn miller
Mercator	Merchant
Mercer	Cloth seller
Meterer	Poet
Mewer	Made cages for hawks
Miller	Miller of corn, cloth miller, saw miller, oil miller (see)
Miller's Carman	Drove cart delivering flour or seed
Milliner	Women's hat maker / seller
Millwright	Designed, built and maintained mills or mill machinery, requiring a variety of skills, from reading plans to diagnosing and solving mechanical problems.
Milestone Inspector	Vagrant – "gentleman of the road"
Milkman	Every morning in the 1950s, like clockwork, the milkman would deliver bottles and jugs filled to the brim with milk. If you were lucky, sometimes he would even deliver other kitchen essentials like eggs and butter. https://www.goodhousekeeping.com/life/g4530/odd-obsolete-jobs/?slide=1
Milner	Worker in a Miln (Mill)
Mine Captain	Senior supervisor or the equivalent of a superintendent in a mining operation
Minister of the Gospel	May also have the initials MOG (Minister of the Gospel); ordained, licensed or commissioned persons preacher, pastor, missionary
Mintmaster / Maker	Issued local currency
Misegatherer	Local tax collector
Mocado Weaver	16-17th Century weaver of wool (mock velvet) for clothing
Modeller	A designer in the pottery industry
Molitor	Miller
Mondayman	Worked for the landowner in lieu of rent - usually a Monday

Monger	Seller of goods (ale, fish, etc.) i.e., fishmonger
Monthly Nurse	An attending woman during the first month after childbirth. Also known as "Confinement Nurse." May also have the initials S.M.S. (Subsidiary Medical Services, i.e., not a doctor, but trained in some way)
Mordant Maker	Made a chemical known as Mordant, used in fixing the dye in cloth. This was obtained, amongst other chemicals, from the vapors given off from "stewing" charcoal
Moss Reeve	A bailiff who received and dealt with claims for land on swamps and mossy areas
Moulder	Made moulds (molds) for castings, brick making, etc.
Mountebank	Seller of fake patent medicines. An impostor
Mudlark	Scratched a living by scavenging river banks at low tide
Muffin Carrier	A street seller of muffins
Mugger	A hawker of earthenware A grimacing comedian
Muggler	Pigman
Mugman	Possibly a variant of "Potman" a term sometimes used for a barman or other helper in an inn or public house
Mule Scavenger / Mudlark	Young children worked some twelve hours a day crouched under working spinning mules, clearing out the debris accumulated there. A very dangerous occupation. In 1904 this job was viewed as unlawful
Mule Spinner	See Spinner
Muleskinner	Teamster
Muleteer	Mule driver
Multurer	Miller
Musicker	Musician
Mustarder / Mustardman	Dealer in mustard
Nailor / Naylor / Nellier	Made iron nails by hand Maintained the teeth (nails) on the carding machine used on wool & cotton before weaving
	2)
Naperer / Napier	Servant in charge of table linen in large houses
Narrow Weaver	Wove ribbons, tapes, etc.
Navvy / Navigator / Navor	Laborer on canals or railways, roads, etc.

Neatherd /er	Cowherd
Necessary Woman	Servant who emptied and cleaned the chamber pots
Necker	Fed the cardboard into box-making machinery
Nedeller	Needle maker
Needle Pointer	Filed or fettled the points in needle manufacture
	Needlepoint craftswoman
	2)
Netter	Net maker
Night Soilman / Nightman	Emptied cesspits, ashpits and outside toilets – "middins" - usually required to work from 9 pm to 5 am. See also Gong Farmer
Nightwalker	Night watchman or bellman
Nimgimmer	Doctor
Nipper	Carter's assistant for delivery of goods
Nob Thatcher	Wig maker
Noon Tender	Guarded quayside goods whilst officers were at lunch
Noterer	Notary
Numbers Runner	A person working for an illegal lottery scheme. Runners carry the money and betting slips between the betting parlors and the headquarters, called a numbers bank.
Nurse Child	A child being looked after by another family for payment
Occupier	Tradesman
Oil Colour Man	Employed in the paint manufacturing trade, mixing pigmented paints
Oil & Colour Man	Dealer in the victualling trade - not to be confused with the above!
Oilman	Lamp oil seller
Oil Miller	Miller of seed to extract oils for food manufacture. Rapeseed, cottonseed, linseed, etc. Cottonseed oil was also used to lubricate the spinning mule.
Olitor	Kitchen gardener – Olitory; a kitchen garden
Oliver Smith/Man	A blacksmith who used a foot operated hammer called an Oliver
Onsetter	Performs the duties of a Banksman, except at the bottom of the shaft
On the Club	This is not an occupation but was seen in census returns. It refers the person being out of work and drawing benefit from "the Club," which was an appropriate insurance scheme.

Orderly	Military batman or officer's servant
Ordinary Keeper	Innkeeper with fixed prices
Orrice Weaver	Designed / wove lace patterns in silk
Osier or Withy Peelers	Peeled bark from willow stems (osiers) for basket weaving - usually women & children
Osler	Bird catcher
Ostiary	Monastery doorkeeper
Ostler / Hostler	Originally, a Hostler was the host of an Inn or (H)ostelry. Later became the man employed to look after the horses of the visitors
Out Crier	Auctioneer
Outworker	Home-worker, particularly in weaving
Overlooker	Overseer or foreman esp. in textile mills
Overman	Colliery supervisor - checked the workers and coal quality
Overmantel Maker	Craftsman who made ornamental structures over a mantelpiece.
Overseer	The officials who performed the assessment and collection of the poor-rates. On large plantations, the person who directed the daily work of the slaves was the overseer, usually a white man but occasionally an enslaved black man—a "driver."
Owler	Smuggler - particularly sheep or wool
Oyster Hawker	Street seller of pickled oysters - 18/19th century
Oyster Dredger	Crew member on an oyster boat
Packman	Itinerant seller - carried the goods in his pack
Pack Thread Spinner	Operated a thread or twine making machine
Pad Maker	Made small measuring baskets
Paintress	Woman who hand painted pottery
Paling Man	Seller of eels
Palister	Park keeper
Pannier Man	Fishmonger
Pannifex	Worker in the cloth trade
Pansmith	Pan maker and/or repairer- metal worker Made and maintained the large, shallow pans in which salt was boiled
Panter	Keeper of the pantry
Pantler	Butler

Pantographer	An engraver who used a Pantograph to transfer the pattern from a drawing to the engraving surface.
Paper Stainer	Printed wallpaper
Paperer	Inserted sewing needles into paper packets ready for sale
Pardoner	Licensed seller of indulgences
Pargeter	Applied pargetting (ornamental plaster) to buildings
Parish Apprentice	Working child of the workhouse
Paritor	Church official attending courts to execute their orders
Parker	Park keeper, usually a game park
Parminster	Worked with Cotswold stone roofing tiles
Passage Keeper	Cleaned the local passageways and alleyways
Pasteler	Pastry chef
Pastor	Shepherd
Patrollers	Slave Control: Patrollers and Overseers

Society at large shared in maintaining the machinery of slavery. In place of a standing police force, Southern states passed legislation to establish and regulate county-wide citizen patrols. Essentially, Southern citizens took upon themselves the protection of their neighbors' interests as well as their own. County courts had local administrative authority; court officials appointed three to five men per patrol from a pool of white male citizens to serve for a specified period. Typical patrol duty ranged from one night per week for a year to twelve hours per month for three months. Not all white men had to serve: judges, magistrates, ministers, and sometimes millers and blacksmiths enjoyed exemptions. So did those in the higher ranks of the state militia. In many states, courts had to select from adult males under a certain age, usually 45, 50, or 60. Some states allowed only enslavers or householders to join patrols. Patrollers typically earned fees for captured fugitive fugitives from slavery and exemption from road or militia duty, as well as hourly wages. Keeping order among enslaved people was the patrollers' primary duty. Statutes set guidelines for appropriate treatment of the enslaved and often imposed fines for unlawful beatings. In rare instances, patrollers had to compensate enslavers for injured enslaved people. For the most part, however, patrollers enjoyed quasi-judicial or quasi-executive powers in their dealings with the enslaved. Source: https://eh.net/encyclopedia/slavery-in-the-united-states/ |
| **Patten Maker/ Pattener** | Made "pattens" to fit under normal shoes for wet/muddy use. Clog-maker |

Pattern Card Maker	Made the cards that set the pattern on weaving looms - the "jacquard" method
Pattern Maker	Makes wood patterns for the construction of steel or other metal objects. Patterns are made for ship construction, for castings, etc.
Paternosterer	Maker of Rosaries
Paver / Paviour / Pavier	Lays paving stones etc. (in use today) also called a Flagger
Pavyler	Erected tents, pavilions, etc.
Pedascule	Schoolmaster
Peddler	A peddler, in British English pedlar, also known as a canvasser, chapman, cheapjack, hawker, higler, huckster, monger, colporteur, or solicitor, is a traveling vendor of goods.
	In England, the term was mostly used for travelers hawking goods in the countryside to small towns and villages; they might also be called tinkers or gypsies. In London more specific terms were used, such as costermonger.
Pedestrian	A Walker, sometimes athlete, sometimes paid for competing
Peeler	Policeman - after Sir Robert Peel, who in 1829, established the London Metropolitan Police Force. He became known as the "Father of Modern Policing."
Pelterer	Worked with animal skins - pelts
Perambulator	Surveyor
Perchemear	Parchment maker
Peregrinator	Itinerant wanderer
Peruker / Peruke Maker	A wig maker
Peon	a Spanish-American day laborer or unskilled farm worker

a person who does menial work; a drudge

a debtor held in servitude by a creditor, especially in the southern US and Mexico

(in South and Southeast Asia) a low-ranking soldier or worker

an attendant or messenger |
| Pessoner | Fishmonger - from the French, poisson |

Petardier	Made Petards - explosive devices used for storming castles
Peterman	Fisherman - biblical
Pettifogger	A shyster lawyer
Petty Chapman	Peddler - itinerant small goods seller
Pew Opener	Opened the doors to private church pews
Pewterer / Pewtersmith	One whose occupation is to make utensils of pewter; plates, bowls, dishes, tankards, pots for the kitchen and table, also larger vessels for inns and businesses. Almost all old wills leave valuable amounts of pewter to members of the family.
Philosophical Instrument Maker	Made Scientific instruments
Phonologist	A person versed in Phonology - the science or doctrine of the elementary sounds uttered by the human voice in speech, including the various distinctions, modifications, and combinations of tones; phonetics. Also, a treatise on sounds.
Phrenologist	Read bumps on the head for character assessment
Picker	Cast the shuttles on a loom
Picker Maker	Made the "Pickers" - strong leather attachments fitted to each side of a weaving loom to drive the shuttle across the loom
Piece Broker	Dealer in fabric remnants
Piece Worker	Worker paid for by the number of articles finished. Usually home workers, and factory workers
Piecemaster	The middleman between employer and pieceworker, who allocated the work
Piecer / Piecener	Employed to piece together broken threads in weaving. Often children.
Pigmaker	Poured molten metal to make "pigs" for distribution of raw metals Pottery worker
Pigman	Crockery dealer Pig herd
Pig Jobber	Bought pigs and then sold them off for profit. A pig trader
Pikelet Maker	Baked Pikelets - small crumpet or pancake

Pikeman	Miller's assistant
	Soldier armed with a pike
	Turnpike worker
Piker	Tramp, vagrant
Pile / Piler	Fitted arrowheads to their shafts (pile was the old term for arrowhead)
Piller	Robber
Pilot	Ship's steersman
Pinder	Dog catcher & pound keeper
Piner	Laborer
Pinner	Pin maker
Pinner up	Dressmaker's assistant
	Sold ballads in the street
Piper	Innkeeper
Pistor	Baker
Pit Brow Lass	Female surface worker at the coalmines
Pitman	Coal miner
Plain Worker	Plain needleworker, as distinct from embroidered work
Plaisterer	Plasterer
Plaiter	Make straw plaits for hat making
Planker	"Planked" or kneaded the felt in hat-making
Platelayer	Laid and maintained railway tracks. The name predates railways, and is derived from the original "plateways" which existed hundreds of years ago, laid for coal mines.
Playderer	Made plaid
Pleacher / Plasher / Platcher / Plaicher	Hedge layer. A skilled job
Plod Weaver / Plaid Weaver	Wove plaid material - Plod was a 16-17th century variant of plaid
Ploughboy	Led the oxen pulling a plough
Ploughwright	Made or repaired ploughs
Plumassier / Plumer	Made ornamental feather plumes or sold feathers - from French, plume
Plumber	Applied sheet lead for roofing and set lead frames for plain or stained glass windows. As lead was the usual material for pipes, the modern term evolved. Plumbium - Latin for lead

Plumbium Worker	Worked with plumbium (lead) - a plumber; from the Latin, plumbium = lead
Plunger	Speculator
Pluralist	A person who had the "living" of more than one parish, or church
Plush Weaver	Wove Plush, a type of textile which has a nap or pile similar to velvet - used in royal courts
Pointer / Pin Pointer	Lace-maker Sharpened needles or pins in manufacture
Pointsman	Changed the points to change the track direction of trains
Poldave Worker	Made "poldave" - a coarse fabric
Poleman	Surveyor's assistant
Polenter / Polentier	Poulterer
Pollard Dealer	Dealer in pollard, bran sifted from flour. Also flour dealer
Poller / Powler	Barber
Ponderator	Weights and measures inspector
Pony Driver	Usually a child, drove the pit ponies drawing the coal tubs
Portable Soup Maker	Made dried soup for transporting
Porter	Door or gate keeper A person who carried baggage in railway stations and other public places Also, Red Caps (railway station porters) The term "porter" has been superseded in modern American usage by "sleeping car attendant."
Portmanteau Maker	Made suitcases / travelling bags
Postillion	Rode as a guide on one of the near pairs of horses drawing a coach or post chaise
Post Boy	Carried mail Guard who travelled on the mail coach Outrider travelling with the coach or a Postillion
Poster	Broke rocks in the quarries
Potato Badger	Potato seller

Pot Boy/man	Cleared away and washed the pots in a public house A Potman was also a street-seller of porter and stout
Pot Burner	Placed completed pots into the ovens for firing
Potato Badger	Potato seller
Potter's Carrier	Chemist or Pharmacist
Potter's Thrower	Potter, using a wheel – "threw" the clay onto the wheel
Poulter / Poulterer	Poultry seller
Pounder	Person how owned the local pound where stray animals i.e., cattle, horses and sheep would be rounded up. The owners of these animals would have to pay the Pounder a fee to retrieve their animals.
Powder Monkey	Young boys - and sometimes women - on war sailing ships who stuffed gunpowder in cannons. employed to supply naval guns with their powder charges from the magazines below the waterline. Boys were usually employed because the gun (Orlop) decks were very low for stability reasons, and grown men would have found it difficult to move around at speed in those situations.
Power Loom Tuner	Maintained the weaving looms
Powler	Barber
Poynter	Lace maker
Preceptor/ Preceptress	School Master / School Mistress
Prentis	Apprentice
Presser Off	A cotton warehouseman employee who gave garments their final pressing before packing
Pressman	Operated a printing press
Prick Louise	Tailor
Pricker	Witch hunter Pattern Maker Horseman
Proctor	University official
Prop Bobby	Checked the pit props in mines
Prothonary	Law clerk
Prow Smith	In shipbuilding, was responsible for laying out the prows and the keel of a vessel
Publican	Innkeeper - still in use
Puddler	Wrought iron or clay worker - see Iron Puddler & Clay Puddler

Puggard	Thief
Pugger	Trod clay to produce the mix for brick making. Often women & children
Pullman porters	Pullman porters were men hired to work on the railroads as porters on sleeping cars. Many passengers called porters "boy" or "George," after George Pullman, regardless of their real names. This was a practice born in the American South where enslaved people were named after their enslaver.
Punky	Chimney Sweep
Purefinder / Pure Gatherer	Old women & young girls who collected dog droppings used in the tanning industry
Purl Seller	Sold purl by boat to other river craft users. Purl was a potent mixture of beer and gin
Putter	Hauled coal tubs in the mines
Putter-in	Input materials in mechanical processes - varied
Pykemonger	Dealer in pike and other freshwater fish
Quarantine (Station)	From 1728, some Customs officials - Quarantines - were given the responsibility of watching quarantine hulks anchored offshore to ensure nobody left them before their period of quarantine had expired on arriving from abroad.
Quarrel Picker	Glazier
Quarrier / Quarry Man	Quarry worker
Quay Clerk	Clerk who worked at a wharf or quay
Quiller	Operated machinery winding yarn onto quills or spools A quill is a reed on to which the thread of the weft was wound when weaving cloth
Quister	One who bleached articles
Raff Merchant	Sold fiber used to make raffia bags, etc.
Raffman	Dealer in "raff" - saleable rubbish
Rag Cutter	Cut rags into small pieces for papermaking
Rag Gatherers	Cleared rags from mill machinery - usually children
Rag Man / Rag and Bone Man	Toured the streets in his cart collecting rags and any old useable discarded items
Rag Picker	Sorted useable items from rag collection
Rag-stabber	Tailor (slang) mid-19th century - also Stab-rag (military slang)
Raker	Street cleaner

Ratoner	Rat Catcher
Rattlewatch	Town watchman
Reacher for Drawing	Specific occupation in the cotton/silk weaving mills. Each thread has to be Drawn through the Eye on a Heald, ready for the loom and then separately picked out from the Beam of warp threads by the Reacher
Rectifier	Distilled alcohol
Red Caps	railway station porters
Redar	Interpreted dreams
Redman / Redeman	Responsible for maintaining the haulageways and passages in a coal mine
Reddleman	Sold the dye used by farmers to mark their sheep
Redsmith	Goldsmith: By the 1700s, American redsmiths were caught redhanded with loads of copper artifacts because that was their job! The term redsmith comes from the shiny bronze color of copper and there are still a handful present today. However, the job title "metalsmith" has become more commonplace.
	https://www.goodhousekeeping.com/life/g4530/odd-obsolete-jobs/?slide=38
Reeder	Used reeds for thatching and hedging
Reedmaker	Made weaving reeds - a reed is a comb-like device for "beating" the weft thread into place as it is passed by the shuttle, the warp threads passing between the teeth of the reed Made reeds or pipes for musical instruments Made reed cloth Made tapestry combs
Reed & Heald Maker	Also Reed Maker (above). Made equipment for the separation of the weft thread on cloth-weaving looms
Reeler	Received yarn on bobbins or paper tubes and arranged them on a shelf above the machine; guided and attached the end of the yarns to swifts (skeleton reels), which revolved and wound the yarn upon themselves in skein form; controlled the power drive on the machine; mended broken threads; removed the hanks or skeins of yarn from the machine when completed Puts woven cloth on to a reel for dyeing (more recent)

Reeve	Churchwarden
	Royal or Manorial elected or appointed official
Reever	Shriever; Sheriff
Regarder	Surveyed woodland, hedges and fences
Registrar	As today - registered events; land purchases, births, deaths, etc.
Relieving Officer	Official of the Poor Law Union to whom the poor or retarded persons in the parish could apply for poor relief
Renovator	Repaired clothing
Resurrection Man	Apart from using the bodies of hanged criminals, dissection was illegal, so 17th century British doctors took to breaking the law. 'Resurrection men' would look for recent burials, dig up the corpse and sell it to a doctor. At the time, you could make a decent living out of the practice. Resurrection men became so unpopular that they ran the risk of being torn to pieces if caught by a mob.
Revenuer / Renenue Man	Tax collector
	A US government official who enforces laws prohibiting the illegal distillation of alcohol
Rice Dressser	Removed the chaff, straw, small grains, etc. to clean up rice grains for human consumption. Rice skins are polished off to give the white grain we normally use
Rickmaster	Captain of Horse
Riddler	Wool stapler
Riding Officer	Employed by the Revenue to patrol 4-10 miles of coastline to detect smugglers. Paid no more than a farmer's laborer and hated, so dangerous. 18th century
Riftere	Reaper
Rigger	Hoist tackle worker - esp. running and dismantling rigging of ships
Ring Spinner	Operated a Ring Spinning Machine - Ring spinning was/ is a method for the continuous spinning of cotton.
Ripper / Rippier	Seller of fish
Riverman	Worked riverboats
Roadman	Worked on building and or maintaining roads - often had a stretch of road which he was responsible for filling in potholes etc. - usually a mile
	A tramp or vagrant was also often referred to as a Roadman
Rockgetter	Rock salt miner

Rockman	Worked in the quarries, usually placing charges
Rodman / Poleman	Surveyor's assistant - held the rod for the surveyor's theodolite observation
Roll Turner	Carded yarn into rolls prior to spinning
Roller Coverer	Covered the rollers in spinning
Rolley Man	Delivery man
Rolleyway Man	Maintained the mine's underground roadways
Roman Cementer / Plasterer	Used "Roman Cement" - used in stuccoing
Rope Runner	Accompanied sets of drams or tubs on the rope haulage system in a Colliery for the purpose of changing over the rope or ropes at the end of the run
Roper	Made rope or nets
	Cotton spinning operative
Rougher	Observed the color of heated iron or steel, determined the rolling temperature, and operated the rougher roll mill to reduce the metal to specified dimensions.
Rover	Archer
	Loaded cotton yarn onto bobbins, giving the yarn a twist, (Roving) after the Carding and Combing processes.
Rubbisher / Rubbler	Sorted small stones in the quarries
Rugman	Dealer in rugs
Rule Maker	Made and calibrated rulers (for measurement)
Rully Man	A Cart man - equivalent to today's lorry or truck driver
Runner	1) Runner or messenger for the magistrates -Bow Street Runner
	2) Smuggler
Sachrist / Sachristan	Person retained in a cathedral to copy out music for the choir and take care of the books. One who is in charge of a sacristy. A sexton
Saddle Tree Maker	Made the wooden frames around which the saddle was formed with leather
Saddler	One who makes, repairs or sells saddles or other furnishings for horses
Safernman	Grower of Saffron

Saggar Maker / Saggar Maker's Bottom Knocker	Made saggars (fired clay containers used to hold ceramic items in the kiln whilst firing.) The Saggar Maker's Bottom Knocker was the saggar maker's assistant, usually a young boy, who was responsible for knocking clay into a large metal hoop using a huge flat mallet called a mawl, to form the bottom of the saggar. The saggar maker would then remove the hoop and form the sides of the saggar onto the base - a much more skilled job than bottom-knocking (testing for cracks by knocking). Some saggar-makers also had a frame filler, who did a very similar job to the bottom knocker but prepared the clay to make the sides of the saggars, rather than the bottom.
Saloonist	Saloon keeper
Salt Boiler	Obtained salt from boiling salt water
Salter / Saucer	Made or dealt in salt
Saltpetre Man	Collected urine and dung, used in the manufacture of saltpetre
Sarcinet Weaver	Silk weaver
Sandesman	Ambassador or messenger
Sawbones	Physician
Sawyer	Timber mill/pit worker, sawing timber
Say Weaver	Made "say" - used in making table cloths bedding, etc.
Scagliola Maker	Made imitation marble
Scappler/Scabbler	Rough-shaped stone before final dressing by a stonemason
Scavelman	Cleaned and maintained waterways and ditches
Scavenger / Scaleraker	Street cleaner Scavenger - also a child employed in a spinning mill to collect loose cotton lying about the floor under machinery
Schrimpschonger	Artisan carving bone, ivory, wood, etc.
Schumacker	Shoemaker
Scotch Draper / Scotchman	Sold goods door to door on instalment payments
Scribe	Clerk - writer
Scriber	Marked bales of cotton on the docks with weight prior to being sold by brokers
Scribler	A person who tends a wool/cotton-combing machine called a Scribler - the first process in carding the yarn
Scribbler	Minor or worthless author

Scrimer	Fencing master
Scrivenor/er	Professional or public copyist or writer notary public
Scrutineer	Election judge
Scutcher/Skutcher	Beat flax to extract the linen fibers. Scutching is the process of extracting linen fibers from flax stems, originally done by hand and later by machine.
Scullery Maid	Female servant who was given the menial tasks
Scullerman	Sculled a boat, (rather than rowing it) in ports/rivers as a ferry
Scullion	Male servant who was given the menial tasks
Sea Fencibles	The Sea Fencibles were established by Order in Council in May 1798 to defend the coast from invasion; they comprised "all such of the inhabitants of the towns and villages of Great Britain as shall voluntarily offer themselves for the defence of the coast." They were taught to use musket, pike and cannon. They were to assist in the manning of defensive positions (Martello towers), plus coastal signal stations and eventually given small boats to patrol harbors. They were to be paid one shilling per day served. It was attractive to fishermen and the like as you were given immunity from being pressed into the Navy. They were organized into districts, commanded by Naval Officers. They grew to their maximum strength in 1810, when there were over 23,000 of them and were disbanded at the end of the wars in 1814.
Seal Presser	Glassmaking - sealed the bath to prevent air spoiling the glass surface
Searcher	Customs man (today called a rummager - self descriptive) who searched for contraband
Secret Springer	Watch spring maker
Seedsman	Sower or dealer in seeds
Seeker of the Dead	During the Plague, older women were employed to diagnose the Plague from the buboes and count the dead to enable the compilation of Bills of Mortality, for which they were paid from 3 to 4 pence per corpse. Risky job!
Self-acting Minder / Self Actor Minder	Watched and minded the 'Self Acting Mule' - the name of a multi thread spinning machine. The original Mule was hand operated and was invented by Samuel Crompton of Bolton in 1779. It was made self-acting by Richard Roberts in 1830. - also see Throstle Spinner and Spinner
Semi Lorer	Made leather thongs

Sempster / Sempstress / Sewster	Seamstress
Seneschal	Senior steward at the manor
Sewer Hunter	Scavenged in the sewers
Sewer Rat	Bricklayer who made and repaired sewers and tunnels
Sewing Clerk	Oversaw and collected clothing piecework
Sexton	Church caretaker - sometimes dug graves or rang the bells
Shagreen Casemaker	Worked with shagreen leather
Shallooner	See Chaloner
Shampooer	Masseur/masseuse in a Turkish baths
Shantyman	Woodman, lumberman
Sharecropper	Tenant farmer whose pay was a fixed part of the crop
Shearer	As today, sheared the fleece from sheep
Shearman / Sherman	Skilled worker who sheared the nap from cloth - also Cropper Cutter of metal
Sheath Maker	Made sword and dagger scabbards
Sheepman	Shepherd
Shepster	Dressmaker Sheep Shearer
Sheriff	Representative of Royal office in a Shire
Shingler	Worked with an Iron Puddler, manipulating puddled balls of iron on an anvil
Ship's Husband	Supplied stores for and maintained ships in dock
Ship Master	Ship's Captain - still used today - often also the vessel's owner
Shipwright	Builder and repairer of ships
Shoe Finder	Sold cobbler's tools
Shoesmith	Cobbler Shoed horses
Shoeshiner	Shoeshiner or boot polisher is an occupation in which a person cleans and buffs shoes and then applies a waxy paste to give a shiny appearance and a protective coating. They are often known as shoeshine boys because the job was traditionally done by a male child. Other synonyms are bootblack and shoeblack.
Shoe Wiper	Polished shoes - a boot-boy

Shook Maker	Woodworker who specializes in the manufacturing of the thin wooden slats used on wooden shipping containers, especially on boxes used to ship fresh fruit.
Shot Firer	Employed blasting in quarries
Shrager	Trimmed and pruned trees
Shrieve / Shriever	Sheriff
Shuffler	Farm yardman
Shunter	Moved - shunted - rolling stock around in railway yards to make up, and break down, goods trains
Shuttle Maker	Made the wooden shuttles for the looms
Shuttle Tip Maker	Made the pointed steel shuttle tips and made in many different designs. A very skilled job as the tips had to withstand being hammered to make the shuttles fly through the yarns from one side of the loom to the other and had to have aerodynamic properties. Forged by hammering red-hot steel
Sick Visitor	Employed by Friendly Societies, who paid benefits to sick people, to ensure they were entitled to receive/ continue to receive benefits.
Sickleman	Reaper
Sidesman	Churchwarden's assistant - esp. in church services
Signalman	A signalman helped manage multiple switches and levers by hand to ensure all trains were moving in the right direction. Once railways were computerized in the late 1960s, signalmen were no longer needed.
Silkman	Person engaged in the manufacture and or sale of silk
Silk Drawer	Drew silk from silk waste for spinning
Silk Dresser	Prepared the silk for weaving
Silk Engine Turner	Worked on automatic silk weaving looms
Silk Mercer	Silk merchant
Silk Piecer	Joined the broken threads in the silk spinning mills
Silk Staff Man	Probably a worker more on a permanent rather than itinerary position
Silk Steward	Manager of a silk weaving/spinning/winding and cleaning room
Silk Thrower/ Throwster	Employed in the silk weaving industry, twisting silk into yarn
Silk Twister	Silk Spinner (from the raw)
Silk Winder	Wound the silk from the silkworm cocoons onto bobbins
Silker	Bound the ends of the silk fabric to prevent fraying

Simpler	Agriculturalist (herbalist)
Sinker	Sunk shafts for mining
Sinker Maker	Made lead weights used with hosiery knitting machines, (Nottingham Area)
Sissor / Cissor	Tailor
Sizer	Applied size to cloth in manufacture
Skepper / Skelper	Beehive maker/seller
Skin Dresser	"Dressed" - prepared animal skins for the manufacture of clothing or footwear
Skinkster	Alehouse tapster
Skinner	Dealer in hides Mule driver
Skip Maker	Made skips (large baskets), used in mining and quarrying, for transporting product or personnel
Skiver	Used a knife to cut out the leather shapes which go to form a shoe or boot
Slapper / Slaper	Pottery worker who prepared the clay for the potter
Slasher	Applied size (Slasher Sizing) to the warp thread in weaving, to strengthen it and facilitate the weaving process.
Slater	Roofer; one who used shingles to make roofs, a roofer
Slate Enameller	Painted decorative slate as used in fireplaces, etc.
Slate River	Was employed to cleave blocks of quarried slate in the making of slates for roofing etc. (River pronounced as in diver.)
Slaymaker	Made the reeds or slays used in weaving. Slays (wooden pegs) or reeds were used to separate the threads on the loom
Sledman	Moved goods by sled
Slinger	Person who used slings for loading goods on ships, wagons, etc.
Slopseller	Slopshop keeper - readymade clothes Basket seller
Slubber	Prepared cotton for spinning, removing the "slubs" or imperfections in the yarn
Slubber Doffer	Removed the empty bobbins from the loom spindles
Slubbing Frame Fitter	Installed and maintained a Slubbing Frame, used in the preparation of cotton ready for spinning
Smallware Maker	Made "smallware" - tapes, braids, ribbons, etc.

Smelter	Smelt fisherman Smelter in an iron foundry
Smiddy	Smith - sometimes still used as a nickname for Smith surname
Smith	Metal worker - see also Engine Smith, Blacksmith, Fender Smith
Smith's Striker	A blacksmith who wielded a hammer whilst another blacksmith held the work-piece with tongs in the right position on the anvil
Smoke Doctor	Specialist in the construction or repair of chimneys
Smugsmith	Smuggler
Snobscat / Snob	Shoe repairer
Snow Boy / Snowy	Ship's crew whose business it is to keep the white flakes caused by the refrigerator appliances from collecting below
Snuffer Maker	Made candle snuffers
Soaper / Soper / Soap Boiler	Soap Maker
Sojourn Clothier	Travelling clothes salesman
Sortor	Tailor
Souter	Shoe maker
Sp Dealer	Enumerators' abbreviation for a Spirit Dealer
Spallier	Tin worker's assistant
Sperviter	Sparrow keeper
Spicer	Spice dealer / grocer
Spindle & Fly Maker	Made the metal Spindles and Fly used in spinning machines
Spinner	Spun the yarn to make cloth
Splitter	Worked a machine splitting stone, timber etc. or did so by hand
Spooner	Spoon maker
Spuller	Inspected yarn, to see that it is well spun, and fit for the loom
Sprig Maker	A weaver of fine lace sprigs applique. e.g., 'Honiton' Lace in Devon
Spring Smith	Made the springs (usually leaf) used in carriages
Spurrer / Spurrier	Made spurs

Squire / Esquire	Country landed gentleman
	Magistrate or justice of the peace
	Knight's attendant
	Professional man
Stabler	Ostler
Stab-rag	Tailor (military slang) mid-19th century - also Rag-stabber (slang)
Stallman	Market stall holder
Stampman	Worked an ore-crushing machine
Stationary Engine Driver	Operated steam factory engine, used for all processes, usually linked by a system of shafts, pulleys and belts
Stationary Engineer	Maintained the factory steam engine and machinery
Statist	Politician
Staymaker	Corset maker
	Made a 'stay' from ash trees, used in bell ringing
Steam Hammer Driver	Operated a large steam-operated hammer to forge iron and steel. Invented in Manchester in 1837 by George Naismith
Steeplejack	Worked on steeples, chimneys, flagpoles etc. - still exists
Steersman	Ship's helmsman
Stenciller	Itinerant tradesmen who travelled around decorating the interior walls of houses with stencils to avoid the prohibitive cost of wallpaper
Stenterer	Worked a cloth finishing machine
Step Boy	Helped passengers on and off coaches
Stick Maker	Made walking sticks
Stick Mounter	Decorated walking sticks with silver, gold, bone or ivory mountings
Still Room Maid	Worked in the Still-Room in a large Victorian household, answerable to both the housekeeper and the cook, where she would concoct the kitchen cleaners, soaps, candles and cosmetics for the lady of the house. It also housed the jams pickles, etc. that the cook would make
Stockinger	Knitter, weaver or seller of stockings
Stock Turner	Turned the wooden stocks used in guns
Stoker	Tended to and fed coal to boilers in mills and aboard ship
Stoker - Refuse Destructor	Fed refuse to an incinerator

Stone Blue Maker	Maker of Bristol Blue glassware
Stone Dresser	Prepared quarried stone for building. This would include cutting it into regular sized blocks with a reasonably even surface
Stone Getter	Stone-face quarry worker
Stone Picker	Removed stones from fields before planting
Stoneman / Stonewarden	Highway surveyor
Stover / Stever/ Staver	The senior member of a partnership of miners and in charge at the surface
Stowyer	Stowed nets on fishing boats
Strawman	(16/17th century) Hired to give false evidence for the prosecution in Court
Straw Joiner	Thatcher (of roofs)
Straw Plaiter	Plaited straw for use in hat-making
Streaker	Laid out bodies for burial
Street Orderly/Boy	Street cleaner
Strickler	Skimmed off the scum from molten iron in a mold
Stretcher / Tenter	Stretched fabrics after weaving on a frame with hooks - origin of saying "on tenterhooks"
Striker / Stryker	Blacksmith's assistant Harpoon man on a whaler
Stripper	Cleaned the carding machines in mills
Stringer	Made bowstrings
Stroller	A vagabond, vagrant; an itinerant beggar or peddler An itinerant actor; a strolling player
Stuff Gownsman	Junior barrister
Stuff Presser	Placed the cloth within sheets of special stiff press paper and passed it into a hot-pressing machine which gave the finish to the cloth
Stuff Weaver	Wove "stuff" - a coarse cloth, more especially of worsted, made of long or "combing wool" distinguished from other woolen cloths by the absence of any nap or pile
Sucksmith	Made Ploughshares
Sugar Baker	Sugar Refiner Made confectionery or cake decorations Fancy baker

Sumner	Summoner or Apparitor
Sumpter	Porter
Supercargo	Officer on a chartered merchant ship who is in charge of cargo and the commercial concerns of the ship (on behalf of the charterers). - Still in use
Surfaceman	A Roadworker
Sutler	Merchant or peddler in an army camp
Swabber	Seaman (slang)
Swailer	Miller Grain dealer
Swain	Herdsman
Swaith Maker	A Swaith / Swathe was (usually) a cotton or silk shroud used for burial
Sweep	Chimneysweep
Swell Maker	Made shallow baskets
Swiller	A basket weaver/maker - an old Cumberland name
Swineyard / Swineherd	Pig Keeper
Swingler	Beat flax to remove the coarse parts
Switchboard Operator	Switchboard operators connected long-distance calls and directed communication before digital exchange switched up the game. By the early '80s the position became obsolete. https://www.goodhousekeeping.com/life/g4530/odd-obsolete-jobs/?slide=10
Sword Cutler	Made swords
Tabernarius	Tavern or innkeeper - from the Latin
Tabler	Boarding Housekeeper
Tackler	Supervisor of weaving shed workers
Taker Off / In	Unhitched coal tubs from an endless rope system - usually children
Tallow Chandler	Candle maker/seller
Tally Clerk	As today, tallied goods into and out of warehouses, ships, etc.
Tallyman / Tally Fellow	Sold goods on installment plan Local official who tallied the allowed number of persons in a dwelling for health reasons - usually 3 adults and four children
Tambour Worker	Worked with embroidery on a (circular) Tambour Frame
Tan Bark Stripper	Collected tree bark used for tanning leather

Tanner	Tanned (cured) animal hides for leather making. Still used
Tanner's Beamsman	Draped part-cured skins over a Tanners Beam, a flat slab of wood or stone, to scrape off the remaining flesh, fat and hair
Taper Weaver	Made candle wicks
Tapiter / Tapicer	Weaver of figured cloth or tapestry
Tapley	Put the taps in ale casks
Tapster	Barman / woman
Tar Boy	Applied tar (antiseptic) to sheep when nicked by shearers
Tasker	Reaper
Tasseler	Made tassels for furnishings
Taverner	Innkeeper
Tawer/Tawyer/Tower	Made white leather
Teamster / Teamer / Teamer Man	Driver of a team horses used for hauling
Teemer	Emptied grain brought by cart Poured molten steel into molds
Teerer/Tierer/Tier Boy	Spread a fresh surface of color on the printer's 'pad' each time he used it to print calico
Teizer	Removed slag from molten glass (18th century glass industry)
Tenter / Tenterer	Tenterer - Someone who, after cloth was dyed, stretched it on a frame, called a "Tent" for drying. This frame was fitted with hooks known as "Tenterhooks" - about which we all know! The term was also used for a person who looked after or watched something, i.e., Tip tenter - person inspecting finished shuttle tips after manufacture. (Tenter - from Tender, to tend)
Textor	Weaver
Thacker / Thatcher	Roof thatcher, using straw or, more usually, reeds
Theemaker	Shoemaker
Thirdborough	Under-constable
Thresher	Separated chaff from grain
Throstle Spinner / Throstle Jobber	Attended a spinning machine known as a Throstle, due to the noise it made, which resembled a lark, or throstle. The machine was used for the continuous spinning of cotton (or wool) simultaneously onto long rows of, perhaps 300 or 400, pirns or bobbins.

Throwster / Thrower	Textile worker attending machine which twisted together strands of fiber into yarn - cotton, silk, wool, etc.
Ticket Porter	Porter wearing badges, or 'tickets,' licensed by the City of London to carry goods, as well as documents and messages. They could be found in the streets and hired when needed.
Tickneyman / woman	Travelling earthenware seller
Tide Gauger / Surveyor	Monitored the state of the tides
Tide Waiter / Tidesman	Customs inspector who boarded ship on arrival to enforce customs regulations
Tiger	Liveried pageboy / groom
Tiler	Worked with roof and floor tiles
Tiller	Farmer
Tillman	Ploughman
Timekeeper	A person responsible for making sure things happened on time e.g., worker
	Arriving or departing, trains, coaches, omnibuses, etc.
Times Ironer	Servant who literally ironed the Times newspaper!
Timoneer	A ship's helmsman (from French, timonier)
Tin Dresser	Processed tin ore
Tinctor	Dyer
Tinker	An itinerant tin pot and pan seller, repairman / knife sharpener - also Iggler
Tinner	Tin miner
	Tinsmith
Tinsmith	Worked with tin
Tinter / Teinter	Artists who tinted photographs before color was available
Tin Streamer	Recovered tin ore by means of 'panning', as in gold panning, from rivers and streams
Tipper	Tipped arrows, etc. with metal
Tippler	Alehouse keeper - It was also the name for an outside "toilet"!! (hole in the ground!)
Tipstaff	Court official
	Policeman

Tirewoman	Female dresser - esp. theatrical Milliner Hairdresser
Tixtor	Weaver
Tobacco Spinner	Made cigars
Todhunter	Employed by the parish to hunt foxes
Toe Rag	Worked in the docks as a corn porter
Toilinet Maker / Knotter	Made "toilinet" - a kind of quilting - The knotter made the knots at the edges.
Toller / Tollie / Tollman / Tollgate Keeper	Collected road tolls at a Toll Gate/House
Tonsor	Barber - from Latin
Tool Helver	Tool handle maker
Topman	Seaman - worked in the "tops" (aloft) on sailing ships
Top Sawyer	Upper man in a sawpit - using a long two-man saw
Topsman	Head cattle drover
Tosher	Scratched a living by scavenging the Victorian sewers
Touch holer	Worked in gun making
Tow Card Maker	Made "tow cards" used in weaving mills
Town Chamberlain	Looked after a town's affairs
Town Crier	"Cried" public announcements and used a bell to get attention
Town Husband	Collected dues from fathers of illegitimate children of the parish for their upkeep
Townsman	Commercial traveler
Townswaiter	Customs man
Tozer	Worked in the mills "tossing" (teasing) the cloth
Trace Maker/Tracer	Worked in a draughting office, copying engineering diagrams, using tracing paper. In the days before photocopying, plans and diagrams for mining and manufacturing industries were copied by hand. It required accuracy, patience and a knack for using the pen without producing ink blots.
Trammer	Young mineworker
Trampler	Lawyer
Tranqueter	Made barrel hoops
Translator	In the shoe trade - a person who translates or remakes old shoe parts into a new shoe. i.e., a cobbler

Tranter	Peddler, often hiring himself out with his horse and cart
Trapper	Opened and shut doors for miners
Traveller	A Gypsy
	Travelling salesman
Travers	Toll bridge collector
Treen Maker	Made wooden domestic goods
Treenail Maker	Made "treenails" - long wooden pins used in shipbuilding
Trencher Maker	Made wooden "trenchers" - platters for serving or cutting food
Trencherman	Cook
Trimmer	Ship's crewman who trimmed coal in ship's bunkers
	Dockworker who trimmed grain or bulk cargo in ship's hold to spread it out evenly
Troacher	Peddler
Troner	Official weigher in markets
Trouchman / Truchman	Interpreter
Trouncer	Drayman's assistant (Brewers)
Trover	Smuggler
Truchman	Interpreter
Trugger / Trug maker	Made "trugs" - shallow baskets
Trusser	Hay baler - made up hay trusses
Tubber	Made tubs and barrels - a cooper
Tubedrawer	Made tubes
Tubman	English barrister
	Court official
	Filled tubs in a coalmine
Tucker	Cleaned cloth goods
Tucker-in	Chambermaid who tucked in the bed-clothing
Turncock	Worked for the local water company, opening and closing the water supply. He also had to inform householders that their water was being turned off.
Turpentine-makers	Turpentine is a thin volatile essential oil obtained by steam distillation or other means from the wood or exudates (material that has oozed out) of certain pine trees and used as a paint thinner, solvent, and medicinally as a liniment.

Turner	Lathe worker
	Gymnast esp. street performers
	In the Potteries; Turns the dried clay ware to the required outline before firing
Turnkey	Jailer
Turning Boy	Weaver's assistant - turned the loom bar
Turnpike Keeper	Collected road tolls
Turnspit	Boy who turned the spit handle, roasting meat. (Medieval)
Tweeny / Tweenie	Maid employed "between the stairs" assisting cook and housemaids
Twiller	Produced a raised diagonal rib appearance in fabric
Twine Spinner	Engaged in ropemaking by hand
Twist Hand	Used a lace-making machine
Twister / Twisterer	Worked a machine twisting the yarns or threads
Tyresmith	Blacksmith who specialized in making the iron bands (tyres) around wooden cartwheels before the introduction of rubber, later pneumatic tyres/tires.
Typist	Typists are still in-demand today, just without the typewriter. In the 1940s, typists were popular positions within the publishing, administrative and clerical industries. The role today has been upgraded with computers.
Ulnager	One appointed to examine the quality of woolen goods to be sold
Upholder / Unholsterer	Furniture seller - mainly chairs and couches
Vacher	Herdsman
Valet	Gentleman's personal male servant
Valuator	Valuer
Vamper	Made up the upper part of a boot or shoe covering the instep and sometimes extending over the toe
Vassal	Lowest order of servant
Vatman	Worked with vats in wine & beer making
	Put pulp into molds for paper-making
Venator / Venur	Huntsman
Verderer	Official in charge of the Royal Forests
Verge Maker	Made spindles for watch and clock-making
Verger	Priest's or Vicar's assistant

Verrier	Glazier - from French
Vestment Maker	Made vestments for the clergy
Viceman	A smith who works at the vice instead of the anvil
Victualler	A tavern keeper - see Licensed Victualler Provided army, navy, or merchant ships with food supplies
Viewer	Manager in the mines
Villein	Paid dues to Lord of the manor for land use
Vintager	Grape grower; wine maker
Vintner / Vinter	Wine merchant
Violin string maker	Made "catgut" violin strings.
Virginal Player	Played the virginal - similar to a harpsichord
Vocalist	A singer
Vulcan	Blacksmith
Wadsetter	(Scottish) Creditor to whom a "wadset" is made. A wadset is a right by which lands, or other heritable subjects, are consigned to a creditor as a security for debt
Waggoner	Wagon or 4-wheeled cart driver
Wailer	Removed impurities and foreign bodies from coal in the mines
Wainwright	Maker or repairer of wagons – "wains"
Waister	Seaman stationed in the waist of the ship
Wait / Wakeman	Night-watchman
Waiter / Tide Waiter	Customs officer who waited on the (high) tide (when vessels arrived) to collect duty on goods imported
Waker	A person whose job was to wake workers in time for early morning work
Walker	"Walked" over cloth after weaving, after wetting, to clean and thicken it - see Fuller
Waller	Brick or dry-stone wall builder In the Cheshire salt-works, makers of coarser grades of salt used in industrial processes, chemicals, fisheries and potteries
Wanter / Want Catcher	Mole catcher
Warder	Jailer
Wardrobe Dealer	Dealer in second-hand clothing

Warper	Set up the "warp" (thread) on looms
	Moved boats by hauling on their "warps" (ropes)
Warrener	A warrener maintains rabbit warrens, traps them and produces rabbit meat for the Laird. Warrens were the property of the lord of the manor.
Washman	Tin coater (tin plater)
Wasteman	Waste remover
	Checked and maintained that mine workings were free of gas
Watch finisher	Assembled time pieces (did not make the parts)
Watcher	Employed as security in Customs bonded warehouses - to Watch the goods
Watchman	Town night-watchman
Watch Making	Various occupations in the Watch-Making Industry
Water Bailiff	Maintained fishing rights on (usually) rivers - still in use
	River based customs official
Water Gilder	Gilded metal surfaces by applying liquid amalgam, the mercury being afterwards removed by evaporation
	Trapped water fowl
Water Leader / Leder / Loder	Transported and sold fresh water
Waterman	Boatman who plies for hire - usually on rivers
	Waterman (waterworks); sluice man, valveman, water valve man controls sluices or valves by which water is let into and out of reservoirs.
	(Also, Drowner) A man who understood irrigation. He was appointed to control the watering of the common water meadows, especially in Dorset, Wiltshire, Avon and Hampshire.
Wattle Hurdle Maker	Made wattle hurdles - panels of wattle fencing
Waulker / Waulkmiller	Cloth worker - see Walker
Waver	Weaver - from regional pronunciation
Way Maker	Road builder
Way Man	Road surveyor
Wayland	A smith
Weather Spy	Astrologer
Weaver	The operative of a loom producing cloth

Webster / Webber	Operator of looms; weaver - originally a female weaver
Weigher / Weigh Clerk	Weighed landed goods on the dockside
Well Sinker	Well digger
Wellmaster	In charge of the village well and responsible for clean drinking water
Wellwright	Made the winding gear for wells
Wet Glover	Leather glove maker
Wet Nurse	Woman who breast-fed babies for others
Wetter	Dampened paper for printing

Glass making worker |
Whacker	Horse or ox team driver
Whalebone Dresser	Prepared whalebones for corsetry and other purposes
Wharfinger	Owner or manager of a wharf
Wheel Tapper	Railway worker - tapped wheels to detect cracks from the resultant ring
Wheeler	Made wheels

Spinning wheel attendant

Led pit ponies underground in the pits |
Wheelwright	Made or repaired wheels; wheeled carriages, etc.
Wherryman	Ran a "wherry" - a large flat-bottomed sailing boat, used typically on rivers
Whig	(Scottish) Horse driver
Whim / Whimseyman	Employed driving mine winding gear carrying men and materials up and down mine shafts.
Whipcord Maker	Whip Maker

Can't get enough? There's more online at https://www.familyresearcher.co.uk/glossary/Dictionary-of-Old-Occupations-Index.html

And see: https://www.berkshistory.org/multimedia/articles/african-american-occupations-in-the-1900s/

Before we complete the discussion on job title listings, I wanted to add as a supplement to the above list, a list of job codes and terms related to the Underground Railroad.

As, more and more, our nation grapples with its history of enslavement of African Americans, more and more documents from those days begin to take on importance. Within the historical records you may encounter unfamiliar terms related to jobs folks did in connection to enslaved people. From the time Africans first set foot on what would become American soil, Black craftspeople worked to produce valued architecture, handicrafts, and decorative items. The proof of Black craftworkers' labors can be found, oddly, in the advertisements calling for their return to bondage. The Black Craftspeople Digital Archive (http://archive.blackcraftspeople.org/) is an online archive of such ads. These show skilled enslaved Black carpenters, needleworkers, sawyers, coopers, brickmakers, caulkers, wheelwrights, tanners, shoemakers, and more. By describing the skills these fugitives from slavery possessed, the ads reveal the valuable level of industry possessed by these people. Further study of enslaved people's efforts to free themselves introduces us to occupational language of a major freedom vehicle, the Underground Railroad. The Underground Railroad was a "secret" and informal network of individuals, safe houses, and escape routes enslaved people in the American South used to gain freedom. Because it was a secretive organization and folks were risking their lives for freedom, code terms were used. The peak time for the Underground Railroad Freedom Movement was between 1820 and 1865.

As you research enslaved ancestors (some of your best sources will be slave narratives, personal letters, diaries, organizational documents and newspaper articles), it is important to be familiar with some of the vocabulary, as you may encounter it and need to interpret the "job" meanings.

Jobs and Terms Associated with the Underground Railroad

Job Name/Code Term	Meaning
Agents	Sympathizers who helped the enslaved connect to the Railroad
Baggage/Cargo/Fleece/Freight/Passengers	Escaped or fugitive slaves
Bundles of wood	Fugitives that were expected
Conductors	Guides on the Underground Railroad
Operator	Person who helped freedom seekers as a conductor or agent
Patter roller	Bounty hunter hired to capture slaves
Shepherds	Folks who encouraged enslaved people to escape and escorted them
Station masters	Those who hid escaping slaves in their homes or a person in charge of a hiding place
Stockholders	Financial supporters who donated to the Railroad

For more on the Underground Railroad, see: https://www.pbs.org/black-culture/shows/list/underground-railroad/stories-freedom/underground-railroad-terminology/ and https://pathways.thinkport.org/secrets/language.cfm

Also see: https://artsedge.kennedy-center.org/~/media/ArtsEdge/LessonPrintables/grade-3-4/harriet_tubman_codes_and_phrases_used_on_the_underground_railroad.ashx

What it took to perform those jobs

As we travel through time and discover the job titles and descriptions of occupations held by our ancestors, it is important to see these job titles in their historical context to understand (not just define) the work our ancestors did.

For example, being a "cook" in the twenty-first century looks very different from being a "cook" in 1920, and very different still than it did in 1820.

Imagine, if you will, today's cook shopping a food market for just the right ingredients for a large meal. They walk the aisles and rows of the market selecting fresh loaves of bread, fruits, and vegetables. Placing them in their reusable tote, popping the goods into the back seat of the SUV, and driving back to the kitchen. Not an unfamiliar or difficult to imagine scene. Now, go back to 1900 in the Southern states.

A White woman hands her Black cook a list. The cook may be illiterate. She walks or is transported into town, where she then stands in a line to be recognized. After being recognized, she hands the paper list to the grocer who gathers the items on the list, places them in a bag, and dismisses the cook. She must then walk or secure some sort of transport to get the bag(s) of groceries back to the house. This has taken half her day. Upon her return, she must clean, wash, sort, and prepare the meal. Once cooked, she then must serve the meal, pick up afterward, wash and dry the pots, pans, dishes, and utensils. Then it's time to travel home for the next thirty minutes or so, since her living quarters would not be close to those of the family who employs her.

You see, we have here the same job title, but at very different times, involving very different activities.

A 1920 census record for my grandma, Fannie Felder, lists her as "cook." And while "cook" may still be listed as an occupation on a modern census, some job titles are a bit less familiar, and perhaps more nuanced than they might appear at first glance, as demonstrated by the exploration of "cook" in the earlier paragraph.

In looking at the early 1900s census records, I saw the term "laundress" frequently listed as a woman's occupation. I assumed that meant that in the days before clothes washers and public laundromats, there were women who did laundry for a living. Sounds simple enough. Then I met Mrs. Vivian Filer.

I attended a session at the UF African American Studies Symposium in February of 2020 and listened with amazement as Mrs. Filer told the story of growing up and working with her mother–a laundress. I will never see this job title the same.

Mrs. Filer told of how, early in the morning, a White man would drive up to her home and drop off a load of white dress shirts to be laundered. The laundress's day began with the making of lye soap.

Next was the drawing of the water. Since there was no indoor plumbing, the water was hand-pumped from a well in the yard. Once all the needed water was secured, Mrs. Filer explained how they then had to make a fire and begin the process of boiling the water.

The washing of the shirts occurred in a ten-gallon galvanized tin tub with ribs on the inside. The ribbing was used as a washboard to scrub any stains or dirt (especially around the collar) of the shirt.

When washed and rinsed, the shirts were hung up to air dry on a clothesline. While the shirts were drying, Mrs. Filer and her mother would begin the process of making starch, and once the shirts were partially dry, they would begin starching them.

With the shirts clean and starched, next came the ironing with a coal-powered iron. Once ironed, they would fold or hang the shirts for pickup. And all this for twenty-five cents.

417

Records for my maternal grandfather, Ned Felder, also revealed he worked as a railroad fireman. On steam locomotives, the term "fireman" was used to describe the person shoveling fuel, typically coal, into the engine's firebox. On U.S. steamships and stationary steam engines, such as those driving sawmills, the term was usually a "stoker" (the British Merchant Navy used fireman). Much of the job is hard physical labor.

Despite the limited upward mobility, Pullman porters, brakemen, and firemen were considered to be prestigious occupations for Black men. In the South, those who held these jobs were respected members of what was, at the time, a fairly small Black middle class. I've come across several references over the years that, for many years in the South, Blacks could become firemen but never be promoted to an engineer. In much the same way, Blacks could be Pullman porters but not Pullman conductors, or could be dining car waiters but not chief stewards. For more on this, check out http://www.worldcat.org/title/association-of-colored-railway-trainmen-and-locomotive-firemen-records-1918-1936/oclc/38477515.

After World War I, my grandfather, Ned, married. Their only child, my mom, remembered "we won the war, but lost the man." Records from Florida State Hospital for the Insane in Chattahoochee, Florida, describe him as a bipolar man with "manic depressive psychosis."

In September 1933 he was transferred to the Tuskegee VA Medical Center. The facility was fully staffed by Whites. His file records portray him as an agitator who "requires restraint to control him."

His records tell us he was "dark brown, muscular, 5 ft 6 in tall, 140 lbs. Missing all teeth, unhealthy gums. 20/20 vision. 6th-grade education ... exceptional for a Negro."

"Since admission he becomes upset; fights other patients or anyone with whom he comes in contact; requires restraint to control him."

"When admitted, did not know anything about his family, nor cared. Good physical condition; much ego."

Understanding his occupations as solider, cook, and fireman sheds light on his physical prowess, which, in turn, paints a vivid picture of his physical description given in the medical records. Knowing his work history gives insight into how he became "muscular" in build, "good physical condition," a man who "requires restraint to control him."

Soundtrack suggestion:
"We Are"
Sweet Honey in the Rock

We are our grandmothers' prayers
and we are our grandfathers' dreamings
we are the breath of the ancestors
we are the spirit of God

Getting a job or doing a job involved more than just doing the job

As strange as it may seem, some folks had issue with the way hair grows out of one's skull naturally. In Louisiana in the 1700s, the Tignon Laws forced Black women to wear head wraps because their hairstyles were considered a threat to the status quo. For Black women entering the workforce in the twentieth century, similar "laws" were observed. These were unspoken until you "crossed the line" and then these laws were articulated clearly. The first rule dealt with hair. Women with kinky hair were required to straighten it so as not to offend coworkers and clients.

In 1786, Spanish colonial Governor Don Esteban Miró enacted the Edict of Good Government, also referred to as the Tignon Laws, which "prohibited Creole women of color from displaying 'excessive attention to dress' in the streets of New Orleans." Instead, they were forced to wear a *tignon* (scarf or handkerchief) over their hair to show that they belonged to the slave class, whether they were enslaved or not. (https://

419

www.vice.com/en_us/article/j5abvx/black-womens-hair-illegal-tignon-laws-new-orleans-louisiana)

Hair styles commonly associated with Black people, such as dreadlocks, cornrows, twists, and Bantu knots, remain an issue of concern now. It was only as recently as 2019 that California Governor Gavin Newsom signed a bill into law that bans workplace and school discrimination against people for wearing their natural hair.

This issue is of particular concern to Black women, whose hair is more likely than White women's hair to be perceived as "unprofessional," according to a 2019 study of 2,000 Black and White women.

The study finds that Black women are also more likely than White women to be sent home from their workplace because of their hair. The same study also found that Black women are more likely to report harsh judgments in the workplace based on looks. Four out of five said they have to change their hair from its natural state in order to fit in with their workplace culture.

In 2019 a New Jersey high school teen wrestler, Andrew Johnson, was forced to cut his dreadlocks in order to participate in a school wrestling match.

He was told by a referee that his hair violated wrestling rules. He received a humiliating on-the-spot cutting of his hair and went on to win the match. State officials opened a civil rights investigation, the *New York Times* reported.

Even now members of Congress are trying to make sure incidents like this never happen again.

Today, but even more so in the past, occupational opportunities are often contingent on appearance. For some of our minority ancestor workers, work meant providing services and labor in spaces our ancestors were not otherwise allowed to occupy. They may have been cooking food in places they could not eat, serving drinks in clubs they were not allowed to sit in and enjoy the show.

Also, for many, a job may involve navigating transportation and parking to get to work. For many of our ancestors, traveling and lodging while in the performance of their craft required the use of "underground" pathways to secure food and lodging. Early Black entertainers used the "Green Book" to find places to eat and sleep while on assignment.

Occupational hazards

> On May 17, 1909, Eighty White Firemen, Members of the Brotherhood of Locomotive Firemen and Enginemen, went on strike against the Georgia Railroad. They charged that the railroad was replacing white firemen with black at lower pay and was granting Negro workers seniority over white. The strike quickly inflamed public opinion; and mobs, attacking trains and beating strikebreakers, soon halted railroad operations completely. (The Georgia "Race Strike" of 1909 by John Michael Matt as seen at https://www.jstor.org/stable/pdf/2206357.pdf)

Some jobs could result in serious injury or worse, as seen in the 1909 Georgia Railroad strike described above. At other times success could get you killed. Such is the case of a relative of mine, Elmore Bolling. Josephine Bolling McCall, the youngest of Elmore and Bertha Mae's seven children, wrote of his story in "The Penalty for Success: My Father Was Lynched in Lowndes County, Alabama."

Elmore started hauling loads of scrap kindling and metal into Montgomery. As time went on, the loads and his business grew.

"He was raising their economic status. . . ." Bolling McCall writes. "They were not as dependent on the cotton and the White farmers. . . . He never wanted to work for anybody."

Word spread in the community of Elmore Bolling's financial gains and the Whites in the area were not happy. Neither were they quiet about expressing their opinion that he was outstepping his place in Southern society. It was a mild winter's night on December 4, 1947, when they discovered his dead body. Bullets riddled his chest, and a shotgun blast had been delivered to his back.

Soundtrack suggestion:
"More than a Paycheck"
by Y.M. Barnwell © 1981

I wanted more pay
But what I've got today
is more than I bargained for
when I walked through that door

We bring more than a paycheck to our loved ones and family
We bring more than a paycheck to our loved ones and family

How race and gender played a part in who did what work

America has a long history of job discrimination. So, if you are researching an ancestor who was a member of a certain minority group, you may save yourself some time by eliminating certain resource sources, as the ancestor may not have been allowed to work in certain jobs and/or certain locations.

"No Irish need apply":

Ireland's potato famine of 1845 launched a wave of immigration across the Atlantic Ocean to the United States. Irish immigrants often entered the workforce at the bottom of the occupational ladder and took on the menial and dangerous jobs that were often avoided by other workers. Many Irish women became servants or domestic workers, while many Irish men labored in coal mines and built railroads and canals. About 4.5 million Irish arrived in America between 1820 and 1930. The Irish often worked dangerous and low paying jobs creating roads and bridges across the country. The Irish workers would follow the construction jobs across the country, and they would work long hours in unsanitary and unsafe conditions. Many Irish men would often work jobs that even black slaves were not allowed to work, because the black slaves were considered valuable property. Irish men were not valued as property and allowed to perform more dangerous tasks. (https://careertrend.com/how-2063600-become-lighthouse-keeper.html)

After 1860, many Irish sang songs about "NINA signs" reading Help wanted—no Irish need apply. (A variation was Irish need not apply, or "INNA"). The 1862 song "No Irish Need Apply" was inspired by NINA signs in London. Later Irish Americans adapted the lyrics and the songs to reflect the discrimination they felt in America.

Historians have debated the issue of anti-Irish job discrimination in the United States. Some insist that the "No Irish need apply" signs were common, but others, such as Richard J. Jensen, argue that anti-Irish job discrimination was not a significant factor in the United States, and these signs and print advertisements were posted by the limited number of early 19th-century English immigrants to the United States who shared the prejudices of their homeland.

In July 2015 the same journal that published Jensen's 2002 paper published a rebuttal by Rebecca A. Fried, an 8th-grade student at Sidwell Friends School. She listed multiple instances of the restriction used in advertisements for many different types of positions, including "clerks at stores and hotels, bartenders, farm workers, house painters, hog butchers, coachmen, bookkeepers, blackers, workers at lumber yards, upholsterers, bakers, gilders, tailors, and papier mache workers, among others." While the greatest number of NINA instances occurred in the 1840s, Fried found instances of its continued use throughout the subsequent century, with the most recent dating to 1909 in Butte, Montana.

Alongside "No Irish Need Apply" signs, in the post-World War II years, signs saying "No Irish, No Blacks, No Dogs" or similar anti-Irish sentiment are reported to begin to appear in the United Kingdom, as discussed by the Irish Studies Centre at London Metropolitan University. (https://en.wikipedia. org/wiki/Anti-Irish_sentiment)

Occupational challenges were compounded if the ancestor happened to be a woman and happened to also be a minority.

Compared with other women in the United States, black women have always had the highest levels of labor market participation regardless of age, marital status, or presence of children at home. In 1880, 35.4 percent of married black women and 73.3 percent of single black women were in the labor force compared with only 7.3 percent of married white women and 23.8 percent of single white women. Black women's higher participation rates extended over their lifetimes, even after marriage, while white women typically left the labor force after marriage.

Differences in black and white women's labor participation were due not only to the societal expectation of black women's gainful employment but also to labor market discrimination against black men which resulted in lower wages and less stable employment compared to white men. Consequently, married black women have a long history of being financial contributors—even co-breadwinners—to two-parent households because of black men's precarious labor market position. (https://www.epi.org/blog/black-womens-labor-market-history-reveals-deep-seated-race-and-gender-discrimination/)

With his New Deal platform, Franklin D. Roosevelt inaugurated the National Recovery Administration in 1933 to draw up industry-wide codes to stop labor strife, ease competition, and get production moving again. Southern Black workers found fault with the codes planned for the textile industry.

From 1934 on, domestic workers denied coverage under NRA and FLSA wrote Washington to ask for help and to inform policymakers about work conditions in the unregulated industry. A representative letter written in pencil on lined notebook paper asked Mrs. Franklin D. Roosevelt to "Please try to help the cooks in private homes to have some kind of working schedule about our jobs."

> We only get a small salary . . . when we keep the house, wash, iron the clothes, cook the meals, come to work at 7 a.m. [and] no limit to the hour we get off. No rest on the job, not an hour to lie down or sit down to rest. But we poor Negro women have to work. Our husbands only get a small salary to pay a few bills, that is rent and a few other utility bills, and we must help. And we don't mind the work, but 18 hours out of 24 hours a day is killing our women. (https://www.archives.gov/publications/prologue/1997/summer/domestics-in-the-depression)

But lest you think that looking for a White female ancestor will be free of discrimination; think again!

"Nine states had marriage [work ban] laws prior to the Depression," writes historian Megan McDonald Way, "and by 1940, 26 states restricted married women's employment in state government jobs." As women around the country struggled to make ends meet during the nation's deepest economic crisis, they became an easy scapegoat for people looking for someone to blame.

And though she is known as one of the architects of the New Deal, Frances Perkins, New York State's Commissioner of Labor, said that negative attitudes toward working women were shared by many who embraced FDR's seemingly liberal economic policies of relief for unemployed workers.

Perkins stated, "Until we have every woman in this community earning a living wage . . . I am not willing to encourage those who are under no economic necessities to compete with their charm and education, their superior advantages, against the working girl who has only her two hands." (https://www.history.com/news/great-depression-married-women-employment) So don't be surprised when you find a wealth of jobless female ancestors during the 1930s.

Earlier examples of the lives of a cook, laundress, or railroad fireman gave us some insight into how race and gender may have played a part in the occupations of our ancestors. Factors of race and gender could often relegate ancestors to the lowest-paying, dirtiest, and most hazardous jobs.

Laws prohibited free Blacks from some activities and occupations and restricted their participation in others. Racism and Klan-like terrorism also made advancement difficult. (https://econpapers.repec.org/article/cupjechis/v_3a59_3ay_3a1999_3ai_3a04_3a p_3a972-996_5f02.htm)

> As segregation tightened and racial oppression escalated across the United States, some leaders of the African American community, often called the talented tenth, began to reject Booker T. Washington's conciliatory approach. W. E. B. Du Bois and other black leaders channeled their activism by founding the Niagara Movement in 1905. Later, they joined white reformers in 1909 to form the National Association for the Advancement of Colored People (NAACP). Early in its fight for equality, the NAACP used the federal courts to challenge disenfranchisement and residential segregation. Job opportunities were the primary focus of the National Urban League, which was established in 1910. (https://www.loc.gov/exhibits/civil-rights-act/segregation-era.html)

A Short History of Colorism

For our non-white ancestors, colorism affected our ancestors' job opportunities and choices. Job opportunities were different according to your race and/or color. (https://www.sciway.net/hist/chicora/freepersons-2.html)

Within the racial classification of Black, there was an issue of colorism. Colorism is a system of practices and ideologies that privileges lighter-skinned Black folks with facial features typically associated with Europeans over their darker-skinned counterparts with more African-associated facial features. (Feliciano, 2016; Reece, 2016). See: https://journals.sagepub.com/doi/10.1177/0034644618770761)

Commonly referred to as the "light versus dark skin issue," colorism within the Black race dates back to slavery in America, where the skin color of slaves was used as the determinant of work chores assigned (Hunter, 2002). Dark-skinned slaves, who were likely of pure African ancestry, were given the more physically demanding tasks in the fields, while lighter-skinned slaves (who had lighter skin because of their biracial status, as it was common for enslavers to rape and have consensual sexual relationships with the females they enslaved) were given more enviable and esteemed positions (Keith & Herring, 1991). This visible division created friction amongst slaves and supported the idea that one was better off if one had a lighter complexion (Ross, 1997).

This mindset was ingrained in the minds of Blacks, and once emancipation occurred, Blacks began buying into and creating their own social divides based on skin tone. For example, Blacks created "blue vein" societies where other Blacks were admitted only if their skin tone was light enough that their veins were visible. Also, the first Black schools, as well as fraternities and sororities, employed the "paper bag test" as a means of admission; if your skin tone was not equal to or lighter than a paper bag, admission was not granted. (http://www.thejuryexpert.com/2010/01/colorism-the-often-un-discussed-ism-in-americas-workforce/)

In 2009 Matthew Harrison introduced a study he conducted on color discrimination in the workplace. Based on his research, Harrison discovered that skin tone is more important than educational background for those seeking jobs. He noted in particular that "a darker-skinned Black male with higher levels of education and past work experience was significantly less preferred than a lighter-skinned Black male with less education and work experience." (*Coloring Inside the Lines: Finding a Solution for Workplace Colorism Claims* in https://scholarship. law.umn.edu/cgi/viewcontent.cgi?article=1147&context=lawine q)

Only the "tall, tan, and terrific" need apply:

> While the club reproduced the racist imagery of the times, often depicting blacks as savages in exotic jungles or as "darkies" in the plantation South, it imposed a more subtle color bar on the chorus girls whom the club presented in skimpy outfits. They were expected to be "tall, tan, and terrific," which meant that they had to be at least five feet, six inches tall, light skinned, and under twenty-one years of age. Duke Ellington, who first played the Cotton Club in 1927, was expected to write "jungle music" for an audience of whites.
>
> See: https://memory.loc.gov/diglib/ihas/loc.music. tdabio.61/default.html and https://www.google.com/ search?client=firefox-b-1-d&ei=rUtlXqSqGqiJytMPm7aU-Ao &q=jobs+that+don%27t+exist+anymore&oq=jobs+that+do n%27t+exist&gs_l=psy-ab.1.1.0l8.9196.17383..19715...0.2..0 .136.2103.11j10......0....1..gws-wiz.......0i71j0i273j0i131j0i67. ZXznJ6lsVws)

Online references related to occupations

- See the list at https://www.ncpedia.org/anchor/ occupations-1860

- https://www.familysearch.org/wiki/en/United_States_ Occupations_Listed_in_Census_Schedules_1850_to_1930_ (National_Institute)

- The *Classified Index of Industries and Occupations* (the "Census Index") was developed to organize and make understandable the many thousands of industries and occupations as obtained from the decennial Census of Population. The 1990 Index lists approximately 21,000 industry and 30,000 occupational titles. The 30,000 titles from the Census Index will fall into one of the 500 occupational classifications used in the National Compensation Survey. (https://www.bls.gov/ncs/ocs/ocsm/comuseindex.htm)

Appendix B – Dead Folk

"You have collected all my tears in your bottle" (Ps. 56:8)

"The Lord is close to the brokenhearted and saves those who are crushed in spirit" (Ps. 34:18).

"A bruised reed He will not break" (Isa. 42:3).

"How would you describe the deceased?"

Genealogy is a look into the past and the lives of folks now dead. You may have gone to a genealogy event and seen folks with t-shirts proclaiming, "I seek dead people." Unfortunately, this seeking can be done with our humanity switch turned to the OFF position. It would be like having a doctor with poor or no bedside manner. Because we are human and folks with hearts, emotions, and feelings, it seemed appropriate for me to talk briefly about a darker aspect of this work, and we begin with a consideration of how you refer to the person you are researching. For you, it may be entirely academic. You are gathering data on a subject. But perhaps for the folks providing you with this information, who may have known your "subject," it is important to consider if your subject may be their "loss."

The Ripple effect of loss

The previous section on Your Folk is intended to help you by discussing some of the ways I found the players in my story, and how you can find your folks, too. I hope that reading about my journey of discovery so far has been both inspirational and motivating for you; motivating enough for you to begin or to dig deeper into your own family narrative. In this section, I want to offer up research tools and tips for you to use as you navigate your own journey of discovery.

Again, we should consider the human or emotional toll of this work. Whereas to you, you are simply gathering data to complete a family tree, for your older relatives, you are asking them to talk about dearly loved and now departed friends and family.

Before you run off to do that interview with Grandma, Grandpa, or your great-aunt or -uncle, please take a moment to consider the ripple effects of death in a family. In particular, let's talk about the idea of "waking the dead," and that of "recognizing and grieving secondary losses."

Waking the Dead

I would not say that I come from a family of great storytellers. They do not tell or retell stories of trauma, violent dying, pain, and grief. Such stories are not common at all, and I can only recall a handful of such stories that surfaced on a regular basis within my family unit.

By far the most common such tale was my mom retelling the story of her dad's demise in the Tuskegee Institute due to insanity. Mom was bitter, and angry at the government and the Jim Crow system that she believes was the root of his "insanity." As she saw it, her loving daddy went off to war, was treated with respect and dignity, then came back to a segregated South diagnosed with "shell shock." He was confined to an institution with all White doctors and caregivers. She would image scenarios where a Southern White doctor entered her daddy's room and asked, "Well, boy, what's your problem?" He dared not say what was really on his mind. That kind of talk could get a Black man killed. So, he'd just say nothing or reply, "fine." Mom knew he died without receiving any real treatment, due to a system that did not respect him as a man.

The other story of loss in my family was, of course, that of my grandmother's dad, A. S. J. Allen. Unlike my mom, Grandma never elaborated or provided much detail in her retelling of A. S. J.'s dying. She would simply say "he was shot by a White man." I believe that if my grandmother ever laid down on a psychiatrist's couch with an expectation to talk and release her pent-up anger, mourning, rage, or sorrow, the session might well have ended with the psychiatrist waking her up. Grandma's way of dealing with stuff was, you didn't talk about it. "Avoidance coping" is what it's called in modern psychiatric circles.

It would be many years after Grandma's death that I would learn the details of my great-grandfather's violent dying that I tell here in this book. Once learning the story, I retold it *ad nauseum* to all who would listen. My son heard the story so many times that he made a film version of it. Not exactly the way I envisioned it, but the story was now clear enough in his mind that he could script it and will thus pass it on to a new generation. The retelling of this violent dying is now family lore. The act of A. S. J. Allen's killing is now a visualization. It is now a memory, and we have, in essence, awakened the dead.

"Memory is not an instrument for exploring the past but its theatre. It is the medium of past experience as the ground is the medium in which dead cities lie interred" (Walter Benjamin, *Berlin Chronicle*).

"Dormant history is awakened when the lament of dead souls breaks through the oppressed layers of memory of the past. Once the dark nights of forgotten memory, especially the ones of violence, are allowed to surface in the light of truth, the dead

souls come to life and begin to speak to their living descendants."
(*Journal of Ritual Studies* 3, no. 2, Korean Ritual Thematic
Issue (Summer 1989): 251-85. Published by Pamela J. Stewart
and Andrew J. Strathern Foundation at: https://www.jstor.org/
stable/44368940?seq=1#metadata_info_tab_contents)

When asking family members about their loved ones, remember
you are awakening memories. Visualizations are being created
around the deceased person's life, and possibly visualizations
and memories of how they died. For them, your interview may be
waking the dead. So, tread with care.

Recognizing and Grieving Secondary Losses

Have you ever thrown a pebble in a still pond and watched what happens? As the stone enters the water, waves expand outward from the point of entry, disturbing the water in ever-growing rings of motion. The one single event of tossing a pebble into the water affects everything in the pond. Death is like that. Death has a ripple effect that sets off a wave that moves across time and space.

The death of someone we care about is a primary event in our lives. It is the pebble in our pond. But the experience of loss doesn't end with the memorial service or the burial. The death sets in motion subsequent losses, called secondary losses, that occur as a result of the primary loss, creating a sense that we are losing more than just the person who died. And it can often feel like that pain will go on forever.

If your relative knew the ancestor you are trying to learn about, remember that for them, retelling the stories of that person's life may be like tossing a pebble back into what had been a calm pond. Your questions and promptings to tell the story may be an invitation to revisit the ripples of an old pain.

Death changes the way we see the world. The changes death brings are physical, personal, social, spiritual, emotional, and psychological. A part of the grieving process is learning how to adjust to a new normal without someone dear. Your family member has been changed by the death of the person you are asking about.

So, again, be cautious, be kind, and be patient.

We human beings are relational creatures. Our identities are contingent on our relationships with others. When we lose someone in our family, it changes those relationships. Now perhaps we are no longer a grandson, son, or nephew in the same way we once were. Our relationships with the person who died might continue after their passing, but the nature of the role has forever shifted and will never be the same again.

435

The following are twenty examples of the types of losses one may experience after the death of a family member. Every individual will not necessarily experience all the losses mentioned here and they may experience additional losses that are not mentioned here. I mention these to prompt you to consider the ripples your questions may create.

- Loss of Family Structure: For siblings, birth order is changed. For parents, a challenge comes when people ask, "How many children do you have?" For spouses, there is no longer another adult in the home. For children, there may now be only one parent.

- Loss of a Primary Relationship: Loss of a significant person who was prominent in your life. The time you spent together, the conversations you had together, and the activities you enjoyed together have ended. There may also be a loss of things you wished you did together but never had the chance to accomplish.

- Loss of the Familiar Way of Relating to Family and Friends: Survivors may find that friends avoid them at social functions, at work, or in the hallways at school. This can bring additional sadness and anger to the bereaved.

- Loss of Support Systems: Loss of friends, family, community organizations, and others who help to sustain and lend strength daily. At a time when we most need extra attention, we often have to develop new systems of support.

- Loss of a Chosen Lifestyle: Being forced to begin a new way of life despite one's personal wishes. For surviving spouses, this means being single again and possibly childless. For siblings, it can mean becoming an only child. For parents whose only child dies, it can mean the loss of future grandchildren.

- Loss of Financial Security: Serious financial loss associated with death. In many cases, the primary wage earner is gone. For others, there can be loss of employment due to the grief process or serious debt incurred by the deceased or as a result of the death.

- Loss of the Past: Inability to share memories of the past journey with the deceased. For survivors who are left alone by the death, there will be no one to talk to about the "remember whens."

- Loss of the Future: The immediate cessation of plans made with the deceased. We mentioned this earlier under "Loss of a Primary Relationship," but even if the loss does not involve a primary relationship, the losses can include (say, for parents) growing old together, having children with that person, watching that person graduate from college, watching them begin their own family, celebrating birthdays/graduations/ marriages of children, being able to resolve unfinished business, and the wish of living happily ever after, to name a few.

- Loss of Dreams: Disillusionment resulting from the disappearance of the plans listed above. This is especially true when a young person dies. Survivors grieve not only a past and present with that person, but also future hopes, goals, and dreams.

- Loss of Identity: Loss of the roles that you no longer fulfill in a relationship. Parents who are now childless may no longer consider themselves parents; surviving spouses are no longer lovers; a surviving sibling may be an only child. This loss of role can be in the home, in the family, at work, among friends, and in the community, as well.

- Loss of a Large Chunk of Self: Loss of the part of the self that was given to the other person in love, and that death seems to have violently ripped from one's being.

- Loss of Self-Confidence: A survivor's failure to recognize his or her own personal self-efficacy. It is easy to make human mistakes on this unknown journey, especially in the initial weeks and months when our attention is completely taken by the death. This can lead to feelings of inadequacy or the thought that we are not able to do anything right.

- Loss of Ability to Make Decisions: The insecurity following the loss of self-confidence that causes the survivor to look for direction and advice from others. Many survivors wonder, "What should I do now?" If the deceased had input in making decisions, there is now a void in the process. Survivors are forced to rely on themselves to make choices without that person which can lead to confusion and indecision.

- Loss of Ability to See Choices: The sense that the survivor has no control over his or her life, leading to an inability to accept that there are still alternatives, options, and allowable preferences. Because the new lifestyle was not a conscious choice, it is harder to see that choices still remain.

- Loss of Trust: Inability to have faith in a positive outcome. Death can shatter our trust in the world, those around us, and ourselves. Trusting enough to open oneself to love again can be very painful and is often avoided by many.

- Loss of Security: Inability to feel safe. Knowing that the world is an unsafe, unpredictable place can lead to feelings of anxiety and vulnerability. It can be accompanied by the uncertainty of what to expect, what will happen next, or how we will react or respond. For survivors who relocate, the changes in homes, sleeping arrangements, schools, churches, and neighborhoods can heighten the feeling of insecurity.

- Loss of a Sense of Humor: The failure to see anything funny. Because of the pain associated with losing an important person in our life, we may not feel like laughing at anything. In the immediate aftermath of the death, we even wonder whether it is still okay to find humor in situations, happiness in events, and enjoyment in life.

- Loss of Patience: The loss of our normal ability to tolerate impaired skills and less-than-ideal reactions. We become impatient with our inability to recover, feel better, and handle normal stress. This can lead to feelings of inadequacy and failure, as the process of grieving normally lasts for several years. Besides, we may find ourselves crying more, yelling more, or arguing more with those we love.

- Loss of Ability to Focus and Function: Loss of concentration due to preoccupation with feelings of pain and sadness. Many survivors report that their ability to focus has become impaired. Focus and full functionality can be difficult to recover, especially if there was trauma involved. There can also be a significant loss of energy, both physically and emotionally. It is estimated by some that one hour of grieving is comparable to eight hours of manual labor.

- Loss of Health: The physical problems resulting from emotional stress, pain, trauma, shock, and grief. Many survivors experience sleep problems, eating problems, heart issues, headaches, stomach problems, depression, anxiety, or all the above. It is a good idea to seek medical attention following a death so that health problems are not compounded.

  Source: 3/21/2013 article by Jill LaMorie https://www.taps. org/articles/19-/secondaryloss

The William Maxwell book, *They Came Like Swallows* (1937), is a realistic, heartbreaking depiction of what happens to a family when the flu kills the mother. The book explores "contagion guilt," where each surviving family member blames himself, in one way or another, for the mother's death.

To review: always remember that we seek dead folks (not data). As you speak with relatives who may hold firsthand knowledge of the people you are researching, remember that it takes time and patience to heal. Awareness of the many secondary losses that can accompany a death may help you to be more patient and caring as you explore the ancestors' lives. Remember that, for them, these stories are personal and may even have a negative or guilty component.

Sick Folk: Aging, Disease, and Death

Aging, medications, illness, and the like: Stories connecting to the keepers of your stories.

There are nine primary record sources you can check to find out about an ancestor's death. These are:

1. State Death Certificate

2. Local Death Record

3. Death Register

4. Cemetery Record

5. Census Mortality Schedule (In the 1850, 1860, 1870, 1880, and 1885 censuses, data was collected on persons who had died the year immediately preceding the enumeration.)

6. Church Death Record

7. Probate Records

8. Obituaries and newspaper death notices

9. Burial Permit (Usually held by cemeteries and funeral homes)

Accidents and killings happen, but perhaps the most common reason there are deadfolk is due to aging and disease which result in death. For our ancestors, sickfolk often resulted in deadfolk. Let's face it, younger folks tend to not be as involved or concerned with collecting family histories as their more "mature" relatives— usually. And when you are young, you usually do not spend a lot of time thinking about aging, diseases, and death. So, let's talk for a moment about how age and the times in which you and your ancestors live will affect your research.

Knowing the cause of death for as many of your ancestors as possible can serve a practical real-time function. This kind of information may inform you of genetic risks you may have inherited. Perhaps cancer, diabetes, heart disease, or some other condition runs in your family. The earlier you know of the possibility, the better your ability to make proactive choices for your own health.

Today we live in a healthier, more wellness-centered culture than that of our ancestors. So when we look through data on our ancestors and discover their "cause of death" there is reason to pause and interpret that cause. Seeing and understanding health trends in the family can be enlightening. As I approached my sixtiethth birthday, I was reminded by my life insurance agent that my existing policy would expire and, if I wanted to continue coverage, I would need to be seen by a nurse/agent and answer a few health questions.

Growing up with my mom, and having my father absent from my life, I had a fairly good knowledge of the diseases and health conditions that ran in my mother's side of the family. But I did not make a connection to my father's side of the family until later on in life and I had no idea of the medical history there. So I emailed my sister and brother and asked, "What kind of health issues did Dad have?" along with the form I was expected to fill out for the life insurance policy. I was both pleased and surprised when both of them responded that Dad was a "private" person and did not talk about his medical issues. However, their observation was that the man seemed to be allergic to *everything*. I smiled and glowed with this newfound information. It explained my life as I, too, found just about *everything* in the natural world to be an irritant. At last I had a justification for my dislike of dogs, cats, flowers, and trees, along with a variety of foods and drinks.

As I write this book, much of America lives under mandatory "stay at home" orders due to the 2020 COVID-19 pandemic. Issues of connection and freedoms are arising in many parts of society. In this era, we have great tools for staying connected to our family. There is email, voicemail, cell phones, FaceTime, Facebook, TikToc, Instagram, and on and on it goes. Apps like FaceTime, Zoom, Skype, Facebook, Twitter, Snapchat, and others are great for communications, although they may present challenges for those unfamiliar. But the simple fact is, there is little to keep us apart.

We have the tools to connect with some of our most vulnerable members—the keepers of our stories—our elders. In times past, this was not the case. So surviving family members may have little information on how an ancestor died. Or how their disease or illness progressed. Most of our Old World ancestors went their entire lives without ever seeing a physician. In 1900 almost 20 percent of children in the U.S. died before age five. Doctors did not keep any sort of "standard" office hours and they generally only paid house calls to the wealthy. Hospitals were places where one went to die, and most folks relied on "snake oils" and patent medicines such as "soothing syrups." These were often addictive concoctions containing morphine, heroin, opium, or laudanum and didn't address the actual cause of the problem.

Diseases, epidemics, and pandemics have always been present in the world. As you search you may be able to associate certain epidemics or a series of diseases within your own family lines. Most of the major U.S. epidemics have involved diseases like yellow fever, measles, influenza, cholera, smallpox, typhus, scarlet fever, and typhoid.

Sick folks with communicable diseases can cause illness to migrate within a family unit as it moves from location to location. There are cases where individuals disappeared from local records such as tax rolls, deeds, or censuses, and the researcher does not know why. In some cases, it could have been that a major epidemic struck the town or village where the ancestor lived, killing them and possibly others in the family. There is also the possibility that one or two family members died from a local epidemic and the other surviving relatives moved away. You may even notice "clusters of deaths," where several family members died within a short period of time. If you do, take a look at the "cause of death" that is listed for each person. This might reveal the common cause of death.

Because of the lack of public health knowledge or even scientific understanding of diseases, there is little wonder that our ancestors' lives were marred by preventable deaths prior to the mid-twentieth century. Death and disease are but two of the many clues we can use to write the stories of our ancestors' lives and to understand the communities they lived in.

Most of the time, the communicable disease was caught and spread as a result of poor hygiene, unclean environments, and even unsafe food practices. Regular bathing didn't really catch on as a common practice until the mid- to late-1800s. Even then, "regular" often meant only once a week, particularly since running water (and hot water) in every home was still decades away. Soap manufacturing for sale in stores happened around the late nineteenth century. Before that era, it was just one of the many items that had to be made at home, and was a fairly involved process that was probably low on the priority list when more important things needed to be done. And without modern refrigeration, food spoilage could present difficulties and lead to illness. (https://www.legacytree.com/blog/disease-epidemics-ancestors)

The life expectancy in 1850 of a White person in the United States was forty; of an enslaved person, it was thirty-six.

As mentioned earlier some of the most prevalent diseases for our ancestors were typhoid fever, scarlet fever, measles, whooping cough, dysentery, consumption (tuberculosis), cholera, pneumonia, cancer, smallpox, and the plague.

Especially noteworthy in the eighteenth and nineteenth century lists are the inclusion of some so-called "Negro diseases."

A quite interesting and enlightening work exploring this topic is *The Negro and the Southern Physician: A study of Medical and Racial Attitudes 1800-1860*, by John S. Haller Jr. An online copy is available at https://

www.cambridge.org/core/services/aop-cambridge-core/
content/view/AF4D580121BEAA7789F9FB5459F1E70E/
S0025727300017737a.pdf/div-class-title-the-negro-and-the-
southern-physician-a-study-of-medical-and-racial-attitudes-
1800-1860-div.pdf.

There are a host of other diseases and ailments that may seem strange to our ears but were almost everyday words to our ancestors. While working on plantations in the southern United States, many enslaved people faced serious health problems. In addition to the conditions mentioned earlier concerning personal hygiene and food refrigeration, for the enslaved, improper nutrition, unsanitary living conditions, and excessive labor made this population more susceptible to diseases than those in the White community. The death rates among the enslaved were significantly higher due to diseases.

Below I've listed disease names you may encounter as "cause of death" in your research, and their meanings. I hope that this listing will help you in your research of your "deadfolk" by offering an understanding of how our ancestors viewed and understood "sickfolk."

Ancient Disease Names Sometimes Used as "Cause of Death."

Ablepsy-Blindness
Ague-Flu or malarial fever, characterized by chills and fever
American plague-Yellow fever
Anasarca-Generalized massive edema
Aphonia-Laryngitis
Aphtha-Thrush
Apoplexy-Paralysis due to stroke
Asphycsia/Asphicsia-Cyanosis and lack of oxygen
Atrophy-Wasting away or diminishing in size
Bad blood-Syphilis
Bilious fever-Typhoid, malaria, hepatitis or elevated
temperature, and bile emesis
Biliousness-Jaundice is associated with liver disease
Black fever-Acute infection with high temperature and dark
red skin lesions and high mortality rate
Black plague or death-Bubonic plague
Black pox-Black smallpox
Black vomit-Vomiting old black blood due to ulcers or
yellow fever
Blackwater fever-Dark urine associated with high
temperature
Bladder in the throat-Diphtheria
Blood poisoning-Bacterial infection; septicemia
Bloody flux-Bloody stools, bloody diarrhea
Bloody sweat-Sweating sickness
Bone shave-Sciatica
Brain fever-Meningitis
Breakbone-Dengue fever
Bright's disease-Chronic inflammatory disease of kidneys
Bronze John-Yellow fever
Bule-Boil, tumor, or swelling
Cachexia Africana (mal d'estomac), or dirt-eating, were
thought peculiar only to the Negro because of his mental
constitution. According to physician James Maxwell,

writing in the *Jamaica Physical Journal of 1835*, dirt-eating had been a practice of many early civilizations, but restricted principally to the black races in the nineteenth century.

Cachexy-Malnutrition

Cacogastric-Upset stomach

Cacospysy-Irregular pulse

Caduceus-Subject to falling sickness or epilepsy

Camp fever-Typhus; aka camp diarrhea

Canine madness-Rabies, hydrophobia

Canker-Ulceration of mouth or lips or herpes simplex

Catalepsy-Seizures/trances

Catarrhal-aka catarrh. Discharge from the nose and/or throat due to a cold or allergies

Cerebritis-Inflammation of cerebrum or lead poisoning

Chilblain-Swelling of extremities caused by exposure to cold

Child bed fever-Infection following the birth of a child (also known as puerperal fever)

Chin cough-Whooping cough

Chlorosis-Iron deficiency anemia

Cholecystitis-Inflammation of the gall bladder

Cholelithiasis-Gallstones

Cholera-Acute severe contagious diarrhea with intestinal lining sloughing

Cholera morbus-Characterized by nausea, vomiting, abdominal cramps, and elevated temperature

Chorea-Disease characterized by convulsions, contortions, and dancing

Cold plague-Ague characterized by chills

Colic-Abdominal pain and cramping

Congestion-Any collection of fluid in an organ, like the lungs

Congestive chills-Malaria with diarrhea

Congestive fever-Malaria

Consumption or galloping consumption-Tuberculosis

Corruption-Infection

Coryza-A cold

Costiveness-Constipation
Cramp colic-Appendicitis
Crop sickness-Overextended stomach
Croup-Laryngitis, diphtheria, or strep throat
Cyanosis-Dark skin color from lack of oxygen in the blood
Cynanche-Diseases of the throat
Cystitis-Inflammation of the bladder
Day fever-Fever lasting one day; sweating sickness
Debility-Lack of movement or staying in bed
Decrepitude-Feebleness due to old age
Delirium tremens-Hallucinations due to alcoholism
Dengue-Infectious fever endemic to East Africa
Dentition-Cutting of teeth
Deplumation-Tumor of the eyelids which causes hair loss
Diary fever-A fever that lasts one day
Diptheria-Contagious disease of the throat
Distemper-Usually animal disease with malaise, discharge
from nose and throat, anorexia
Dock fever-Yellow fever
Drapetomania-Considered a "Negro disease" in the mid-
1800s. Mental illness that made enslaved people desire to
run away. Treated with whippings.
Dropsy-Edema (swelling) often caused by kidney or heart
disease
Dropsy of the brain-Encephalitis
Dry bellyache-Lead poisoning
Dysaesthesia Aethiopica, laziness, or "rascality"-Considered
a "Negro disease" in the mid-1800s. Treated with
whippings.
Dyscrasy-An abnormal body condition
Dysentery-Inflammation of colon with frequent passage of
mucous and blood
Dysorexy-Reduced appetite
Dyspepsia-Indigestion and heartburn. Heart attack
symptoms
Dysury-Difficulty in urination
Eclampsy-Symptoms of epilepsy, convulsions during labor

Ecstasy-A form of catalepsy characterized by loss of reason

Edema-Nephrosis; swelling of tissues

Edema of lungs-Congestive heart failure, a form of dropsy

Eel thing-Erysipelas

Elephantiasis-A form of leprosy

Encephalitis-Swelling of the brain; aka sleeping sickness

Enteric fever-Typhoid fever

Enteritis-Inflation of the bowels

Enterocolitis-Inflammation of the intestines

Epitaxis-Nose bleed

Erysipelas-A contagious skin disease, probably due to streptococci; characterized by bulbous lesions

Extravasted blood-Rupture of a blood vessel

Falling sickness-Epilepsy

Fatty liver-Cirrhosis of the liver

Fits-Sudden attack or seizure of muscle activity

Flux-An excessive flow or discharge of fluid like hemorrhage or diarrhea

Flux of humour-Circulation

Frambesia or "yaws"-A tropical infection of the skin, bones, and joints

French pox or great pox-Syphilis (also known as "bad blood")

Gathering-A collection of pus

Glandular fever-Mononucleosis

Great pox-Syphilis

Green fever sickness-Anemia

Grippe/grip-Influenza-like symptoms

Grocer's itch-A skin disease caused by mites in sugar or flour

Heart Sickness-Condition caused by loss of salt from the body

Heat stroke-Body temperature elevates because of surrounding environment temperature and the body does not perspire to reduce the temperature

Hectical complaint-Recurrent fever

Hematemesis-Vomiting blood

Hematuria-Bloody urine
Hemiplegy-Paralysis of one side of the body
Hip Gout-Osteomylitis
Horrors-Delirium tremens
Hydrocephalus-Enlarged head, water on the brain
Hydropericardium-Heart dropsy
Hydrophobia-Rabies
Hydrothroax-Dropsy in the chest
Hypertrophic-Enlargement of organ, like the heart
Impetigo-Contagious skin disease characterized by pustules
Inanition-Physical condition resulting from lack of food
Infantile paralysis-Polio
Intestinal colic- Abdominal pain due to improper diet
Jail Fever-Typhus
Jaundice-Condition caused by blockage of intestines
King's evil-Tuberculosis of neck and lymph glands
Kruchhusten-Whooping cough
Lagrippe or grippe-Influenza or symptoms similar to
influenza
Lockjaw-Tetanus or infectious disease affecting the muscles
of the neck and jaw
Long sickness-Tuberculosis
Lues disease-Syphilis
Lues venera-Venereal disease
Lumbago-Back pain
Lung fever-Pneumonia
Lung sickness-Tuberculosis
Lying in-Time of delivery of an infant (aka confinement)
Malignant fever or malignant sore throat: Diphtheria
Mania-Insanity
Marasmus-Progressive wasting away of the body, like
malnutrition
Membranous croup-Diphtheria
Meningitis-Inflations of the brain or spinal cord
Metritis-Inflammation of uterus or purulent vaginal
discharge
Miasma-Poisonous vapors thought to infect the air

Milk leg-Postpartum thrombophlebitis
Milk sickness or milk fever, aka "the milksick"-Disease
resulting from drinking the milk of cattle that had eaten
white snakeroot plant
Mormal-Gangrene
Morphew-Scurvy blisters on the body
Mortification-Gangrene of necrotic tissue
Myelitis-Inflammation of the spine
Myocarditis-Inflammation of heart muscles
Nascentium-"Nine-day fits" or Trismus nascentium-
stiffness of the jaw muscles in a newborn child
Necrosis-Mortification of bones or tissue
Nephrosis-Kidney degeneration
Nepritis-Inflammation of the kidney
Nervous prostration-Extreme exhaustion from an inability
to control physical and mental activities
Neuralgia-Described as discomfort, such as "headache" was
neuralgia in the head
New money fever-Pneumonia (often called pneumonie fever
and seen and heard as "new money fever")
Nostalgia-Homesickness
Palsy-Paralysis or uncontrolled movement of controlled
muscles
Paroxysm-Convulsion
Pemphigus-Skin disease of watery blisters
Pericarditis-Inflammation of heart
Peripneumonia-Inflammation of lungs
Peritonotis-Inflammation of abdominal area
Petechial fever-Fever characterized by skin spotting
Phthiriasis-Lice infestation
Phthisis-Chronic wasting away or a name for tuberculosis
Plague-An acute, febrile, highly infectious disease with a
high fatality rate
Pleurisy-Any pain in the chest area with each breath
Podagra-Gout
Poliomyelitis-Polio
Potter's asthma-Fibroid pthisis

Pott's disease-Tuberculosis of the spine
Puerperal exhaustion-Death due to childbirth
Puerperal fever-Elevated temperature after giving birth
Puking fever-Milk sickness
Putrid fever-Diphtheria
Putrid sore throat-Strep throat
Quinsy-Tonsillitis
Remitting fever-Malaria
Rheumatism-Any disorder associated with pain in joints
Rickets-A disease of the skeletal system
Rose cold-Hay fever or nasal symptoms of an allergy
Rubeola-German measles
Sanguineous crust-Scab
Scarlatina-Scarlet fever
Scarlet fever-A disease characterized by a red rash
Scarlet rash-Roseola
Sciatica-Rheumatism in the hips
Scirrhus-Cancerous tumors
Scotomy-Dizziness, nausea, and dimness of sight
Screws-Rheumatism
Scrivener's palsy-Writer's cramp
Scrofula-Tuberculosis of neck lymph glands. Characterized
by slow progression, abscesses, and pistulas
Scrumpox-Skin disease, impetigo
Scurvy-Lack of vitamin C. Symptoms of weakness, spongy
gums, and hemorrhages under skin
Septicemia-Blood poisoning
Shakes-Delirium tremens
Shaking-Chills, ague
Shingles-Viral disease with skin blisters
Ship fever-Typhus
Siriasis-Inflammation of the brain due to sun exposure
Sleeping sickness or brain fever-Encephalitis
Sloes-Milk sickness
Smallpox-Contagious disease with fever and blisters
Softening of brain-Result of stroke or hemorrhage in the
brain, with a result of the tissue softening in that area

Sore throat distemper-Diphtheria or quinsy
Spanish influenza-Epidemic influenza
Spasms-Sudden involuntary contraction of muscle or group
of muscles, like a convulsion
Spina bifida-Deformity of the spine
Spotted fever-Either typhus or meningitis
Sprue-Tropical disease characterized by intestinal disorders
and sore throat
St. Anthony's fire-Also erysipelas, but named so because
affected skin areas are bright red in appearance
St. Vitas dance or chorea-Disease characterized by
convulsions, contortions, and rapid complex jerking
movements done involuntarily
Stomatitis-Inflammation of the mouth
Stranger's fever-Yellow fever
Strangery-Rupture
Sudor anglicus-Sweating sickness
Summer complaint-Diarrhea, usually in infants caused by
spoiled milk
Sunstroke-Uncontrolled elevation of body temperature due
to environmental heat. Lack of sodium in the body is a
predisposing cause
Swamp sickness-Could be malaria, typhoid, or encephalitis
Sweating sickness-Infectious and fatal disease common to
the UK in the 15th century
Tetanus-Infectious fever characterized by high fever,
headache, and dizziness
Thrombosis-Blood clot inside a blood vessel
Thrush-Childhood disease characterized by spots on mouth,
lips, and throat
Tick fever-Rocky Mountain spotted fever
Toxemia of pregnancy-Eclampsia
Trench mouth-Painful ulcers found along the gum line,
caused by poor nutrition and poor hygiene
Tussis convulsiva-Whooping cough
Typhus-Infectious fever characterized by high fever,
headache, and dizziness

Variola-Smallpox
Venesection-Bleeding
Viper's dance-St. Vitus Dance
Water on brain-Enlarged head
White swelling-Tuberculosis of the bone
Winter fever-Pneumonia
Womb fever-Infection of the uterus
Worm fit-Convulsions associated with teething, worms,
elevated temperature, or diarrhea
Yellowjacket-Yellow fever

Source: https://www.citizen-times.com/story/
life/2015/07/05/asheville-genealogy-granny-call-
illness/29733993/, https://en.wikipedia.org/wiki/Slave_
health_on_plantations_in_the_United_States, and http://
www.usgennet.org/usa/ar/county/greene/olddiseases1.htm

Two websites for those who want to see more obsolete diagnoses:

http://www.olivetreegenealogy.com/index.shtml
http://www.homeoint.org/cazalet/oldnames.htm

Unusual or Odd Deaths

The subject of an ancestor's death is a serious one. As you search the deaths of your ancestors, you may discover unusual or odd findings. Our ancestors may have held to ideas about health, wellness, and plausible causes of death that we might find sad, macabre, or even humorous. While we may smile at some of these, remember, at the time of their use, these "medical" terms were quite serious. Therefore, we see that ancient coroners have attributed death to causes that seem bizarre to you and me as modern readers.

Some death causes come with a story that may be passed down (at times with embellishment) as "fact." You be the judge. A few more famous examples of odd deaths and causes follows.

An 1880 census mortality schedule from Leadville, Colorado, shows that J. Nash died from "Sore Eyes."

Jack Daniel's 1911 death certificate only lists "blood poisoning from operation," as cause of death, but the full story of the famous distiller's death is a bit odd. The story goes that in frustration at not being able to open his safe, he kicked it, injuring his toe. This resulted in an infection which was ultimately responsible for his death.

In January 1919 a storage tank burst in Boston's North End, releasing a wave of molasses which killed twenty-one people and injured one hundred fifty.

The 1927 violent death of dancer, Isadora Duncan, was caused from a broken neck. Her untimely death at age fifty occurred while riding in an open-top Amilcar model automobile in Nice, France. The flowing scarf she wore became tangled in the car's open-spoke wheels, throwing Duncan from the vehicle and snapping her neck.

In 1920 Ray Chapman played shortstop for the Cleveland Indians. He was killed when a spitball-style pitch from the Yankees' Carl Mays struck his temple. Chapman is the only professional baseball player to be killed by a pitch.

Last, Dick Wertheim, a tennis linesman, died in 1983 after a ball struck him in the groin and he fell out of his chair.

Grief, memorials, museums

Soundtrack suggestion:
"Fly Like an Eagle"
Steve Miller Band
Songwriters: Steven Haworth Miller
Fly Like an Eagle lyrics © Sailor Music

Time keeps on slippin', slippin', slippin'
Into the future
Time keeps on slippin', slippin', slippin'
Into the future

Time keeps on slippin' into the future so we cannot afford to wait to do those interviews and collect those oral histories and family stories. One day our family elders will be gone; and if we have not collected their stories, we may lose a valuable part of our past.

"If history were taught in the form of stories, it would never be forgotten" (Rudyard Kipling).

Genealogy is about looking at and studying the dead. Much of my activity over the years has been less about genealogy and more about family history. Family history is about honoring and acknowledging the fact that such folks actually *lived*. I always try to find the stories of the deceased person's life.

What's good about them?

"The evil that men do is remembered after their deaths, but the good is often buried with them." (From the speech, "Friends, Romans, countrymen, lend me your ears," spoken by Marc Antony in Shakespeare's *Julius Caesar*)

When death occurs, loved ones typically experience a time of grief and sorrow. Many times, the grief expressed is in proportion to the closeness of the relationship; but not always.

In my lifetime I have experienced a lot of death in my family. An exercise I do is to chart my feelings of grief. In doing so, I have learned that sometimes I grieved more over someone who was a distant relative than someone with whom I was well acquainted.

Thus, the nature of the human heart and grief. I don't have an answer to why I mourn the violent dying of my great-grandfather, A. S. J., (whom I did not know) more than I did that of a cousin whom I knew well and communicated with often. Grieving is emotional. It is not a mechanical function that you can control or predict. By charting grief experiences as I do above, I do not mean to imply that I loved one person more or less than another. I've noticed that when I create a chart and then, six months later, create another, the intensity bars are different. Grief, like every other emotion we have, changes over time.

Expressions of grief must have an outlet. Holding in the emotions because you don't think they are proper, it's not the right time, not the right place, or for other reasons, can have unwanted outcomes. Grief will find a way out. If you suppress it, it will often find expression at a time or place you least expect or want to welcome it.

> "Moses took the bones of Joseph with him because Joseph had made the Israelites swear an oath. He had said, "God will surely come to your aid, and then you must carry my bones up with you from this place." (Exod. 13:19 [NIV])

One way to deal with grief is by making or visiting memorials. For many folks, a way to do this is to create space in a burial site, often near relatives. In Genesis 49:29-32, we read Jacob's instructions about his burial place.

> "I am to be gathered to my people; bury me with my fathers in the cave that is in the field of Ephron the Hittite, in the cave that is in the field at Machpelah, to the east of Mamre, in the land of Canaan, which Abraham bought with the field from Ephron the Hittite to possess as a burying place. There they buried Abraham and Sarah his wife. There they buried Isaac and Rebekah his wife, and there I buried Leah—the field and the cave that is in it were bought from the Hittites."

Memorials

A *memorial* is a special space for grief. It can be an object which serves as a focus for the memory or the commemoration of something, usually an influential, deceased person or a historical, tragic event. Popular forms of memorials include landmark objects or works of art such as sculptures, statues or fountains, and parks. Our world has many examples of public memorial spaces.

- The Door of No Return, Senegal

- Gettysburg Battlefield, Pennsylvania

- Lincoln Memorial, Washington, D.C.

- The United States Memorial Arch, Valley Forge, Pennsylvania

- The Marine Corps War Memorial, Washington, D.C.

- Pro Football Hall of Fame, Canton, OhioNational Baseball Hall of Fame and Museum, 25 Main Street, Cooperstown, New York

- Rock and Roll Hall of Fame and Museum, Cleveland, Ohio

- Country Music Hall of Fame, Nashville, Tennessee

- Basketball Hall of Fame, Springfield, Massachusetts

- NASCAR Hall of Fame, Charlotte, North Carolina

- The Great Pyramid of Giza (also known as the Pyramid of Khufu)

- Gateway Arch, St. Louis, Missouri

- The Vietnam Veterans Memorial, Washington, D.C.

- USS *Arizona* Memorial, Honolulu (Pearl Harbor), Hawaii

These memorial spaces often contain museums that display historical artifacts dedicated to cultural preservation or to telling the stories and contributions of the folks represented there. Visiting a museum is a great way to get a hands-on feel for history. Museum tours can be great ways of learning about the accomplishments of the ancestors.

Visits to burial grounds—cemeteries and graveyards

Simply put, a cemetery or graveyard is a place where the remains of the deceased are buried or otherwise interred. The term graveyard is often used interchangeably with cemetery, but a graveyard primarily refers to a burial ground within a churchyard or on the property adjacent to a church building. If your ancestors are interred in accessible burial grounds, how can you honor them? I think of this as a two-part process that involves historical discovery and preservation.

Step one is discovery. Where are they? To begin, you will not need to start at the actual cemetery. Before you visit the land where your ancestor is buried, start your search online. Below are resources on how to search a cemetery.

Tips on visiting a real cemetery:

When it comes to locating a relative or ancestor in a cemetery there are a few things I'll call "cemetery manners" or "cemetery etiquette" that I believe everyone should know. Here are a few tips on how to search a cemetery, along with some dos and don'ts.

Step two is about preservation and how to visit responsibly.

Once you discover the site, how do you visit it in a way that does no harm to the site and ensures that you and others can visit in the future?

Three Tips on Cemetery Etiquette:

When visiting a cemetery, good manners, or etiquette, will serve you well. Here are three things you should keep in mind to honor the dead and the living. These three tips on cemetery etiquette are here to help keep you from being insensitive or breaking any laws, and generally to make sure you enjoy a peaceful experience.

1) Follow the Rules:

The only way to do this is to know the rules. So, you must make contact and get permission from the managers or owners of the cemetery property!

Contact the funeral home and/or the cemetery. Tell them who you are looking for and what you are hoping to find. Most cemeteries have a sign posted near the entrance listing rules specific to the property such as opening and closing hours. Many cemeteries are open from dawn until dusk. Try not to remain in the cemetery after dark.

A few months ago, I got word of a reunion happening in my hometown. This was a great opportunity to go back home and visit the gravesites of my grandmother and mother. I had not been to the cemetery for many years. I discovered a cemetery society web page for the cemetery and used the contact information available on the site to contact the owner. Within a few days, she emailed me back with the news that she had located my ancestors.

Also, since gravesites do not come with street addresses, I would need some assistance in locating the graves. She was very responsive and offered to meet me at the cemetery when I got into town. Once there she walked me to the sites. As I mentioned, the cemetery often does not come with named or marked streets, or gravesites with addresses, so having a guide is important.

2) Walk and Drive with Care:

The second tip is to drive and walk with care. Just because you have a clear line of sight to a monument or headstone you want to visit, you might not want to just head out in a straight line walking to it. Careful inspection of the terrain might reveal hidden gravesites; holes in the ground left from moved, or even vandalized, tombstones; or other trip hazards.

Follow the roadways and don't drive your vehicle on the grass. Drive slowly and watch out for folks who might not be paying attention. If the lane is narrow and another car approaches, offer to move your car until the other driver can get through.

3) Respect and Document the Graves:

Don't handle any monuments or headstones; this may cause damage to the memorials, especially older ones. Never remove anything from a gravestone, such as flowers, coins, or tributes that have been left by family or friends.

You should document the resting places of the folks you are

researching. But this should be done thoughtfully and with care to offer respect to the deceased and to avoid damaging the memorials.

Tombstone rubbings are prohibited in some areas. A state, county, municipality, or a cemetery itself can set rules regarding tombstone rubbings. Be sure to find out what is allowed in the specific location you are visiting.

Historic cemeteries and those popular with tourists will often prohibit tombstone rubbings because of the potential deterioration and damage that repeated rubbings of a stone can cause over time.

There are other common practices that you should avoid when documenting the cemetery you are visiting. Primary among my list of don'ts is something a well-meaning visitor to one of my relatives has done. To better see the writing on the stones, they have rubbed chalk on the stone. The writing is easier to read, as the letters stand out better, however, this is not a good idea as chalk is not biodegradable.

To better view the writing on gravestones, I've encountered suggestions involving the use of shaving cream, baby powder, chalk, or flour dusted onto the front of the gravestone. The problem with such methods is this. Flour promotes mold growth, and shaving cream leaves an acid residue that eats away at the stone. And remember, no matter how well you believe you wash away your dusting material when you're done, gravestones are full of nooks and crannies into which these materials can deposit and continue to do damage over time. You mustn't cause harm to the graveyard you are trying to document!

Instead of rubbing or powdering a stone, try water. Pouring clean water over an old stone may be all it takes in some circumstances. Wetting the stone makes the inscription appear darker. For the best solution, however, take along a good digital camera. Use that iPhone, iPad, smart phone, or camera and take lots of images. Even subtle shadows can be emphasized in most digital software packages.

The Unmarked Grave

I do not want to leave the topic of burial grounds without a mention of the "unmarked grave." An unmarked grave is one that lacks a marker, headstone, or nameplate indicating that a body is buried there. In cultures like ours here in America that mark burial sites, the phrase unmarked grave has taken on a metaphorical meaning. As a figure of speech, a common meaning of the term unmarked grave is that the person buried here is consigned to an ignominious end.

I would like to end this section about respecting the graves by addressing an issue that many times can cause stress and even guilt. That is the issue of the unmarked grave. You have contacted the cemetery officials, you have been careful to observe all the rules, and you get to the gravesite only to discover that your ancestor's grave is unmarked. There is nothing to document or photograph but a patch of grass.

You may discover that the cemetery your ancestor is buried in has a plot map. Since gravesites do not have street addresses or numbers posted on them, you may need to locate your ancestor by counting x steps from a permanent marker. While the typical gravesite in the United States is marked with a permanent memorial marker (typically placed within a year of burial), there are plenty of cases in which a grave remains unmarked for much longer, maybe for decades. The reasons for the unmarked grave are usually as valid as they are varied.

There can still be a bit of stigma attached to an unmarked grave. In times past, criminals were deliberately placed in unmarked graves so that no honor could be bestowed upon them, even in death. On the other end of the spectrum, we find many celebrities and famous folks buried in unmarked graves as a deterrent to vandalism, trophy hunters, and unwanted attention from fans and the general public.

My point is this: there should be no shame in discovering an ancestor in an unmarked grave. During your visit, you may decide to leave behind a flower or a photo, or some other token on the clear site. You may choose to purchase a marker, or you can leave the site undisturbed, at peace, and unmarked. I have numerous ancestors buried with no permanent markers. I know the places, and my children know where they are. I prefer to leave them as they are so that they may rest in the shadows just as they once lived in the shadows. "Now's no time to become a show off!" I hear them say.

To recap, begin your search online using virtual cemetery data sites, burial, and death records. When you decide to visit a physical cemetery, consider these three tips to honor the dead and ensure a safe and positive visit.

Why now?
Because all we have is today.
Myth: We've got time. We can talk about this later.

> Soundtrack suggestion:
> "Cat's in the Cradle"
> Harry Chapin

> *My child arrived just the other day*
> *He came to the world in the usual way*
> *But there were planes to catch, and bills to pay*
> *He learned to walk while I was away.*

After a series of stanzas where the son grows to be a man, the song continues with the haunting refrain of *Cat's in the Cradle*:

And the cat's in the cradle and the silver spoon
Little boy blue and the man in the moon
"When you coming home, Dad?" "I don't know when.
But we'll get together then,
You know we'll have a good time then."

The song ends with the singer, now an old man, singing

And the cat's in the cradle and the silver spoon
Little boy blue and the man in the moon
"When you coming home, son?" "I don't know when.
But we'll get together then, Dad,
We're gonna have a good time then."

I stumbled upon a website called simply "See Your Folks," or www.seeyourfolks.com, that drives this point home. The site seeks to address our "but we'll get together then" attitude by showing us how short "then" is. When you visit the website, you enter, on average, how many times you see your parents in a year. This is done by first selecting the country your parents live in. Then you enter the age of each of your parents. Then, based on information from the World Health Organization Life Expectancy Data (2014), the site tells you how many times you would likely see your parents before they die.

The site reveals in the "Why are we doing this?" section that "We believe that increasing awareness of death can help us to make the most of our lives. The right kind of reminders can help us to focus on what matters, and perhaps make us better people."

Soundtrack suggestion:
"Let Her Fly"
Dolly Parton, Loretta Lynn, and Tammy Wynette

There's a wreath on the door
She don't live here no more
As of today, she flew home
And we all gathered here
In sorrow and tears
It won't be the same with her gone

463

Gathering stories can be cold data collection. I believe most of us do it not for this, but because these narratives connect us with our ancestors. We long to hear what they have to say. A. S. J. worked for the benefit not only of his nine children but for the good of all Black and White children in the South after the Civil War. That was his story. You, too, may have an ancestor who was a mentor, teacher, or influencer of young minds. This sort of investment in the future has generated much prose and poetry, all of which can assist us in honoring the ancestors who did this work.

In the movie *Dead Poets Society*, Mr. Keating hands Gerard Pitts the poem, *To the Virgins, to Make Much of Time*:

Gather ye rosebuds while ye may,
  Old Time is still a-flying;
And this same flower that smiles today
  Tomorrow will be dying.

The glorious lamp of heaven, the sun,
  The higher he's a-getting,
The sooner will his race be run,
  And nearer he's to setting.

That age is best which is the first,
  When youth and blood are warmer;
But being spent, the worse, and worst
  Times still succeed the former.

Then be not coy, but use your time,
  And while ye may, go marry;
For having lost but once your prime,
  You may forever tarry.

Source: Robert Herrick-1591-1674, https://poets.org/poet/robert-herrick

And who can forget the scene in front of the school trophy cases as he tells the boys to lean in and listen to the boys of classes from long ago as they whisper, "*carpe diem*."

Our confrontation with "The Dead" should remind us of our own immortality and tell us to make the most of our lives.

Why do mentors care?
Because if youth don't know the truth, they may believe a lie.
Myth: The past is unimportant in the growth and development of children.

Soundtrack suggestion:
"Teach Your Children Well"
Crosby, Stills, Nash, and Young

You who are on the road
Must have a code that you can live by
And so become yourself
Because the past is just a good-bye.
And you, of tender years,
Can't know the fears that your elders grew by,
And so please help them with your youth,
They seek the truth before they can die.

Human beings are hard-wired for narrative. In the absence of a story, we will make one up. A frequently heard reason for youth joining street gangs is that the young person is seeking family. Seeking a story to belong to and call their own. Many children and adolescents are motivated to join a gang for a sense of connection or to define a new sense of who they are.

Consider the following taken from the Los Angeles Police Department website:

- Gang members join a gang by either committing a crime or undergoing an initiation procedure wherein they are beaten by fellow gang members to test their courage and fighting ability. Their motivations for joining the gang are varied, but usually fall within one of the following:

- Identity or Recognition. Being part of a gang allows the gang member to achieve a level of status he/she feels impossible outside the gang culture.

- Protection. Many members join because they live in the gang area and are, therefore, subject to violence by rival gangs. Joining guarantees support in case of attack and retaliation for transgressions.

465

- Fellowship and Brotherhood. To the majority of gang members, the gang functions as an extension of the family and may provide companionship lacking in the gang member's home environment. Many older brothers and relatives belong or have belonged to the gang.

  Source: Official Site of the Los Angeles Police Department http://www.lapdonline.org/top_ten_most_wanted_gang_ members/content_basic_view/23473

It is vitally important to tell your story. Before your young one goes out seeking a family, be sure that they understand the richness of the family they may be deciding to leave.

"How, then, can they call on the one they have not believed in? And how can they believe in the one of whom they have not heard? And how can they hear without someone preaching to them? And how can anyone preach unless they are sent? As it is written: 'How beautiful are the feet of those who bring good news!'" (Rom. 10)

Biography – Alonzo Felder

Alonzo Felder was a full-time IT Analyst with a career spanning over thirty-seven years at Duke University. He spent his days providing end user-level computer support and troubleshooting computer related issues. He is now retired.

Over the last four decades, Mr. Felder has become versed in a number of disciplines, including legal, historical, and investigative research methods. He has co-authored, co-investigated, and edited scientific articles, journals, and medical research studies. He has conducted historical research for use in a variety of presentations and publications, and has presented on family history research at numerous workshops and presentations. His most recent presentation was for the Stanford L. Warren Branch Library, where he explored motivations for family history research, as well as pitfalls to discovery and ways to overcome "brick walls" in research.

He is an online participant and contributor on a number of public genealogy-oriented forums and social media venues, including GenForum, Finding Your Roots, AfriGeneas Genealogy and History Forum, Genealogy.com, and Ancestry.com, just to name a few. His work has been featured at THE LoDi PROJECT museum in Raleigh, North Carolina.

Mr. Felder and his research work are referenced in the following publications:

- *Emancipation Betrayed: The Hidden History of Black Organizing and White Violence in Florida from Reconstruction to the Bloody Election of 1920*, by Paul Ortiz.

- *Old South, New South, or Down South? Florida and the Modern Civil Rights Movement*, edited by Irvin D. S. Winsboro.

Mr. Felder has contributed to the *Finding Your Roots* TV show website, "The Race Card Project," by Michele Norris of NPR's *All Things Considered*. In 2017 he presented the event "Let's Talk Roots," a panel discussion about the impact family history has in our community, in Raleigh, North Carolina. He has also given numerous presentations on the importance of grandparents and seniors for a variety of senior faith-based groups.

In 2015 Mr. Felder founded My Roots Foundation and currently serves as its president. My Roots Foundation is a 501(c)3 non-profit organization based in Durham, North Carolina. The mission is to honor ancestors and promote awareness of the importance and impact of family history through discovering, preserving, and sharing the stories of the forebears.

Work mentioned in *Psychology Today*'s online publication posted April 2, 2017.

"The Stories of Our Lives" section by Robyn Fivush, Ph.D.
"Cultural stories provide roots for growth
Being part of a cultural group through storytelling is beneficial."

Link: https://www.psychologytoday.com/us/blog/the-stories-our-lives/201704/cultural-stories-provide-roots-growth_=_

Mr. Felder actively works as a participant and workshop presenter for DiversifyIT, a voluntary group of Duke University professionals working in the information technology (IT) field who seek to address issues of diversity in the IT workforce. https://diversifyit.duke.edu/

Active contributor to the DGHI Community, Diversity and Inclusion Committee, and member of the DGHI Equity Task Force.

Participant/Member of Cohort 4 of the Duke University School of Medicine and Duke Health's Teaching and Leading Equity Now (TEN) series, a part of the Duke Office of Diversity and Inclusion.

Mr. Felder has been featured in a variety of newspaper and magazine publications, including "Foundation helps people discover–and celebrate–their family history" by Lewis Beale.

> Correspondent
> October 21, 2015, 05:10 p.m.
> Updated October 21, 2015, 10:48 p.m.
> link: https://www.newsobserver.com/news/local/
> article40763325.html#storylink=cpy
>
> Triangle Gives: My Roots Foundation connects generations
> to strengthen families | News & Observer
> By Corbie Hill
> newsobserver.com Nov 22, 2017
>
> "I realized...how to deal with racism."
> by Alonzo Felder
> *Duke Magazine* photos by Author; Illustration by James
> Boyle
> September 26, 2020, Special 2020 issue